The Arab Winter

In 2011, the world watched as dictators across the Arab world were toppled from power. In Tunisia, Egypt, Libya, Yemen, Syria, and Iraq, ordinary Arab citizens mobilized during the Arab Spring to reinvent the autocratic Arab world into one characterized by democracy, dignity, socio-economic justice, and inviolable human rights. This unique comparative analysis of countries before, during, and after the Arab Spring seeks to explain the divergent outcomes and the disappointing and even harrowing results of efforts to overcome democratic consolidation challenges from the tentative democracy in Tunisia, to the emergence of the Islamic State, to civil war and authoritarian retrenchment everywhere else. Tracing the period of the Arab Spring from its background in long-term challenges to autocratic regimes, to the mass uprisings, authoritarian breakdown, and the future projections and requirements for a democratizing conclusion, Stephen J. King establishes a broad but focused history that refines the leading theory of democratization in comparative politics and realigns the narrative of the Arab Spring by bringing its differing results to the fore.

STEPHEN J. KING is an associate professor of government at Georgetown University and the author of *Liberalization Against Democracy: The Local Politics of Economic Reform in Tunisia* (2003) and *The New Authoritarianism in the Middle East and North Africa* (2009), and coeditor of *The Lure of Authoritarianism: The Maghreb after the Arab Spring* (2019). He has published multiple articles and book chapters on the politics of economic reform and regime transition processes in the Arab world.

The Arab Winter

Democratic Consolidation, Civil War, and Radical Islamists

STEPHEN J. KING
Georgetown University

CAMBRIDGE
UNIVERSITY PRESS

CAMBRIDGE
UNIVERSITY PRESS

University Printing House, Cambridge CB2 8BS, United Kingdom

One Liberty Plaza, 20th Floor, New York, NY 10006, USA

477 Williamstown Road, Port Melbourne, VIC 3207, Australia

314–321, 3rd Floor, Plot 3, Splendor Forum, Jasola District Centre,
New Delhi – 110025, India

79 Anson Road, #06–04/06, Singapore 079906

Cambridge University Press is part of the University of Cambridge.

It furthers the University's mission by disseminating knowledge in the pursuit of
education, learning, and research at the highest international levels of excellence.

www.cambridge.org
Information on this title: www.cambridge.org/9781108477413
DOI: 10.1017/9781108769792

First published 2020

Printed in the United Kingdom by TJ International Ltd, Padstow Cornwall

A catalogue record for this publication is available from the British Library.

Library of Congress Cataloging-in-Publication Data
Names: King, Stephen J. (Stephen Juan), 1961– author.
Title: The Arab winter : democratic consolidation, civil war, and radical Islamists /
    Stephen King.
Description: Cambridge, United Kingdom ; New York, NY : Cambridge University Press,
    2020. | Includes bibliographical references and index.
Identifiers: LCCN 2019040406 (print) | LCCN 2019040407 (ebook) | ISBN 9781108477413
    (hardback) | ISBN 9781108708661 (paperback) | ISBN 9781108769792 (epub)
Subjects: LCSH: Democratization–Arab countries–History–21st century. | Civil war–Arab
    countries–History–21st century. | Islam and politics–Arab countries–History–21st century. |
    Arab Spring, 2010- | Arab countries–Politics and government–21st century.
Classification: LCC JQ1850.A91 K56 2020 (print) | LCC JQ1850.A91 (ebook) |
    DDC 909/.097492708312–dc23
LC record available at https://lccn.loc.gov/2019040406
LC ebook record available at https://lccn.loc.gov/2019040407

ISBN 978-1-108-47741-3 Hardback
ISBN 978-1-108-70866-1 Paperback

For the Next Arab Spring

Contents

Abbreviations[*]

ABM	Ansar Bayt al-Maqdis
ABM/WS	Ansar Bayt al-Maqdis/Wilayat Sinai
ALMP	Active Labor Market Programs
AQAP	al-Qaeda in the Arabian Peninsula
AQIM	al-Qaeda in the Islamic Maghreb
ASC	Anbar Salvation Council
AUC	American University in Cairo
BPC	Basic People's Congress (Libya)
BTI	Bertelsmann Stiftung Transformation Index (Country Reports)
CAPMAS	Central Authority for Public Mobilization and Statistics (Egypt)
CFAD	Tunisian Center for Training and Support
CAOA	Central Agency for Organization and Administration (Egypt)
CBL	Central Bank of Libya
CIA	Central Intelligence Agency
CPA	Coalition Provisional Authority (Iraq)
CPR	Congress for the Republic (Tunisia)
CSF	Central Security Forces (Egypt)
CSO	Central Security Organization (Yemen)
DFI	Development Fund for Iraq
DSE	Directorate of State Security (Tunisia)
ECESR	Egyptian Center for Economic and Social Rights
ENA	National School of Administration (Tunisia)
ERRADA	Egyptian Regulatory Reform and Development Activity
FJP	Freedom and Justice Party (Egypt)
FLOSY	Front for the Liberation of Occupied South Yemen

[*] Abbreviations that do not follow the word order presented follow the word order of other languages (French in the case of Tunisia and Kurdish in the case of Iraq).

viii

FSA	Free Syrian Army
GCC	Gulf Cooperation Council
GDP	Gross Domestic Product
GNA	Government of National Accord (Libya)
GNC	General National Congress (Libya)
GPC	General People's Congress (Libya, Yemen)
GSS	General Security Services (Iraq)
HOR	House of Representatives (Libya)
HT	Hizb al-Tahrir
IGC	Iraqi Governing Council
IFI	International Financial Institution
IMF	International Monetary Fund
IAI	Islamic Army of Iraq
IS	Islamic State
ISIL	Islamic State in Iraq and the Levant
ISIS	Islamic State of Iraq and al-Sham
JCP	Justice and Construction Party (Libya)
JMP	Joint Meeting Parties (Yemen)
KDP	Kurdistan Democratic Party
KRG	Kurdistan Regional Government
LGBT	Lesbian, Gay, Bisexual, and Transgender
LIFG	Libyan Islamic Fighting Group
LNA	Libyan National Army
LNSF	Libyan National Salvation Front
LPA	Libyan Political Agreement
LROR	Libya Revolutionaries Operations Room
LTDH	Tunisian Human Rights League
MB	Muslim Brotherhood
MI6	Military Intelligence, Section 6 (Great Britain)
MOI	Ministry of the Interior
MTI	Islamic Tendency Movement
NCA	National Constituent Assembly (Tunisia)
NDC	National Dialogue Conference (Yemen)
NDF	National Defense Forces (Syria)
NDP	National Democratic Party (Egypt)
NFA	National Forces Alliance (Libya)
NGO	Non-governmental Organization
NLF	National Liberation Front (Yemen)
NOC	National Oil Corporation (Libya)

NSA	National Security Apparatus (Egypt)
NSB	National Security Bureau (Yemen)
NSF	National Salvation Front (Egypt)
NTC	National Transitional Council (Libya)
PDP	Progressive Democratic Party (Tunisia)
PDRY	People's Democratic Republic of Yemen
PFG	Petroleum Facilities Guard (Libya)
PIL	Political Isolation Law (Libya)
PMF	Popular Mobilization Force (Iraq)
POMEPS	Project on Middle East Political Science
RCC	Revolutionary Command Council (Libya, Iraq)
RCD	Constitutional Democratic Rally (Tunisia)
RC	Revolutionary Committee (Libya)
ROY	Republic of Yemen
SAA	Syrian Arab Army
SCAF	Supreme Council of the Armed Forces (Egypt)
SCC	Specialized Criminal Chamber (Tunisia)
SCC	Supreme Constitutional Court (Egypt)
SCIRI	Supreme Council for Islamic Revolution in Iraq
SOI	Sons of Iraq
SSC	Supreme Security Council (Libya)
SSI	State Security Intelligence (Egypt)
SSO	Special Security Organization (Iraq)
TCD	Temporary Constitutional Declaration (Libya)
TDC	Truth and Dignity Commission (Tunisia)
TIMEP	Tahrir Institute for Middle East Policy (Egypt)
UAE	United Arab Emirates
UAR	United Arab Republic
UCLG	United Cities and Local Governments
UGTT	Tunisian General Labor Union
UN	United Nations
UNDP	United Nations Development Programme
UNSMIL	United Nations Support Mission in Libya
USAID	United States Agency for International Development
UTICA	Tunisian Confederation of Industry, Trade, and Handicrafts
VPN	Virtual Personal Network
WB	World Bank
YCR	Yemeni Congregation for Reform

YEC	Yemen Economic Corporation
YMCO	Yemen Military Economic Corporation
YPG	Kurdish People's Protection Units
YSP	Yemeni Socialist Party

Introduction

The Arab Winter: Democratic Consolidation, Civil War, and Radical Islamists

STEPHEN J. KING

The Arab World has decided to reinvent itself. This decision did not come from the top. It was claimed by each and every one of us, from the most famous to the anonymous.

–Fares Mabrouk

The Arab Spring surprised the world when it began in late December 2010.[1] Arabs sought to topple their political regimes and to reinvent themselves in a region characterized by persistent authoritarianism, widespread corruption, and the world's worst record on protecting human rights. The initially peaceful mass uprisings – which toppled dictatorships in Tunisia, Egypt, Libya, and Yemen while deeply threatening Bashar al-Assad's Syria – envisioned transforming the region into one characterized by respect for human dignity, democracy, socioeconomic justice, and inviolable human rights. The George W. Bush administration's "war of choice" in Iraq, which began in 2003, attempted to use foreign military power to impose the same goals. That conflict merged into the volatile democratic transition dynamics of the Arab Spring.

Unfortunately, even sadly, the manifest will of the vast majority of Arabs is yet to be realized. In 2019, nine years after the start of the Arab Spring, only Tunisia can tentatively be considered a consolidated democracy. A military coup in Egypt ended their democratic experiment and ignited a new phase of violent conflict between the state and Islamist groups, which saw the military's generalized repression of any opposition. Libya, Yemen, and Syria descended into civil wars. One can only hope that current international negotiations to end these civil

---

[1] The above quote is taken from Huffington (2013). Fares Mabrouk is Co-Founder and Director of the Arab Policy Institute.

1

wars and restart transitions to democracy will bear fruit. The US invasion and occupation of Iraq in 2003 led to over a decade of insurgency, civil war, and partial state collapse. It also created territory and added motivation for an al-Qaeda mutation – one even more brutal than its predecessor – to seize real estate and declare an Islamic Caliphate in parts of Iraq and neighboring Syria. In its attempt to reimpose its interpretation of the seventh-century Golden Age of Islam, the Islamic State has been totalitarian, bloodthirsty, theatrically barbaric, and influential enough to foster allegiance by violent cells and religious fanatics in every country in the region – and beyond.[2] The group often murders ordinary Muslims whom they deem apostates.

Why has the attempt by the vast majority of Arabs to reinvent themselves and to transition to democracy and the human rights standards and socioeconomic justice associated with it been so difficult to achieve? The short answer is that the challenges facing participants in the Arab Spring were steep. Transitioning to democracy is a multi-stage and difficult process. Scholars usually divide it into three phases: authoritarian breakdown, democratic transition, and democratic consolidation. Democratic consolidation is the most complex and difficult of the three phases. Challenges associated with democratic consolidation go a long way toward explaining the contours and disappointing results of the Arab Spring.

Authoritarian Breakdown

Authoritarian breakdown in Tunisia, a small predominantly Arab country in North Africa, triggered the Arab Spring. On December 17, 2010, Mohamed Bouazizi – a deeply frustrated street vendor in rural Tunisia – lit himself on fire in protest of the confiscation of his wares and the harassment and humiliation inflicted on him by a local municipal official. His act galvanized feelings of solidarity against a brutal regime that had deprived people of their dignity, grown rich from corruption, and ruled autocratically. Mass demonstrations and riots spontaneously erupted throughout Tunisia. Aided by the organizational power of social media, the mobilized public anger intensified

---

[2] Also known as the Islamic State of Iraq and the Levant (ISIL), the Islamic State of Iraq and al-Sham (ISIS), and the Islamic State of Iraq and Syria (ISIS). The Arabic acronym Daesh is also used (al-Dawla al-Islamiyya al-Iraq al-Sham). In this book, I will refer to the Islamic State and to ISIS.

until then-President Zine El-Abidine Ben Ali stepped down on January 14, 2011, and fled to Saudi Arabia. He had been in power for 23 years.

Tunisians' shocking ability to break down an entrenched authoritarian regime was a catalyst for mass uprisings throughout the region. On January 25, 2011, organizers in Egypt turned "National Police Day" into the date marking the beginning of the Egyptian Revolution. Demonstrations, riots, labor strikes, and public plaza occupations mounted in number and intensity until President Hosni Mubarak, in power since 1981, stepped down on February 11. Once protests had reached critical mass in Tunisia and Egypt, neither president-for-life was able to convince his military to inflict mass murder upon their fellow citizens in order for them to remain in power.

The Yemeni Uprising occurred simultaneously to the Egyptian Revolution on January 25, 2011. A major demonstration took place in Sanaa, Yemen's capital, on January 27, 2011. The protestors demanded the resignation of Yemeni President Ali Abdullah Saleh, who had been in power for 33 years. Instead, the regime began shooting live rounds at protestors. The government's reaction led to mass defections from the military, effectively rendering much of the country outside government control. Witnessing a growing civil war, the Gulf Cooperation Council (GCC) brokered a power transfer deal with Saleh in November 2011. A presidential election was held in Yemen on February 21, 2012, formally ending Saleh's authoritarian regime.

On February 15, 2011, the uprising against the government of Muammar Qaddafi began in Benghazi. After army defections, the protests quickly turned into a civil war. The Libyan loyalist forces were attempting to score a decisive victory against the opposition in Benghazi when Western powers, authorized by a United Nations Security Council resolution to protect civilians, established a no-fly zone that bolstered the rebel forces' power. After a bloody fight, the rebels won. Qaddafi was captured and killed on October 20, 2011. Opposition forces declared the liberation of Libya and the official end of the war on October 23, 2011. This ended an authoritarian regime, which Muammar Qaddafi had ruled since 1969.

The Syrian Uprising began in earnest on March 15, 2011, after young boys in the southern city of Daraa – who had written the slogan "The people want the regime to fall" on city walls – were arrested and reportedly tortured. In response to the Daraa incident and the violent crackdown on other protests, activists declared March 15, 2011, a "day of rage" and staged protests throughout the country, all of which called for the removal of President Bashar al-Assad, democratic reforms, and greater freedoms. The regime's ferocious response to peaceful protests led to a cycle of violence and an ongoing civil war, which has killed more than 560,000 people and led to the worst refugee crisis since World War II (Haaretz and Reuters 2018).

Authoritarian breakdown in Saddam Hussein's Iraq took place through the initiative of former US President George W. Bush's "war of choice," "Operation Iraqi Freedom" (2003–2011) (Sullum 2011). US and British forces, with small contributions from other allies, broke down Saddam Hussein's regime quickly. The postwar US mission prominently included "securing and stabilizing a new democracy in Iraq" (Caryl 2013). However, instead of freedom and democracy, an insurgency emerged to oppose what they declared to be occupying foreign forces and the newly formed Iraqi government beholden to them.

The post-invasion Iraqi Civil War has claimed at least 60,000 Iraqi lives and perhaps 10 times that number (Caryl 2013). Between 2003 and 2012, 4,486 US military personnel lost their lives in Iraq as well. The United States has spent at least $800 billion in the Iraqi conflict in addition to having up to $2 trillion of war-related expenditures (Caryl 2013). Still, democracy has remained elusive in Iraq, and communal violence continues. The emergence of the Sunni extremist group, ISIS, which at one time controlled a third of Iraqi territory and parts of Syria, highlights the risks of failed democratic transitions.

In sum, mass uprisings seeking socioeconomic justice, democracy, and human rights broke down four authoritarian regimes during the Arab Spring. Operation Iraqi Freedom removed another. President Bashar al-Assad's brutal authoritarian regime in Syria has survived to date by unleashing state violence that has cost more lives than any conflict in the region in decades. To a lesser extent during the Arab Spring, other autocrats in the Arab world faced mass uprisings as well.

Democratic Transition

After authoritarian breakdown, a change of government through free and fair elections is the most important benchmark of a democratic transition. The founding elections of Tunisia's democratic transition took place on October 23, 2011. As a result of these Constituent

Assembly elections, a coalition dominated by a moderate Islamist political party took control of the Tunisian government. Moderate Islamists also won founding elections in Egypt, with Muslim Brotherhood member Mohamed Morsi becoming Egypt's first popularly elected president in June 2012. Founding elections in Libya's transition took place on July 7, 2012. The National Forces Alliance (NFA), a predominantly liberal and secular coalition, won the majority of seats in Libya's General National Congress (GNC) elections. An election in February 2012 replaced long-time Yemeni president and strongman Ali Abdullah Saleh with his vice-president, Abdrabbuh Mansur Hadi.[3] Post–Saddam Hussein governments have also been chosen through competitive elections.

The final phase of a democratic transition – democratic consolidation – has been the most difficult to achieve during the Arab Spring. Democratic consolidation brings into play challenges in state–society relations that stretch far beyond the electoral arena.

Democratic Consolidation

Of the three processes embedded in democratization – authoritarian breakdown, democratic transition, and democratic consolidation – the latter is the least studied and understood. Scholars have debated over aggregate and disaggregate interpretations of democratic consolidation (Encarnación 2000). The aggregate approach aims to capture democratic consolidation by examining its final outcome in terms of political institutions and the behavioral norms of elites and the masses. The focus in this approach is on electoral politics and similar aspects of the formal institutionalization of democracy. Transitions to democracy are considered consolidated when free and fair elections are conducted and surveys reveal that elites and masses regard democratic institutions as the only legitimate framework to choose the country's most important policymakers.

By contrast, the disaggregate approach unpacks democratic consolidation by identifying the multiple spheres in which the process takes place. These spheres stretch beyond the formal electoral arena into other areas that are important for sustaining democracy. A disaggregate approach also provides more insight into the internal

---

[3] Hadi ran unopposed in these elections.

dynamics of democratic consolidation and assists in measuring the extent of democratic progress.

Here, I refine and extend a disaggregate approach to democratic consolidation found in *Transitions from Authoritarian Rule: Tentative Conclusions about Uncertain Democracies* (O'Donnell and Schmitter 1986). In a book widely recognized as the founding work of what became known as the democratic transitions literature, Guillermo O'Donnell and Philippe Schmitter emphasized the concept of pacts. Pacts are negotiated compromises or efforts at national consensus designed to address conflicts that could derail a democratic transition.

Based on studies of democratic transformation in Southern Europe and Latin America, O'Donnell and Schmitter highlighted three pacts: military, political, and socioeconomic. Military pacts are national efforts to get the military back to their barracks and subject to civilian control. Political pacts are democratic bargains committing all political parties to competition based on the rules of political democracy. Socio-economic pacts emphasize inclusive policymaking to legitimize emerging democratic regimes. Effectively extending O'Donnell and Schmitter's democratic consolidation approach to the Arab world – which I do below – requires refinements of the three pacts they discuss and the addition of two other pacts: nation-state pacts and transitional justice, human rights, and rule of law pacts.

Democratic Consolidation: Military Pacts

O'Donnell and Schmitter conceptualized democratic transitions as involving a sequence of "moments" – military, political, and economic – with each moment corresponding to negotiated efforts to establish enough national consensus or pacts to prevent the derailment of democratic outcomes. The first moment is devoted to a military extrication pact that ensures military impartiality in political processes.

A history of military involvement in politics poses a major challenge to a democratic transition. The majority of democratic transition failures have historically been attributed to military coups designed to prevent a loss of military power in a country's politics and economy (Trinkunas 2000). The threat of military intervention in fragile democratic transitions makes civilian control of the military indispensable for the establishment of democratic rule.

In the context of developing countries, civilian control over the military can be especially challenging because the competition for control over the state between different political forces, including the military, may still be largely unsettled. The expectation that governments should be civilian may not exist or may not be fully engrained. This is especially true in the Arab world, a region that has experienced more tension, civil strife, and armed conflict than anywhere else on the planet. This experience has empowered the role of military officers in politics. In addition, even when the military has not directly intervened in politics, there are many cases in which military tutelage, prerogatives (including economic prerogatives), and contestation of civilian authority persist. This creates informal or indirect military rule.

Ultimately, the potential for sidelining a powerful military during a democratic transition depends on the degree of the armed forces' political influence prior to the transition, as well as on the steps taken by civilian elected officials to establish control over core decision-making areas. In this light, civil–military relations in the Arab world can be placed along a continuum with a polarization between full civilian control on one side and full military rule on the other. Cases in which political decision-making power is divided between civilians and the military are positioned somewhere along the continuum.

Beyond this continuum of civil–military relations, there is a need for a full framework to empirically assess the concrete state of civil–military relations at one point in time and longitudinally so that progress in the institutionalization of civilian control can be captured in the analysis. Following Croissant and colleagues (2011), civilian control here is understood as one pole on the continuous distribution of decision-making power between civilians and the military. Their framework distinguishes five decision-making areas and identifies whether the formal or informal authority to decide in each area rests with civilians or the military:

1) Leadership Selection: civilian control is undermined if active military personnel are eligible for public offices and soldiers influence governments' formation and dissolution.
2) Policy-making: this area comprises the rules and procedures of policy-making, agenda-setting, policy formulation, policy adoption, and policy implementation. Military influence over the national budget is crucially important in this decision-making area.

3) Internal Security: this area entails the decisions and concrete actions regarding the preservation and restoration of domestic law and order, including counterinsurgency operations, counterterrorism and domestic intelligence-gathering, daily law enforcement, and border control.
4) National Defense: this area includes all aspects of defense policy, ranging from the development of security doctrines to the deployment of troops abroad and the conduct of war.
5) Military Organization: this area comprises decisions regarding all organizational aspects of the military's institutional, financial, and technological resources, and decisions regarding military doctrine, education, and personnel selection.

Military intervention in decision-making for leadership positions and policymaking poses a greater threat to democratic consolidation than military influence in internal security, defense policy, and military organization. Countries in which the military dissolves governments and dominates policymaking cannot be categorized as democracies. The aim in security, defense, and military organization is to develop a professional military subject to elected civilians' control.

Civilian control over all five decision-making areas is consolidated when elected officials craft institutions that permanently shift power away from the military to bureaucracies that civilians control. In consolidated democracies, these institutions sustain civilian leverage over the military. Developing these institutions is crucial if civilians are to govern without military interference.

A number of institutions can aid civilian control over the military in emerging democracies. For example, in South Korea two ex-generals, Park Chung-hee and Chun Doo-hwan, seized power and then created a civilian-dominated agency, the National Defense Security Command (NDSC), to monitor military officers in order to keep them out of politics (Moon and Rhyu 2011). Later civilian rulers maintained this institution. Civilian leaders can also create legislative oversight committees with permanent staffs, civilian defense secretariats, and independent intelligence agencies. They can strengthen police forces and create multiple intelligence and security agencies. Temporary strategies can become institutionalized as written rules governing military relations. These rules may emerge from a new constitution, executive decrees, legislative actions, or court decisions (Trinkunas 2000).

Powerful international actors and domestic populations mobilized in support of elected governments' efforts to gain control of the military and police can also contribute to developing institutions that extract the military from politics (Bermeo 2003). Once created, these institutions help civilian leaders monitor military leaders – and sanction them if necessary.

Democratic Consolidation: Political Pacts

To successfully consolidate a democracy, political party leaders must strike a democratic bargain or political pact. The political pact involves a package deal among the leaders of a spectrum of electorally competitive parties that represent the country's major factions. The parties agree to compete according to the rules of political democracy and to forgo appeals to mass mobilization, violence, and military intervention to alter electoral outcomes. By accommodating vital interests, political pacts enable warring elite factions to deliberately reorganize their relations through negotiated compromises over their most basic disagreements (Burton et al. 1992).

During the Arab Spring, political elites sought compromises over class, region, tribe, ethnicity, sect, and other conflicts. However, conflicts over the role of religion (Islam and Islam's religious law, *Shari'a*) in politics have posed the most frequent challenge to democratic bargains. Similar to nineteenth-century Europe, when Christian political movements emerged in the wake of the spread of modern democratic ideas, a range of Islamic political movements have developed alongside the more recent spread of democratic aspirations in the Arab Middle East. One current of political Islam, which grew to accept democracy, mirrors a transition by Christian movements from being hostile toward liberal democracy to being tolerant and accepting of the emergence of "Christian democracy" and Christian democratic political parties:

Contemporary Christian democratic parties evolved from Catholic confessional parties created in the second part of the nineteenth century and the first part of the twentieth century. These parties emerged out of a largely anti-liberal...mass Catholic movement that challenged the ascendancy of liberalism in Europe from a "fundamentalist" and theocratic perspective...Although initially opposed to democracy [Catholic activists] quickly realized that their interests lay in the consolidation and further expansion of parliamentary and electoral democracy, institutions that provided them social and political power. (Kalyvas and Van Kerbergen 2010: 185)

Similarly, in a form of "Muslim Democracy," Muslim activists have realized that the rise of democratic institutions and electoral democracy offers them a chance to gain social and political power. Many have embraced this opportunity and democratic norms. However, other currents of political Islam reject democracy. Some reject nonviolence as a means to achieve their goals as well. Salafis, for example, challenge democracy from a fundamentalist and theocratic perspective. They want to replicate their interpretation of the spirit, principles, and worldview of the First Muslims, the first three generations of believers, who were closest to the Prophet (*al-salaf al-salih*). Salafis are theocratic in that they oppose liberal and democratic interpretations of early Islamic history. Instead, they assert that democracy, to humanity's detriment, replaces God's laws (*Shari'a*) with man-made laws.

Some Salafis, quietist or Scripturalist Salafis, are not directly political. They seek to Islamize society before attaining the political power that is Islamization's natural outcome. To do so, they focus on education and teaching. In contrast, Jihadi Salafis are directly political and are willing to use violence to attain political power. Some Jihadi Salafis are referred to as Takfiri Salafis (a Takfiri is a Sunni Muslim who accuses another Muslim of apostasy, excommunicates them, and calls for them to be put to death). They believe that *jihad* must be waged not only against non-Muslims, but also against supposedly apostate Muslim rulers in Muslim countries *and* even against ordinary Muslims within their own homelands. The pronouncement of apostasy by Takfiri Salafis targets the accused – ruler or ruled – for death.

In the early stages of the Arab Spring, Jihadi Salafis like al-Qaeda adherents were in retreat. Muslim democratic parties like Ennahdha in Tunisia and the Muslim Brotherhood in Egypt demonstrated that they could attain political power through the ballot box, so there was no need for violence.[4] However, struggles at democratic consolidation gave new life to both the violent and nonviolent currents of Salafism.

In Iraq and in Syria, Takfiri Salafis – Islamic State adherents and others – reject Shia Islam as an authentic form of Islam and have

---

[4] There is a debate in the Arab world and in scholarship about the degree of commitment to democracy held by the Muslim Brotherhood and Ennahdha.

engaged in the mass murder of Shia Muslims, who are 15% of the world's Muslim population and the majority in Iraq, Bahrain, and Iran. In addition, the United Nations (UN) has formally accused ISIS of perpetrating genocide against minority Yazidis in Iraq. The expansive use of *takfir* by ISIS against fellow Muslims even spurred condemnation from al-Qaeda.

In sum, the advancement of democratic norms in the Arab Middle East led to political parties that combined traditional Islamic teachings with modern democratic ideas. However, minority currents, including some that readily use violence for political ends, reject both democracy and the nation-state. Instead, they seek a theocracy and a return to an Islamic empire. State collapse (or near collapse) during the Arab Spring in Libya, Yemen, Syria, and Iraq provided the terrain for Jihadi and Takfiri Salafis to attempt to put their beliefs into practice.

Extremists aside, compromise between Islamist and secular-oriented parties that formally accept democracy but distrust each other's intentions is the main challenge to achieving democratic bargains in the Arab Middle East. These parties represent the vast majority of the region's populations. Alfred Stepan (2012) has called the successful striking of a democratic political bargain between secularist and religious-based political parties the "twin tolerations." In the first, religious citizens must accord democratically elected officials freedom to legislate and govern within the bounds of the constitution and human rights without having to confront denials of their authority based on religious claims – such as the claim that "only God, not man, can make laws." In the second, as long as Islamist parties follow democratic norms, secular-oriented citizens must tolerate religious political parties' participation in elections. Thus, secularists must accept elected Islamist governments' legitimacy and the policies they generate as long as their actions do not impinge negatively on other citizens' liberties or violate democracy and the law.

Implied in the twin tolerations is the need for moderate Islamists to coax Islamic extremists toward moderation and democracy through dialogue and persuasion. The same is true on the other side in terms of moderate and authoritarian secularists. All of the state's coercive capacities have to be brought to bear against the recalcitrant Jihadi and Takfiri Salafis, who have far too often turned Arab hopes for the Arab Spring into bloody nightmares.

Democratic Consolidation: Socioeconomic Pacts

Most successful democratic transitions involve simultaneous political and economic reforms (Amin et al. 2012). In the Arab world, as elsewhere, the democratic aspirations of people participating in mass uprisings against authoritarian rule cannot be separated from expectations that changes in government will bring jobs and greater prosperity. Given the need for dual transitions, a group of economists, with regional expertise, have advanced an economic reform program with the potential to help consolidate emerging democracies in the Middle East and North Africa (Amin et al. 2012). Their modified market reform strategy takes advantage of the opportunities for economic growth provided by global markets and a vigorous private sector, while avoiding the simpleminded application of market liberalization, privatization, and a minimal state, which resulted in the crony-capitalist forms of authoritarian rule that have characterized the Arab world's political economy in recent decades (King 2009).

The recommended reforms can be conceptualized as five economic transitions. The first is the forging of a developmental state that avoids elite capture, limits corruption and is capable of implementing an industrial policy within the framework of a market-oriented model of development:

There is still a strong demand for a developmental state role in Arab economies and a significant suspicion over the impact of liberal economic reforms that, under the old regimes, served to benefit only a few well-connected private groups. The diagnoses of what is needed in terms of an economic transition is one of eliminating elite capture – the shaping of rules of the game and institutions of the state for the benefit of a few – rather than a need for fundamental reform of the economic model. In this, the Arab economic transitions differ markedly from economic transitions in Eastern Europe where the overall vision of a decisive move toward a market-oriented economy quickly became a consensus. Instead, in Arab economies, the key reforms…[reflect] the process of policymaking (voice and accountability concerns), the effectiveness of government institutions (the quality of the bureaucracy in formulating policies and delivering public services), and the control of corruption. (Amin et al. 2012: 7)

The second economic transition is in the private sector. Today, large elements of the private sector in the Arab world are seen as synonymous with corruption. To regain society's confidence, private sector leaders must set aside rent-seeking activities and direct all their energy to production and innovation. In turn, since there is no sustainable economic model for the region that does not have the private sector playing a leading role, governments need to gain the private sector's confidence and create an environment in which large, medium-sized, and small enterprises can operate equally. This requires reducing administrative discretion and petty corruption and strengthening competition policy.

Third, market-oriented reforms that can aid democratic consolidation also require a vigorous social policy (Przeworski 1991). Social policy has to address unemployment, poverty, and wage trends. There is so much unemployment and underemployment in the region that democratic governments must prioritize creating employment opportunities. If market forces are left to operate freely, wage earners and potential wage earners will be left out of rising national income for far too long for any possible political acceptance (Sheahan 1986). In addition to wage policies, needed social policies include health, education, and income maintenance programs. Without creating incentives to remain idle, income protection must be sufficient to cover basic needs and facilitate job searches and training. For countries with large informal sectors, social policies can facilitate access to the formal labor market. A subsidized credit system to promote self-employment would benefit small-scale entrepreneurs.

Social policy in the Arab world has to have a special focus on the young (Amin et al. 2012). The size of the youth base in the region is unprecedented; almost two-thirds of the population in the Arab world is under 30. High unemployment levels among the young drove the Arab Spring as much as anything else. The region also needs a major revamp of the education system for the young to acquire the skills to contribute to a competitive economy.

The fourth economic transition is in the approach to the world and the region. Arab countries need to improve their approach to the rest of the world, including the International Financial Institutions (IFIs): The World Bank (WB) and the International Monetary Fund (IMF). Successful emerging economies take advantage of the opportunities provided by global markets and the services provided by global institutions. However, Arab countries undergoing democratic transitions harbor a suspicion of the WB and the IMF because of the validation and support they provided to the old regimes, even in the face of rampant corruption and deteriorating governance.

For optimal success, both sides have to address this tension. The IFIs need to make independent assessments of the likely benefits of economic reforms for the majority of the people. Fruitful change will require that the IFIs undertake analyses of corruption, cronyism, and the potential capture of the state by special interest groups. In this vein, it would be useful if the IFIs worked more closely with civil society and emerging democratic parliaments in the region.

On the other side, Arab countries undergoing political transitions can benefit from a more constructive engagement with IFIs, the global economy, and the region. In other areas of the world, regional agreements have played a key role in anchoring economic transitions. While there are vast differences across the region – and past efforts to create regional projects have foundered – *that* the Arab Spring occurred almost simultaneously throughout the region suggests the existence of an Arab identity that should not be ignored (Amin et al. 2012). The effort to develop good and feasible policies to deal with what is manifestly a regional challenge has to be a backdrop to national approaches.

Finally, for economic transitions to succeed and contribute to democratic consolidation, politics is as important as policy. In their transitions framework, O'Donnell and Schmitter emphasize the importance of seeking national compromise and consensus about major social and economic decisions (i.e., a socioeconomic pact):

Getting the military back to the barracks and subject to civilian control, and getting political parties to compete according to the rules of political democracy are sufficient achievements to ensure significant regime change...however there is evidence that these accomplishments must be supplemented by another type of concertive effort: some sort of socio-economic pact. (O'Donnell and Schmitter 1986: 45)

For very good reasons, "economic transitions" need to be discussed and implemented within a broad national dialogue. Negotiations and compromise among key actors are critical because for the economic policies to succeed they must meet two opposing requirements (Sheahan 1986: 154). The first entails restraining the public demands of mobilized populations. The second implies concessions to these very same groups. Without some agreement on socioeconomic policies among business, government, and labor during the upheaval of democratic transitions, governments risk falling into a cycle of demands (strikes and protests for state benefits) and capitulation that threaten economic viability. Thus, national dialogues and the institutionalization of bargaining rights among business, labor, and government (corporatism) can produce socioeconomic pacts that create the possibility of a sustainable balance between demands on the economy and possibilities for sustained economic growth. In this way, economic transitions can support democratic transitions.

Democratic Consolidation: Nation-State and Weberian-State Pacts

In addition to managing military, political, and socioeconomic challenges during the Arab Spring, political leaders and their followers often had to attempt to forge national unity and attributes of modern states at the same time. The nation-building and state-building challenges complicated and sometimes overwhelmed the other elements of democratic pact-making.

National unity has long been an important variable in studies of regime transitions. For Dankwart Rustow, democracy is not possible without national unity (Rustow 1970). National unity, in this sense, means that "the vast majority of citizens in a democracy-to-be have no doubt or mental reservations as to which political community they belong to." Without national unity, it may be impossible to contain conflicts in new democracies. The introduction of competitive elections may trigger communal violence if antagonistic groups fear unbearable setbacks from losing elections. Thus, competing "nationalities," in a sustainable way, may not be willing to accept the basic principles that make democracy feasible:

In a democracy, representatives must at least informally agree that those who win greater electoral support or influence over policy will not use their temporary superiority to bar the losers from taking office or exerting influence in the future, and that in exchange for this opportunity to keep competing for power and place, momentary losers will respect the winners' right to make binding decisions. (Schmitter and Karl 1991: 82)

O'Donnell and Schmitter's transitions framework does not examine national unity challenges. Likely, this is because their framework was developed from democratic transitions in Southern Europe and Latin America, where national unity and modern state attributes were largely established before the democratic transitions began. However, in some of the Arab Spring transitions, this was decidedly not the case.

Arab nation-states largely owe their origins to European colonialism and imperialism. Post–World War I, after the defeat of the Ottoman Empire, Europe divided most of the Arab Middle East into many small, weak states with haphazard territorial boundaries drawn to favor European interests. The forced fragmentation of the Arab world led to the persistence of sub- and supra-state identities that weakened national unity (Hinnebusch 2006).

While no Arab states have definitively broken apart during the Arab Spring, the introduction of electoral competition in Arab majority countries without fully consolidated national identities has exacerbated communal conflicts. Elections turned into violent competition between Shias and Sunnis in Iraq. Regional rivalries between the former North Yemen and South Yemen, which unified in 1990 to form the Republic of Yemen, violently erupted after the introduction of competitive elections. Two sets of competitive elections could not prevent, and probably contributed to, post–Qaddafi civil war in Libya. In contrast, more consolidated national identities in Tunisia and Egypt probably limited violence during their tumultuous transitions. While there was loss of life, even the military coup in Egypt that removed the democratically elected Muslim Brotherhood from power did not lead to a cycle of violence on the scale of Syria that some feared.

Supra-state identities have also infused violence into the introduction of democratic institutions. The breakdown of authoritarian regimes during the Arab Spring emphasized the artificiality of some territorial boundaries. Without brutal tyrants and police states holding the "nation" together, dissatisfaction with the incongruence of identity communities with state boundaries has surfaced. For example, most Kurds want – and are willing to fight for – a Kurdistan regardless of how democratic Syria and Iraq become.

The Arab Spring has also reopened debates about the nation-state itself. In earlier decades, Pan-Arabism and Pan-Islamism challenged the European-imposed Arab nation-state system. During the Arab Spring, the Islamic State pointedly began creating their "Caliphate" (Islamic empire) by carving out territory across Iraqi and Syrian borders.

National unity challenges are not unsolvable, but they often require complex negotiations, pacts, consociational agreements, and possibly territorial realignments (Linz and Stepan 1996). If violent conflicts are to be limited during periods of democratic transition, the task of finding the best answers to national "disunity" is of crucial importance. Summarizing a generation of research, David Laitin (1995) finds such answers in institutional arrangements and political strategies that have federalism at their core – including holding national elections before regional and local elections in order to support both national unity and local autonomy. He concludes that democracies in multinational states will be different from those in homogenous states, but it does not mean that culturally or nationally heterogeneous societies are not viable candidates for successful democratization.

Ultimately, forging national unity while attempting to consolidate democratic procedures may be overwhelming for even the most gifted and devoted (to democracy) political elites. Yet, this is the position in which transitional elites of several countries – Libya, Yemen, Iraq – found themselves during the Arab Spring. Still, the literature suggests that the murders of Shias, Kurds, and Yazidis by Sunnis, as well as the murders of Sunnis by Alawites and other Shia groups during the Arab Spring, were not "natural" events born of primordial conflicts and inevitable "nationalist" movements. Instead, the violence between these groups requires a political explanation – and a political solution.

Similar to national unity, the role of the character of the state has drawn the attention of analysts seeking to explain the consolidation of democratic transitions. Scholars build on Max Weber's three core characteristics of modern states: a military that monopolizes the use of force within the state's territory, a rational-legal bureaucracy, and a tax collection apparatus able to pay for the military and bureaucracy. For Lisa Anderson, the capacity of the state to extract adequate resources, implement public policy, and maintain law and order constitute important conditions for both the adoption and consolidation of democratic regimes (Anderson 1999). Juan Linz and Alfred Stepan assert that "democracy is a form of governance of a modern state. Thus, without a modern state, no modern democracy is possible" (Linz and Stepan 1996: 17).

Attempting to democratize without a modern state means that elites must engage in state-building while introducing competitive politics. These state-building policies must aim to bolster extractive capacity, increase state capacity and good governance, and professionalize the military and secure its monopoly of violence within the country's borders while also subordinating it to civilian control. They must do so to protect citizens' rights and safety and deliver the basic services they demand. As we have witnessed in Libya, Yemen, and Iraq, establishing a monopoly of coercion may require surmounting the daunting challenge of unifying and subordinating a range of armed groups, including some brigades and militias that were never under state control.

States without enough bureaucratic capacity to deliver public services and implement the policy preferences that emerge from competitive elections also severely hinder democratic prospects. Governments in fragile new democracies need to be able to deliver on the policy goals that brought them to power. The new democratic order's legitimacy is at stake if elected governments lack a modern state that can envision the impact of various policy alternatives and guarantee their successful implementation. Political elites who lack a modern state during democratic transitions are forced to hurriedly implement policies that foster rational-legal bureaucracies while they are attempting to institutionalize political democracy.

Some argue that democratic consolidation is virtually impossible without the presence of a modern state prior to the start of a democratic transition:

It is neither plausible nor reasonable to expect that elites whose societies have little semblance of the bureaucratic capacity, military power, or international recognition we associate with statehood in the contemporary world would be able to initiate and sustain a democratic transition. (Anderson 1999: 11)

During the Arab Spring, political elites whose societies have little semblance of the military power or bureaucratic capacity we associate with modern statehood attempted to initiate and consolidate democratic transitions. After authoritarian breakdown, they had little choice but to attempt, on the fly, to create national unity, professional militaries under civilian control, and rationalize bureaucracies *while* attempting to institutionalize political democracy. This was the case in Libya, Yemen, and Iraq. Tunisians and Egyptians, with national unity forged across the centuries, have states that are closer to the Weberian ideal.

In sum, in contrast to the Western European and Latin American experience, the Arab Spring erupted in places where Weberian states and nation-states could not be taken for granted. For democratic consolidation to succeed in the region, nation-building and state-building measures often have to be undertaken at the same time as the implementation of competitive elections. This would be an enormous challenge for any group of people, anywhere in the world.

Democratic Consolidation: Transitional Justice, Human Rights, and Rule of Law Pacts

Dignity (*Karamah*) was a frequent demand in the Arab Spring uprisings. The call for a different relationship between citizens and government has encapsulated the revolts: a rejection of corrupt, repressive regimes that treated citizens as subjects without rights, paired with outrage at the capture of most economic benefits by government officials and their cronies (Dunn 2013). The authoritarian regimes that provoked the Arab Spring often engaged in unlawful imprisonment, violence, torture, and killing. In addition, during the Arab Spring, hundreds of thousands of people, many of them children, have been killed during armed conflicts, including the civil wars in Syria, Libya, Yemen, and Iraq. The level of bloodshed and brutal repression had been so high during the Arab Spring – and prior to it – that the introduction of competitive elections without transitional justice, national reconciliation, and a national effort to improve human rights and the rule of law risked gutting democracy of meaning.

"Transitional justice" refers to processes of dealing with a past of state-sponsored oppression and violence (Teitel 1990; Uprimny and Saffon 2006). It addresses the problem of how a society should face a legacy of grave crimes against humanity. Should it punish perpetrators? Should it forget atrocities in order to favor reconciliation? Under international law, transitional justice includes four elements:[5]

1) Truth: establishing the facts about violations of human rights that occurred and ending the culture of impunity;
2) Justice: investigating past violations, and if enough admissible evidence is gathered, prosecuting the suspected perpetrators;
3) Reparation: providing full and effective reparation to the victims and their families; and
4) Guarantees of nonrepetition and changes in relevant laws and practices.

---

[5] These can be found in United Nations Security Council (2004).

Some scholars and activists also highlight the need for the public telling of truths and apologies along with a process of reconciliation, clemency, and education of the public.[6]

While transitional justice is often vital for democratic consolidation, national reconciliation can be as well. Leaders of transitions from authoritarianism to democracy face the difficult task of solving the tension between the imperative to punish the perpetrators and the pragmatic demand of amnesty imposed by transitional contexts. Banning all "members" of the regime (defined in the broadest terms possible) from public and political life, which occurred in Iraq's "de-Baathification" and with Libya's Political Isolation Law, has been a recipe for disaster.

To address the need for peace and national reconciliation during regime transitions, the concept of restorative justice has been advanced as a replacement for transitional justice. The restorative justice model evolved most significantly in the South African context during a climate of political pragmatism and compromise between the African National Congress (ANC) and South Africa's ruling Afrikaans National Party at the end of the Apartheid era. The South African Truth and Reconciliation Commission (TRC, established by the Promotion of National Unity and Reconciliation Act of 1995) made the case for conditional amnesty based on truth-telling instead of on the prosecution of those responsible for crimes committed prior to the transition (Frederiksen 2008). Bishop Desmond Tutu made the argument in ethical and practical terms by asserting that justice should not be understood in purely retributive and punitive terms. Instead, Tutu advocated "another kind of justice – a restorative justice which is concerned not so much with punishment as with correcting imbalances, restoring broken relationships – with healing, harmony, and reconciliation" (Frederiksen 2008).

Transitional justice and restorative justice can be conceptualized complementarily so that the needs of peace and reconciliation are met without drastically weakening the requirement of justice, including punishment (Uprimny and Saffon 2006). Finding an equilibrium between justice and peace would not entail general amnesties for atrocious crimes, nor would it impose absolute and inflexible

---

[6] Widely reported advice given by the former president of South Africa, Nelson Mandela, to Tunisian transition leaders.

punishment of crimes and the stripping of democratic rights for alleged perpetrators. Pardons for perpetrators would proceed on an individual basis and only when it is the only mechanism to achieve the objectives of peace and national reconciliation.

Democratic transitions also offer the opportunity for formerly authoritarian regimes characterized by acute repression to reset human rights according to the highest international standards and establish the rule of law – an essential ingredient of democratic regimes. This includes equal citizenship rights for all. Upgrading human rights in countries where their violation has been pervasive and establishing the rule of law require judicial and security sector reforms that replace brutal state–society relations in the service of ruling-cliques and narrow patronage networks with democratic norms in which the state protects human rights and the rule of law.

In the Arab autocracies, instead of being the cornerstone of the rule of law, the judiciary has been one of the institutions that autocrats have used to establish and maintain power. There has been no separation of powers. The executives have dominated the other two branches of government. Constitutional courts in the region have conferred misleading constitutional legitimacy to cover up despotic regime projects, such as amendments that limit electoral competition and allow presidents to remain in office for life. These courts have also enabled vast corruption. Instead of delivering justice, they have facilitated unlawful detentions and other violations of human rights in the interests of autocratic regimes.

To establish the rule of law, protect human rights, and support democratic consolidation, the judiciary may have to be dismantled and reconstructed. Old regime figures resistant to change have to be removed. The branch's independence and professionalism have to be constructed in theory and in practice through personnel changes, new constitutions, and possibly new advisory bodies for the judicial framework.

To foster democratic consolidation, establish the rule of law, and improve human rights, the security sector has to be addressed as well. Repression has been essential to the crony-capitalist forms of authoritarian rule that dominated the Middle East prior to the Arab Spring. Security apparatuses in Arab states have been extensions of the ruling autocratic regimes rather than instruments of the state and servants of the people. Security forces have operated with impunity – there has been no judicial recourse for abuses of human rights. The Ministries of the Interior and partially hidden internal security infrastructures have proven to be surprisingly resistant to change, creating an avenue for the return to dictatorship in Arab Spring transitions.

In many ways, the Arab Spring was a regionwide reaction against the violations and abuses of the *mukhabarat* state (Ashour 2013). In Tunisia, Mohamed Bouazizi's self-immolation, which triggered the country's revolution and the Arab Spring in late 2010, followed a day of insults, attempted bribes, and beatings by security officials in his hometown of Sidi Bouzid (Fahim 2011). Egypt's uprising was framed and amplified by two policemen's brutal murder of an Internet activist, Khaled Said. A photo of his grotesquely beaten face was uploaded to a Facebook page by Egyptian Google executive, Wael Ghonim. Demonstration leaders created a "We are all Khaled Said" campaign and intentionally chose Egypt's National Police Day, January 25, 2011, as the start of the revolution.

Libya's Spring was also spurred by abuses in the security sector. In June 1996, Muammar Qaddafi's security forces gunned down 1,236 political prisoners in Abu Salim Prison. In February 2011, the arrest of Fathi Terbil, a human rights lawyer who for years had represented the families of the victims of the massacre, sparked the Libyan Revolution. In Syria, sadistic abuses against children and teenagers committed by Assad's security forces in March 2011 in Daraa triggered the protests that ignited the country's ongoing civil war. Loyalist security forces in Yemen turned protests into a war when they fired on peaceful, mostly young, demonstrators in early 2011.

To consolidate democracy, the mission of the security sector has to be redefined from a brutal instrument of internal repression designed to protect authoritarian rule and narrow patronage networks to a neutral public authority that protects citizens' rights and safety. Members of the security sector have to be subject to the rule of law. Greater transparency has to be established. Citizens have to trust the police, not fear them.

At a minimum, security sector reforms in support of democracy need to establish government and parliamentary control over the security services. Professionalism, efficiency, and integrity need to be inculcated and financially supported. The most compromised protectors of the old regime need to be removed along with gross systematic abuses of human rights. The public needs to be made aware of the responsibilities and limits of security institutions in a democratic society. These are fundamental changes that could benefit from a national dialogue that leads to the drafting and implementation of a new code of conduct for the internal security services. The drafting of such a code would come after wide consultation inside and outside the security sector, and it would take into account the new mission of internal security services in a postauthoritarian era (ICG 2015).

The Arab Spring uprisings provided an opportunity to upgrade human rights in the Arab world, including freedom from torture; freedom from forced disappearance; freedoms of speech, press, assembly, and religion; the right to equal protection under the law, due process, and fair trial; bodily integrity; and the right to life. The uprisings also mobilized groups seeking equal citizenship rights for women and all minorities.

Finally, the recent "awakening of Muslim democracy" (Cesari 2014) is seemingly producing "unsecular democracies" with broad elite and mass consensus about free and fair elections, the right to political opposition and organization, the right to express political opinions, and, to an extent, freedom of the press. However, some individual freedoms (sexual orientation and the right to exit or criticize Islam) are limited on religious grounds (Cesari 2014). These are generally considered to be human rights in modern democracies.

Looking Ahead

The Arab Winter's case study chapters begin with challenges to the Middle East and North Africa's autocratic regimes before the Arab Spring. This is followed by an analysis of authoritarian breakdown, democratic transition, and democratic consolidation in each country. Thereafter, I expand on my argument that challenges associated with democratic consolidation helped turn the Arab Spring into the Arab Winter.

Chapter 1 describes how Tunisia's unique success has been based on comparative strength in national unity and state capacities, along with an apolitical military and Islamist and secular political parties exceptionally willing to work together to sustain a democratic bargain. Latent threats to Tunisia's democracy remain in a security sector fighting reform, socioeconomic struggles, and the resurgence to power of pre–Arab Spring political and economic elites.

In Chapter 2, I describe how Egypt entered the Arab Spring with relative strength in national unity and state capacities. However, during the country's democratic transition, its military took advantage of conflicts between Islamists and secularists in order to stage a coup and reassert its historical dominance of Egypt's political economy. Both Islamist and secular-oriented political parties were at fault in failing to forge the "twin tolerations" necessary for a political pact or democratic bargain in Egypt. Witnessing the victory of Islamists in transitional elections, secularists turned to the streets and the military to overturn electoral outcomes. For their part, after winning Egypt's post-Mubarak founding elections, President Morsi and the Muslim Brotherhood made decisions and appointments that raised questions about their commitment to democracy and their willingness to share power at the most delicate point of a democratic transition, the period that includes constitution-writing.

The Libyan case study in Chapter 3 reveals how harrowing the introduction of democratic elections can be in countries without national unity or any of the attributes of a modern state. Qaddafi's ideology of a stateless, egalitarian society based on an idiosyncratic blend of Islamic and Marxist concepts left Libya's transitional regime largely without a bureaucratic apparatus to implement policies (Pargeter 2012). Qaddafi also reinvigorated Libya's tribal system by favoring his own tribe and punishing the regions and tribes that were the base of support for the prior monarchical regime.

Competitive elections in Libya were implemented in a country without a national military that could monopolize the use of violence. In its place, during the civil war, a welter of regional, local, tribal, and ideological militias – some more powerful than the "national military" – emerged and prevented transitional governments from being able to provide peace and security for Libyans. There is also a military strongman in Libya, General Khalifa Haftar, seeking to utilize the near anarchic conditions to forge a military authoritarian regime by reining in the militias and providing desperately needed security.

National "disunity" revealed itself quickly during the Libyan Revolution. In that environment, competitive elections sparked bloody communal conflict with both political power and access to the country's rich oil reserves at stake.

Chapter 4 tracks Yemen's democratic transition and descent into civil war. Like Libya, Yemen entered the Arab Spring with severe national unity and state-capacity challenges. National unity collapsed in Yemen when the military fired on protestors and when some soldiers and officers defected to the uprising.

In addition, in Yemen, during the democratic transition, potent political parties never emerged to represent the secular youth who spearheaded the regime. Houthi rebels, the main challengers to the prior regime under Saleh's rule, also felt left out of the transition process. Lastly, political parties also failed to forge a consensus on how to resolve conflicts between the former North Yemen and South Yemen, which prevented a democratic bargain or political pact from forming.

Yemen is also the poorest country in the region, making it exceptionally vulnerable to socioeconomic challenges. Yemen's failed democratic transition has been costly. In 2018, the UN declared Yemen the site of the worst humanitarian suffering in the world (Ferguson 2018). Nearly 100,000 Yemenis are living under famine conditions, and millions more risk dying from hunger. Years of war have destroyed the economy and have caused widespread starvation and disease. The fighting blocks supply routes to the desperate.

Chapter 5 focuses on broken nation-states during the Arab Spring – Iraq, Syria, and the Islamic State – the human suffering that broken states cause (even if they "broke" during efforts to implement and sustain democratic politics), and how elites have tried to put the states back together again. Syria's grinding civil war, which began after President Bashar al-Assad chose to ruthlessly repress the country's Arab Spring uprising, has killed over 560,000 people, including more than 100,000 civilians (Syrian Observatory for Human Rights 2019). More than half of the country's prewar population – over 12 million people – have been killed or forced to flee their homes. Families are struggling to survive inside Syria or to make new homes in neighboring countries. Syrian refugees have also risked life and limb to reach European shores.

Internationalizing the conflict, Iranian and Russian support helped Assad survive when he was on the precipice of defeat. The opposition has largely accepted that, with foreign help, Assad has won, and they are now seeking merely to survive. Making matters worse, Assad is using his current control of the postconflict order to brutally reimpose a minority regime that is at war with most of Syrian society.

In Iraq, Iraqis have endured nearly two decades of bloody communal strife, including the temporary loss of one-third of its territory to the

Islamic State. Hundreds of thousands of Iraqis have died in this time period.

Democratically elected governments in Iraq and the US-led occupation have worked against national unity and done little to create a modern state. The result has been competitive elections and fragmentation, but not democratic consolidation. An elected government led by the Shia majority won transitional elections, but discriminated against Sunnis enough to contribute to an insurgency and support for ISIS among Iraqi Sunnis. Kurds have voted for secession from Iraq and the declaration of an independent "Kurdistan" in northern Iraqi territory. The governments in power have used violence and negotiations to prevent full Kurdish independence and to retake control of the oil resources in the regions that the Kurds currently occupy.

Mass murder – including of other Muslims – is central to ISIS's identity. Inevitably, the Caliphate that it founded gradually lost all of its territory in Iraq and Syria to its numerous enemies in the Arab world and the West. In response, it has gone underground in both countries, sponsored cells in other countries with nation-state issues, returned to guerilla warfare, and become more al-Qaeda-like in targeting its far-enemy in the West with terrorist attacks.

Chapter 6, the final chapter, summarizes what we learn from the case studies about democratic consolidation. In light of the disappointing results of the Arab Spring, using comparative experience and research to identify the challenges and possible solutions to democratic consolidation can be disheartening. However, in addition to providing current depictions of the polities in the region, *The Arab Winter* illuminates these difficult challenges and highlights the (sometimes heroic) attempts to meet them during what has come to be called the Arab Spring.

References

Amin, M. et al. 2012. *After the Spring: Economic Transitions in the Arab World*, Vol. 2. New York: Oxford University Press.
Anderson, L. 1999. "Introduction." In L. Anderson, ed., *Transitions to Democracy*. New York: Columbia University Press, pp. 1–13.
Ashour, O. 2013. "Finishing the Job: Security Sector Reform after the Arab Spring." *Brookings.edu*, 28 May. www.brookings.edu/articles/finish ing-the-job-security-sector-reform-after-the-arab-spring/.

Bermeo, N. 2003. "What the Democratization Literature Says – or Doesn't Say – about Postwar Democratization." *Global Governance*, 9(2), 159–177.

Burton, M. et al. 1992. "Introduction: Elite Transformations and Democratic Regimes." In J. Higley and R. Gunther, ed., *Elites and Democratic Consolidation in Latin America and Southern Europe*. Cambridge: Cambridge University Press, pp. 1–37.

Caryl, C. 2013. "The Democracy Boondoggle in Iraq." *Foreign Policy*, March 6. www.foreignpolicy.com/2013/03/06/the-democracy-boondoggle-in-iraq/.

Cesari, J. 2014. *The Awakening of Muslim Democracy: Religion, Modernity, and the State*. Cambridge: Cambridge University Press.

Croissant, A. et al. 2011. "Conceptualizing Civil–Military Relations in Emerging Democracies." *European Political Science*, 10(2), 137–145.

Dunn, T. M. 2013. "The Failings of Liberal Modernisation Theory." PhD diss., University of Nottingham.

Encarnación, O. 2000. "Beyond Transitions: The Politics of Democratic Consolidation" *Comparative Politics*, 32(4), 479–498.

Fahim, K. 2011. "Slap to a Man's Pride Set Off Tumult in Tunisia." *New York Times*, 21 January. www.nytimes.com/2011/01/22/world/africa/22sidi.html.

Ferguson, J. 2018. "Fighting, Starvation and Disease Yield Grim Crisis in Yemen." *PBS*. December 28. www.pbs.org/newshour/show/fighting-starvation-and-disease-yield-grim-crisis-in-yemen.

Frederiksen, E. A. 2008. "Reconstituting Political Community: Truth Commissions, Restorative Justice and the Challenges of Democratic Transition." Paper presented at the Annual Meeting of the Canadian Political Science Association, Vancouver, BC, June 4–6.

Haaretz and Reuters. 2018. "560,000 Killed in Syria's War according to Updated Death Toll." *Haaretz.com*, December 10. www.haaretz.com/middle-east-news/syria/560-000-killed-in-syria-s-war-according-to-updated-death-toll-1.6700244.

Hinnebusch, R. 2006. "Authoritarian Persistence, Democratization Theory, and the Middle East: An Overview and Critique." *Democratization*, 13 (3), 373–395.

Huffington, A. 2013. "Marhaba! Introducing Al Huffington Post Maghreb." *HuffPost*, June 26. www.actionnews.ca/newstempch.php?article=/entry/introducing-al-huffington-post-maghreb_b_3492847.html.

International Crisis Group (ICG). 2015. "Reform and Security Strategy in Tunisia, Middle East and North Africa Report." *Crisisgroup.org*, 23 July. www.crisisgroup.org/middle-east-north-africa/north-africa/tunisia/reform-and-security-strategy-tunisia.

Kalyvas, S. and K. Van Kerbergen. 2010. "Christian Democracy." *Annual Review of Political Science*, 13, 183–209.

King, S. J. 2009. *The New Authoritarianism in the Middle East and North Africa*. Bloomington: Indiana University Press.

Laitin, D. 1995. "Transitions to Democracy and Territorial Integrity." In A. Przeworski, ed., *Sustainable Democracy*. Cambridge: Cambridge University Press, pp. 19–33.

Linz, J. and A. Stepan. 1996. *Problems of Democratic Transition and Consolidation: Southern Europe, Latin America, and Post-Communist Europe*, Vol. 1. Baltimore: Johns Hopkins University Press.

Moon, C. and S. Rhyu. 2011. "Democratic Transitions, Persistent Civilian Control over the Military, and the South Korean Anomaly." *Asian Journal of Political Science*, 19(3), 250–269.

O'Donnell, G. and P. C. Schmitter. 1986. *Transitions from Authoritarian Rule: Tentative Conclusions about Uncertain Democracies*. Baltimore: Johns Hopkins University Press.

Pargeter, A. 2012. *Libya: The Rise and Fall of Qaddafi*. New Haven, CT: Yale University Press.

Przeworski, A. 1991. *Democracy and the Market: Political and Economic Reforms in Eastern Europe and Latin America*, Vol. 1. Cambridge: Cambridge University Press.

Rustow, D. 1970. "Transitions to Democracy: Toward a Dynamic Model." *Comparative Politics*, 2(3), 337–363. doi:10.2307/421307.

Schmitter, P. C. and T. L. Karl. 1991. "What Democracy Is and Is Not." *Journal of Democracy*, 2(3), 75–88.

Sheahan, J. 1996. "Economic Policies and the Prospects for Successful Transitions from Authoritarian Rule in Latin America." In G. O'Donnell, P. C. Schmitter, and L. Whitehead, ed., *Transitions from Authoritarian Rule: Comparative Perspectives*. Baltimore: Johns Hopkins University Press, pp. 154–164.

Stepan, A. 2012. "Tunisia's Transition and the Twin Tolerations." *Journal of Democracy*, 23(2), 89–103. www.journalofdemocracy.org/articles/tunisias-transition-and-the-twin-tolerations/.

Sullum, J. 2011. "Obama's War of Choice." *Reason.com*, March 23. www.reason.com/2011/03/23/obamas-war-of-choice-2.

Syrian Observatory for Human Rights 2019. "Syria Death Toll for January 2019 Nearly at 900." *Syriahr.com*, February 3. www.syriahr.com/en/?p=115251.

Teitel, R. 1990. "How Are the New Democracies of the Southern Cone Dealing with the Legacy of Past Human Rights Abuses?" Paper presented at the Council on Foreign Relations Latin American Project, New York, May 17.

Trinkunas, H. A. 2000. "Crafting Civilian Control in Emerging Democracies: Argentina and Venezuela." *Journal of Inter-American Studies and World Affairs*, 42(3), 77–109. doi:10.2307/166439.

United Nations Security Council. 2004. *The Rule of Law and Transitional Justice in Conflict and Post-Conflict Societies*. Report of the Secretary-General S/2005/616. New York: United Nations. www.un.org/ruleof law/blog/document/the-rule-of-law-and-transitional-justice-in-conflict-and-post-conflict-societies-report-of-the-secretary-general/.

Uprimny, R. and M. P. Saffon. 2006. "Transitional Justice, Restorative Justice and Reconciliation: Some Insights from the Columbian Case." Working paper. Bogota: National University of Columbia.

1 | Tunisia

While the eruption of the Arab Spring came as a surprise to the world, the academic literature had shown that Arab majority regimes were deeply unpopular and faced serious economic and political challenges (Gause 2011). Tunisia under former president Zine El Abidine Ben Ali was no exception. I begin this chapter with a description of the authoritarian regime Ben Ali led and major challenges to it prior to the Arab Spring.

As the country that began the Arab Spring by forcing Ben Ali out of power, Tunisia also invites inquiry into authoritarian breakdown. The regime transitions framework discussed in the Introduction highlighted tensions between regime elites as the catalyst. However, there were no obvious signs that Ben Ali's authoritarian regime was splitting between hardliners and softliners when the desperation and defiance of a Tunisian fruit and vegetable vendor, Mohamed Bouazizi, triggered the Arab Spring. Instead, Tunisia's transition was initiated by a mass uprising, the pivotal role of a martyr (Bouazizi), and social media.[1] Copycat attempts at "revolution" in the rest of the Arab Middle East demonstrated the potency of regional dynamics in regime transition processes.

In terms of democratic consolidation, Tunisia has been the only relative success story of the Arab Spring. Post-authoritarian breakdown, military, political, and nation-state pacts in Tunisia have ensured significant regime change. However, socioeconomic issues continue to threaten democratic progress in the country, as does resistance to judicial and security sector reforms, which hinder transitional

---

[1] The role of a martyr, social media, and regional dynamics stand out when integrated into existing comparative studies of transitions. Anchored in studies of Latin America and Southern Europe, the transitions literature's emphasis on conflicts between hardliners and softliners within authoritarian regimes tracked empirical realities. Authoritarian breakdown in Africa and Eastern Europe largely shared the Arab world's genesis in mass uprisings. See Bratton and van de Walle (1994) and Bunce (2003).

justice, improvements in human rights, and ultimately the establishment of the rule of law.

Crony-Capitalist Authoritarian Rule: Tunisia under Ben Ali, 1987–2011

Under President Ben Ali (1987–2011), a crony-capitalist form of authoritarian rule was consolidated. In addition to a liberalizing economy dominated by the distribution of state assets – companies and land – to the extended family members and cronies that became his regime's social base, Ben Ali orchestrated a façade of multiparty politics while cultivating an ideology of developmentalism and state protection from the dangers of radical Islam. His obsession with security and control led to the general shutdown of political space and possibly the most restrictive media in the Arab world.

Crony capitalism in Tunisia has been fully exposed since the revolution. Every regime's ability to govern is underpinned by a set of allied interests and coalition partners (Waterbury 1989). In the Tunisian case under Ben Ali, privatization policies based primarily on political considerations forged allied interests – a ruling coalition – with crony capitalists and large landowners (King 2009). In addition, state elites used their positions to coerce private-sector actors to include them in any profitable enterprise.

Ben Ali's economy was mafia-like: "More than half of Tunisia's commercial elites were personally related to Ben Ali through his three adult children, seven siblings, and his second wife's 10 brothers and sisters, the widely reviled Trabelsi clan. This network became known in Tunisia as 'the Family'" (Anderson 2011: 3). After the revolution, judicial authorities banned travel for 460 businessmen suspected of involvement in corruption cases with the president's in-laws (Lewis 2011). It has been estimated that the Ben Ali and Trabelsi families controlled up to 40% of the Tunisian economy (Lewis 2011). This level of predation occurred in a country of approximately 11 million people with a Gross Domestic Product (GDP) of around $45 billion in 2013.

Ignoring the impact of rampant corruption, Ben Ali portrayed himself as the steward of an economy widely viewed by the International Financial Institutions (IFIs) – the World Bank (WB) and the International Monetary Fund (IMF) in particular – as a model of economic development for Arab and African countries (WB 1995, 1996; Pfeifer 1999).The IFIs' reports issued during Ben Ali's time in power highlighted sound macroeconomic policies, a 6% on average annual growth rate in the decade prior to the revolution, a growing middle class with high levels of home ownership, and social policies that kept poverty levels below 7%. The WB cited Tunisia as an exemplary case of equitable growth (WB 1996). If only this were true.

After a revolution calling for socioeconomic justice, the depiction of the Tunisian economy by the IFIs and Ben Ali's regime was wildly inaccurate. Poor data partly explains the puzzle. Repressive regimes maintain their grip on power partly by controlling the availability and accuracy of information. This holds true even in deals with the IFIs that provide autocratic developing countries like Tunisia with development aid to fight poverty and promote economic growth. For example, Tunisia's National Institute of Statistics reported poverty rates below 7%, and WB publications championed it. However, new postrevolution statistics released in May 2011 by the Tunisian Ministry of Social Affairs set the actual poverty rate at 24.7% of the population (WB 2011).

Tunisian national statistics were also probably off in other areas. Despite a very young population (55% of Tunisians are below the age of 24), official unemployment under Ben Ali, at its high-water mark, was probably reported as no more than 14%. A reality-based recasting of Tunisia's development profile just prior to the January 2011 revolution would be as follows. More than 24% of the Tunisian population lived below the poverty line, and unemployment was likely around 20%. Unemployment for the young (ages 15–24) has been recalculated and was over 30% in 2005 (Index Mundi n.d.). Unemployment among university graduates was distressingly high. Additionally, under Ben Ali, Tunisia suffered from sharp disparities in regional development. The coastal regions fared far better than the interior of the country.

Ultimately, cultivating cronies provided the regime with a base of support in an economy that was faring much worse than official accounts would have one believe.

To maintain social control and forge some domestic and international legitimacy, Ben Ali established a façade of multiparty politics dominated by his ruling party, the Constitutional Democratic Rally (RCD), and affiliated corporatist institutions – that is, various labor and employer associations.

Like most elections in the Arab world prior to the Arab Spring, Tunisian elections under Ben Ali were rigged and produced legislatures with little power. The RCD never received less than 80% of the vote in elections that occurred every five years beginning in 1989. The direct presidential elections Ben Ali instituted were also never competitive. In the 1989, 1994, 2004, and 2009 elections, he never received less than 90% of the official vote tally. He seemed to have had in mind a form of consensual authoritarianism in which opposition political parties supported the regime, accepted that they would never be competitive electorally against the RCD, and backed Ben Ali as president-for-life. In exchange, they received limited policy input and state patronage benefits.

Politics in Tunisia under President Ben Ali was also marked by intensive political repression. The security and judicial sectors were deployed to protect the narrow group of elites that dominated the country's political economy. Ben Ali used state violence and intimidation to devastate all forms of resistance from Islamism (in all its manifestations) to independent trade unionism (Mullin and Patel 2013). Some 35,000 men and 1,500 women, mainly Islamists, were detained and tortured under Ben Ali (Mullin and Patel 2013). In addition, in a small country with a small population, the regime maintained some 80,000 secret police (Cole 2013).

Ben Ali thus constructed a crony-capitalist police state in which freedoms of press, association, and speech did not exist and in which all institutions that could constitute countervailing powers to the regime – trade and employer unions, the judiciary, parliament, voluntary associations, political parties, universities, etc. – were systematically placed under government control (Reporters sans Frontieres 1999).

While robust, authoritarianism in Tunisia under Ben Ali was challenged at times, especially by labor, human rights organizations, and Islamists. The Tunisian Human Rights League (LTDH) was the first independent human rights association in the Arab world (Chayes 2014). However, its independence came at a price. To repress the organization's activities and meetings, the regime-dominated courts ruled against it on numerous trumped-up charges (HRW 2009). Human rights defenders and the dissidents they sought to protect faced surveillance, arbitrary travel bans, dismissal from work, interruptions in phone service, and physical assaults; torture in prison was common, as were charges of disturbing the public order (HRW 2009). Notably, after Ben Ali fled to Saudi Arabia, a former president of the LTDH, Moncef Marzouki, would go on to become president of the Tunisian Republic.

Historically, the Tunisian General Labor Union (UGTT) has been a powerful political force. Formed in 1946, it made major contributions to the independence struggle that was led by Tunisia's first postindependence president, Habib Bourguiba, and his Neo-Destour Party. In negotiations with France, he was one of the official interlocutors who oversaw the state's creation (Bellin 2002). The UGTT's first president, Farhat Hached, was assassinated in 1952 for his work on behalf of Tunisian independence. The UGTT's decision to support Bourguiba during a conservative challenge at a crucial 1955 party conference secured the president's rise to power (Bellin 2002). While Bourguiba attempted to emasculate the UGTT and turn it into just one more state-controlled "national organization," its domination by the ruling party was never complete (Bellin 2002). In 1978, it led an unprecedented national strike that shook the regime.

In response to the 1978 national strike, the entire leadership of the UGTT was put on trial and replaced by regime loyalists (Omri 2014). This led to riots that were repressed by the army, which resulted in many deaths. Like Habib Bourguiba, during his twenty-three years in power, Ben Ali also attempted to suffocate independent trade union activity, primarily by co-opting its leadership. He, too, was not completely successful. Six months of protests by phosphate mine workers in the southern town of Gafsa in 2008 (known as the Gafsa revolts) are widely seen as a precursor to the Tunisian Spring.[2] Rising discontent prompted the radical local wing of the UGTT to organize an occupation of its regional office by Gafsa workers (Lee and Weinthal 2011). In addition, once the Arab Spring uprisings began, organized labor did not wait for orders from above; their spontaneous solidarity with the revolution helped to maintain the momentum for change across the country (Toensing 2011).

Once the UGTT had been brought back under regime control in 1978, Islamism took its place as the most powerful force in opposition to the government. Tunisia's main Islamist movement began in 1970 as

---

[2] This point was made during a series of interviews undertaken by the author after Ben Ali's departure.

the Quranic Preservation Society, an apolitical organization dedicated primarily to encouraging piety and faithfulness (Hamdi 1998). However, witnessing the power of and potential for change that the UGTT manifested in the 1978 national strike, several Islamists – led by Rachid Ghannouchi – broke away from the Quranic Preservation Society and formed the overtly political Movement for Islamic Renewal, which was renamed the Islamic Tendency Movement (MTI) a year later. The MTI's platform called for equitable economic reform, an end to one-party rule, and a return to the "fundamental principles of Islam." The group requested recognition as a political party under Bourguiba but was denied; most of its leaders were jailed.

Ben Ali came to power in 1987 promising reform and democratization. That promise turned into a façade of multiparty politics and the prohibition of any political party with a name containing the words Islam or Islamic. In response, the MTI renamed itself Hizb Ennahdha (Ennahdha), the Renaissance Party, but Ben Ali still refused to allow the organization to openly participate in politics. After years of generalized harassment, imprisonment, and torture of Ennahdha members, Ben Ali violently repressed Ennahdha in 1991 with the intention of uprooting it once and for all. Its leaders were either jailed, or, like Ghannouchi, forced to flee into exile. Ghannouchi returned to Tunisia shortly after Ben Ali's first abdication of power on January 14, 2011. Ennahdha was the primary winner of the democratic transition's founding elections in October 2011.

Authoritarian Breakdown

Under Ben Ali, potentially destabilizing protests followed a general pattern. They typically began in the poorer southern and central parts of the country, but were usually shut down by security forces before they could spread to the capital and coastal cities.[3] The pattern is evident in what most Tunisians regard as the real start of their revolution: the 2008 revolts in the southern phosphate-mining region of Gafsa near the Sahara.[4] Those protests focused on corruption and working conditions and were organized by the radical wing of the

---

[3] Interview with Tunisian journalist, March 2011.
[4] This was the most common answer given to questions about the genesis of the revolution in interviews conducted in Tunis and Sidi Bouzid, the cradle of the Tunisian Revolution.

UGTT (Ben Moussa 2012). Six months of sporadic demonstrations led to hundreds of arrests, several deaths, and many injuries at the hands of security forces. However, in a common strategy of authoritarian maintenance, the Tunisian government imposed a successful information blackout during the Gafsa revolts – journalists were not allowed in the region, the state-controlled media ignored them, and little information and few images to inspire similar protests managed to get out.[5]

The stifling of dissent in the south before it reached the coastal population centers in northern Tunisia finally failed during the Arab Spring. Two factors seem to have enabled the countrywide mass protests in late 2010 and early 2011 to finally overcome the regime's southern strategy and bring an end to Ben Ali's dictatorship.

The first was the role played by a martyr.[6] In despair, Mohamed Bouazizi, a struggling fruit and vegetable vendor in impoverished rural Tunisia, poured paint thinner over his body and lit himself on fire to protest the arbitrary confiscation of his produce and further humiliations by local officials. Bouazizi's desperate act inspired a sense of solidarity and focused anger against the regime that led to mass protests in his hometown of Sidi Bouzid and in the surrounding area.

The second was social media and cell-phone technology, which had spread throughout Tunisia by 2010, helped protestors overcome the regime's media bans, and helped organize a nationwide revolution. Ben Ali's regime used every tool in the police-state tool kit to prevent the type of countrywide information flow and civil society strength that contributed to the regime's ouster in early 2011. However, social media made a powerful contribution to the Tunisian Revolution because it enabled the construction of a parallel "cyber civil society" out of the regime's reach and beyond its understanding. Social media and Bouazizi's martyrdom were crucial factors in the success of the Tunisian Revolution.

The social media process that led to the successful circumvention of a police state at the end of 2010 can be traced back to 1998, when two Tunisians known as Foetus and Waterman (names used to protect their anonymity) began what they called a cyber think tank, Takriz (Arabic

---

[5] Interview with Tunisian journalist, March 2011.

[6] No literature that I am aware of asserts the causal role of galvanizing, solidiaristic martyrdom. The power of social media and the internet received some attention before the Arab Spring.

street slang for "frustrated anger").[7] Takriz's goals included freedom of speech and affordable Internet access. Foetus, Takriz's chief technology officer, is a skilled hacker who began hacking because he could not afford Tunisia's then-exorbitant phone and Internet costs. The founders recognized that the Internet was the only form of media in Tunisia not completely controlled by Ben Ali. The Internet also provided relative safety for dissidents through anonymity.

By 2000, Takriz had grown into a loose network of thousands, and their criticisms of the Tunisian regime led to their website being blocked in the same year. Takriz used various tactics – from serious political analysis to leaked documents and fierce polemic – to reach multiple audiences. Its leaders turned to Arabic slang, obscenities, and street culture to stir up street youth. They also organized protests at football stadiums, one of the few venues with lax political control. Its members were hunted and exiled for years under Ben Ali. Their cyberactivism increased dramatically after 2009, when Ben Ali orchestrated yet another five-year term in office. Takriz's founders saw this as the last straw, as they could imagine another decade of Ben Ali and his rapacious family mafia looming, with the formal opposition and general public afraid to act.[8]

Zouhair Yahyaoui, one of the members of Takriz, deserves special note. Yahyaoui, known online as Ettounsi ("the Tunisian"), started TUNeZine, a political webzine and forum that inspired many with humor, such as in the following notice of a "competition":

TUNeZine is launching a competition for jokes, reserved for young people, about
Ben Ali and his party:

First prize: 13 years in prison.
Second prize: 20 years in prison.
Third prize: 26 years in prison.

TUNeZine made Ettounsi famous in Tunisia, but it also led to his arrest and torture. He was jailed in 2000, after inviting readers to vote on whether Tunisia was "a republic, a kingdom, a zoo, or a prison."

---

[7] This depiction of the development of Tunisia's cyber civil society is based on Pollock (2011) and on interviews with Tunisian cyberactivists conducted by the author.
[8] Ibid.

According to his family, he was sent to one of the worst prisons in the country – with 120 people in one room, just one bathroom, and hardly any water. He became ill and was beaten when he asked for a doctor. He went on several hunger strikes. He was released that year in extremely poor physical condition and died shortly afterward. Reporters without Borders gave Zouhair Yahyaoui its first Cyber-Freedom Prize in 2003. The PEN American Center (now PEN America) gave him its Freedom to Write Award that same year.

The life of Zouhair Yahyaoui was the primary catalyst for the emergence of Nawaat (Arabic for "the nucleus" or "the core") in 2004.[9] Its four founders were affected by Yahyaoui's articles and were committed to his tradition of cyberactivism. Nawaat began as a webzine and Nawaat Forums. Later, it became a collection of bloggers. In time, members of Nawaat became adept at all the social media tools: blogs, forums, Facebook, Twitter, YouTube, and various livestreaming applications. They learned quickly, for example, that Facebook provided an empty space to fill with information better than older platforms like WebZine, where all users read one editor's comments. They understood that the power of Facebook and some blogs was in the interaction between writers and readers. Along with blogs and Twitter, Nawaat used Facebook to create a cyber civil society: activist platforms with followers, citizen journalism, and social interaction that could partially replace the civil society confiscated by Ben Ali's regime. The social media platforms provided a public space, and between 2007 and 2010 there was an explosion in the number of Tunisians regularly using social media, which provided the public for this new public space.

Ironically, Ben Ali – himself a computer geek who was an electronics technician in the army – may have contributed to the creation of this dissident public sphere. In his fifteenth development plan, released in 2001, he announced a policy of extending Internet connection to 100% of the country. Under his rule, the number of cybercafés increased dramatically due to government credits and grants to the unemployed that funded these ventures. The Tunisian version of the Internet that became available to many Tunisians was heavily censored (reportedly, Ben Ali's wife, Leila, owned the .planet domain through

[9] Most of the information to follow comes from a personal interview carried out in April 2012 with the founders of Nawaat.

which all Tunisian emails passed). However, Ben Ali's technology push got large numbers of Tunisians online. In addition, his daughter, Cyrine Ben Ali Mabrouk, brought third-generation (3G) developments in wireless technology to Tunisia in 2010 (Le Monde 2011). Her company, Orange, spread mobile Internet services throughout the country. The 3G technology she introduced vastly improved live-streaming capabilities in Tunisia.

Technology to evade Internet censorship also rapidly became wide-spread in Tunisia. Hot-spotting technology, which allowed users to stay anonymous, spread to the masses, and when the regime broke down in 2011, thousands posted "hot-spotting, we won't forget you" on their Facebook pages. Well-trained cyberactivists associated with Nawaat were technically able to avoid detection by the secret police by, for the most part, using a VPN (Virtual Private Network). The bloggers used Facebook's news feed function to share information and develop and maintain thousands, if not tens of thousands, of followers. These bloggers frequently adapted a revolutionary tone toward the Ben Ali regime.[10]

Between 1998 and the 2010–2011 Tunisian Revolution, social media tools gradually created an alternative public sphere, a civil society online in a country that did not allow street demonstrations, associational life, free speech, or independent political parties. That civil society had become committed to political power based on free and fair multiparty elections.

Through its organizational capabilities, Tunisia's cyber civil society contributed to the nationwide mass revolt between December 17, 2010, and January 14, 2011, that ended the dictatorship in Tunisia and inspired the Arab Spring. The emergence of a martyr that caused feelings of solidarity and anger focused enough to trigger a mass rebellion against the regime was the second major factor that led to authoritarian demise in Tunisia.

On December 17, 2010, Mohamed Bouazizi, a fruit and vegetable vendor in the impoverished central Tunisian region of Sidi Bouzid, set himself on fire to protest the confiscation of his goods and his constant harassment and humiliation by municipal officials and police officers.

---

[10] Among the most prominent were Fatima Arabica, Slim Amamou, Yassine Ayari, Malek Kadhraoui, and Riadh Guerfali. Fatima Arabica's blog was mainly literary; however, she was arrested in 2009, which may have been an attempt on her part to send a message to other bloggers.

With its symbol of exasperation with arbitrary rule, Bouazizi's actions led to immediate protests, beginning with members of his extended family or "tribe" (as well as with his fellow fruit vendors).[11] Bolstered by a second suicide in Sidi Bouzid a few days later, the protests accelerated.[12] (Another young man committed suicide, this time by electrocuting himself on a utility pole. His mother wailed and cried in the streets for hours.)

Unlike in 2008, due to social media the local protests in 2010–2011 spread throughout the country. In one of the first videos of the protests from Sidi Bouzid in December 2010, you can hear someone saying, "I'm going to post this on Facebook tonight."[13] On December 25, 2010, anonymous bloggers organized the demonstration in Tunis. To gather critical mass, they hacked into Tunisia's National Trade Union Federation's website to announce the demonstration's date and time. This allowed them to reach the rank and file of an organization whose leadership had long been co-opted by Ben Ali.

A member of Nawaat, Slim Amamou, filmed the Tunis protests, which Al Jazeera broadcast. This was the first time that people from Sidi Bouzid realized that their protests had reached the capital. In early January 2011, a group of cyberactivists called Anonymous hacked official government websites, including the president's and the prime minister's, to demonstrate the vulnerability of the regime. Between December 17, 2010, and January 14, 2011, over 500 videos of Tunisian protests were posted on Facebook, blogs, Twitter, and YouTube. Due to social media, social interaction across the country had become too supple for the Tunisian police state. "*Like, Comment, Share, Tweet*" became acts adapted to Tunisian circumstances, circumstances characterized by anger and a powerful desire to end an unpopular dictatorship.

The Ben Ali regime made a last-ditch effort to stop cyberactivism, but they were largely unsuccessful. Protestors mocked their efforts with slogans such as "Free from 404" (404 being Internet error message for when a file cannot be found).[14] Bloggers posted videos of events in Sidi

---

[11] Citizens in Sidi Bouzid interviewed by the author in April 2012 offered both accounts.

[12] Ibid.

[13] I was unable to verify that degree of intentionality in Mohamed Bouazizi's act of self-immolation.

[14] See https://www.anonymoustunisie.com/.

Bouzid as they occurred: violent images of state murder, the photos of martyrs, the executions of citizens by Ben Ali's thugs. They also provided the names of arrested militants.

Despite the banning of YouTube, videos of Tunisian demonstrations appeared on the platform. And tweets were issued under the hashtag #sidibouzid (Ryan 2011b). Activists filmed confrontations between protestors and Tunisian riot police all over the country and successfully posted them online and/or had them broadcast on Al Jazeera. Of particular importance was a YouTube video showing the military refusing to shoot at a crowd of protestors and even running interference between protestors and the police and security forces, who had killed dozens in the rebellion's early days (Bellin 2011). Convinced that the military would not shoot to protect Ben Ali's regime, popular mobilization increased dramatically. By the time that mass demonstrations were taking place in major Tunisian cities in early 2011, few Tunisians were unaware of the events that began in Sidi Bouzid, and many were participating in them.

On January 13, 2011, Ben Ali delivered a televised speech promising democracy, freedom, and lower prices for all staples. The speech was anchored by the repetition of the phrase, "I've understood you," a construction Charles de Gaulle used with Algerians during their independence struggle that rang sour on Tunisian ears. The next day, Ben Ali acknowledged the end and fled to Saudi Arabia.

Democratic Transition

A pattern of relations developed during Tunisia's democratic transition. It consisted of government actions or statements, a public response demanding more radical changes, and then an accommodating government reaction (Hafaiedh and Zartman 2015). Immediately after Ben Ali's flight into Saudi Arabian exile, the remaining members of the Old Order negotiated among themselves to follow constitutional provisions for filling his vacancy: under article 57, which dealt with permanent incapacity, Fuad Mebazza, the speaker of parliament, became president and cobbled together a caretaker government under the continuing prime minister, Mohammed Ghannouchi. The government attempted to guide the transition; however, continuing protests led to Ghannouchi's resignation.

Following Ghannouchi's fall, Mebazza appointed Beji Caid Essebsi, a lawyer and prominent figure during Habib Bourguiba's administration, as interim prime minister. After announcing his intention to respect the Tunisian Revolution's principles and spirit, Essebsi formed an interim government, which he expected to guide the transition (Tunisia Weekly 2012). The interim government focused on reestablishing security and the economy. Essebsi made a promise that no members of the interim government would be allowed to participate in upcoming elections, a promise that he kept.

Essebsi's promises and actions did not fully satisfy a wary Tunisian public. Continuing protests led to the formation of the Higher Political Reform Commission, which was composed of representatives of all political parties and civil society organizations. The commission, led by legal expert Yadh Ben Achour, oversaw Tunisia's democratic transition. The remarkably effective body became known as the Ben Achour Commission (Stepan 2012).

The Ben Achour Commission decided that the first popular vote to be held would be to choose the members of a constituent assembly charged with drafting (for voters' approval) a new constitution that would set up a presidential, semi-presidential, or parliamentary system. The National Constituent Assembly, as a legitimately elected body, would possess powers like those of a parliament: it would select a government that would be responsible to the Assembly until elections under the new constitution could be held, ostensibly within one year.

The Commission chose a pure proportional representation electoral system for its anti-majoritarian, democracy-facilitating implications. Under this system, a broad range of political parties would have a chance to be elected to the Constituent Assembly. A proportional representation electoral system also would also encourage coalition-building among political parties. To ensure women's strong participation in the constitutional drafting process, the Commission agreed to aim for male–female parity in candidates. Ben Ali's official party, the RCD, and some of its most important members were banned. However, to avoid the exclusion of a large group of citizens from political participation, former RCD party members were allowed to form new parties. Finally, to ensure that all the contesting parties would have confidence in the electoral results' fairness, the Commission decided to create Tunisia's first independent electoral commission. It also invited many international electoral observers and gave them extensive monitoring prerogatives.

As discussed in the following section, the founding election of Tunisia's democratic transition established the predominance of its relatively moderate Islamist political party, Ennahdha, in the Constituent Assembly. Ennahdha formed Tunisia's first elected government by creating an alliance with two smaller secular parties. Signifying a real democratic transition, the rise to power of Ennahdha would have been unthinkable as late as early December 2010.

Democratic Consolidation: Political Pact

Political pacts contribute to democratic consolidation by enabling warring elite factions – whose conflicts could derail a democratic transition – to deliberately reorganize their relations through negotiated compromises over their most basic disagreements. In successful political pacts, all parties agree to compete according to the rules of political democracy and to forgo appeals to mass mobilization, violence, or military intervention to alter electoral outcomes.

In Tunisia's democratic transition, a political pact has had to temper potentially violent polarization between Islamist and secular-oriented political forces. Politicians have navigated their way through mistrust, polarization, and terrorist attacks with pragmatic consensus politics. Both sides have had to learn to tolerate each other and to seek compromise and consensus within the emerging democracy. Establishing and maintaining the "twin tolerations" in Tunisia has not been easy, but it has been successful – so successful, in fact, that after two electoral cycles, consensus politics – a cross-ideological alliance of Islamists and secularists governing the country with little opposition and similar policies – has become a threat to democratic consolidation.

Without a doubt, the twin tolerations, cross-ideological coalitions, and compromise among political parties helped democracy survive in Tunisia during the early, delicate, constitution-making process on through most of the term of the first government elected under the Constitution. However, serious concerns have arisen about a political pact that has overwhelmed any opposition, has failed to address the basic socioeconomic issues that catalyzed the revolution, and has stunted political party development in the name of quelling polarization and meeting economic and security challenges (Grewal and Hamid 2018).

Tunisia's path to the twin tolerations began long before the Arab Spring erupted. Islamist and secular political parties began negotiating a post–Ben Ali democratic future, with room for both of them, in the early 2000s (Stepan 2012). In 2003, representatives of four nonregime political parties – Ennahdha, the secular-oriented Congress for the Republic (CPR); Ettakatol, the Democratic Forum for Labor and Liberties; and the Progressive Democratic Party (PDP) – met in France to negotiate and sign a "Call from Tunis." This document reflected the twin tolerations. Two fundamental principles were endorsed:

1) any future elected government would have to be founded on the sovereignty of the people as the sole source of legitimacy; and 2) the state, while showing respect for the people's identity and its Arab-Muslim values, would provide guarantees of liberty of beliefs to all and the political neutralization of places of worship. (Stepan 2012: 96).

Ennahdha and representatives of other political parties met again in 2005 to produce another document, "The October 18 Coalition for Rights and Freedoms in Tunisia." By signing it, the parties reached a consensus on a number of crucial issues. Historically, general principles of *Sharia*, Islamic law, governed such matters as marriage, divorce, family maintenance, paternity, and custody of children. Shortly after independence, President Habib Bourguiba reformed Tunisia's family law code to grant more equality to women. In the October 18 document, Ennahdha and the more secular-oriented political parties agreed not to change Tunisia's liberal family code. They also declared that any future democratic state would have to be a "civic state…drawing its legitimacy from the will of the people." Finally, the manifesto asserted that "there can be no compulsion in religion. This includes the human right to adopt a religion or not" (Stepan 2012: 96).

While there were bumps along the road – some cutting against the compromises made by Islamist and secular political party leaders during Ben Ali's time in power – overall, developments toward the twin tolerations continued after the Arab Spring began.

After Ben Ali fled to Saudi Arabia, Tunisia's National Constituent Assembly (NCA) elections took place on October 23, 2011. The NCA was charged with governing and with producing a constitution within one year. Parties representing all four of Tunisia's dominant ideological orientations – Islamist, leftist, liberal, and nationalist (with either a leftist or liberal bent) – organized to contest the founding elections of the country's democratic transition.

Despite progress toward the twin tolerations, it quickly became clear that political competition in postrevolutionary Tunisia would be dominated by battles between Islamists and secularists, with both fearing the other's political and social projects for the country's future:[15]

In this second phase of the Tunisian uprisings [after the exceptional and ephemeral moment of national unity and shared goals among all participants and sympathizers] anxious interrogations about the place and role of Islam and secularism in Tunisia took over the newly opened and variegated field of political competition... Tunisians who referred to Islam as a normative element of social life and politics demanded the liberation of the discourses and institutions of Islam from state control [Under Ben Ali and his predecessor, Habib Bourguiba, the public interpretations of Islam and secularism were essentially defined and authorized by the state]. They also wanted to impose limits on what they considered to be non-Islamic behaviors [alcohol consumption, gender mixing in public, dress, artistic portrayal of religious figures, blasphemy, etc.]. Tunisians [with a more secular orientation] demanded the liberation of expression in almost all its forms, but often wanted to impose limits on some expressions of Islam they deemed dangerous or incorrect. (Al Mogaz 2014)

Ennahdha emerged as the dominant political force in the NCA elections, winning 89 of 217 seats. However, their margin of victory was not large enough to form a government on their own. Notably, to form a government Ennahdha added two secular partners, the Congress for the Republic (CPR) – which won 29 seats in the NCA – and Ettakatol, the Democratic Forum for Labor and Liberties – which won 20 seats. The ruling alliance became known by the name Troika. Ennahdha's Hamdi Jebali became prime minister, the most powerful role in the government, though the movement's spiritual leader, Rachid Ghannouchi, remained closely involved in the transition's politics. CPR leader Moncef Marzouki became president, and Ettakatol's leader Mustapha Ben Jaafar became the Speaker of Parliament (president of the NCA).

[15] All translations appearing in this book are my own unless stated otherwise.

The Troika varied somewhat in terms of its preferred economic and social policies (Ottaway 2012). Ennahdha is liberal in this regard, while the CPR and especially Ettakatol are more center-left. All three ruling parties favored aggressively addressing corruption and increasing the state's focus on development in the impoverished interior regions of the country and the poor outer suburbs of the capital, Tunis. Ettakatol's party platform emphasized economic and social reforms that would boost investment and enhance small and medium-sized enterprises. Ultimately, their differences were surmountable because the alliance was not built to advance any particular political platform. Instead, the Troika was formed largely to overcome divisions between Islamists and secularists to create a national consensus supporting political democracy.

From the start, Ghannouchi and Marzouki asserted that the Troika alliance should serve as a model during transitions across the region because it helped to overcome the secular–Islamist divide that threatened democratic progress everywhere in the Arab Middle East (Ryan 2012). Convenience also underpinned the coalition. Ennahdha needed partners to make a majority, and the two lesser parties wanted to keep Ennahdha's power in check (Hafaiedh and Zartman 2015).

Empowered by electoral success, Ennahdha's commitment to democracy was tested in how it handled more extreme interpretations of Islam that were hostile to democracy. With some influence from abroad, Scripturalist and Jihadi Salafis, previously rare in Tunisia, had made their presence known in the more open political environment. The nucleus of the small Tunisian Salafi movement that was intent on establishing a theocracy developed during Ben Ali's time in power (Touched 2012). In 2006 in Suleiman, there were armed clashes between Jihadi Salafis and Tunisian security operatives. The clashes lasted about a week. The security services named Khatib Idrissi, who was born in Sidi Bouzid, as the spiritual leader of the Suleiman Jihadi Salafis. He was jailed for two years on charges of issuing *fatwas* that sanctioned jihadist actions and covering up terrorist activities. Many of his associates were jailed as well. Idrissi received his religious education in Saudi Arabia and has published several religious books.

The jailed Jihadi Salafis were freed after the 2011 Revolution. During the period of the the Troika coalition, Scripturalist and Jihadi Salafis (with some overlap between the two) posed a direct threat to the success of Tunisia's democratic bargain. Some used violence against those who held different opinions, especially if these opinions were in any way linked to religion. Most rejected democracy and elections as un-Islamic. All wanted to use state power to impose a highly politicized version – their own – of *Sharia* law.

Many Tunisians suspected that Ennahdha, despite public proclamations supporting democracy, was sympathetic to both Scripturalist and Jihadi Salafis and that it ultimately aimed to impose a theocratic state similar to Iran's (Hafaiedh and Zartman 2015: 60). As leader of the elected governing coalition and as an Islamist movement, Ennahdha was held responsible for both groups' actions when they threatened lives and rejected both individual freedoms and democracy. The two secular members of the Troika ruling coalition were also put on the defensive due to the behavior of some Salafis and to Ennhada's reaction to it. At times, this destabilized the coalition.

Public views that were skeptical of Ennahdha's moderation were not completely off base. There were ideological divisions within Ennahdha between a doctrinaire and sometimes extremist wing that sought to rule alone after its October 2011 electoral victory, and a pragmatic wing seeking to build coalitions across Islamic and secular lines (Hafaiedh and Zartman 2015). Party discipline and the leadership of Rachid Ghannouchi, who ultimately favored pluralism, smoothed over the ideological divisions within Ennahdha's 120-member ruling Consultative Council (*shura*) (Hafaiedh and Zartman 2015).

Post–Ben Ali, Salafi activities led Ghannouchi and the Troika to harden their views toward them. Initially, they tended to emphasize the small number of Jihadi Salafis in Tunisia and pointed out that there were extremists in every country, especially during the tense times shortly after the end of a dictatorship (Sky News Arabiya 2013).

The Troika preferred dialogue and persuasion to repression in dealing with Salafis (Sky News Arabiya 2013). In their view, they were capable of socializing radical Islamists of every stripe toward moderation and democracy. Repression, they argued, closed the door on evolution in Salafi thought toward the legitimacy of democracy. It would be a repeat of Ben Ali's police state and antithetical to the atmosphere of freedom and inclusion promised by the revolution. Ennahdha leaders declared that the state would not violently battle any religious current, stressing that the era of exclusion and security campaigns in Tunisia had ended (Arab News 2012c).

In an interview, discussing for the first time in public the rise of both the Scripturalist and Jihadi Salafi currents in Tunisia, Ennahdha spiritual leader Rachid Ghannouchi urged Salafis to operate within the emerging legal democratic framework and stated that dialogue with them would lead them in that direction:

The government has begun consultations with the *Salafists*. I have spoken personally with many [Salafi] elders and encouraged them to work within the [Tunisian] legal framework pertaining to associations and political parties. It is not a problem if they receive some votes in elections [he has estimated their total numbers to be no more than 5,000]. The important thing is to avoid confrontation. I do not think *Salafists* pose a terrorist threat. There are extremists of course, but they know that terrorism would be a suicidal path. And you must know that not all *Salafists* are the same. Most reject violence and do not accuse Ennahdha of disbelief. Dialogue is possible with these people. (Arab News 2012a)

Four events changed Ennahdha's tolerant stance toward Tunisian Salafism. First, on September 14, 2012, hundreds of protestors, furious about a film produced in the United States denigrating the Prophet Muhammad, ransacked the US embassy in Tunisia. This was days after US Ambassador to Libya Chris Stevens had been killed during an attack on the US embassy compound in Benghazi.

The protestors in Tunisia started fires, broke windows, destroyed property, and raised a black flag indicative of a connection to al-Qaeda that read, "No god but the God and Muhammad is his Prophet." They also set fire to the nearby American Cooperative School of Tunis. No Americans were hurt, but in restoring order security forces killed four protestors and injured dozens. Both President Marzouki, a secular member of the ruling Troika, and Ennahdha's spiritual head, Rachid Ghannouchi, expressed shock at Salafi violence in a Tunisia known for moderation (Marzouki 2013).

After receiving heavy criticism that Ennahdha's permissive attitude allowed Jihadi Salafi groups to flourish, Ghannouchi spoke out in strong terms against them at a press conference: "Our country is in a state of war against Islamic extremist groups. Now is not the time for dialogue. Terrorism has no future in Tunisia. It is time to cleanse our country of arms raised against the state" (Arab News 2013). He added, however, that if they put down their arms dialogue would be possible: "I call on *Salafi* extremists implicated in acts of violence to distance themselves from terrorism and engage in peaceful political action." He added: "We hope that the phenomenon of *Salafism* in Tunisia will evolve toward the formation of political parties and the acceptance of democracy as it has in Egypt and Algeria." Finally, Ghannouchi stated that the only place for *jihad* in Tunisia is *jihad* for economic development and democracy.

Second, on February 6, 2012, Chokri Belaid, secretary general of the Nationalist Party and leader of the left-wing secular coalition Alliance of the Popular Front, was assassinated in front of his home. There were immediate protests alleging that the attack was part of the violent Islamization of the country. The incident shook the government formed by the Troika. Prime Minister Hamadi Jebali reacted by stating his attention to dissolve the government and form a new technocratic government of national unity. However, Ennahdha rejected his proposalz and he resigned. Ali Laarayedh replaced him as prime minister.

Third, on July 25, 2012, a second secular opposition leader, Mohammed Brahmi, was assassinated. He too was killed outside his home – shot four14 times in front of his wife and children by two assassins on a motorbike. Mass protests followed the second assassination as well.

Fourth, Jihadi Salafis waged battles against the security forces and the military along the western border of Algeria and in other isolated areas of the country. Salafis, on occasion, also employed violence against fellow Tunisians for violating what they considered to be Islamic norms in terms of dress, the consumption of alcohol, mixed dancing, and other matters. In a related vein, groups calling themselves the Leagues for the Protection of the Revolution cropped up in many neighborhoods. Some Tunisians accused them of being Ennahdha's private militias (Patel and Belghith 2013).

The largest Jihadi Salafi group in Tunisia goes by the name of Ansar al-Sharia. The group was formed just after the fall of the Ben Ali dictatorship. They have connections with the Suleiman group that battled security forces near the end of Ben Ali's time in power. Their leader, Saif Abdullah bin Hussein (also known as Abu Ayyad), was born in a suburb of Tunis. He received military training in Afghanistan from al-Qaeda operatives and was jailed for years under Ben Ali (Arab News 2012b). Ansar al-Sharia was initially a legal association. However, in May 2013, due to security concerns, they were not permitted to have their annual meeting in Kairouan, the religious capital of Tunisia, nor in the poorer Tunisian suburbs (Al Nadhif 2013).

In late August 2013, the Tunisian prime minister, Ali Laarayedh, held a press conference and told the audience that Ansar al-Sharia had become a terrorist organization. He accused the group of killing both Chokri Belaid and Mohamed Brahmi. He also blamed them for the attacks on the army near the Algerian border and linked the group to the September 2012 attack on the US embassy and the American school. Abu Ayyad fled from Tunisian authorities. He was subsequently captured by US forces in the city of Misrata in Libya (Mosaiquefm 2013).

Beyond ordering security and military operations to contain Jihadi Salafis, Ennahdha also had to forge a democracy-sustaining national consensus about the role of *Sharia*, Islamic law, in the emerging political system. The twin tolerations – and democracy – cannot be sustained if legislation has to be based on *Sharia*, God's law.

After contentious constitutional debate, Ennahdha, with some dissent within its ranks and despite pressure from Salafis, agreed to exclude any reference to *Sharia* law in the constitutional text. In the only mention of Islam, they kept the formulation of the 1959 Tunisian Constitution, which stipulated that Tunisia is a free, independent, sovereign nation. It is a Republic, whose religion is Islam and whose language is Arabic.

Ennahdha's position on *Sharia* caused great consternation for many who shared an Islamist political orientation. Some went their own way. The Troika granted two Salafi groups the right to form political parties after they renounced the use of violence. Hizb al-Tahrir strove to create an Islamic Caliphate and impose it interpretation of *Sharia* within it. Jabhat al-Islah stated that it prioritized Islam but that it would also seek to forge a democracy (Zelin 2012). In December 2013, Hizb al-Tahrir and Jabhat al-Islah joined together to establish a coalition of political parties and Islamic movements under the name The High Council to Support the Revolution (Smadhi 2013). Despite the two parties' hostility toward or ambivalence about democracy, Ennahdha supported their authorization because of the harsh crackdown it had faced as an opposition party under Ben Ali and because of various practical considerations of governing a country polarized along religious lines (Smadhi 2013).

Presumably, Ennahdha also believed that bringing conservative Salafi groups into the formal political system signaled that, if one wants to take part in shaping Tunisia's future, one must buy into the democratic process and be open to the role of *Sharia* within it.

In justifying the decision to exclude *Sharia* law from the Constitution, Ennahdha leader Rachid Ghannouchi stressed the need for national consensus over partisan politics in Tunisia's fragile new democracy. Ennahdha, in the name of national consensus, also did not press for changes in Tunisia's Code of Personal Status, which is the most gender-equal and 'secular' set of regulations on family law in the Arab world. Gender equality issues emerged in another way during the drafting of the Constitution by the 2011 National Constituent Assembly. Islamists in the NCA proposed describing women as complements to men, with a primary role in the family. Opposition activists argued that the description fell short of recognizing women and men as equals (Daragahi 2012). In response, Ennahdha agreed to remove the offending language.

In addition to the role of *Sharia* in the Constitution and to gender equality, Ennahdha compromised on blasphemy concerns. Despite strong internal support for adding provisions to the Constitution prohibiting blasphemy and criminalizing attacks on religion – that is, on its values and figures – opposition within the Troika and broader Tunisian society led Ennahdha to drop the blasphemy clause it had proposed (Sofi 2019).

Islamist forces in Tunisia have thus made significant strides toward achieving their half of the twin tolerations.[16] The Troika coalition showed leadership in forging a democratic national consensus. The model of moderate Islamist and secular political parties governing together seems like the best vehicle with which to navigate religious polarization in Arab countries. The Islamist-dominated Troika learned while in power that they had to use force and repression in addition to dialogue when dealing with Jihadi Salafis, despite the echoes of Ben Ali's police state. Conflicts about gender equality, blasphemy, and the

---

[16] This point can be overstated. While the presidency and the speaker of the house position went to secular allies, Ennahdha members took control of all other key ministerial positions, including prime minister, in addition to placing its own members in the administrative, political, and diplomatic apparatus. Some viewed this as an attempt to dominate and control the post–Ben Ali political arena (Sofi 2019).

role of *Sharia* in politics were largely resolved in a manner supportive of democracy.

While religious extremists tested Ennahdha's commitment to a democratic bargain with secularists, secular-oriented political parties wavered on the twin tolerations as well. By the end of 2012, secular-oriented political parties (those outside the Troika alliance with Ennahdha) had regrouped from their poor showing in the National Constituent Assembly elections to form a new political party: Nidaa Tounes ("Call for Tunisia").

Founded in 2012 by Beji Caid Essebsi, who had served as interim prime minister during the period between Ben Ali's ouster and NCA elections, Nidaa Tounes is a self-styled big-tent secularist party that patched together diverse actors with no shared political ideology or vision for the country's ailing economy other than to curb the dominance of Ennahdha over the political and public spheres of the country (Ajroudi and Allahoum 2018). The party includes wealthy businessmen, former regime members, progressive liberals, secular leftists, and organized labor. Over time, Nidaa Tounes has revealed itself to be a party that at its core represents the interests of the political and business elite of the old Ben Ali era (McCarthy 2018).

The assassination of the second secular opposition leader, Mohamed Brahmi, on July 25, 2013, occurred shortly after a second popular uprising in Egypt that ended in a military coup removing elected Islamists from power. This tempted Nidaa Tounes members and other secularists in Tunisia to follow a similar path of mass mobilizations and appeals for a military coup to take over political power. However, they could never generate the degree of political mobilization experienced in Egypt, and the Tunisian military, historically uninvolved in politics, remained that way.

Still, in the summer of 2013, Tunisian protesters, pointing to the NCA's failure to produce a constitution within its one-year mandate, called for the end of the rule of their elected Islamist-dominated government and demanded the immediate dissolution of the National Constituent Assembly. Ennahdha countered with proposals to hold elections by the end of 2013. That offer did not end the conflict. The crisis prompted more than 70 members of the NCA to resign. The secular leader of the Troika and NCA speaker, Mustapha Ben Jaafar, announced the suspension of the NCA on state television. After some deliberation, Ennahdha's leader, Rachid Ghannouchi, accepted the suspension of the NCA so that a new national unity government of technocrats could be formed. His agreement hinged on first reaching a consensus on the Constitution and the dates for the next elections. However, the opposition demanded the immediate resignation of the Islamist-led government and the appointment of a nonpartisan administration before final negotiations on the Constitution or on the timing of new elections (Al Jazeera 2013).

Witnessing growing instability and the impasse between Ennahdha and Nidaa Tounes dragging on, the powerful UGTT (the Tunisian General Labor Union) and three civil society partners – Tunisia's employer association, the Tunisian Confederation of Industry, Trade, and Handicrafts (UTICA); the Tunisian Human Rights League; and the Tunisian Order of Lawyers – began holding informal talks with both sides about proposals to end the political deadlock. In early October 2013, the National Dialogue Quartet, led by the UGTT, drafted their own proposal to resolve the political crisis (Al Jazeera 2013). The negotiators produced a three-phase roadmap agreement signed by Ennahdha and major opposition parties. In the first phase, the negotiators agreed to form a nonpartisan government (which would include a new prime minister), after which the Ennahdha coalition would formally step down. In the second phase, the negotiators were required to form a commission of experts to finalize the draft of a new constitution. The 2011 NCA was required to adopt the new charter by a two-thirds majority. In the third phase, the negotiators and NCA members agreed to form an independent electoral body tasked with organizing new legislative and presidential elections by drafting and adopting a new electoral law and setting the dates for the new elections.

Yet, the roadmap to restart Tunisia's democratic transition ran into difficulties (Al Jazeera 2013). The agreement was signed on October 5, 2013. Roadmap deadlines specified one month from the first session of talks to finish the Constitution and three weeks for the resignation of the current government and its replacement by a technocratic government. Early dates for elections were also set to reassure Tunisians that politicians would work together quickly to reach a consensus for Tunisia. The roadmap also set a timetable of one week after the commencement of national dialogue to appoint a new prime minister.

It took nearly two months to appoint a new prime minister. Finally, the Minister of Industry, Mehdi Jomaa, took over that role. The deadline for a new constitution was pushed back to January 14, 2014. The Constitution was finally passed on January 26, relieving the nationwide political tensions caused by a prolonged stalemate (News Assabah 2014). For its efforts, the National Dialogue Quartet won the 2015 Nobel Peace Prize.

Elections for parliament and the presidency under the new Constitution were held in late 2014. Ennahdha and the Troika paid a price for having made little progress in revitalizing the economy and in providing security. The secular opposition also had some success painting Ennahdha as retrograde and uncultured. In the parliamentary elections of October 26, 2014, the secular-oriented coalition party Nidaa Tounes gained a plurality of votes, winning 85 seats in the 217-seat chamber. Ennahdha won 69 seats. The next most successful party, the Free Patriotic Union, won 16 seats. A month later, Nidaa Tounes founder Beji Caid Essebsi won the presidency by 10 points over the CPR's Moncef Marzouki.

The 2014 elections continued Tunisia's pattern of cross-ideological – Islamist and secularist – governing coalitions. After internal debate, and despite winning a plurality of votes, Nidaa Tounes invited its main rival, Ennahdha, to join the governing coalition. In a weakened position after losing the parliamentary elections – and in fear of being forcibly removed from the political system after a military coup in Egypt in 2013 had removed the Muslim Brotherhood's Muhammad Morsi from the presidency – Ennahdha accepted Essebsi's offer. As a minority partner, Ennahdha became invested in the government's success and intent on deferring to Essebsi and Nidaa Tounes (Grewal and Hamid 2018).

Essebsi and Nidaa Tounes took advantage of their 2014 electoral success in a second way. The 2014 Constitution created a quasi-parliamentary political system with shared executive powers dominated by the prime minister. Essebsi has since used Ennahdha's support and an agreement with Ghannouchi to strengthen the largely ceremonial power of the presidency in an attempt to dominate governments headed by the prime minister:

Tunisia's 2014 constitution [to prevent a return to autocracy dominated by the presidency] established a quasi-parliamentary political system, which grants the Head of Government top executive powers. Indeed, whereas the

President of the Republic controls defense and foreign affairs issues, The Head of Government controls most other government sectors. Due to this power balance, incumbent President Beji Caid Essebsi of Nidaa Tounes and leader of Ennahdha...Rachid Ghannouchi have governed Tunisia through an unwritten political consensus since the constitution's implementation. (Mastouri 2018)

Power-sharing between Tunisia's two largest parties has been justified on two fronts (Grewal and Hamid 2018). First, Essebsi and Ghannouchi sought to quell the polarization that had plagued Tunisia in 2013. Second, they claimed that economic and security challenges facing the country required political stability and unity.

The "Grand Coalition" faltered early, though. The government of (initial) Prime Minister Habib Essid received a vote of no-confidence after two mass suicide attacks and continuing economic struggles. On March 18, 2015, three religious extremists attacked the Bardo National Museum in Tunis. Twenty-two people, mostly European tourists, were killed. On June 26, 2015, a mass shooting occurred on a beach near Sousse. Thirty-eight people, 30 of whom were British, were killed by a gunman, Seifeddine Rezgui.

To address steep security and economic challenges, after the Essid vote of no-confidence, nine political parties and three leading labor unions signed an agreement known as the Carthage Declaration, which called for a new national government that would prioritize the fight against terrorism, anticorruption measures, and economic revitalization (Feuer 2018). That coalition government, which included Ennahdha, took power under the leadership of Prime Minister Youssef Chahed from Nidaa Tounes in August 2016.

In addition to a security-oriented approach to terrorism, Prime Minister Chahed has taken steps to fight corruption and revitalize the economy through IMF- and WB-backed economic reforms. His economic vision envisages high economic growth, massive public investment, and the modernization of government functioning (ICG 2019).

In his loan agreement with the IMF, he received $2.9 billion against a number of steps such as reforming the public sector, balancing the budget, canceling subsidies, and devaluing the currency (Mazel 2018).

The austerity measures hurt in the short term. Protests, including highly destabilizing national strikes led by the UGTT, followed the implementation of the measures. Chahed has been largely undeterred in his twin goals of implementing far-reaching economic reforms and fighting corruption at the cost of growing opposition inside his own party and great popular unrest (Mazel 2018).[17] While never comprehensive, the anticorruption measures have so far targeted big financial supporters of Nidaa Tounes, causing some to argue that Chahed was using the party for reasons of self-aggrandizement.

To advance his agenda, and without consulting his party, Chahed attempted a partial government reshuffle in November 2018, which included appointing some of his own ministers after dismissing some of the ministers put in place by Essebsi and other leaders of Nidaa Tounes. This contributed to division within the party.

The 2019 legislative and presidential elections could not arrive fast enough to prevent Nidaa Tounes from splintering into factions. The Nidaa Tounes-Ennahada coalition government also fell apart prior to the 2019 elections. Much of the turmoil in the run-up to the 2019 elections was due to socioeconomic conditions that had not improved, painful IMF-backed austerity measures, municipal elections, and a plethora of demonstrations and protests that suggested a large population alienated from all the country's main political parties. And in addition to all this, there was a struggle against hereditary politics.

Five months prior to the end of his term, on July 25, 2019, ninety-two-year-old President Caid Essebsi died in office. Prior to his death, he had taken steps to pave the way for his son, Hafedh Essebsi, to replace him in office. When Essebsi became president, by law he was no longer able to remain head of Nidaa Tounes. In his place, he put his son, Hafedh Essebsi, as secretary general of the party. Much of the general public and many of his own party members sensed that the point was to prepare Hafedh, who had little prior experience in politics, to succeed his father as president of Tunisia and restore autocratic rule. Prime Minister Chahed is among those who are against Hafedh and any notion of hereditary succession. Hafedh Essebsi and Prime Minister Chahed have since become political archenemies.

By mid-2018, the economic reforms doggedly pursued by Chahed were still delivering little more than pain to the population. That May, municipal elections – the first free and fair local elections in the

---

[17] Chahed has relented on wages. See the section on socioeconomic pacts.

country's history – were held to begin a process aimed at ushering in more legitimate and transparent local authorities with greater control over regional development (Debate 2018). Those elections also provided a view of the political field ahead of the 2019 legislative and presidential elections. The results were poor for Nidaa Tounes, who received 20.8% of the vote. Ennahdha did slightly better at 28.6%. Reflecting disenchantment with the lack of socioeconomic progress and alienation from the Nidaa Tounes–Ennahdha Grand Coalition, Independents won the day with 32.2% of the vote.

Another lesson to draw from the municipal elections is the lack of a strong secular-progressive alternative in Tunisia (Sasmaz 2018). A potential leftist and Arab nationalist alliance petered out. The leftist Popular Front only received 4% of the vote. The Civil Alliance garnered 1.7%. Former President Moncef Marzouki's populist Al-Irada Party received 1.3%, belittling Marzouki's claim that his party is the most attractive alternative to Ennahdha and Nidaa Tounes (Bajec 2018).

Indeed, the only well-known alternative to Nidaa Tounes and Ennahdha, going into the 2019 national elections, was a splinter party from Nidaa Tounes, Tahya Tounes ("Long Live Tunisia") led by Prime Minister Chahed. In general, all three electorally viable Tunisian political parties shared the same political agenda: security and economic growth via IMF-backed reforms.

Shortly after the May 2018 municipal elections – in the midst of economic stagnation and an electoral reminder of the people's frustrations – the fractures in Nidaa Tounes broke into full public view. Hafedh Essebsi exploded at Chahed's partial government reshuffle. A newly named secretary general of Nidaa Tounes, Slim Riyahi, accused Chahed of attempting a military coup. Both Essebsi(s) called for a vote of no-confidence and the full replacement of the Chahed government ostensibly for failing to revitalize the economy. President Caid Essebsi suspended Chahed from Nidaa Tounes. Disturbed by the potential of father-to-son succession, nearly half of the members of Nidaa Tounes left the party and joined Chahed's newly formed Tahya Tounes ("Long Live Tunisia").

In a surprising twist in his struggle against father and son Essebsi, Chahed forged an alliance with Ennahdha to prevent losing power. Ennahdha claimed that it broke its alliance with Nidaa Tounes to support Chahed because the removal of the prime minister and a full government change would be destabilizing for the country.

Furious about Ennahdha's backing of Chahed, Caid Essebsi ended the Nidaa Tounes–Ennahdha coalition government. He claimed that Ennahdha remained culturally and religiously retrograde, and that the consensus relationship between him and Ennahdha had ended after they chose to form a secret relationship with Youssef Chahed, which was essentially a coup attempt (Ajroudi and Allahoum 2018).

In the midst of this political struggle for power, President Essebsi organized national negotiations between trade unions and political parties, including both Nidaa Tounes and Ennahdha. Carthage II amended the Carthage Declaration and produced 65 agreed-upon social and economic reforms. The agreement was signed by all, but the consensus quickly broke down over the fate of the Chahed government (Feuer 2018).

In a meeting at Carthage Palace convened by President Beji Caid Essebsi on May 22 [2018], Nidaa Tounes, the Secular Free Patriotic Party, the UGTT, and the National Union of Tunisian Women all called for Chahed's resignation and a complete change in government. In response, Ennahdha, the centrist National Destourian Initiative, al-Massar, and the Tunisian Union of Agriculture and Fisheries pushed back, agreeing to a partial government reshuffle but insisting that Chahed retain his post. Consequently, the Carthage II Agreement was suspended indefinitely on May 22, and the UGTT withdrew from talks in protest against Chahed remaining in office.

Overall, in the run-up to the late 2019 legislative and presidential elections, the machinations within Nidaa Tounes and between Nidaa Tounes and Ennahdha left the Chahed government still in place and three main political forces in the Tunisian Parliament: With 44 MPs, Tahya Tounes out-ranked Nidaa Tounes (41MPs), and became the second-largest political force in parliament after Ennahdha (68 MPs) (Dumas 2019).

Tunisia held parliamentary elections on October 6, 2019. The results were fragmented, delivering no clear mandate to any single party (Tharoor, 2019 please add to references, https://www.washingtonpost.com/world/2019/11/05/world-crisis-tunisias-democracy-marches/). Ennahda won the most seats–52 out of 217–and has begun tricky negotiations to form the next government and choose a prime minister. The moderate Islamist party has publicly ruled out a new alliance with Nidaa Tounes, which in its fragmented and diminished state won only 3 parliamentary seats. Ennahda is also reluctant to form an alliance with Heart of Tunisia, a new secularist party formed by media mogul and presidential candidate, Nabil Karoui, that won 38 seats. Current Prime Minister Chahed's party, Tahya Tounes, won 14 seats. To form a government, Ennahda will cobble together a coalition of other secularists, leftists, and Islamists (Tharoor, 2019).

In a rejection of the status quo symbolized by the alliance between Caid Essebsi and Rachid Ghannouchi, two outsiders received enough votes to trigger a run-off in 2019 presidential elections. Mogul Nabil Karoui faced Kais Saied, a culturally conservative retired law professor and political independent. Saied, promising to address the economy and corruption, won in a landslide with over 70 percent of the vote. Ennahda has reached out to Saied and made the case that they are in the best position to help him govern and enact his agenda (Tharoor, 2019).

In sum, Power-sharing, consensus government, the twin tolerations, and cross-ideological coalitions have buffeted the Tunisian democratic transition and helped it survive fundamental party conflicts that could have derailed democratic consolidation and caused widespread violence during democracy's fragile emergence. The apparent end of power-sharing – Tunisia's Grand Coalition composed of Ennahdha and its strongly secular rival Nidaa Tounes – prior to the 2019 electoral cycle worries many.

On the other hand, the argument has been made that coalition governments have served their purpose in Tunisia and that, at this stage in democratic consolidation, the end of consensus rule may be a positive development (Grewal and Hamid 2018).

The alliance between Tunisia's two largest parties has been justified as a way to quell violent polarization. In addition, party leaders have claimed that the economic and security challenges facing the country required political stability and unity. While the agreement struck in 2013 between Rachid Ghannouchi and Caid Essebsi likely prevented a democratic collapse, the desire for consensus has undermined democracy in its own right (Grewal and Hamid 2018).

With over 80% of the Parliament in the ruling coalition, there has been no real opposition to exert a check on government. With this excessive power, the ruling coalition passed a pair of unpopular laws, one of which backslides on human rights (the Counterterrorism Law) and the second of which protects those who committed economic crimes in the Ben Ali era (the Economic Reconciliation Law). The one party that was large and organized enough to prevent these initiatives – Ennahdha – was *in* the government, was invested in the government's success, and, at the time, was intent on deferring to Essebsi and Nidaa Tounes: "Too much consensus facilitated the counterrevolutionary tendencies and interests of Nidaa Tounes and the remnants of the former autocratic regime" (Grewal and Hamid 2018).

The politics of consensus in Tunisia has also narrowed the range of ideological and policy alternatives for a population desperate for new social and economic projects that will yield success. For many Tunisians, both parties, as well as Chahed's Tahya Tounes, have little to offer but strong-arm security and the promises of the same liberal economic reforms that operated as corrupt crony capitalism under Ben Ali and that seem to have offered little more than painful austerity since his departure from the scene.

With few policy differences between the main political parties, Tunisians no longer feel represented by them; this is evident in surveys, in countless strikes and demonstrations, and in the results of the May 2018 municipal elections that were dominated by Independents. The same message can be taken from the 2019 presidential elections which featured millions heading to the polls to choose between two political outsiders. 2019 Parliamentary elections also demonstrated contempt for the nation's political establishment that has not delivered on stability or the economy.

At this point, it's not yet clear what type of coalition government will emerge from the 2019 parliamentary elections, including the extent of "consensus" governing. In terms of democratic consolidation, however, it is clear that Tunisia's nascent party system would benefit from having the main political parties retreat to their voter bases and develop competing economic and political agendas, including as needed, an alternative to the economic reforms proselytized by the IFIs.

Democratic Consolidation: Military Pact

Military coups pose the greatest threat to democratic transitions. However, the history of military–civilian relations in Tunisia makes that a relatively remote possibility. The state of civilian control over the military in Tunisia can be evaluated for the Bourguiba era (1956–1987), the Ben Ali era (1987–2011), and the transitional period to date. Under President Habib Bourguiba, civilians had more control over the military than perhaps in any other Arab state. During the nationalist movement to end French colonialism, the military followed the policies of Bourguiba and other civilian leaders within the Neo-Destour Party. As president, Bourguiba conscientiously created a military establishment supportive of his secular, republican, civilian-led nationalist ideals (Ben Kraiem 2014).

Under Bourguiba's leadership, the Tunisian military also developed into a nonpraetorian, highly professional body of officers and soldiers. During that era, the military was described as an establishment "dedicated single-mindedly to defense of the national territory from all enemies foreign and domestic" (Ware 1985: 37). However, in terms of national defense, Bourguiba kept the military small and relied on former colonial power France for military advice and assistance.

To fully understand the distribution of decision-making power between civilians and the military, one must examine five decision-making areas. Leadership selection and policymaking are the most important. In both, under Bourguiba's leadership, civilian control was high. During the struggle for independence from France, the army acted as an adjunct of the nationalist party and followed policies made by civilians (Mansour 2012). Unlike their counterparts in many other Arab states, the Tunisian military did not spearhead efforts to modernize the country. Bourguiba and the ruling party played that role. The military also did not involve itself in economic-development schemes that would expand its core interests and goals beyond national defense (Barany 2011).

Bourguiba used the Constitution of 1959 and his leverage as nationalist hero and leader of the state party to institutionalize civilian control over leadership selection and policymaking (Ware 1985). The military answered to the authority of civilians controlling the state through the intermediary of a civilian Minister of Defense. Bourguiba disenfranchised the officer and enlisted corps by denying their right of political association, even within the ruling party. The military never took part in making political decisions under Bourguiba until the crisis-laden period at the end of his rule (Barany 2011).

Internal security, as the third decision-making area, entails the decisions and concrete actions regarding the preservation and restoration of domestic law and order, including counterinsurgency operations, counterterrorism, domestic intelligence gathering, daily law enforcement, and border control. Bourguiba denied the military a primary role in the suppression of internal dissent, relying instead on the separate forces of a gendarmerie, a National Guard, and a special paramilitary Brigade of Public Order (Ware 1985). In 1978 and 1984, Bourguiba commanded the army to restore order following nationwide civil disturbances. (They did so under his orders.) Both times, the generals were said to have resented assuming police functions and were happy to have their men return to barracks as soon as the crises passed (Barany 2011).

The fourth decision-making area, national defense, includes all aspects of defense policy ranging from the development of troops abroad to the conduct of war. Under Bourguiba, civilians controlled this area as well, partly by relying on the French for national defense. In addition, in developing the officer corps, the civilian leadership decided who to send abroad for training and where to send them, usually to France or to the United States (Ware 1985). Algerian threats to the autonomy of its smaller neighbor – and even more menacing provocations by Muammar Qaddafi in Libya next door – were the greatest national defense concerns in Tunisia under Bourguiba. In both conflicts, Bourguiba and his civilian Minister of Defense dominated policy, not the military brass.

Finally, the fifth decision-making area is military organization, which covers all organizational aspects of the military's institutional, financial, and technological resources, as well as all aspects of matters to do with doctrine, education, and personnel selection. Bourguiba and his inner circle kept tight control over their budgets and influenced officer selection.

For most of the period when Habib Bourguiba led Tunisia, then, civilian dominance of the military was manifest in all five important decision-making areas. However, Tunisia went through a protracted and in-depth crisis in the mid-1980s, which threatened its stability and enabled greater military intervention in politics. The economy stagnated for most of the early 1980s. The powerful Tunisian General Labor Union (UGTT) organized a destabilizing national strike. Qaddafi tried to foment a revolution in the southern mining town of Gafsa. An Islamist movement became explicitly political and attacked the regime on multiple levels. To control growing social chaos, Bourguiba relied heavily on his head of internal security and Minister of the Interior at the time, General Zine El-Abidine Ben Ali. In particular, Bourguiba ordered the harsh repression of Islamists. By 1986, the conflict between Islamists and the state appeared to be moving toward civil war. In early 1987, Bourguiba named Ben Ali prime minister. On November 7, 1987, Ben Ali overthrew Bourguiba in a bloodless coup.

During the difficult period of the 1980s, some speculated that the Tunisian military as an institution might be on a path to a military coup in which it would take over the Tunisian state: "There was a risk that senior officers would begin to exercise surveillance over important civilian posts and then simply ease the civilians from authority" (Ware 1988). However, Ben Ali's coup did not lead to the military as an institution taking over the state. He turned out to be a military officer with political ambition who attained presidential power, acted as a civilian in power, and continued Bourguiba's policy of keeping the armed forces on the political sidelines (Barany 2011). Moreover, the military played an important political role in Ben Ali's ouster. Army Chief of Staff General Rachid Ammar used his troops to prevent Ben Ali's security forces from violently suppressing the Arab Spring's mass uprising.

The new era of democratic transition, which began on January 14, 2011, has provided many opportunities for the Tunisian military to play an important role in politics, but so far it has maintained the tradition of civilian control of political decision-making. During the Arab Spring, it protected civilians from Ben Ali's police and security forces. After the revolution, it moved back to the sidelines as soon as an interim civilian government took over the state. The initial interim government was composed of many members from the Ben Ali regime. Mass protests returned to force a change. A second interim government with more popular support took power without resorting to military intervention.

Recall that in October 2011 Tunisians voted for a constituent assembly charged with the writing of a new constitution and electoral rules. Their mandate was for one year in which new elections were to take place. The Islamist party, Ennahdha, won a plurality of the vote. More secular-oriented Tunisians began grumbling about a need for a military coup to prevent the Islamization of Tunisian society and politics under Ennahdha, but the military did not intervene after its electoral victory.

The refusal to intervene at Tunisian secularists' urging is not to say that elements of the military and some politicians were not concerned about a potential Ennahdha victory in founding elections. Prior to NCA elections, Farhat Rajhi, the Minister of the Interior in the first interim government of the transition (January 27 to March 28, 2011), leaked statements on Facebook saying that political elites would ask General Rachid Ammar to organize a coup if Ennahdha were to win the election (Ryan 2011a). The Minister of Defense denied Rajhi's claims immediately. In a report released on October 11, 2012, the Tunisian Minister of Defense communicated that the military had been and always would be apolitical. He asserted that the national army was neutral with respect to different parties and political sensitivities in Tunisia (Ryan 2011a).

Tunisian interim governments, including the Troika, largely kept the military out of politics. Both post–Ben Ali presidents – Marzouki and Essebsi – have communicated that the Ministry of Defense and the army prefer to concentrate their resources in territorial defense rather than the continuous effort to enforce national order. However, instability has prevented the military from returning fully to its main goal.

Many strikes and protests, sometimes violent, over poor economic conditions and unemployment have taken place throughout Tunisia since the transition began in 2011. However, the military has not used these conditions to usurp political power. For example, in late November and early December 2012, there were violent confrontations between police and protesters in the flashpoint town of Siliana. More than 300 people were injured. The government used the army to restore order. However, as soon as the peace was restored, the soldiers followed government orders to withdraw and return to their barracks.

As we have seen, Tunisia's democratic transition has been marred by polarization and some violence between Islamists and secularists. The assassinations of secular opposition leaders Chokri Belaid and Mohamed Brahmi ignited mass protests by the secular opposition to the Islamist-dominated government. The military did not intervene in these major conflicts between Islamists and secularists, even when these conflicts were intensified by the Egyptian coup on July 3, 2013, that forcibly removed an elected Islamist government from power.

Drafts of the new Tunisian Constitution express the civilian leadership's desire to maintain and institutionalize an apolitical military in the emerging democratic regime. Article 16 states that the national army is a military force based on discipline and the law. It is obligated to maintain political neutrality. Its sole mission is to defend the independence of the nation and its territorial integrity. The military supports civilian authority according to conditions defined by law. Article 17 spells out the duties of the forces of national security, which also operate under civilian authority. Article 76 names the civilian executive as commander of the armed forces.

Tunisia may be the least coup-vulnerable country in the Arab world. Historically, the military has not been involved in the country's politics. The military has not developed significant economic assets to protect. The military prefers to focus on external threats and the development of professionalism. Civilian leaders past and present in Tunisia have sought to institutionalize civilian control over the military. Finally, authoritarian breakdown and the tumultuous democratic transition in Tunisia has opened up many opportunities for the military to intervene and carve out a greater role for itself in the Tunisian political system, yet the military has eschewed taking the country down that path.

Democratic Consolidation: Nation-State and Weberian-State Pact

National unity prior to the Arab Spring has helped consolidate Tunisia's new democracy. The country has a homogenous population of 98% Arab (or Arabized Berber) Sunni Muslims of the Maliki rite, which is overwhelmingly committed to a single political community forged across the centuries. In that sense, Tunisia is a fully realized nation-state. Unlike the case of its neighbor Libya, for example, political elites seeking to consolidate Tunisia's democracy have not had to engage in a nation-building pact at the same time as they attempted to institutionalize competitive elections.

For the region, Tunisia is also relatively advantaged as a Weberian or modern state. Max Weber argued that modern states are characterized by a military that monopolizes violence within the state's territorial boundaries, a rational-legal national administration, and a tax collection apparatus to pay for the military and the bureaucracy. Tunisia has been singled out among Arab countries for historical developments that produced comparative advantages in creating a modern state (Anderson 1980). While there are major concerns to be addressed and reforms to be implemented, the Tunisian state had enough bureaucratic capacity, military power, and tax collection ability to avoid state collapse and attempt democracy after the Arab Spring uprising brought down Ben Ali's regime. Still, democracy can be deepened in Tunisia through reforms in all three abovementioned areas of the modern state.

Military that Monopolizes the Legitimate Use of Violence

To guarantee respect for individual freedoms and citizens' physical and mental integrity, democracy requires that force must be exercised only by official state armed forces within the framework of the rule of law. For the Arab world, the Tunisian military is comparatively professional and largely able to uphold citizens' safety and security. The gravest threat to the Tunisian military's monopoly on (legitimate) force has occurred in the forested Mount Chambi region of the Kasserine governorate in the center of the country along the Algerian border (Arabic News 2013a). There, Jihadi Salafis have established a stronghold, ringing the area with land mines and bunkers. They have thus far managed to hold off military and security forces. In periodic raids sweeping the area, the military and security forces have found caches of weapons, ammunition, and food rations along with encrypted communications between Jihadis organized by al-Qaeda in the Islamic Maghreb (AQIM) looking to establish a foothold in Tunisia.

Jihadi violence, though at a weaker level, is also being combated in the south, along the Libyan border, and in the cities of Kef and Sfax (Arabic News 2013b). Most of the arms these terrorists use have crossed over the border from Libya, where Jihadi Salafis, al-Qaeda, and ISIS, some of whom are of Tunisian origin, have taken advantage of the civil war and continuing fragile political situation. Several members of the military and security forces have been killed and dozens seriously injured in these battles. Dozens of Jihadis have been killed, injured, or captured.

Security deficits in Tunisia have been highlighted by four dramatic terrorist acts that garnered international attention. On March 18, 2015, three militants attacked the Bardo National Museum in the Tunisian capital, Tunis. They killed 22 people, mostly European tourists. Around 50 others were injured. Then, on June 26, 2015, a Jihadi Salafi killed 38 people, 30 of whom were British, in a mass shooting in a tourist resort in Sousse. This was the deadliest nonstate attack in the history of modern Tunisia. Third, on November 24, 2015, ISIS claimed responsibility for a bomb attack on a bus carrying Tunisian presidential security guards. The bombing, on a principal road in Tunis, killed 12 guards. Finally, on March 7, 2016, Jihadi Salafis crossed the Libyan border to attack a Tunisian National Guard base and army barracks in the southern border town of Ben Gardane. At least 45 attackers – supported by sleeper cells in the city and wielding heavy weaponry, including RPGs (rocket-propelled grenades) – were killed (Al Jazeera 2016). Ten Tunisian soldiers and seven Tunisian civilians were killed as well. While the Jihadis were repulsed by the Tunisian military, some feared that this was the start of an insurgency, with ISIS militants attempting to seize the coastal city and establish an Emirate there (Paton 2016).

Tunisia's inability to fully secure its Algerian and Libyan borders and put an end to destabilizing (not to mention tourism-killing) terrorist attacks by AQIM- and ISIS-linked groups have led to secret cooperative military and security relations between the United States and Tunisia, including missions by US special forces (Blaise et al. 2019).

Bureaucratic Capacity

Since the 2011 Revolution, Tunisia has tried to improve its bureaucratic capacity – the quality of the bureaucracy in formulating policies and delivering public services. The country has also – due to recalcitrant economic and political elites from the Ben Ali era – struggled to control corruption and eliminate the elite capture of economic policies.

Despite relatively high levels of bureaucratic capacity for the region, the Tunisian bureaucracy has also drawn attention since Ben Ali fled the country. Public administration reforms have been high on the agenda. Many attribute Tunisia's revolution to disparities between the relatively wealthy coastal areas and the impoverished interior with a widespread belief that the central government had favored the former. Strengthening local government (i.e., decentralization) is viewed as an important corrective that would bring decision-making responsibilities closer to the people. It is also thought to deepen democracy and ensure more efficient public service provision if local actors are empowered and provided with resources to serve their communities.

The 2014 Tunisian Constitution included an article dedicated to decentralization (Article 131). The article states that local and regional governments chosen by a universal and transparent vote will have their own legal personality as well as administrative and financial competence and autonomy (UCLG 2014). For political reasons (e.g., rivalries), implementation of a decentralization law has been delayed for several years. The Islamist Ennahdha Party dominates municipal and regional governments – though Independents have emerged as a force in those areas – while the more secular-oriented Nidaa Tounes dominates the central government, urban areas, and the coast, making them reluctant to decentralize.

Also, the Ministry of the Interior (MOI), tasked with controlling local areas under Ben Ali, has been reluctant to cede local control.[18] In addition, there are concerns that local governments lack the bureaucratic skill and trained technocrats (including economists) to manage a redistribution of power.[19] Still, local government officials, civil society in the Tunisian periphery, and Tunisian residents in the country's rural interior are anxious to start playing a greater role in their political and economic destiny.

Finally, on April 26, 2018, Parliament passed the Local Authorities Code, which now governs the entire decentralization process. Just 10 days later, elections were held for 350 municipalities. This marked a major change from the Ben Ali era, in which local and regional officials were not competitively elected. In that period, central authority figures within the dreaded MOI had the most power and resources in local areas. Decentralization would change that, though the law was passed so close to municipal elections that winning candidates may not yet know the full extent of their powers and their access to resources (Yerkes and Muasher 2017). In fact, decentralization is a long process, and the Tunisian government estimates that it will take 27 years to fully devolve power to local officials and to bring the most poorly performing municipalities on par with the rest of the country (Yerkes and Muasher 2017).

On a more general level, the Tunisian government has initiated a range of programs to improve its bureaucracy since the democratic transition began (UNDP 2015). The National School of Administration in Tunis (ENA), which provides civil service candidates with

---

[18] Interviews by the author for a decentralization study in Spring 2015.
[19] Interview with former Minister of Economic Infrastructure and Sustainable Development Hédi Larbi.

training and preparation for the administrative entrance examinations, received additional funding after the revolution. In 2011, ENA received financing from the European Union for six months to strengthen the Tunisian Center for Training and Support for Decentralization's (CFAD) institutional capacity. In 2012, reforms to increase funding for and the administrative management of ENA took place. The Ministry of Employment and Vocational Training created the Administrative Leadership Institute, which trains top-level administrators and seeks to modernize public administrative management.

Tax Collection Apparatus

Under Ben Ali, Tunisia's tax collection apparatus was sufficient to fund the military and the bureaucracy. Still, to rationalize tax policy, modernize tax administration, and undertake other fiscal reforms to secure a sound fiscal foundation for economic stability and long-term growth – with the support of the WB, the IMF, and USAID – Tunisia must take further action in this regard (USAID 2018). Most observers are concerned about tax evasion. Due to a shortage of field inspectors to enforce the law against tax evaders, tax evasion, already rampant, has increased since the revolution (Bouazza 2019).

Tunisia did not have national unity issues. It was a consolidated nation-state long before the Arab Spring. In terms of a Weberian state, its military is professional but has struggled, on the margins, to monopolize violence against international and domestic terrorists. Compared to other Arab bureaucracies, the Tunisian bureaucracy has received praise, though reforms since the revolution to rationalize it, make public service delivery more effective, and limit corruption have had uneven success. To meet the goals of the 2011 Revolution – especially the goal of eliminating toxic regional disparities – Tunisia has begun decentralizing its highly centralized administrative system to better provide public services, bring government closer to citizens, and make it more accountable and responsive to their needs. However, for political reasons, the move to empower local governments and give them greater control over their budgets has been slowed. The MOI has been reluctant to relinquish long-standing powers in towns, cities, and villages throughout the country. Political party rivalries have contributed to the delay as well. However, the passing of a decentralization law and the holding of local elections in 2018 means that serious decentralization – and hopefully its contribution to building a more modern Tunisian state – is underway.

Democratic Consolidation: Socioeconomic Pact

A failure to secure a new socioeconomic pact in Tunisia – nine years after the fall of Ben Ali – has become the greatest peril to the consolidation of the country's emerging democracy.

Nearly a decade after Ben Ali's departure, most Tunisians still feel like outsiders in a fundamentally unchanged, corrupt crony-capitalist economy. They are angry about it. They have made their voices heard through individual, group, and national protests – roadblocks, sit-ins, strikes – that have grown steadily: 5,000 in 2015, more than 11,000 in 2017, and more than 13,000 in 2018 (Brésillon 2018). Following the path of Mohamed Bouazizi, several Tunisians have self-immolated in protest of socioeconomic conditions. Disappointed in the revolution, a journalist, Abderrasak Zorgui, explicitly tied his suicide to frustration at high unemployment rates and widespread poverty. Protestors are returning to the main slogan of the Arab Spring uprising in Tunisia: "Get out you gang of thieves" (ICG 2015). Desperate and angry Tunisian youth are seeking to illegally migrate to Europe in droves – hundreds have died en route – or to join ISIS cells in Libya, Syria, or Iraq (more Tunisians have joined ISIS than any other nationality).

To meet the socioeconomic challenge, Tunisian governments since the revolution – backed by the IMF and the WB – have officially supported an economic reform program designed to create a true market-oriented economic model led by a vigorous private sector taking advantage of the opportunities for inclusive economic growth in competitive domestic, regional, and global markets. That economic reform program entails five economic transitions, although little progress has been made in any of them to date.

The first transition is to control corruption and forge a developmental state that avoids elite capture and is capable of implementing an industrial policy within the framework of a market-oriented model of development. Little has been done since the 2011 Jasmine Revolution to reform the state to eliminate elite capture of economic policies for their own benefit and at the expense of society as a whole. In fact, the opposite may be the case: the country's unnecessarily heavy regulatory burden stifles opportunity and initiative, allowing inefficient firms to gain unfair advantages via privileges and corruption (WB 2014). Apparently, the World Bank "found evidence that the regulations themselves were in fact being adjusted in response to personal interests and corruption. This reflects an environment, still largely in place three years after the revolution, where cronyism and rent extraction (rather than competition and performance) drive economic success" (WB 2014: 313).[20]

Also largely in place is the discretionary implementation of customs regulations and tariff evasion, both of which have resulted in an annual state revenue loss of $100 million (WB 2014). The banking sector offers more of the same. While cronies have had unrestricted access to cheap credit – if the loans are paid back at all – ordinary businesses have struggled and continue to struggle to gain access to finance (WB 2014). According to the WB, "there is strong evidence that these problems may have even worsened since the revolution. These practices have a cost beyond the corruption itself – they prevent the success of the best-performing firms, and thereby lower the performance of the entire economy" (WB 2014: 17).

Restrictions on market competition, in the lingering Ben Ali economy, have cut potential investments in half: "Pervasive restrictions to the number of firms allowed to operate in the domestic market... coupled with many legal monopolies and undue regulatory constraints, severely limit competition, such that investment faces restrictions in over 50 percent of the economy" (WB 2014: 17). While efficient firms are stunted, crony firms in Tunisia receive huge rents and make astounding profits (WB 2014: 115). Also, the country's competition law needs a major overhaul. In its current form, it stifles economic growth by hampering private initiative and discouraging innovation and productivity (WB 2014).

Finally, Tunisia's new Administrative Reconciliation Law (initially, the Economic Reconciliation Law), which grants amnesty to public officials involved in corruption during the Ben Ali era, amounts to an excellent strategy for Ben Ali–era crony capitalists and political elites to reinvigorate the networks within the state that allowed elite capture of the benefits of economic policy in the first place (WB 2014).

Clearly, the economic and political elites who benefited from corruption under Ben Ali are contributing to corruption in the present. In

---

[20] These conditions remained largely in place in 2019.

addition, since his departure, corruption has expanded from elite circles to the broader society (WB 2014). These trends go against what is needed for vigorous private-sector-led growth: leveling the playing field for small, medium-sized, and large-scale companies and ending the need for political connections (WB 2014). The lack of competitive pressures results in lower job creation and productivity, as well as in higher prices for consumers and firms (WB 2014).

Corruption and regulatory abuse thus remain critical development challenges in Tunisia. Cronyism and rent extraction – rather than competition and performance – continue to drive economic success. Political connections matter more than firms' economic efficiency. Post–Ben Ali, the shaping of the "rules of the game" and the state's institutions tilting toward the benefit of a few are still occurring.

In terms of an industrial policy, the WB, the IMF, and Tunisian transitional governments have largely focused on limiting the state and its institutions to their regulatory and administrative missions (WB 2014). They also consider the role that the government can play in facilitating structural transformation – from agriculture to industry – and economic development by supporting the growth of high-potential industries in which Tunisia has "revealed" a comparative advantage (WB 2014: 222). Textile, mechanical, and electrical products have the most potential. Tunisian governments, to date, do not appear to be close to implementing an effective industrial policy.

The second economic transition is in the private sector. In Tunisia, as elsewhere in the Arab world, the private sector has become synonymous with corruption. To regain society's confidence and to contribute to vigorous economic growth, private sector leaders need to set aside rent-seeking activities via cronyism and corruption and direct all their energy to production and innovation. That transition has not yet occurred.

After the revolution, Tunisian judicial authorities banned travel for 460 businessmen suspected of involvement in corruption cases with the president's in-laws. With vast amounts of illicit wealth stolen during the Ben Ali era still outstanding, and a private sector that is still not weaned off rent-seeking, it is startling that President Beji Caid Essebsi and other lawmakers passed an economic reconciliation law that granted immunity to corrupt businesspeople. Amnesty was granted to public officials who were involved in corruption during the dictatorship but "who claim they did not personally gain from it." The law does not lay out a process for determining whether their claims are true (Gantri 2017).

Certainly, the two dozen most powerful Tunisian private sector actors have resisted changing their crony-capitalist habits:

According to most ordinary Tunisians and experts alike, the main culprits [resisting the transformation of the Ben Ali economy] are the country's corrupt and squabbling politicians and an oligarchic business elite – around 22 families allegedly monopolize the country's wealth – who are loath to relinquish their privileges. Remnants of Tunisia's pre-revolutionary deep state, a murky constellation of bureaucrats and members of the security services, among others, are said to be determinedly torpedoing attempts at reform. (Zaman 2019)

Essebsi's party, Nidaa Tounes, clearly depends on Ben Ali–era economic elites as the core of its social base. The party has no intention of forcing them – in order to drive the country's economic success – to exchange rent extraction, monopolies, and cronyism for competition and performance. Ennahdha, in a coalition government with Nidaa Tounes, voted for the Economic Reconciliation Law – the version that passed – as well. Prime Minister Chahed and his new party, Tahya Tounes, have targeted some corrupt businesspeople, but some close observers suggest that the purpose was part of his battle against Nidaa Tounes and Hafedh Essebsi rather than the serious beginning of a crackdown against corruption. Chahed was also in power when the Administrative Reconciliation Law passed.

Clearly, Ben Ali's business cronies have not been weaned off rent-seeking and corruption. Neither has the rural elite, who he favored in policy at the expense of equity and economic growth. Tunisia's Arab Spring uprising began in the country's impoverished rural interior. While the corruption of the private sector under Ben Ali is discussed widely, less well-known are land privatization policies that concentrated landownership in the hands of the wealthy much to the detriment of the small peasantry (King 2003). While state-owned enterprises and other state assets were going into Ben Ali's and his cronies' hands, upward land reform was implemented in the countryside. The privatization of state farms to large landowners (instead of to the small peasantry who worked on them) deprived numerous rural families of an important part of their livelihood in areas like Sidi Bouzid, where the Arab Spring began. It is also well known that small and medium-sized farms – partly due to cheap family labor – are generally more productive than large farms (King 2003).

Former state lands were targeted during Tunisia's Jasmine Revolution. Right after January 14, 2011, a large number of state farms (more than 100), which had been transferred to private investors (large landowners typically with ties to Ben Ali and his cronies) were attacked, causing major damage and destruction (Gana 2012: 208). Several of these farms were occupied by farm workers who denounced the privatization of state farms and demanded that the transition government redistribute the land in their favor. Some small farmers demanded to get back the land of their ancestors that was first confiscated by French colonialists and then nationalized by the state after independence.

Using former state assets to provide the poor with better access to land could make a real difference in a Tunisia riven by the poverty of the rural interior. Since the revolution, trade unions and some political parties have supported small farmers' and agricultural laborers' protests over land rights. Under Nidaa Tounes and President Caid Essebsi, a mechanism was set up for occupiers of former state lands, who had invested in them in the years after Ben Ali's downfall, to appeal for permanent land rights.[21] Nevertheless, Tunisia's postrevolution governments have not attempted to recast land tenure and other agricultural policies in favor of the small peasantry. Following a neoliberal narrative, they continue to justify the hardship in the countryside on the grounds that boosting agricultural exports requires policies that favor large landowners' and investors' prerogatives (Ayeb and Bush 2016).

The third economic transition focuses on improving the relationship between the Tunisian government, the International Financial Institutions, the region, and the world. Despite harboring some suspicion of the WB and the IMF because of the validation and support they provided to the old regime, even in the face of rampant corruption and deteriorating governance post–Ben Ali, Tunisian governments have been open to the resources, advice, and economic services of the IFIs – along with the possibilities for economic growth provided by regional and global markets. The dominant political configurations in

[21] Interview by the author on May 13, 2017, with former Minister of Economic Infrastructure and Sustainable Development Hédi Larbi.

Tunisia, Nidaa Tounes, Prime Minister Chahed's Tahya Tounes, and Ennahdha, are largely on the same page in that regard.

The IFIs see possibilities of dynamic growth in Tunisia via an industrial policy and an agricultural policy targeting products for the European market. They dismiss hope for regional integration in North Africa (WB 2014). Recall that the WB and the IMF have been criticized for ignoring the elite capture, cronyism, theft of state assets, and corruption that emerged during the implementation of their recommended liberal economic policies under Ben Ali. They have responded by undertaking their own analyses of corruption, cronyism, and the potential capture of the state by interest groups. Much of this section is based on their country reports. Still, there is little evidence that Tunisian governments will undertake the reforms necessary to end those practices and few signs that the IFIs will force them to do so through conditionality for their loans.

The fourth economic transition, the implementation of an effective social policy, has stalled as well. Certainly, Tunisian transitional governments (nine since 2011) have been aware of widespread and volatile feelings of social, regional, and economic exclusion. They know that they need a vigorous social policy that addresses poverty, wage policies, and unemployment – especially when it comes to the young and educated Tunisians that spearheaded the Arab Spring.

Social policy under the Chahed government relies on economic reforms to improve inclusive private-sector-driven growth. In addition, transitional governments and the IFIs have reached agreements to reform social protection programs so they are better targeted toward those most in need (WB 2015), which will free up income for state investments and labor market programs to support private sector efforts to increase well-paid, value-adding labor.

Despite analysis, formal commitment, and planning, Tunisia's social protection and labor policies have not followed the script. To address unemployment, Tunisian governments have used the public sector to buy short-term peace since 2011. Instead of a vigorous private sector creating jobs, the public sector has recruited en masse. Between 2011 and 2017, the public sector saw the addition of 200,000 jobs, raising the wage bill from 10.8% to 15% of GDP, one of the highest ratios in the world (Brésillon 2018). To calm frequent protests, Tunisian governments have also created (low-paying) jobs through construction and environmental projects (Brésillon 2018).

Unemployment declined in Tunisia from 18.9% (officially) in 2011 to 15% in 2014, but the decrease was mainly due to increases in public sector recruitment and not to the creation of decent-paying jobs by a vigorous private sector (WB 2015). Unfortunately, this public sector spending has not resolved Tunisia's social issues; it has also stifled the government's ability to invest and has caused a major crisis in public finances (Brésillon 2018). There are also Active Labor Market Programs (ALMPs) in post–Ben Ali Tunisia (subsidies for job training mainly), but they have not sufficiently boosted job placement – even in sectors that have created jobs (WB 2015).

Tunisia's powerful national labor federation, the UGTT, has successively bargained for wage increases during the transition and has maintained pressure on successive governments to resist cutting public sector jobs. This has provided relief for its members, but the UGTT has resisted pressure to include the more vulnerable informal sector workers, who make up 30%–40% of the Tunisian workforce, in their mission (WB 2015).

To protect the poor, post–Arab Spring social policy in Tunisia has continued Social Safety Net (SSN) programs in place since the 1980s (WB 2015). Beyond that, under IMF guidance, Tunisian governments have begun to reform and better target universal price subsidies on energy and basic commodities (WB 2015). Subsidies for energy have received the most attention. They are viewed as inequitable (pro-rich) and costly, depriving the state of resources needed to boost private-sector-led job growth and reinforce the sustainability of social programs (WB 2015). There have also been discussions to start an unemployment benefits system.

The fifth transition is the implementation of socioeconomic dialogue and collective bargaining. Because they have become part of Tunisia's social dialogue process, it's helpful to take into account Tunisia's macroeconomic stabilization policies backed by IMF loans.

The austerity measures, in the short term, are increasing many Tunisians' economic vulnerability. Partly due to high inflation during the transition (7%–8%, the highest in two decades), Tunisians' purchasing power has fallen sharply since the revolution. Successive Tunisian governments have turned to the IMF for help (Brésillon 2018). Tunisian transitional governments also hope that engagement with the IMF can address debt, budget deficits, unemployment, dwindling foreign exchange reserves, and weak economic growth.

The most recent IMF loan in 2016 was for $2.9 billion over four years. In exchange for the loans, Tunisia must restore balance to its public finances, raise interest rates, increase some taxes, cut the public sector wage bill, devalue the currency, raise the price of fuel every quarter to reduce the cost of subsidies, and reform pensions (Brésillon 2018). Tunisia was also forced to adopt the principle of central bank independence and prioritize controlling inflation over promoting economic development (Brésillon 2018).

Cutting the value of the currency was intended to make exports more competitive and to help restore foreign exchange reserves. However, in reality, the dinar's fall has mainly boosted inflation and further penalized consumers (Brésillon 2018). Overall, the macroeconomic stabilization policies are meant to cut inflation, rebuild public finances, give the state a surplus to invest, and stimulate exports and economic growth. However, what is actually happening is more like a sharp economic slowdown, with austerity, rising prices, curtailed investment and consumption, and higher deductions (Brésillon 2018).

Social dialogue in Tunisia has been hampered by the austerity policies. To support democratic consolidation, "economic transitions" need to be discussed and implemented within a broad Tunisian national dialogue, while the stabilization through austerity policies seems to have been made by the IMF.

Negotiations and compromise are necessary because the economic policies must meet two opposing requirements to succeed (Sheahan 1980). First, they must have the consistency necessary for a viable economy that can achieve some economic growth. That requirement implies restraints: the government needs the ability to limit claims that would seriously damage economic efficiency. The second is the ability to answer enough of the economic expectations of the politically aware groups in society to gain and hold their acceptance (Sheahan 1980).

In other terms, a vigorous social policy addressing employment, wages, and poverty within the context of a viable economic model can help prevent the cycle of demands (strikes and protests for state benefits) and government capitulations that commonly threaten economic viability during democratic transitions. Theoretically, social dialogue and collective bargaining provide the opportunity to both restrain and answer the demands of a popular uprising seeking economic justice and opportunity.

The WB supports national social dialogue in Tunisia's efforts to make the radical changes – essentially the five economic transitions discussed above – needed to create a healthier economic environment:

The post-revolution transition still represents a unique opportunity for Tunisians to revisit their economic system and agree to bold changes to open up economic opportunity to all Tunisians, accelerate shared growth, create quality jobs, and promote regional development. This requires a national social dialogue to discuss the radical changes needed to create a healthier economic environment that can promote investment and enable firms to increase their productivity and be competitive, and thereby accelerate creation of good quality jobs. At the same time, Tunisians need to decide what level of redistribution may be appropriate to share fairly the benefits of economic growth and to ensure that no one is left behind. (WB 2014: 18–19)

There is a paradox in social dialogue and collective bargaining in Tunisia. On the one hand, the country has a history of tripartite negotiations and bargaining – government, labor, employers – on which to build. Since the revolution in 2011, a number of steps have been taken to expand on that legacy to support democratic consolidation. On the other hand, to date none of these efforts have stopped the cycle of worker demands and government capitulation that is hindering the emergence of a viable post–Ben Ali economy.

In a country of 11.5 million people, 200,000 have been added to the public sector payroll since 2011. Yet, there were 11,000 demonstrations, protests, and strikes in 2018. A national strike for higher public sector wages and against subsidy cuts, including energy, brought the country to a standstill in early 2019.

The government's decision to follow unpopular IMF austerity policies has alienated the UGTT and most Tunisians. How can labor, employers, and the Tunisian government negotiate socioeconomic policies if the IMF is the most powerful economic decision-maker in Tunisia? That question has to be important to Prime Minister Chahed, who is caught between the IMF and the Tunisian people.

Chahed has begun to cut and target energy and other subsidies, but working at cross-purposes with an IMF mandate to reduce the state budget, he recently agreed to raise the minimum wage for industrial and agricultural workers in addition to raising the pensions of thousands of private sector retirees by 6.5% (Amara 2019).

Social dialogue post–Ben Ali had a promising beginning. A social tripartite contract was agreed to in January 2013 (WB 2015). However, the political assassinations and political crisis of 2013 sidelined socioeconomic dialogue, and little progress has been made since at implementing a new social contract.

For the delay, the national employer's association, the Tunisian Confederation of Industry, Trade, and Handicrafts ((UTICA) partly blames the UGTT for a traditional socialist attitude and for not sufficiently coming to grips with new economic realities, in which the state has become less powerful and competitive constraints on the private sector have become more difficult (EU 2016). The UGTT blames the government for being puppets of the IMF and for supporting the return to power of Ben Ali cronies, who have not returned the wealth they stole from the state. They proclaim moderation and a balanced approach concerning the country's socioeconomic realities:

This balanced approach is reflected in its continuous attempts to put pressure on employers and/or the government (as public sector employer), including the use of strikes, but to maintain also a good social climate and relationship with employers and government, in which the country's socio-economic realities (unemployment issues, inflation, capacity to pay) are recognized and taken on board as part of the bargaining agenda. (EU 2016: 57)

The intensification of social dialogue is on the horizon in Tunisia. If successful, the country could make progress on all five economic transitions. In 2017, the Tunisian Parliament passed a law creating the National Council for Social Dialogue. The council, with a rotating presidency, has tripartite representation with members from the government, the UGTT, and UTICA. It's too soon to judge its effectiveness. Notably, the informal sector has been left out of these negotiations.

Notable as well, in addition to traditional tripartite negotiations and bargaining among the government, labor, and employers, social dialogue in Tunisia has taken the form of talks and agreements between trade unions, the government, employers, and political parties.

As discussed above in the section on political pacts, the Chahed government took power in 2016 after the signing of The Carthage Declaration, which included economic and social policy guidelines. By 2018, the continuation of economic and social woes under Chahed, and his personal battle with father and son Essebsi, led the elder

Essebsi to call for Chahed's dismissal, as well as to a second Carthage agreement. Unhappy with Chahed's IMF-backed economic austerity policies, the UGTT also supported Chahed's removal. However, Essebsi did not have enough support to oust Chahed. Instead, he suspended the Carthage Declaration and scuttled plans for a Carthage II agreement. In response to the failure of negotiations, the UGTT secretary general, Noureddine Taboubi, announced that, moving forward, "I am not bound to anything" (Mazel 2018).

The economic system that existed under Ben Ali has not been changed significantly – and the demands of Tunisians for access to economic opportunity have not yet been realized. Tunisia has not implemented substantive and effective socioeconomic reforms, in line with the spirit of the democratic transition, in the nearly 10 years that have passed since authoritarian breakdown. Certainly, Tunisians perceive that the economic crisis is worsening, and they are exhibiting the stress of the stifling crisis in the form of social, economic, and political behavior that signed socioeconomic pacts by the main political players have not been able to contain (Laghmari and Al-Atrush 2019).

Democratic Consolidation: Transitional Justice, Human Rights, and Rule of Law Pact

Delays in establishing a transitional justice, human rights, and rule of law pact is the second biggest threat to democratic consolidation in Tunisia.

A process that began favorably is succumbing to backlash by the ruling elite under Ben Ali. A call for a different relationship between citizens and government encapsulated the Arab Spring. Mohamed Bouazizi illustrated this when he self-immolated after having his wares taken, being slapped, and being humiliated by local government officials. So too did the spontaneous mass uprising that was inspired by his martyrdom – in Tunisia and across the region – and that defied collective action hurdles and broke the barrier of fear instilled by cruel autocratic regimes across decades.

Thus, in Tunisia and across the region, people rejected corrupt, repressive regimes that treated citizens as subjects without rights. This rejection was paired with outrage at the capture of most economic benefits by government officials and their cronies (Dunn 2013). Along with a fair and independent judiciary, participants in the Arab Spring anticipated that democracy would forge a new relationship between the people and the state.

Tunisia under Ben Ali was widely viewed as a police state in which the judicial and security sectors operated to protect narrow patronage networks that dominated the country's economy (Bouguerra 2014). Many laws were promulgated in the form of presidential decrees, which was a way to legally bend the security forces and shape their main functions to protect the regime instead of the people. The political police force was Ben Ali's greatest weapon. He used this network of organizations and individuals inside and outside government – including most members of his ruling RCD political party – to terrorize and intimidate his political opponents. Under the leadership of the Directorate of State Security (DSE), multiple intelligence bodies supported surveillance and targeting for purposes of political control. An umbrella organization composed of various local police units reported on citizens' political activities, as well as on diplomats' and foreign journalists' daily activities (Bouguerra 2014).

In addition to bending the security sector to his will, the executive firmly controlled the judiciary during the Ben Ali era (Bouguerra 2014). The constitutional courts conferred misleading constitutional legitimacy to regime projects that limited electoral competition and made Ben Ali "president-for-life." The courts also enabled vast corruption. Instead of delivering justice, courts facilitated unlawful detentions and other human rights violations that sustained authoritarian rule: "Judges commonly accepted as evidence confessions obtained under torture, and forensic assessments were generally either absent or falsified without any accountability" (Bouguerra 2014).

The economic and human rights crimes under Ben Ali were linked. Corruption and economic crimes were perpetrated in concurrence with (or through the perpetration of) civil, political, and human rights abuses; the Ben Ali regime propped itself up through mass corruption and economic crimes by severely oppressing large swathes of the population who voiced their dissatisfaction with the dire state of economic inequality (Aboueldahab 2018).

There were high hopes for transitional justice when Tunisia's Truth and Dignity Commission (TDC) was created in 2014 to investigate human rights violations and economic crimes in the country between 1955 and 2013. It documented the suffering of 33,154 victims (Volkmann 2019). The crimes cited in the report include torture, rape, murder, forced disappearance, detention without trial, and massive economic corruption. Political opponents' families were harassed as well.

Before Tunisia's old political and economic guard – *les anciens nouveaux* (Aboueldahab 2018) – began hijacking the country's transitional justice process around 2013–2014, when Essebsi's Nidaa Tounes was in ascent, there was a three-year period of "revolutionary justice" for economic and human rights crimes in pre–Arab Spring Tunisia and during the uprising (ICG 2015).

Tunisian governments and civil society undertook many initiatives aimed at addressing past financial corruption and preventing it in the present and future (Yerkes and Muasher 2017). Through these efforts, they have retrieved billions of dollars in stolen state assets and wealth from the Ben Ali era. For example, 662 firms owned by the Ben Ali family were confiscated in the first anticorruption efforts after the revolution (Rijkers et al. 2017). Decree Law 2011-13 addressed

114 people: Ben Ali, his family, his in-laws the Trabelsi family, and others close to him. It covers the period from 1987 until the revolution and has seized 550 properties, 48 boats and yachts, 40 stock portfolios, 367 bank accounts, and [hundreds of enterprises] at an estimated value of $13 billion (the equivalent of 25 percent of the 2011 Tunisian gross domestic product), as well as $28.8 million held in a Lebanese bank account by the former first lady. (Yerkes and Muasher 2017)

Freezing and returning stolen assets deposited abroad by Ben Ali's kleptocracy have proven to be more difficult. Transparency International (2018) estimates that up to $42 billion in assets was misappropriated and siphoned off and sent abroad by Ben Ali and others. I focus here on the main national effort at transitional justice for economic crimes and at reconciling with the past that was undertaken by the TDC. This body's economic mission has come under attack by political elites tied to the Ben Ali era, including President Caid Essebsi. In 2015, Essebsi proposed an economic reconciliation law that would have removed all financial cases from the jurisdiction of the TDC (Yerkes and Muasher 2017). He claimed that the law was necessary to find investment to get the economy moving again after the instability of the revolution and early transition. He also emphasized a need for Tunisians to move forward and stop dwelling on the past.

Transparency International (2015) condemned the draft economic reconciliation law, which it believed would allow people who stole public funds to be given amnesty for past crimes. The proposed bill would have stopped prosecutions and halted trials for corrupt former officials, crooked businessmen, and their cronies if they revealed their stolen wealth to a new Arbitration and Reconciliation Committee. However, the law did not have a clear way to reveal the full amount stolen, nor did it have a way to prevent fraud, which would have enabled the corrupt to hide their wealth (Transparency International 2015). There was nothing in the proposed law to make the corrupt name the cronies or high officials in the Tunisian government who helped them steal; this likely allowed the most corrupt in Tunisia to escape justice (Transparency International 2015).

Widespread protests prevented the passage of the economic reconciliation law. A revised version, the Administrative Reconciliation Law, passed in 2017. Only mildly watered down, the law provides amnesty to civil servants who could argue that they had no choice but to obey their superiors' orders for fear of retribution (Transparency International 2018). The law does not oblige them to make public apologies or to publicly reveal their crimes. The group of civil servants who would be granted amnesty is not required to undertake any procedure to do so, and the law does not offer the state or the Tunisian people anything in exchange for the impunity given to this group (Yerkes and Muasher 2017).

Despite broad civil society and public rejection of the proposal, and with tens of billions of dollars siphoned off by Ben Ali's cronies still unaccounted for, the law was passed with elite support from both Nidaa Tounes and Ennahdha. Essentially, the Administrative Reconciliation Law created a transitional justice process that runs counter to the TDC's mandate and to the Tunisian Constitution; the law effectively stripped the TDC of one of its primary responsibilities – to expose and account for corruption at all levels – to the greatest extent possible (Aboueldahab 2018).

Transitional justice for human rights crimes has followed the same path as transitional justice for economic crimes: from promise to massive disappointment. Shortly after authoritarian breakdown in 2011, Ben Ali and other defendants, including former ministers of the interior, several high- and mid-level state-security officers, and several police officers were charged with human rights abuses that included murder, though many were issued questionable acquittals, or had their sentences significantly reduced (Aboueldahab 2018).

Between 2014 and 2019, the Truth and Dignity Commission received over 65,000 complaints and heard thousands of testimonies detailing the horrors of atrocities that have been committed since Tunisian independence in 1956 (Aboueldahab 2018). The TDC created Specialized Criminal Chambers (SCCs) to prosecute individuals accused of human rights crimes. More than 170 cases of gross human rights violations were referred to the SCCs by the end of 2018 (HRW 2019). A series of televised public hearings were held at the TDC, which triggered a lively national debate about reckoning with the painful past (Aboueldahab 2018).

However, by the time the TDC's report was issued in 2019, revived Ben Ali–era political, economic, and administrative elites appeared on the verge of ending hope for robust truth-telling, justice, reparations, national reconciliation, human rights, and the rule of law in Tunisia. Their strategies were publicized in a joint letter from Tunisian and international nongovernmental organizations (NGOs) to Mr. Fabian Salvioli, Special Rapporteur on the promotion of truth, justice, reparation, and guarantees of non-recurrence at the United Nations (HRW 2019).

The greatest alarm in the letter was expressed over the proposed law to shut down the SCCs after only a handful of defendants had been forced to face justice. The law would quash judgments delivered in cases of human rights violations and corruption, provided the perpetrator issues an apology before the TDC. There is no role for victims in the process that would amount to granting amnesties for all perpetrators of all gross human rights violations – torture, rape, arbitrary detention, arbitrary killing – over which the SCCs were created to have jurisdiction.

Tunisian authorities have also curtailed transitional justice, including the work of the TDC by preventing it from accessing the archives of the Presidency and Ministry of the Interior and ignoring the TDC's numerous requests for information about the identity of police agents allegedly involved in gross human rights violations. Military courts have refused to cooperate as well.

The Head of the Truth and Dignity Commission, Sihem Bensedrine, believes that the commission has operated with a low budget and an uncooperative government (Aboueldahab 2018). In 2018, Parliament refused to extend the TDC's mandate by one year. Eight years after the revolution, the judiciary hardly ever successfully prosecutes security officials. A state-of-emergency law – imposed after the terrorist attack on the Bardo Museum that killed 20 foreign tourists and four Tunisians in 2015 – has been abused to violate human rights and continue the culture of impunity within the security services.

Since the fall of Ben Ali, a welter of new police and security sector unions have used strikes and political activities to stymie the revolutionary desire for purging and reforming the security sector (Grewal 2019). They successfully pressed for a counterterrorism law with an overly broad definition of terrorism that could extend to peaceful political activity (Grewal 2019). A follow-up draft law by the MOI entitled "Repression of Attacks against the Armed Forces" would institutionalize impunity and authorize security forces to use lethal force to protect property (not just life); the bill would also criminalize the unauthorized disclosure of publication of any information, data, and documents relating to national security, with no protections for whistleblowers or journalists (Grewal 2019). Security and police unions threatened to not protect parliamentarians if they did not quickly bring the draft law to a plenary session (Grewal 2019).

Supporters of the Truth and Dignity Commission fear inaction on the Commission's recommendations for police, security sector, and judiciary reforms aimed at exposing and eliminating the institutional networks that facilitated the committing of human rights violations over the five decades preceding the 2013 Transitional Justice Law that created the TDC. The recommendations also seek to ensure the rule of law and prevent a return to authoritarianism.

Even prior to the new government proposal on "transitional justice," the SCCs encountered many difficulties in serving arrest warrants and summonses for the accused and witnesses to appear. Because the accused include high-ranking police officers, the police often refuse to serve the warrants. Some security unions refuse to protect SCC trials based on claims that they are out for revenge (Volkmann 2019). In general, The MOI has been hostile to the TDC initiative. Although the law obliges them to do so, the MOI has refused to provide the TDC with files from the political police (Aboueldahab 2018). The failure of political elites, the security apparatus, the police, and to an extent judges to cooperate with the goals of transitional justice has unsurprisingly led many Tunisian perpetrators of economic and human rights crimes to ignore proceedings against them.

For their part, security forces claim that they believe in fundamental reforms, but without oversight by democratic political institutions (government or Parliament) (ICG 2015). They tend to view politicians as incompetent on security matters and deny the government's right and obligation to assert its control or to hold recalcitrant officers accountable. Many security services members believe that they are the only ones qualified to handle security matters, all the more so as they consider themselves the primary targets of Jihadi Salafis and social protests. In contrast, many self-proclaimed democratic forces dismiss the security forces as supporters of dictatorship and of counterrevolution.

In 2019, Tunisia is still fundamentally a police state. Despite the TDC's legal authority, judges do not always cooperate with it (ICG 2015). The police and security sector has not undergone the deep overhaul that is needed to change a strong-arming police force that protected a narrow corrupt regime to one that protects all citizens (Volkmann 2019).

By law, within a year from its 2019 release date, the Tunisian government is supposed to implement the recommendations of the Truth and Dignity Commission's final report. Yet, Prime Minister Chahed has called it a failure and President Essebsi its biggest enemy. In contrast, the TDC head, Sihem Bensedrine, counters that the report provides all the tools necessary to reform the state to achieve transitional justice and impose the rule of law (Heberg 2019). However, support from civil society *and* political parties seeking voters for 2019 parliamentary and presidential elections will be needed to reverse the current negative direction of transitional justice.

Indicative of Tunisia's impasse on transitional justice and the rule of law is the fact that, five years after its creation in the 2014 Constitution, Tunisia's new Constitutional Court remains vacant. Once formed, the Constitutional Court will face many difficult tasks. The Constitution contains a number of conflicting articles, and the Constitutional Court will have to harmonize existing Tunisian law with the former's main principles (HRW 2015). It will have to take the lead role in reforming the judiciary. As Tunisia moves to a decentralized political system, the Constitutional Court will have to referee a struggle between the MOI, which preserved authoritarian rule at the local level by exercising its legal authority over regional administration, and newly elected, financially empowered local government officials. The high court will also have to clarify the powers of the president and the prime minister and address an antiterrorism law that affects the balance between freedom and security.

Individual freedom and equal citizenship rights are important in democracies. The 2014 Tunisian Constitution guarantees gender equality, but the existing Personal Status Law does not. President Essebsi has at least proposed a law guaranteeing gender equality in inheritance, which would be a big step toward gender equality and which would make Tunisia the first Arab country to pass such a law.

After a jarring spike in racism, and the mobilization of Black Tunisians and African migrants, a law was passed making racism illegal (King 2019). Lesbian, Gay, Bisexual, and Transgender (LGBT) people in Tunisia are mobilizing against anti-LGBT discrimination – both male and female same-sex sexual activity are illegal in Tunisia. Freedom of speech and blasphemy laws will continue to be tested in the country. Transitional justice, human rights, and rule of law issues do not just detract from Tunisia's emerging democracy, they threaten its very existence.

Summary

Tunisia's revolution inspired the Arab Spring. Keeping the military out of politics and subject to civilian control, and getting political parties to compete according to the rules of political democracy were sufficient achievements to have ensured significant democratic consolidation in Tunisia. In addition, relative to other countries in the region, Tunisia was blessed with national unity and other attributes of modern states entering the Arab Spring.

Still, Tunisia is vulnerable to authoritarian regression. With economic despair as important to participants in the Arab Spring uprising as democracy, most alarming is the lack of progress on producing a new socioeconomic pact. Ten years after the 2011 Revolution, Tunisians are furious that the Ben Ali economy – corrupt, crony, rent-seeking, and dominated by ruling elites – has largely remained intact.

The ruling elite under Ben Ali – gradually revitalized since authoritarian breakdown – is also threatening democratic consolidation by slowing, or even reversing, progress in terms of transitional justice, judicial and security reforms, and the fuller establishment of the rule of law.

References

Aboueldahab, N. 2018. "Navigating the Storm: Civil Society and Ambiguous Transitions in Egypt, Libya and Tunisia." In J. Brankovic and H. van der Merwe, ed., *Advocating Transitional Justice in Africa: The Role of Civil Society*. Cham, Switzerland: Springer, pp. 183–204. doi:10.1007/978-3-319-70417-3_9.

Ajroudi, A. and R. Allahoum. 2018. "Tunisia's Nidaa Tounes in Shambles amid Political Turbulence." *Al Jazeera*, December 5. www.aljazeera .com/indepth/features/tunisia-nidaa-tounes-shambles-political-turbu lence-181202090020299.html.

Al Jazeera. 2013. "Ennahdha Lays out New Tunisia Government Terms." *Al Jazeera*, August 26. www.aljazeera.com/news/africa/2013/08/ 2013826194458461726.html.

   2016. "Tunisia: Deadly Clashes Erupt in Ben Gardane near Libya." *Al Jazeera*, March 7. www.aljazeera.com/news/2016/03/tunisia-ben-gar dane-clashes-160307070914234.html.

Al Mogaz. 2014. "Tunis- Istithna' Dīmoqrātī Tahtha Wat'at 'Istiqtāb 'Ilmānī 'Islāmī" [Tunisia – A Democratic Exception under a Secular Islamic Polarization]. *Al Mogaz*, November 25.

Al Nadhif, A. 2013. "Tūnus Tamna' Ansār Al Sharī'a Min 'Aqd Mo'tamarihā Bi Al-Qairawān." [Tunisia prevents Ansar al-Sharia from holding its conference in Kairouan]. *Al Arabiya*, May 18.

Amara, T. 2019. "Tunisia Raises Minimum Wages, Pensions to Tackle Discontent." *Reuters*, May 1. www.reuters.com/article/uk-tunisia-wages-idUKKCN1S73UC.

Anderson, L. 1980. *The State and Social Transformation in Tunisia and Libya: 1830–1980*. Princeton, NJ: Princeton University Press.

   2011. "Parsing the Difference between Tunisia, Egypt, and Libya." *Foreign Affairs*, 90 (3), 2–7. doi:10.1080/00472336.2013.780471.

Arab News. 2012a. "Ennahdha Calls Salafis to Work within the Country's Legal Framework." *Arab News*, April 3.

   2012b. "Who Is Abu Ayyad?" *Arab News*, September 23.

   2012c. "Ghannouchi Retracts Previous Statements on Salafi Militants." *Arab News*, September 27.

2013. "Ghannouchi: Terrorism Has No Future in Tunisia." *Arab News*, May 10.

Arabic News. 2013a. "Mine Strategy, Tunisia Becomes Platform for Launching Jihadists." *Arabic News*, May 1.

2013b. "90% of the Jihad Salafi Group's Weapons Enter from Libya." *Arabic News*, May 11.

Ayeb, H. and R. Bush. 2016. "Small Farmer Uprisings and Rural Neglect in Egypt and Tunisia." *Middle East Report*, 272. www.merip.org/2014/09/small-farmer-uprisings-and-rural-neglect-in-egypt-and-tunisia/.

Bajec, A. 2018. "Tunis Attack, a Wake-up Call for Tunisia's Political Leaders." *Al Jazeera*, October 30. www.aljazeera.com/news/2018/10/tunis-suicide-attack-wake-call-tense-politics-181030130301913.html.

Barany, Z. 2011. "Comparing the Arab Revolts: The Role of the Military." *Journal of Democracy*, 22(4), 24–35. doi:10.1353/jod.2011.0069.

Bellin, E. 2002. *Stalled Democracy: Capital, Labor, and the Paradox of State-Sponsored Development*. Ithaca, NY: Cornell University Press.

2011. *Lessons from the Jasmine and Nile Revolutions: Possibilities of Political Transformation in the Middle East?* Middle East Brief. Waltham, MA: Crown Center for Middle East Studies, Brandeis University. https://www.brandeis.edu/crown/publications/meb/MEB50.pdf.

Ben Kraiem, B. 2014. "Bourguiba et L'armée Tunisienne : Les raisons d'une méfiance." *Facebook: Association des Anciens Officiers de l'Armée Nationale*, February 3. www.facebook.com/AnciensOfficiersDeLarmee NatinaleTunisienne/photos/bourguiba-et-larm%C3%A9e-tunisienne-les-raisons-dune-m%C3%A9fiancepar-le-colonel-boubaker-/681914991831388/.

Ben Moussa, A. S. 2012. "West Tunisia: The Revolution Boiled in Secret." *Arabic News*, February 23.

Blaise, L., et al. 2019. "Why the US and Tunisia Keep Their Cooperation Secret." *New York Times*, March 2. www.nytimes.com/2019/03/02/world/africa/us-tunisia-terrorism.html.

Bouazza, R. 2019. "Tunisia Struggles with Scourge of Tax Evasion." *The Arab Weekly*, April 21. www.thearabweekly.com/tunisia-struggles-scourge-tax-evasion.

Bouguerra, B. 2014. *Reforming Tunisia's Troubled Security Sector*. October 27. Washington, DC: Atlantic Council. www.atlanticcouncil.org/in-depth-research-reports/issue-brief/reforming-tunisia-s-troubled-security-sector/.

Bratton, M. and N. van de Walle. 1994. "Neopatrimonial Regimes and Political Transitions in Africa." *World Politics*, 46(4), 453–489. doi:10.2307/2950715.

Brésillon, T. 2018. "Tunisia, Divided and Unequal." *Le Monde Diplomatique*, November 1. www.mondediplo.com/2018/11/05tunisia.

Bunce, V. 2003. "Rethinking Recent Democratization: Lessons from the Postcommunist Experience." *World Politics*, 55(2), 167–192. doi:10.1353/wp.2003.0010.

Chayes, S. 2014. "How a Leftist Labor Union Helped Force Tunisia's Political Settlement." *Carnegie Endowment for International Peace*, March 27. www.carnegieendowment.org/2014/03/27/how-leftist-labor-union-helped-force-tunisia-s-political-settlement-pub-55143.

Cole, J. 2013. "Why Tunisia's Arab Spring Is in Turmoil." *Informed Comment*, February 9. www.juancole.com/2013/02/tunisias-spring-turmoil.html.

Daragahi, B. 2012. "Term Used for Women in Tunisia's Draft Constitution Ignites Debate, Protests." *Washington Post*, August 16. www.washington post.com/world/middle_east/term-used-for-women-in-tunisias-draft-consti tution-ignites-debate-protests/2012/08/16/c6045e24-e7bf-11e1-a3d2-2a0 5679928ef_story.html.

Debate, S. 2018. "Tunisia's Municipal Elections." *Carnegie Endowment for International Peace*, May 10. www.carnegieendowment.org/sada/ 76299.

Dumas, M. 2019. "Nidaa Tounes 'Is No Longer Part of the Picture.'" *Middle East Eye*, March 28. www.middleeasteye.net/news/nidaa-tounes-no-longer-part-picture.

Dunn, M. C. 2013. "Editor's Note." *Middle East Journal*, 67(4), 507–508.

European Union (EU). 2016. "Strengthening EU Support for Tunisia." EU–Tunisia Joint Communication, September 29. www.eeas.europa.eu/ headquarters/headquarters-homepage_en/10746/EU%20%E2%80% 93%20Tunisia%20Joint%20Communication.

Feuer, S. 2018. "Reshuffle, Rinse, and Reform: Tunisia's Government under Strain." *The Washington Institute*, June 12. www.washington institute.org/fikraforum/view/reshuffle-rinse-and-reform-tunisias-gov ernment-under-strain.

Gana, A. 2012. "The Rural and Agricultural Roots of the Tunisian Revolution: When Food Security Matters." *International Journal of Sociology of Agriculture and Food*, 19(2), 201–213. halshs-01165135.

Gantri, S. E. and M. De Figueiredo. 2017. "Talking Policy: Salwa El Gantri on Transitional Justice in Tunisia." *World Policy*, July 21. www.world policy.org/2017/07/21/talking-policy-salwa-el-gantri-on-transitional-justice-in-tunisia/.

Gause, F. G., III. 2011. "Why Middle East Studies Missed the Arab Spring." *Foreign Affairs*, 90(4), 81–90. www.jstor.org/stable/23039608.

Ghosh, B. 2019. "Lessons from the Only Remaining Arab Spring Democracy." *Bloomberg*, February 7. www.bloomberg.com/news/articles/2019-02-07/lessons-from-the-only-remaining-arab-spring-democracy.

Grewal, S. 2019. "Military Defection during Localized Protests: The Case of Tataouine." *International Studies Quarterly*, 62(2), 259–269. doi:10.1093/isq/sqz003.

Grewal, S. and S. Hamid. 2018. "Tunisia Just Lost Its Anchor of Stability. That's a Good Thing." *Foreign Policy*, October 12. https://foreign policy.com/2018/10/12/tunisia-just-lost-its-anchor-of-stability-thats-a-good-thing/.

Hafaiedh, A. B. and I. W. Zartman. 2015. "Tunisia beyond the Ideological Cleavage: Something Else." In I. W. Zartman, ed., *Arab Spring: Negotiating in the Shadow of the Intifadat*. Athens: University of Georgia Press, pp. 56–60.

Hamdi, M. E. 1998. *The Politicisation of Islam: A Case Study of Tunisia*. Boulder, CO: Westview Press.

Heberg, H. 2019. "Tunisian Truth Commission Releases Final Report Detailing 50 Years of Dictatorship." *The Organization for World Peace*, April 7. www.theowp.org/tunisian-truth-commission-releases-final-report-detailing-50-years-of-dictatorship/.

Human Rights Watch (HRW). 2009. "Tunisia: Events of 2008." *Human Rights Watch*, n.d. www.hrw.org/en/world-report-2009/tunisia.

2015. "Tunisia: Law Falls Short on Judicial Independence." *Human Rights Watch*, June 2. www.hrw.org/news/2015/06/02/tunisia-law-falls-short-judicial-independence.

2019. "Joint Letter to Mr. Fabian Salvioli, Special Rapporteur on the Promotion of Truth, Justice, Reparation, and Guarantees of Non-Recurrence." *Human Rights Watch*, April 30. www.hrw.org/news/2019/04/30/joint-letter-mr-fabian-salvioli-special-rapporteur-promotion-truth-justice.

Index Mundi. n. d. "Tunisia – Economy – Youth Unemployment Rate." www.indexmundi.com/tunisia/youth-unemployment-rate.html.

International Crisis Group (ICG). 2015. "Reform and Security Strategy in Tunisia, Middle East and North Africa Report." *International Crisis Group*, 23 July. www.crisisgroup.org/middle-east-north-africa/north-africa/tunisia/reform-and-security-strategy-tunisia.

2019. "Tunisia in 2019: A Pivotal Year?" Brussels: International Crisis Group, February 4. www.crisisgroup.org/middle-east-north-africa/north-africa/tunisia/tunisia-2019-pivotal-year.

King, S. J. 2003. *Liberalization against Democracy: The Local Politics of Economic Reform in Tunisia*. Bloomington: Indiana University Press.

2009. *The New Authoritarianism in the Middle East and North Africa.* Bloomington: Indiana University Press.

Laghmari, J. and S. Al-Atrush. 2019. "Arab Spring's Lone Democracy Teeters as Economy Refuses to Heal." *Bloomberg*, February 5. www.bnnbloomberg.ca/arab-spring-s-lone-democracy-teeters-as-economy-refuses-to-heal-1.1209759.

Lee, E. and B. Weinthal. 2011. "Trade Unions: The Revolutionary Social Network at Play in Egypt and Tunisia." *The Guardian*, February 10. www.theguardian.com/commentisfree/2011/feb/10/trade-unions-egypt-tunisia.

Lewis, A. 2011. "Tracking down the Ben Ali and Trabelsi Fortune." *BBC News*, January 31. www.bbc.com/news/world-africa-12302659.

Mansour, A. M. A. H. 2012. "Al 'Askar Wa Al Siyāsah Fī Tūnus" [Military and politics in Tunisia]. *Al Shourouq*, September 17.

Marzouki, M. 2013. "Renaissance Unable to Rule Tunisia?" *Arab News*, January 24.

Mastouri, A. 2018. "Infighting in Nidaa Tounes: A Danger to Tunisia's Democracy?" *The Washington Institute*, November 6. www.washingtoninstitute.org/fikraforum/view/infighting-in-nidaa-tounes-a-danger-to-tunisias-democracy.

Mazel, Z. 2018. "Is Tunisia on the Verge of Anarchy?" *The Jerusalem Post*, December 23. www.jpost.com/Opinion/Is-Tunisia-on-the-verge-of-anarchy-575222.

McCarthy, R. 2018. *Inside Tunisia's Al-Nahda.* Cambridge: Cambridge University Press.

Mosaiquefm. 2013. "Alqabd ala Abu 'Ayyad in Libya." [The arrest of Abu Ayyad in Libya]. *Mosaiquefm*, December 30.

Mullin, C. and I. Patel. 2013. "Political Violence and the Efforts to Salvage Tunisia's Revolution." *Al Jazeera*, August 5. www.aljazeera.com/indepth/opinion/2013/08/20138310271198303.html.

News Assabah. 2014. "Mabrūk Li Tūnus: Al Musādaqa 'Ala Al Dustūr Fī Qirā'atin 'Ūlā."[Congratulations to Tunisia: Ratification of the constitution in its first reading]. *News Assabah*, January 26.

Omri, M.-S. 2014. "The UGTT Labor Union: Tunisia's Powerbroker." *Tunisia Live*, January 22. www.tn-news.com/v4_portal/article/view/69143364.

Ottaway, M. 2012. "The Tunisian Political Spectrum." *Carnegie Endowment for International Peace*, June 19. www.carnegieendowment.org/2012/06/19/tunisian-political-spectrum-still-unbalanced-pub-48478.

Patel, I. and S. Belghith. 2013. "Leagues for the Protection of the Tunisian Revolution." *Open Democracy*, 25 June. www.opendemocracy.net/en/leagues-for-protection-of-tunisian-revolution/.

Paton, C. 2016. "Tunisia: Isis Seeking to Create Emirate in Ben Guerdane after 53 Killed in Raid from Libya." *International Business Times*, March 8. www.ibtimes.co.uk/tunisia-isis-seeking-create-emirate-ben-guerdane-after-53-killed-raid-libya-1548185.

Pfeifer, K. 1999. "How Tunisia, Morocco, and Even Egypt Became IMF 'Success Stories' in the 1990s." *Middle East Report*, 210, 23–27. doi:10.2307/3012499.

Pollock, J. 2011. "Streetbook: How Egyptian and Tunisian Youth Hacked the Arab Spring." *MIT Technology Review*, August 23. www.technologyreview.com/s/425137/streetbook/.

Reporters sans Frontieres. 1999. "Silence, on réprime." *Reporters sans Frontieres*, June 1. www.rsf.org/fr/rapports/silence-reprime.

Rijkers, B. et al. 2017. "All in the Family: State Capture in Tunisia." *Journal of Development Economics*, 124(C), 41–59. uri:hdl.handle.net/10986/25014.

Ryan, Y. 2011a. "Former Tunisia Minister Warns of Coup Risk." *Al Jazeera*, May 5. www.aljazeera.com/news/africa/2011/05/2011551812282786.html.

  2011b. "How Tunisia's Revolution Began." *Al Jazeera*, January 26. www.aljazeera.com/indepth/features/2011/01/2011126121815985483.html.

  2012. "Building a Tunisian Model for Arab Democracy." *Al Jazeera*, November 27. www.aljazeera.com/indepth/features/2012/11/20121127143845980112.html.

Sadiki, L. 2016. "The Arab Spring: The 'People' in International Relations." In L. Fawcett, ed., *International Relations of the Middle East*. Oxford: Oxford University Press, pp. 325–355. doi:10.1093/hepl/9780198708742.003.0016.

Sasmaz, A. 2018. "Who Really Won Tunisia's First Democratic Local Elections?" *Washington Post*, June 1. www.washingtonpost.com/news/monkey-cage/wp/2018/06/01/who-really-won-tunisias-first-democratic-local-elections/.

Sheahan, J. 1980. "Market-Oriented Economic Policies and Political Repression in Latin America." *Economic Development and Cultural Change*, 28(2), 267–291. doi:10.1086/451172.

Sky News Arabiya. 2013. "Tunis: Mutalabah Bi Ta'addud Al Zawjāt Wa Man' Al 'Khtilāt." [Tunisia: Demand for polygamy and gender segregation]. *Sky News Arabia*, December 18.

Sofi, M. D. 2019. "From Past to Present, Al-Nahdah's Journey in Tunisia." *Daily Sabah*, March 7. www.dailysabah.com/op-ed/2019/03/07/from-past-to-present-al-nahdahs-journey-in-tunisia.

Stepan, A. 2012. "Tunisia's Transition and the Twin Tolerations." *Journal of Democracy*, 23(2), 89–103. doi:10.1353/jod.2012.0034.

Toensing, C. 2011. "Tunisian Labour Leaders Reflect upon Revolt, Middle East Research and Information Project." *Middle East Research and Information Project* 258. www.merip.org/2011/04/tunisian-labor-leaders-reflect-upon-revolt/.

Touched, E. 2012. "The Mysterious World of Salafis in Tunisia Sunday." *Arab News*, January 2.

Transparency International. 2015. *Asset Declarations in Tunisia Illicit Enrichment and Conflicts of Interest of Public Officials*. Berlin: Transparency International. www.transparency.org/whatwedo/publication/asset_declarations_in_tunisia_illicit_enrichment_and_conflicts_on_interest.

2018. *Corruption Perceptions Index 2018*. Berlin: Transparency International. www.transparency.org/cpi2018.

Tunisia Weekly. 2012. "March 2011–October 2011: Tunisia under Beji Caid-Essebsi." *Tunisia Weekly*, February 18. www.tunisiaweekly.wordpress.com/2012/02/18/march-2011-october-2011-tunisia-under-beji-caid-essebsi/.

United Cities and Local Governments (UCLG). 2014. "Local Governments in Tunisia's New Constitution." *UCLG*, February 7. www.uclg.org/en/media/news/local-governments-tunisia%E2%80%99s-new-constitution.

United Nations Development Programme (UNDP). 2015. *The Political Economy of Public Administration Reforms: A Study of the Arab Transitions*. New York: UNDP.

United States Agency for International Development (USAID). 2018. *Fiscal Reform for a Strong Tunisia (FIRST) Fact Sheet Tunisia*. Washington, DC: USAID. www.usaid.gov/tunisia/fact-sheets/first.

Volkmann, E. 2019. "Human Rights Report Traces Tunisia's Bloody Past, Demands Plan for Justice." *Al-Monitor*, April 18. www.al-monitor.com/pulse/originals/2019/04/tunisia-transitional-justice-report-violations-presidents.html.

Ware, L. B. 1985. "The Role of the Tunisian Military in the Post-Bourguiba Era." *The Middle East Journal*, 39(1), 27–47. www.jstor.org/stable/4326972.

1988. "Ben Ali's Constitutional Coup in Tunisia." *The Middle East Journal* 42, no. 4: 587–601. www.jstor.org/stable/4327834.

Waterbury, J. 1989. "The Political Management of Economic Adjustment and Reform." In J. Nelson, ed. *Fragile Coalitions: The Politics of Economic Adjustment*. New Brunswick, NJ: Transaction Books, pp. 39–56.

World Bank (WB). 1995. *Republic of Tunisia: Growth Policies and Poverty Alleviation*, 2 vols. Washington, DC: World Bank Group.

1996. *Tunisia's Global Integration and Sustainable Development: Strategic Choices for the 21st Century*. Washington, DC: World Bank Group.

2011. *Tunisia – Participatory Service Delivery for Reintegration*. Washington, DC: World Bank Group. www.documents.worldbank.org/curated/en/367321468120534989/Tunisia-Participatory-Service-Delivery-for-Reintegration-Project.

2014. *The Unfinished Revolution: Bringing Opportunity, Good Jobs, and Greater Wealth to all Tunisians*. Washington, DC: World Bank Group. www.worldbank.org/en/country/tunisia/publication/unfinished-revolution.

2015. *"Consolidating Social Protection and Labor Policy in Tunisia: Building Systems, Connecting to Jobs."* Washington, DC: World Bank Group. www.worldbank.org/en/country/tunisia/publication/consolidating-social-protection-and-labor-policy-in-tunisia-building-systems-connecting-to-jobs.

Yerkes, S. and M. Muasher. 2017. "Tunisia's Corruption Contagion: A Transition at Risk." *Carnegie Endowment for International Peace*, October 25. www.carnegieendowment.org/2017/10/25/tunisia-s-corruption-contagion-transition-at-risk-pub-73522.

Zaman, A. 2019. "Tunisia's Democracy on Life Support as Politicians Squabble." *Al-Monitor*, January 24. www.al-monitor.com/pulse/originals/2019/01/tunisia-democracy-life-support-revolution-economy.html.

Zelin, A. 2012. "Who Is Jabhat al-Islah?" *Carnegie Endowment for International Peace*, July 18. www.carnegieendowment.org/sada/48885.

2 | *Egypt*

Similar to Tunisia, Egypt entered the Arab Spring as a long-established nation-state with comparative advantages as a Weberian state. While national unity, bureaucratic capacity, and the monopoly of violence by the military and security apparatus came into play during the Arab Spring in Egypt, elites largely did not have to engage in nation-state building pacts while attempting to institutionalize political democracy. Nevertheless, Egyptians, who sought democracy in early 2011, have been profoundly disappointed in the results. Hopes were doomed when Islamist and secular political parties failed to sustain the twin tolerations necessary to forge a political pact in support of the country's emerging democracy. That failure facilitated the return of an authoritarian regime dominated by the Egyptian military.

Polarization between Islamists and secularists played into the hands of a military that had been reeling enough from the Arab Spring – and their unwillingness to commit mass murder to repress it – to allow a democratic transition dominated by the Muslim Brotherhood and its Freedom and Justice Party (FJP). In power, the Muslim Brotherhood demonstrated some ambivalence about democracy, as did the secular opposition, who used mass street demonstrations and support for a military coup to overturn electoral outcomes.

After the coup on July 3, 2013, the military outlawed the Muslim Brotherhood and brutally repressed its members.

Secularists, who had hoped to dominate electoral politics and reset the country's democratic transition after the military coup, instead faced a military intent on establishing a more comprehensive dictatorship than the one that had prevailed during Hosni Mubarak's tenure. Transitional justice, human rights, and the rule of law are weaker under military strongman and "elected" President Abdel Fattah El-Sisi than they were under Mubarak. Instead of a socioeconomic pact aimed at delivering inclusive, private-sector-driven economic growth, El-Sisi has used economic policies to deepen the military's – partially hidden, crony-ridden, and noncompetitive – share of the Egyptian economy.

Challenges to Mubarak's Regime

Just before the Arab Spring erupted, a ruling coalition composed of the military, large landowners, rent-seeking capitalists, and a self-aggrandizing political elite characterized authoritarianism under Mubarak. That coalition had been enriching itself through privatization policies during Mubarak's last decade in power (King 2009). Business cronies associated with Mubarak's son, Gamal, had gobbled up state-owned enterprises with little concern for market competitiveness. Political elites did the same, with the combined results yielding mostly monopolies. In addition, in a backward land reform, inefficient rural notables took land away from the small peasantry.

The crony capitalism in Egypt under Mubarak had two branches: one civilian (organized around Gamal Mubarak), the other military (dominated by officers). By intention, the exact extent of the military's economic empire in relation to Egypt's Gross Domestic Product (GDP) is unknown – estimates range from 3% to 40% (Abul-Magd 2017). Undoubtedly, under Anwar Sadat and Hosni Mubarak, the military acquired economic autonomy vis-à-vis the regular state budget and acquired substantial economic resources; it was thereby able to maintain a vast network of patronage and economic privileges (Hauslohner 2014). The Egyptian military penetrated almost every area of the "civilian" economy:

It owns factories for pasta, home appliances, cement, steel, jeep cars, fertilizers, and much more. It bakes subsidized bread, produces foodstuffs in vast farms, builds bridges and roads, constructs social housing, erects football stadiums, and so on. It runs hotels with lucrative summer-houses, and apartment buildings along with lavish villas. It runs gas stations, shipping firms, domestic cleaning companies, and spacious parking lots. It constructs toll highways to collect daily fees. (Abul-Magd 2017: 228)

In addition to the fact that it has a business empire, the Egyptian military is also the country's largest single landowner (Springborg 2017). Operating in a black box that it refuses to share with the public, the military has a share of the economy that is immune from official oversight and regulation (Abul-Magd 2017). Military- and officer-owned companies also benefit from a host of subsidies and preferential treatments, including turning soldiers into laborers for their productive enterprises, tax-free status, and favoritism in government contracting (Springborg 2017).

Egypt under Mubarak combined crony capitalism with a façade of multiparty politics. The state party, the National Democratic Party (NDP), and affiliated corporatist organizations were used to maintain social control. Turnovers in power were not possible through the periodic parliamentary and presidential elections held in Mubarak's Egypt. Opponents have said that Mubarak had the powers of a Pharaoh (Lesch 2011). He could appoint and remove the prime minister and his cabinet. He could dissolve the bicameral Parliament at any time, veto laws, and bypass the legislature by putting issues to a vote in public referenda. In addition, Mubarak appointed all governors, mayors, and deputy mayors. The winner-take-all system to elect local councils guaranteed the NDP's monopoly of power and encouraged widespread corruption among local government officials.

The façade of multiparty politics under Mubarak was paired with a repressive security apparatus and affronts to the rule of law, including a state-of-emergency law that lasted decades, the lack of due process, military trials for civilians, torture, and forced disappearances.

Perhaps it was the Egyptian Movement for Change, also known as the "Enough" (Kefaya) movement, that marked the beginning of the end of the deeply illegitimate Mubarak regime. In late 2004, Mubarak made constitutional changes to enable a fifth six-year-term to begin in 2005 and to prepare the terrain for the transfer of power to his son (Nazif 2009). In response, the Kefaya movement was formed (Shaaban 2007). The movement's name resonated profoundly among both the masses and elites. Its initial message was a simple declaration: "No to a fifth term and no to hereditary rule." It was a revolutionary message because it broke the barrier of direct confrontation between Egyptians and their president, his son, and the repressive, corrupt regime they helmed. Analyzing the internal dynamics of the Kefaya movement, journalists noted:

No one could get anywhere near the President. No one could talk about the prolongation of the presidency as if he were a Pharaoh who lives and possesses the throne forever. The Kefaya movement had the audacity and bravery to pull the Pharaoh down from his sacred untouchable status to one within the human sphere where we could say to him: "No. We do not want you forever. We do not want your son. We do not want a hereditary throne." (Oweidat et al. 2008: 24)

Kefaya served notice that Egyptians of all social backgrounds and political persuasions wanted an end to Mubarak's rule, the prevention of his intention to hand over power to his son, Gamal Mubarak, and true democratic transformation.

In addition to anger at the prospect of a hereditary dictatorship, widespread economic hardship played an important role in galvanizing the Egyptian uprising on January 25, 2011. Labor strikes demanding better wages, improved working conditions, and greater rights and benefits increased dramatically in the five years before the revolution (Abdalla 2012). The snowballing protests spread from factory to factory, mill to mill, until they covered the country. On April 6, 2008, a general strike was launched in El Mahalla. The workers protested rising prices, low wages, and the privatization of public sector firms (Ekram 2012b).

Thanks to the general strike, the April 6 Youth Movement was born. This activist group was organized to support the workers and foster mass participation in their strike. It used social media – Facebook, Twitter, and Flickr – to convince many Egyptians, the young and educated primarily, to participate in politics for the first time (Radsch 2012). The organization continued to operate after the strike, dedicating itself to advocating for free speech while criticizing nepotism and Egypt's stagnant economy (Shapiro 2009).

Protests by the small peasantry occurred at the same time as labor strikes. In a process that began in the late 1990s, tenant farmers – whose tenancies were permanent and inherited – lost all rights established under land reforms enacted in the 1950s (Lesch 2011). Landowners took back the land or imposed rental rates too high for tenants to pay. Thus, under Mubarak the rural poor's protests joined those of labor and the urban poor.

Before the Arab Spring, Islamists had long been a potent opposition force to the authoritarian secularism of Gamal Abdel Nasser, Anwar Sadat, and Hosni Mubarak. Jihadi Salafis included Ayman al-Zawahiri, a leader of Al-Jihad in Egypt before becoming the current leader of al-Qaeda. In 1997, the main Jihadi groups within Egypt renounced the use of violence but continued to challenge the regime (Al-Sayyid 2003).

The mainstream Society of Muslim Brothers, shortened to the Muslim Brotherhood (MB), was established in Egypt in 1928. In recent decades, the MB have used charitable activities to obtain political influence (Fareg 2011). Under Mubarak, the MB often filled gaps in social service provision at the grassroots level. As Egypt's public service scheme deteriorated, the MB played an increasingly central role as an alternative provider of services. The group operated hospitals, schools, emergency relief, and programs to support widows and orphans across Egypt.

The MB's charitable activities led to political influence. It attained dominance over Egypt's professional associations and skirted the law against religious parties to become the most potent opposition force in the multiparty elections of the authoritarian regime. In Mubarak's later years, conceivably, the MB served as a shadow government and plausible alternative to his rule, an alternative captured by their slogan "Islam is the solution" (El-Hadini 2011).

Challengers to Mubarak's regime faced comprehensive and sometimes fierce repression (HRW 2011). Under a state of emergency, which was in effect all throughout Mubarak's time in power, security personnel could restrain individuals' movement, search persons or places without warrants, tap telephones, monitor and ban publications, forbid meetings, and detain suspects without trial (HRW 2011). The state could choose to refer civilians to criminal courts, Emergency State Security Courts, or draconian military courts. Civilians were prosecuted in emergency and military courts for nonviolent offenses. To curtail freedom of assembly, gatherings of more than five people were illegal. Security and police personnel harassed people on the streets, demanded bribes, and seized and beat people to coerce false confessions. Torture was systematic in police stations, prisons, and in State Security Intelligence (SSI) detention centers.

Authoritarian Breakdown

Prolonged dictatorship with the prospect of a father-to-son handover in power, economic hardship, corruption by the political elite, harsh repression, and the availability of a shadow government and counter-elite all contributed to Egypt's mass revolt in January 2011. However, the two most proximate causes were the demonstration effects of the successful Tunisian Revolution, which swiftly sent long-term president, Zine El Abidine Ben Ali, into exile on January 14, 2011, and the "We are all Khaled Said" campaign.

Khaled Said was a 28-year-old Egyptian man who lived in Alexandria. In June 2010, Said was beaten to death in the streets by two police officers because he possessed video footage of them sharing the spoils of a drug bust (Ahram Online 2012). A family member took a picture of his brutalized face in the morgue: "The face was unrecognizable, almost grotesque. The jaw was dislocated, little gaps remained where once his teeth used to be, the nose was broken and the eyes stared vacantly ahead. The expression was one of horror, frozen forever" (Ahram Online 2012).

A few days after his death, an Egyptian executive for Google, Wael Ghonim, uploaded the picture and launched the "We are all Khaled Said" Facebook page. Instantly, it became one of the most popular places of political dissent for Egyptians on the Internet.

Egyptians had been following the unfolding revolution in Tunisia. Activists had noted how Mohamed Bouazizi's self-immolation had galvanized a popular revolt that stunningly forced their dictator into exile. As excited Egyptians watched Tunisia's revolution unfold, Ghonim decided to use the "We are all Khaled Said" Facebook page to organize a similar revolt in Egypt. If Mohamed Bouazizi could become the symbol of the Tunisian Revolution, Khaled Said could become the face of the Egyptian Revolution.

Ghonim chose January 25, Police Day in Egypt, as the official launch day of Egypt's Arab Spring revolution. In response to Ghonim's request, on January 25, 2011, tens of thousands of people demanding an end to President Hosni Mubarak's 30-year rule filled the streets of several Egyptian cities (Fahim and El-Naggar 2011). The size and intensity of the demonstrations, which were led by secular-leaning youth, seemed to shock even the protestors, yet the demonstrations continued to grow all day. In the following days, members of the Muslim Brotherhood and organized labor joined the protests.

In response to the increasing numbers, the police intensified the use of rubber bullets to disperse protestors, who began setting fire to buildings belonging to the police, government, and the ruling NDP (Fahim and El-Naggar 2011). Violence grew sharply on January 27. Civilian casualties mounted. To prevent continued protests, the authorities interrupted broadcasts on Facebook, Twitter, and You-Tube, as well as text messaging. On Friday, January 28, which was deemed the Day of Rage, police forces were overwhelmed by the intensifying mass revolt; military forces were deployed to maintain security.

By this point, a majority of Egyptian citizens clearly wanted to end Mubarak's regime. They were fully mobilized in the streets to do so. No amount of state brutality deployed at that stage could have stemmed the tide and saved Mubarak's dictatorship. Ultimately, the military leadership decided not to unleash their firepower against non-violent protestors. Instead, they protected citizens participating in the mass uprising. The protests continued through early February. On February 11, the eighteenth day of mass protests, Mubarak finally stepped down. People power had been enough to end his dictatorship and force the military to consider moving itself far enough away from politics to enable democracy.

Democratic Transition

Islamists and the secular opposition largely worked together during the 18 days of Egypt's Arab Spring uprising that led to Mubarak's resignation (Utvik 2017). In addition, instead of shooting down protesters, the Egyptian military presented itself as defenders of the January 25 Revolution, and the demonstrators' backers declared democratic aspirations. However, the transition engendered dynamics revealing ambivalence about democracy among Islamists, secularists, and the military. The military partially showed its hand at the outset of the transition by forcibly taking over the transition process through the Supreme Council of the Armed Forces (SCAF), which took over governing the country after Hosni Mubarak fell.

Founding democratic elections in Egypt took place in stages: a SCAF-imposed constitutional referendum in March 2011, parliamentary elections for the Lower House and Upper House in 2011–2012 (with both houses responsible for selecting members of a Constituent Assembly assigned to write a new constitution), a second constitutional referendum for the 2012 Constitution, and presidential elections in June 2012.

The MB and allied Islamist political parties dominated all of these elections, most notable of which included the election of Muhammad

Morsi as president. Due partly to Mubarak-era policies, secular-oriented political parties suffered from a lack of organizational strength and connection to broad constituencies – both strengths of the Muslim Brotherhood, which quickly formed the Freedom and Justice Party (FJP), which turned out to be an electoral juggernaut. Fear of the MB's mobilizational capacity led secularists to turn to street demonstrations and ultimately a military coup to oust the Islamists from the formal political arena (Utvik 2017). Secure in its electoral strength, the MB only half-heartedly sought to sustain the Islamist–secularist coalition that brought down Mubarak's regime. Instead of democratic consolidation, all three groups' ambivalence about democracy culminated in a new military authoritarian regime.

Democratic Consolidation: Political Pact

The broad coalition that brought down Mubarak's military-backed authoritarian regime and that convinced the military to initially support a transition to elected civilian rule achieved a few other goals in 2011 before intense polarization between Islamists and secularists doomed hopes of a democratic bargain.

Notably, early in the transition, pressure from an Islamist–secularist alliance exacted from the SCAF the dissolution of the Mubarak-era Parliament, the dissolution of his National Democratic Party, and the designing of an election law in such a way as not to open too much room for the old regime forces (Utvik 2017).

However, despite evidence that mass mobilization was the only effective way to threaten pillars of Mubarak's autocracy – the military, the Ministry of the Interior (MOI) with its police and security forces, the judiciary, business cronies, and rural notables – mere days after the 18-day Egyptian Revolution the Islamist–secularist alliance began to break down (Utvik 2017).

Several issues contributed to overwhelming polarization between the two social forces and also revealed their ambivalence about democracy: differences in Islamists' and secular organizations' mobilizational capacities; the transition roadmap; coalitions and electoral results; the formation of a Constituent Assembly; presidential elections; the writing of a new constitution; a constitutional declaration made by President Muhammad Morsi of the Muslim Brotherhood; and the lack of inclusivity in bodies controlled by elected Islamists.

Mobilizational Capacity and the Transition Roadmap

Young, mostly secular-oriented people spearheaded the Arab Spring in Egypt before Islamists joined them in mass protests in Tahrir Square and in other squares in Cairo and the rest of the country. The secular activists were not acting as part of any particular political party and somewhat idealistically were reluctant to join or form any after Mubarak's fall. However, after authoritarian breakdown and the prospect for genuinely competitive elections emerge, political parties become central in democratic transitions (O'Donnell and Schmitter 1986). Unfortunately for secularists in Egypt, young or old, Islamists had major advantages in forming effective political parties upon entering the Arab Spring.

Through repression and co-optation, political liberalization under Sadat and Mubarak aimed to keep all opposition political forces/ parties poorly organized, dependent on the state, and deprived of deep links to the Egyptian population (Utvik 2017). The former presidents largely succeeded, with the exception of the Islamists – in particular the Muslim Brothers, who had, despite harsh repression, preserved a nationwide organization with strong roots in large parts of the population. That legacy meant that as founding elections of Egypt's new democracy approached, only the Muslim Brotherhood and the old regime rulers possessed networks able to rapidly mobilize widespread support (Shehata and Stacher 2006).

Facing organizational and mobilizational disadvantages, secularists sought a slower transition pace than the better-organized Muslim Brotherhood and their newly created Freedom and Justice Party. In this instance, the military, in control of the transition, sided with the Islamists. Shortly after Mubarak's fall, the ruling Supreme Council of the Armed Forces appointed a committee of eight judicial experts to suggest revisions to the Constitution to enable free and fair elections. The group of eight, led by a respected judge and moderate Islamist, Tariq al-Bishri, also included a member of the MB, but no other members of the opposition (to Mubarak) – Islamist or secularist.

The Bishri committee's proposals and the SCAF's announcement of dates for parliamentary and presidential elections became the roadmap for Egypt's democratic transition (Utvik 2017). The proposals included a reduction of presidential terms from six to four years (plus a two-term limit), the restriction of emergency laws, and full judicial supervision of elections. In addition, after fresh elections for these bodies, the committee stipulated that a new constitution would be prepared by a 100-member assembly to be appointed by a joint meeting of the two houses of the Egyptian Parliament. The SCAF ultimately ordered parliamentary elections to be held between November 2011 and February 2012 and for presidential elections to be held between May and June 2012.

The proposed amendments to the Constitution were put to a referendum on March 19, 2011, less than two months after the revolution of January 25, 2011. Secularists, needing time to develop favorable links to the Egyptian population, sought to delay the referendum and have a written constitution before any elections (Utvik 2017). They argued that, in countries emerging from decades of authoritarian rule, the ground rules of a democratic system – a new constitution – was needed before elections. However, they struggled to justify their position when confronted with the questions of who should make the new constitution and by what means these people should be selected. They also argued that rapid elections would favor groups that already possessed a strong organization (i.e., the MB), while other groups needed an extended period to build their capacity for outreach.

The Muslim Brothers countered that for a future constitution to be legitimate it must be made by an assembly elected by the people. They also held that rapid elections would support democratic consolidation because they would quickly end rule by an autocratic military council.

Once the SCAF enforced March 19, 2011, as the referendum date, secularists called for a no-vote. However, the result was a landslide victory in favor of the proposed amendments: 77% in favor and only 23% against.

Coalitions and Electoral Results

Though they knew they needed more time to become embedded in the Egyptian population, secularists organized in political parties were chilled by Islamists' electoral power, which was demonstrated by the Constitutional Referendum's success on March 19, 2011. Polarization only increased from there. Islamist forces won resounding victories in both houses of Parliament and the presidency. Because the Muslim Brotherhood had promised not to run a presidential candidate to avoid dominating all branches of government and the Constituent Assembly, the candidature and election of Muhammad Morsi as president alarmed the military and secular political forces.

Demonstrating ambivalence about democracy and a failure of the twin tolerations, instead of actively negotiating with Islamists to maintain the alliance they shared during the Egyptian Uprising, secularists turned to street demonstrations and calls for military intervention to overturn Islamist electoral victories.

For their part, Islamists – aware of their organizational and electoral advantages – revealed some ambivalence about democracy by making only weak attempts to be inclusive.

The Tunisian case had demonstrated the benefits of cross-ideological – Islamist and secularist – campaign coalitions and consensus-governing during early transitional elections in the Arab world. From the standpoint of democratic consolidation, early transitional elections benefit from ideological cooperation more than later elections because they determine the rules of the democratic game (i.e., the Constitution). They can also help develop trust and the twin tolerations between polarized Islamist and secular forces.

In the run-up to parliamentary elections in Egypt, attempts – largely unsuccessful – were made to create a grand coalition of Islamists and secularists that was similar to the Tunisian Troika, which included the rough equivalent of the Muslim Brotherhood, Ennahdha, and Ennahdha's two junior secular partners, Ettakatol and the Congress for the Republic.

From November 2011 to February 2012, elections were held for the Lower House of Parliament, the People's Assembly. In the run-up to those elections, the Muslim Brotherhood's Freedom and Justice Party formed an electoral coalition, the Democratic Alliance, with Egypt's historic secular party, the Wafd, which had been active in the pre-Nasser pluralist era (Dunne and Hamzawy 2017). Other, smaller, secular parties including the Nasserist Dignity (Karama) Party and the Tomorrow of the Revolution joined the alliance. There were also smaller Islamist parties in the coalition. This coalition fell apart after secular parties withdrew over differences regarding the total number of candidates fielded by each of them and conflicts over religion's place in the election platform (Dunne and Hamzawy 2017). Recall that in Tunisia, despite electoral dominance, Islamists in the Ennahdha political party removed polarizing language from a draft constitution that designated a role for *Sharia* in law-making and the state. The Muslim Brotherhood proved much less willing to make such concessions.

Reacting to the MB-led Democratic Alliance, the Egyptian Bloc emerged as a well-funded anti-Brotherhood secular electoral coalition campaigning on separating religion from politics and state affairs (Dunne and Hamzawy 2017). An additional Islamist alliance organized by conservative Salafis, The Nour (Light) Party, formed to compete in parliamentary elections as well.

Islamist forces dominated founding elections in Egypt's People's Assembly. The Muslim Brotherhood's FJP took 43% of the seats. Shockingly, conservative Salafis in the Nour Party took 24%, and 2% went to smaller Islamist parties – meaning that 68% of the Assembly seats went to Islamists of various hues. The fragmented secular opposition won at most 24%, with the remainder going to offshoots of Mubarak's dissolved NDP and to Independents (Utvik 2017).

Most secularists perceived the Islamist domination of the assembly as a major defeat; and in response acted in a manner unfavorable to the twin tolerations. They ruled out possibilities of consensus building with Islamists, and by doing so moderate Islamists became less moderate. As Dunne and Hamzawy note:

Facing a fragmented and somewhat hostile secular spectrum, the Muslim Brothers, who originally viewed the Salafis as their competition and toyed with the idea of collaborating with secular groups – moved closer to Salafis and, in doing so, endorsed more of the Salafis' ultra-conservative platform. They called forcefully for the application of Sharia and denounced secular views as blasphemous. (Dunne and Hamzawy 2017: 15)

Elections to the Shura Council, the Upper House of Parliament, followed the elections to the People's Assembly. Historically devoid of any real power, the SCAF-imposed Constitutional Amendments made the Shura Council members partners with Popular Assembly members in the selection of the 100-member Constituent Assembly tasked with writing the new constitution. Islamists – a combination of the FJP and the Nour Party – won 150 seats in elections to the Upper House. Secularists won only 30 seats and realized that they were confronting not only a vast Islamist majority but also a majority involving a quarter of the parliamentary seats, in both houses, being filled with people even more religiously conservative than the Muslim Brothers (Utvik 2017).

Presidential elections, which were held between May and June 2012, further increased Islamist–secularist polarization. In a demonstration of their ambivalence about democracy, the Muslim Brothers announced that they would indeed field a candidate, Muhammad Morsi, who became president of Egypt in June 2012 (Dunne and Hamzawy 2017). This was after promising that the MB would not attempt to monopolize both the legislative and executive branches of government and that it would restrict itself to participation in Parliament and the Constituent Assembly.

The presidency, along with dominance of both houses of Parliament, gave the Islamists electoral legitimacy to (temporarily) rule Egypt. However, secular-oriented political parties and old regime autocrats within the military and judiciary were unwilling to tolerate formal Islamist political power. With military backing, the Supreme Constitutional Court (SCC) dissolved the People's Assembly. Secularists chose to ally with the military and the SCC, and they backed the destruction of the country's first genuinely elected body since the early 1950s.

Constituent Assembly Formation

Constituent assembly elections – because they produce the rules of the political game for all political forces – constitutions – are different from other elections within democracies that can be based on majority rule more or less without question. Islamist–secularist conflicts vis-à-vis the selection of a constituent assembly increased Islamist–secularist polarization in Egypt (Utvik 2017). Based on the 2011 Constitutional Amendments and composed of 100 members chosen by the houses of Parliament, the Constituent Assembly was charged with writing the country's new democratic constitution. Fifty of the members would be MPs in proportion to the electoral weight of the various parties. The 50 others were to be selected from outside Parliament. Basic conflicts over the composition of the Constituent Assembly made it difficult to form the group (Utvik 2017).

On March 25, 2012, the two chambers of Parliament produced a list of 100 people who would be charged with writing the new constitution. Most secularists, and ominously a representative from the SCC, were unwilling to accept the selection, which they deemed to be dominated by Islamists. Most secularists urged withdrawal from the

Constituent Assembly in protest. The secularists' posture indicated that most of them refused to acknowledge the elected assemblies' right to form the Constituent Assembly (Utvik 2017). Instead of negotiating with Islamists within the body, they appealed to autocratic forces – the courts and the SCAF – to blunt Islamist electoral power within the Constituent Assembly.

On the other hand, Islamists acted as though they did not recognize that a constitutional assembly is different from a regular parliament because it produces the rules of the game and therefore requires all parts of society to be represented, roughly equally, within it.

Court action, backed by the military and supported by most secularists, dissolved the first Constituent Assembly and the elected Lower House of Parliament, the People's Assembly.

A second Constituent Assembly failed to resolve Islamist–secular differences, and again secularists called for members to withdraw from it in protest. Thus, Muhammad Morsi of the Muslim Brotherhood took over the Egyptian presidency in June 2012, lacking an elected supportive Parliament, with a Constituent Assembly under attack, and facing obstruction by the military, secular forces, and Mubarak's hostile judiciary. In addition, the SCAF still controlled the transitional government. Nevertheless, Morsi shepherded a new constitution into being.

The 2012 Egyptian Constitution

Secularists criticized the Muslim Brotherhood's 2012 Constitution in terms of process and content (Awad 2011). In broad lines, secularists and Islamists diverged on the place of *Sharia* in the political system, on the powers of the executive, and on rights and freedoms, in particular those of women. Instead of compromise, Islamists ultimately imposed their preferences in all these areas, including adding an article addressing more concretely "how" the principles of *Sharia* would be the main source of legislation – as the second article in Egypt's 1971 Constitution declared. To ensure that the article would be legally binding, a new article added that "the principles of *Sharia* include its general proofs, its fundamental and legal rules, and its sources within the Sunni schools" (Trager 2016: 219).

In terms of process, secularists – while participating in the Constituent Assembly – complained about a lack of transparency and about contradictions between circulating versions of the draft constitution. They also charged that amendments and suggestions that secularist members submitted were being ignored.

Morsi's Constitutional Declaration

Arguing – plausibly – that he needed to protect the revolution from reactionary forces, including the courts and their military backers, in November 2012, President Muhammad Morsi issued a constitutional declaration that ended any dwindling possibility that secularists would tolerate Islamists' right to rule – temporarily – based on electoral results.

Morsi's decree gave the president nearly unlimited powers and immunized the Constituent Assembly and the Upper House of Parliament from dissolution by any court or other entity until the country had a new constitution and a new parliament had been elected (Utvik 2017). Morsi also intervened in the judiciary by appointing a new public prosecutor, and he even replaced leaders of the SCAF, making General Abdel Fattah El-Sisi its head.

Taking advantage of Morsi's decree, the Constituent Assembly rushed through a draft of the 2012 Constitution before the military and the SCC could regroup. That draft passed in a two-round referendum, which took place on December 15 and December 22, 2012. Morsi's decree also gave the Shura Council, which his party dominated, legislative powers in the absence of a lower house.

Morsi's constitutional declaration hit a galvanizing nerve with secularists. By making his decrees immune to judicial review, Morsi, according to secularists, was taking powers not claimed even by Mubarak. A viable secularist coalition, the National Salvation Front (NSF), emerged from the controversy (Dunne and Hamzawy 2017). The NSF brought together parties such as the Wafd, the Unionists, the Free Egyptians, the Social Democrats, the Democratic Front, the Congress Party, the Popular Alliance, and Dignity. The coalition demanded that Morsi rescind his constitutional declaration and launch a national dialogue to address key challenges facing Egypt's democratic transition (Al-Sudany 2015).

Morsi countered with an offer of a national dialogue, but by this time it had become clear that secularists would reject all calls coming from Morsi, the Muslim Brotherhood, and Salafi parties to participate in electoral coalitions, national dialogues, constitutional consultations, and participation in the executive branch of government (Dunne and Hamzawy 2017). Instead, they turned away from electoral politics and toward the streets, and ultimately toward the military in hopes of increasing their own power during the country's democratic transition.

For its part, the MB exhibited bad faith by offering only token participation to secularists in the cabinets of its governments and other appointments. "The last straw came in June 2013 when Morsi named Adel al-Khayat as the governor of Luxor. Al-Khayat was more than just an Islamist. He was a terrorist who had massacred 62 people, most of them tourists, in 1997 at the Temple of Hatshepsut" (Totten 2016).

The mobilization of the NSF melded into Tamarod ("Rebellion"/ "Revolt"), a grassroots movement – funded and backed by the military, the security agencies, and wealthy Mubarak supporters – that was founded to oppose President Morsi and force him to call early elections. The biggest protests were scheduled for June 30, 2013, on the one-year anniversary of Morsi's rise to power.

Due to Islamist–secularist polarization and the failure of these two sides to develop the twin tolerations, then, Egypt was approaching a point of uncontrolled instability by the spring of 2013 (Dunne and Hamzawy 2017). That instability culminated in the El-Sisi–led military coup of July 3, 2013.

Democratic Consolidation: Military Pact

Democratic consolidation challenges were more difficult in Egypt than in Tunisia. In part, this is because the military had an expansive role in politics – and the economy – prior to the Arab Spring. In Egypt, democratic hopes hinge largely on extricating the military from politics and placing it under civilian elected officials' authority and control. This is a tall task partly because, prior to the Arab Spring, the Egyptian military had the guns *and* the (in)formal authority to make decisions in all five core governing areas. In Mubarak's Egypt, the military dominated or interfered in leadership selection, policymaking, internal security, national defense, and military organization instead of civilians.

Incredibly (and instructively), despite the military's stranglehold on politics and deep economic interests, after 18 days of a cross-ideological mass uprising, the Egyptian military seemed to have accepted as inevitable a transition from military to elected, civilian rule (Utvik 2017).

Post-Mubarak, after the Muslim Brotherhood racked up electoral victories, former President Morsi began to extricate the military from politics. However, after campaign promises to establish elected-civilian authority over the military, including its budget, and after actually taking the step of replacing the SCAF's senior leadership, Morsi lost leverage; progress was reversed before any steps to subordinate the military could be institutionalized. Instead, the breakup of the Islamist–secularist alliance, which had brought down Mubarak, enabled the reassertion of military authoritarian power. Secularists, as fearful of Islamist electoral power as the military, did not trust that the Muslim Brotherhood's FJP and its Islamist allies would surrender power if they lost subsequent elections. Instead of maintaining an alliance with Islamists to extricate the military from politics, they turned to the military and to the streets to overturn electoral results. Having greater electoral strength, Islamists contributed to secular doubts and lost secular support for extricating the military from politics by pushing for elections before secularists could organize and connect with constituents, as well as by declining to seriously share power in the fragile earliest stage of Egypt's democratic transition.

Once the MB had been subdued by the coup on July 3, 2013, secularists seemingly believed that the military would carry on reforms on behalf of the January 25 Revolution: it would modify the Constitution, hold multiparty elections, and institutionalize democratic government (Bayat 2013). Instead, the military demonstrated that it would only make democratic concession in the face of a cross-ideological mass uprising. All Egyptians, more or less, had wanted to end Mubarak's military-backed crony-capitalist authoritarian regime. However, the military took advantage of the split between Islamists and secularists in order to reinstall authoritarian rule with an even stronger role for the military in core decision-making areas than the one that had prevailed under Mubarak.

The Egyptian military's opportunistic behavior, secularists' naïvety, and the actions of Islamists within the MB (who apparently shared power with the military rather than vigorously attempt to maintain a coalition with secularists) invite a tracking of the military's ambivalence about democracy and its underlying preference for military rule. Ultimately, the military's support of the people's revolution proved to be weak: it only took the first opportunity to reassert its power without mass bloodshed – the split between Islamists and secularists – for it to do so.

A Military-Guided Democratic Transition?

In Tahrir Square, the heart of the Egyptian Revolution, which took place on January 25, 2011, the army rank-and-file sympathized with protesters, and the leadership proved unwilling to order its troops to fire on demonstrators (Bumiller 2011).[1] In exchange, the Egyptian military enjoyed popular support. The military claimed to be acting in compliance with the will of the people, and its popularity increased when the SCAF issued a formal statement that supported the protestors' main demands: dissolving Mubarak's feeble Parliament and his NDP, suspending the Constitution, and calling for competitive elections within six months.

While the SCAF statement indicated support for democracy, on the other side of the ledger *how* it managed the transition – assuming direct control and demonstrating concern about the disruptive power of sustained street protests and organized political forces, first and foremost the Muslim Brotherhood – suggests instead ambivalence about democracy and a gradual approach to managing change with the hope of creating a deeper military authoritarian regime than the one that had existed under Mubarak (Roll 2015).

Recall that, in Tunisia, the military also gave democracy a chance by refusing to shoot demonstrators en masse. However, it then backed away from the political scene and allowed opposition forces to take control. Civil society actors and representatives of newly emergent political parties formed a commission to manage the transition to democracy. The commission, generally known as the Ben Achour Commission (named for its chairman, attorney Yadh Ben Achour), made fundamental decisions during Tunisia's transition that protected and enhanced democratic prospects (Stepan 2012).

In contrast, beginning with its announcement that the military would take over the state and government after removing Mubarak

---

[1] A credible Egypt specialist asserts that the military was involved in allowing attacks against the protesters by pro-Mubarak forces on horseback and camels – but not by the army, so as not to taint it in the public eye (Bumiller 2011).

from power (ostensibly to comply with the people's demand for democratic transformation), the Egyptian military SCAF made decisions
during the transition that sabotaged democratic prospects (Roll 2015).

The Military's Constitutional Declaration

Immediately after Mubarak's ousting, two SCAF decisions bespoke
ambivalence about democracy (Roll 2015). First, instead of following
the Tunisian example and kicking off the transformation process by
electing an assembly to draft a new constitution, the SCAF worked on
the basis of the constitution in force. On March 19, 2011, it amended
and successfully submitted to referendum nine articles composed by a
Mubarak-regime-dominated technical committee.

Second, a mere 11 days after a successful referendum designed to
create an interim constitution by modestly updating the previous one,
the SCAF issued a declaration of 63 articles to describe how Egypt
would be governed during the provisional period as citizens waited for
a new leadership to be elected and a new constitution to be written
(Brown and Stilt 2011).

In addition to giving the amendments that passed by referendum the
force of law, the SCAF's constitutional declaration appointed the
SCAF as the ultimate decision-maker and manager of the transformation process. The latter's scope remained more or less obscure and
gave the SCAF de facto last word over the beginning of the constitutional process after the election of a new parliament (Roll 2015). The
constitutional amendments approved by popular referendum, though,
had reserved that right for the president, implying that the drafting of a
new constitution would not start before legislative and executive
powers were transferred to elected politicians. As Stephan Roll
observes, "by changing the rules of the game some ten days after the
referendum, the SCAF gave the first indication of its attitude towards
due process and democratic procedures. It did not even try to open a
debate or achieve national consensus, but put itself in charge of determining the path of transformation" (Roll 2015: 27).

Notably, the 2011 constitutional referendum and the military declaration 10 days later revealed an implicit alliance between the military
and the Muslim Brotherhood, and ambivalence about democracy by
both actors. The MB backed the military's referendum and call for

quick elections – which they knew they would dominate over secular forces. In return, the generals could tamp down revolutionary dynamics and spearhead the transformation process with the backing of the country's best organized political force (Roll 2015).

The MB's tacit alliance with the military was brief. Islamist dominance in parliamentary elections shook the military, and the MB confronted a military that limited the power of the newly elected parliament and insisted on control of the constitution-writing process (Roll 2015).

On June 16, 2012, the SCAF issued an addendum to its 2011 constitutional declaration. This supplementary constitutional declaration increased military leadership's powers vis-à-vis the presidency (El-Sadek 2012). The provisions therein took away the president's authority to appoint the Minister of Defense and commanders of the main branches of the armed forces. They limited the president's power to declare war and granted the SCAF more power in internal security. One article allowed the SCAF to retain legislative powers in the event of the dissolution of Parliament and established the SCAF's right to form a new constitutional assembly if needed. Finally, an amendment obliged newly elected presidents to take their oath of office before the Supreme Constitutional Court, instead of in the presence of Parliament.

These additional provisions reinforced the SCAF's own ultimate authority over the military and provided it full legislative powers in the absence of an elected parliament (Roll 2015).

Dissolving an Elected Parliament

The military and Mubarak's judiciary were alarmed enough by the manifestation of Islamist electoral power, and ambivalent enough about democracy, that they took concrete steps to combat it. In addition to the two constitutional declarations, they dissolved the elected Lower House of Parliament, the People's Assembly. With military backing, and on dubious technical grounds involving fairness between political parties and Independents in electoral rules, the SCC dissolved the People's Assembly that had been constituted based on the results of the parliamentary elections held between November 28, 2011 and January 11, 2012 (Roll 2015).

Presidential Elections

The SCC's decision to dissolve the People's Assembly and the military's additional constitutional amendments occurred days before voting in the second and decisive round of presidential elections began. Either military candidate Ahmed Shafiq or the Muslim Brotherhood's Muhammed Morsi was poised to win.

In light of its history of orchestrating favorable elections, it's clear that the military had enough respect for – or fear of – mass mobilization and organized opposition by the Muslim Brotherhood to not directly interfere with democratization and a 52% versus 48% victory for Morsi. Instead, it decided to clip his wings by dissolving Parliament and maintaining control of legislating and government formation as long as possible. It also forced Morsi to pledge his oath of office in front of an implacably hostile Supreme Constitutional Court that days earlier had formally dissolved an elected parliament dominated by his party and Islamist allies.

SCAF-Appointed Governments

To guide the transition process in favor of its interests, the SCAF appointed successive "technocratic" governments dominated by military officials rather than form transitional governments that included all relevant Egyptian political and social forces (Roll 2015). Even after Muhammad Morsi won the presidency in June 2012, the SCAF continued to dominate government formation until Morsi took back this right of elected officials through his controversial constitutional declaration.

Morsi's Constitutional Declaration

Leading up to Morsi's constitutional declaration of November 22, 2012, the newly elected president began a counterattack against the reassertion of autocratic powers by the military, security agencies, and the judiciary (Roll 2015). Morsi's ability to assert electoral power demonstrated that the Muslim Brotherhood, then an embedded organization and electoral juggernaut, could still threaten autocratic resurgence – or at least demand a share in power with some success.

On August 8, after religious militants killed 16 Egyptian soldiers in the Sinai (which sparked a lot of public anger), Morsi fired the country's intelligence chief and several other high-ranking officers in the MOI. Four days later, the president nullified the SCAF's June constitutional declaration and replaced scores of older generals with younger officers, which included the removal of the SCAF's commander-in-chief, Muhamad Tantawy, who was replaced by General Abdel Fattah El-Sissi.[2]

Notably, despite the power Morsi displayed in the SCAF reshuffle and the nullification of the SCAF's constitutional declaration, he did not follow up with measures to institutionally subjugate the military to civilian authority, a crucial step in consolidating a democracy-enhancing military pact that extricates the military from politics.

In addition, after campaigning on promises to place the military and its budget under the oversight of civilian elected officials, Morsi did neither: the 2012 Constitution did not contain any such provisions (Brown and Dunne 2013). Article 197 in the 2012 Constitution established a National Defense Council that would continue to shroud Egypt's military institutions and its massive economic ventures in secrecy and keep them above the law. Article 198 constructed a vague standard for crimes "that harm the Armed Forces" to provide a continuing justification for military trials of civilians. Article 234 gave the SCAF the power to appoint its own Minister of Defense. Article 152 prevented the president from declaring war without first consulting the SCAF. The military also remained the de facto ultimate decision-maker on all questions of national security.

Rather than subordinate the military to elected civilian rule, the back-and-forth between the SCAF and the Muslim Brotherhood during the transition probably indicated an ultimately unsuccessful attempt to work out a power-sharing deal that put certain areas under presidential authority and others under military authority (Roll 2015).

Morsi's November 2012 constitutional declaration upped the stakes in the struggle for power and control among Islamists, secularists, and the old regime. None acted in a way that wholeheartedly supported democracy. The declaration, at least temporarily, put the president above the law and immunized the constitution-drafting process against

---

[2] Some Egypt specialists believe that the military, in a step to revamp its own leadership, for reasons of its own, tacitly okayed the shuffling of military officers.

judicial interference (Kirkpatrick 2014). It also gave the president legislative and executive powers, including the power to enact laws to defend the revolution, national unity, and national security. It also shielded any laws, measures, and decrees adopted by the president from appeal. In addition, the president protected the partly elected, partly appointed Muslim-Brotherhood–dominated Upper House of Parliament, and then turned to it to form a government to replace the SCAF's appointed government.

Notably, Morsi took these steps as an elected official seeking to override the unelected SCC's and military's decisions. He also did so without "democratic" allies. The secular opposition supported the SCC's dissolution of an elected parliament and had long shown signs of support for military intervention to end Islamist electoral power.

With military backing, the SCC, which had dissolved the Lower House of Parliament on specious grounds, set its sights on disbanding the Constituent Assembly that had been chosen by elected members of both houses of Parliament.[3]

Most of the non-Islamist opposition called for its members to withdraw from the Constituent Assembly they viewed as unfairly constituted, and supported the move of the SCC to disband the Constituent Assembly, which was an autocratic holdover power from the Mubarak era. In addition, infuriated by a presidential declaration that gave Morsi even more power than Mubarak, secularists created a coalition, the National Salvation Front (NSF), that turned to the streets to remove him from power.

Finally, in another expression of ambivalence about democracy, Morsi rushed constitution-writing and the (ultimately successful) referendum backing the 2012 Constitution. He did not convincingly seek measures to address secular complaints about the composition of the Constituent Assembly and the need for ideological balance in a body charged with writing the rules of the game for an emerging democracy.

---

[3] For tactical reasons, the SCC and secularists were already attacking the Muslim Brotherhood and criticizing the Constituent Assembly vehemently; the SCAF remained in the Constituent Assembly and claimed to be apolitical.

Tamarod

The hostile popular reaction to his constitutional declaration, secular complaints about the 2012 Constitution, and the formation of the NSF pushed Morsi to seek a national dialogue with secularists and to compromise on some parts of his decree. But it was too late, and the secular opposition fundamentally did not trust Morsi and his word. The declaration ignited sustained public opposition to Morsi's government that culminated in his removal by the military after one year in power (Jumet 2017).

In addition to the NSF, a mass movement called Tamarod ("Rebellion") claimed to have attracted 22 million signatures and mobilized an estimated 12 million people to go into the streets for a mass demonstration on June 30, 2013, in order to force Morsi to end his rule early on his one-year anniversary in power (Al-Arabiya 2013). The military staged a coup a few days later on July 3, 2013.

The Military and Core Decision-Making in Egypt

To successfully stage its coup to remove the Muslim Brotherhood's threat to its political and economic power, the military co-opted and funded Tamarod (Jumet 2017). Tamarod gave the Egyptian military a path to claim that it was staging a coup in support of a faltering democratic transition. The disappointing reality that the military had used the polarization between Islamist and secular social forces – and secular support for its coup against an elected government – to revive and deepen a military authoritarian regime did not fully sink in for the secular opposition until General El-Sisi announced his intentions to run for the presidency in March 2014 (Utvik 2017).

On July 3, 2013, the Supreme Council of the Armed Forces in Egypt took power again (Roll 2015). That night, El-Sisi and the opposition figures from Tamarod who had met with him within the previous 48 hours held a news conference in which El-Sisi announced his roadmap to the Egyptian public. El-Sisi said that Morsi had been ousted and the head of the Supreme Constitutional Court, Adli Mansour, was now the president and that he (El-Sisi) was Minister of Defense. The government and the Shura Council were disbanded, and the Constitution was suspended.

The new president was charged with forming a new government, announcing a date for parliamentary and presidential elections, and running the country temporarily. The opposition figures surrounding El-Sisi – including members of the Islamist Nour Party, which had developed a rivalry with the Muslim Brotherhood and most secular-oriented political parties – announced their support for the roadmap and called for Egyptians to stop fighting (Al-Qurashy 2013). The National Salvation Front was represented by former Nobel Peace Prize winner Mohamed ElBaradei, who agreed to serve as interim vice-president.

El-Sisi made numerous calls to other countries, explaining the situation and seeking international support. The Muslim Brotherhood immediately responded in a statement that Egypt had just undergone a military coup and asked its supporters to back electoral legitimacy by protesting peacefully.

On July 7, interim President Mansour issued a constitutional declaration defining the framework of the transitional period and the elections and laying out a new process of constitution-making. Mansour appointed a committee of 10 legal experts, who prepared recommendations for constitutional change. A 50-member government-appointed Constituent Assembly, which notably did not include any members of the Muslim Brotherhood, drafted a new constitution, which passed by referendum in a dubious 98% landslide in early January 2014 (France 24 2014).

The 2014 Constitution gave more decisive power to the military than previous constitutions regarding questions of operational and leadership autonomy, national security, budget matters, and military justice (El-Din 2013). In doing so, the military was no longer treated as part of the executive branch of government but rather a branch in and of itself (Brown and Dunne 2013). Defense Ministers had to come from the ranks of the military and are subject to SCAF approval. The military budget was walled off from legislative scrutiny.

In terms of religious issues, the 2014 Constitution removed from the 2012 charter a provision requiring lawmakers to consult Al-Azhar in matters pertaining to Islamic law. Both the 2012 and 2014 constitutions state that the principles of *Sharia* are the principal sources of legislation. However, the 2014 Constitution eliminated the article that was written to define "principles of *Sharia*" and how *Sharia* could be implemented in a practical way.

The 2014 Constitution also eliminated the Shura Council, the Upper House of Parliament. It stipulated that the president, not the prime minister, would appoint several powerful ministers, namely, those for defense, foreign affairs, the interior, and justice. Presidential terms were limited to two four-year terms. Presidential elections were scheduled for May 26–May 28, 2014. Parliamentary elections were to be held in two phases from October 17 to December 2, 2015.

On March 26, 2014, El-Sisi resigned from the military and announced that he would be running for the presidency. According to official Egyptian figures, he was elected with 97% of the vote. Obviously, despite initial appearances, instead of extricating the military from politics and supporting elected civilian rule, El-Sisi staged a coup to deepen military influence in Egyptian leadership selection, policymaking, internal security, national defense, and military organization.

Under Mubarak, military rule was more indirect than it has been under El-Sisi. The military protected its institutional autonomy and concealed its economic interests from public view and accountability under Mubarak. However, the generals preferred to preserve their own interests by acting as political veto players working behind the scenes with the capacity to interfere in political life should its interests become threatened (Albrecht and Bishara 2011).

As part of the core elite under Mubarak – alongside business cronies, high judicial figures, the MOI, and its security and police forces – Mubarak's ruling National Democratic Party also represented military interests (Roll 2015). However, El-Sisi rose to power after the collapse of Mubarak's civilianized presidency and the public rejection of the NDP. In the face of that political vacuum, El-Sisi seems to be constructing political institutions that build on the SCAF's decision to take more direct political responsibility immediately after Mubarak's fall from power instead of retreating to its reserved powers.

In terms of leadership selection, top army officials "okayed" El-Sisi's 2014 run for the presidency well before his announcement to the public (Saleh 2014). As Mubarak did before him, El-Sisi may attempt to distance himself from his military roots, civilianize the executive branch, and develop a ruling party to link to society. However, currently El-Sisi seems to be more intent upon further militarizing the Egyptian state, its economy, its formal politics, and its society (Abul-Magd 2017).

Currently, the military brass also seems more intent on maintaining active control of the executive branch than it has been in the past (Roll 2015). Among other things, 2019 amendments to the 2014 Constitution appear designed to justify – based on the amended Article 200, which gives the military the duty to protect the Constitution and democracy – military intervention in politics, any future removals of heads of state by the military, cancellations of free elections, and interruptions of any democratic process (HRW 2019). The dubiously passed amendments also overturned two-term presidential limits and increased the terms from four to six years to allow President El-Sisi to remain in office until at least 2030.

In terms of leadership selection within the façade of multiparty politics that he has reorchestrated, El-Sisi does not rely on a single ruling or state party as Mubarak, Sadat, and Nasser did before him. El-Sisi has not endeavored to replace Mubarak's banned NDP. Instead, to create parliamentary backers willing to change his policies into legislation without question, El-Sisi relies more on Independents and a small array of supporting parties, none of which appear to be building a strong organizational base, constituent networks, or a patronage distribution system akin to those deployed by Mubarak's NDP (Dunne and Hamzawy 2017).

The electoral system for the 2015 election directed voters toward individual candidates rather than party-based lists. The law gave individual candidates 448 seats and party-list candidates 120 seats. For some, this indicates that it is more the military than any political party that has taken the NDP's place in El-Sisi's Egypt: "Sisi's lack of interest in civilian politics is one of several reasons why there has not been a new nationalist political party to replace Mubarak's National Democratic Party" (Dunne 2015).

El-Sisi apparently chose an electoral system dominated by Independents because it produces a parliament composed of individuals only seeking personal economic advantage; such a body is less capable of providing a check on the presidency than even the Mubarak Parliament (Dunne 2015). Regime co-optation, repression (the Muslim Brotherhoods' FJP was banned), boycotts, and pro-state parties and individual candidates characterized the 2015 parliamentary elections (Dunne and Hamzawy 2017). Here are the results:

Independent candidates dominated by pro-regime figures:

- 300 seats in the 2015 parliamentary elections (Fawzy et al. 2015).

Explicitly pro-state parties:

- For the Love of Egypt (120 seats)
- The Nation's Future (53 seats)
- Protectors of the Nation (18 seats)
- Republican People's Party (13 seats)
- Congress (12 seats)
- Conservatives (6 seats)
- Democratic Peace (5 seats)
- Egyptian National Movement (4 seats)
- Modern Egypt (4 seats)
- Freedom (3 seats)
- Egypt My Country (3 seats)
- Unionist (1 seat)

Co-opted parties:

- Free Egyptians (65 seats)
- Wafd 35 (seats)

Oppositional parties:

- Reform and Development (3 seats)
- Egyptian Social Democratic Party (4 seats)
- Guardians of the Revolution (1 seat)

A number of oppositional political parties boycotted the 2015 sham elections:

- Egyptian Socialist Popular Alliance
- Egypt Freedom, Justice
- Tomorrow of the Revolution
- Constitution
- Strong Egypt
- Bread and Freedom

Beyond any strategy of electoral domination by a remerging military authoritarian regime, 2019 constitutional amendments are redrawing the Egyptian political system and removing the last pretense of separation of powers or the subordination of the military to elected civilian governments (HRW 2011).

In addition to dominating leadership selection, the military also has increasing influence in policymaking under El-Sisi, which is perhaps clearest in the economic realm (Roll 2015). In addition to walling off its budget and economic enterprises that constitute up to 40% of Egypt's GDP from public scrutiny, the policy of giving public contracts to military entities or military-controlled companies without competitive bidding, which was formally implemented after the El-Sisi-led coup, culminated in a new, huge Suez project that probably would have gone to Gamal Mubarak's business cronies under Hosni Mubarak and to Gulf allies under Morsi (Kalin and Saleh 2014). The project included the expansion of the existing canal as well as the development of a huge international industrial and logistics hub in the Suez Canal Zone by a consortium of companies affiliated with the Egyptian army. The military, which was formally in charge of the nontransparent mega-development scheme, gave subcontracts to members of Egypt's business elite, but only according to terms set by the SCAF (Roll 2015).

Since the SCAF took over after Mubarak's fall, the military brass has remained the de facto decision-maker on all questions of national security in Egypt. In the 2014 Constitution and the 2019 amendments, the MOI and its police and security forces lost to the military part of the direct influence on decision-making that they had acquired during the Mubarak era (Roll 2015).

Finally, given the military's increasing dominance of leadership selection, policymaking, and internal security under El-Sisi, the military has clearly maneuvered itself in such a way as to maintain dominance over civilians – elected or not – in decision-making for national defense and military organization issues.

Democratic Consolidation: Nation-State and Weberian-State Pact

In terms of democratic consolidation, Egypt will always be relatively blessed as a long-established nation-state with – for the region – comparative advantages as a Weberian state. Egypt has been a nation-state for nearly 5,000 years. That consolidated national identity was an asset in the country's failed democratic transition. It contributed to the unwillingness of the military to commit mass murder to protect Mubarak. National unity also probably limited bloodshed and blocked the emergence of a civil war after the military coup on July 3, 2013. Centuries as a nation state and relative strength as a Weberian state will support democratic consolidation in any future Egyptian democratic transition.

Egypt was one of the earliest countries to establish national unity. Millennia ago, Egyptians united into one nation-state by connecting the scattered settlements and regions of ancient Egypt under a central government (Alim 2011). Throughout history and despite foreign occupations and varying religious and political ideologies, Egyptians remained united under their established state. In the 1919 Revolution, Egyptians held and repeated the slogan "Religion is for God; the nation is for everyone" to mark yet another era of national unity among people from all religions and ideologies.

However, at times, extremists have challenged Egyptian national unity. Some 10% of Egyptians are Coptic Christians. There are also small numbers of Beja, Nubians, Dom, and Berber Egyptians, and small Shia and Bahai communities in the overwhelmingly Sunni Muslim country of over 94 million people. Attacks on churches and clashes between Muslims and Christians have occurred sporadically down through the centuries. Recent attacks against Christians culminated in the All Saints Church bombing on New Year's Day 2011, just before the January 25 Revolution. The bombing at Alexandria's Coptic church killed at least 21 people and injured 70. It triggered a mass wave of anger by both Christians and moderate Muslims. President Mubarak went on state television to express his shock: "This act of terrorism shook the country's conscience, shocked our feelings and hurt the hearts of Muslim and Coptic Egyptians" (BBC News 2011).

Some violence and attacks on Christian houses of worship occurred during the 18 days of the January 25 Revolution. However, hundreds of pictures and videos filmed in Tahrir Square showed young Muslim men protecting Christian houses of worship. Christian youth were also seen protecting Muslim youth while they prayed in the Square.

Yet, in the years following the revolution, attacks on churches and Christians have increased. The Maspero Square Massacre was the most prominent and discouraging for Egyptian Christians (Tadros 2011). Copts had gathered in Cairo on October 9, 2012, to protest the destruction of a church near Aswan. About 10,000 protestors planned a march to Maspero Square. Marchers had to pass hostile Muslim crowds and upon arrival were crushed by military armored vehicles and soldiers firing rifles to cheers from some Muslim onlookers (Lane 2012). In all, 27 Christians were killed as a result of the Maspero incident.

The SCAF, then in charge of the country, channeled the Maspero investigation and trial of military officers into military courts. Three soldiers were sentenced to three years in jail for involuntary manslaughter. The verdict inspired derision from the media: "The fact that the SCAF was ruling the country, in charge of officers who attacked the protestors, and at the same time investigating the case … was an astonishing conflict of interest. How can a military court rule in a situation where military personal are accused in a civil case? This could only lead to a massively biased verdict" (Ekram 2012a).

Military rulers displayed more conviction in their persecution of the media covering the attacks and some of the marchers (Ekram 2012a). The military took civilians to military courts, including bloggers and activists, on charges of using violence against the armed forces, stealing weapons, and possession of weapons. During the events, state TV channels argued that protestors were attacking the military and asked citizens to come out and defend their armed forces, which led to more violence against Copts.

Prospects for improved conditions for Egypt's minorities (i.e., primarily its Coptic Christians) remained low under the rule of Morsi and the Muslim Brotherhood. Security forces were criticized for intervening too late in a clash that led to the death of five Copts in a town near Cairo in April 2013 (BBC News 2013). Subsequently, clashes first between a mob and protesters-turned-mourners, and later between the mourners and security forces, marred these five Copts' funerals in St. Mark's Cathedral (Taylor 2013). Other incidents targeting minorities and weakening national unity during Morsi's rule included the killing of four Shia Egyptians by a Salafi-led mob in Giza in June 2013. Once again, police forces were present but did not intervene to stop the massacre (Hellyer 2013).

Morsi and the Muslim Brotherhood were criticized for doing little, if anything, to counter sectarianism and foster national unity in Egypt. Morsi's removal from power was followed by attacks on more than 40 churches and a number of affiliated buildings across Egypt by his supporters (Miller 2016a). Security forces did little to prevent this destruction, because it revealed the MB's violent inclinations. The military used this to justify their forced exclusion from the political scene after the July 2013 military coup that removed Morsi from power (HRW 2015).

Quick to recognize the importance of winning over Egypt's Copts, El-Sisi took a pioneering move in paying the Coptic Pope a visit during the Christmas mass (Ahram Online 2015), doing so again in his second year in power. More importantly, he promised the renovation of churches destroyed in the earlier waves of violence within a year (Ahram Online 2016). Although such steps have certainly had positive impacts on Egypt's Copts, other problems persist, which include the chronic postponement of laws governing personal status and church construction, as well as a culture of prioritizing reconciliation over justice in the aftermath of sectarian clashes (Al-Masry Al-Youm 2016).

Despite the bloody conflicts between Egyptian Muslims and Christians and other minorities, holes in national unity did not prevent democratic consolidation during Egypt's Arab Spring. There is a strong enough sense among the vast majority of Egyptians that Egypt is a single political community, a single nation-state, for the consolidation of a democratic political system.

Is Egypt enough of a Weberian state for democratic consolidation to succeed? The Egyptian military is considered more professional than most in the region, but following the 2011 Revolution, and to an extent beforehand, the state has not always monopolized violence within the country. A Sinai insurgency, originally named Ansar Bayt al-Maqdis ("Supporters of Jerusalem," ABM), has evolved over the last 15 years (Ashour 2016). In the early 2000s, ABM's stated goal shifted from supporting Palestinian armed groups to controlling areas in northeast Sinai and fighting Egyptian security and military forces there.

Since Mubarak's removal from power, Egyptian governments have been more concerned with resolving the country's economic and political problems than safeguarding the Sinai Peninsula, which has become a near lawless region that has allowed Jihadi and Takfiri Salafis to operate relatively freely (Tuitel 2014). There have been frequent attacks, murders of civilians, kidnappings of soldiers, and ambushes of checkpoints in the region. Islamist militants have also used the weakened central authority in the Sinai to carry out attacks in Israel, and Sinai Bedouins have carried out attacks and kidnappings to free jailed tribesmen that they claim have been sentenced unfairly on charges ranging from terrorism to drug dealing.

As discussed above, in response to the security vulnerabilities in the Sinai and as a way to assert civilian control over the military, President Morsi removed key leaders of the SCAF and fired the intelligence chief, General Murad Muwafi. Morsi, and military rulers after his removal, launched several operations, none completely successful, to contain radical Islamist militants in the Sinai. In late 2014, the Sinai insurgent group, ABM, declared allegiance to ISIS and rebranded itself Wilayat Sinai ("the State of Sinai," WS). ABM/WS claimed that it killed more than a thousand pro-regime figures in 2014–2015. The Egyptian government's humiliation and repression of the Sinai population and counterinsurgency blunders have helped give ABM/WS ready access to a large pool of recruits (Ashour 2016).

The military's reassertion of power and control after the Morsi period was partly driven by popular societal sentiments yearning for stability. Many believed that Morsi's ouster had unleashed terrorist groups like ABM/WS to conduct attacks outside of the troubled Sinai and well within Egypt's capital and major cities. In late January 2014, the capital was shaken by four deadly car bombings, raising fears that Egypt was entering a prolonged and violent struggle between the military-backed government and a growing Islamist insurgency, though the cycle of violence has been more limited than the worst fears (Kirkpatrick 2014).

At times, ABM/WS has been less random in their attacks (Al-Ahram 2013). For example, Egypt's former minister of the interior, Mohamed Ibrahim, survived a failed assassination attempt by ABM/WS in September 2013. When the army responded with an operation in Sinai, ABM/WS shot down a military helicopter in January 2014, killing five soldiers (Al-Arabiya 2014a). In October 2014, two suicide attacks killed 29 soldiers at a checkpoint in Sheikh Zuweid in North Sinai, after which El-Sisi declared a state of emergency and imposed a curfew in the governorate.

After ABM morphed into Wilayat Sinai of the Islamic State in 2014, terrorist attacks increased (Kingsley et al. 2014). In a report on violence in Egypt, the Tahrir Institute for Middle East Policy (TIMEP) noted a surge in the monthly attack count from 30 in 2014 (already quadruple that of prior years) to 100 in 2015. This staggering increase has been accompanied by a diversification in terror acts, such as the assassination of the Prosecutor-General in June 2015, the explosion near the Italian consulate in Cairo in July 2015, the beheading of a Croatian oil worker in August 2015, the scandalous Russian airplane explosion over Sinai in October 2015, and the targeting of judges residing at a hotel in al-Arish in November 2015 (TIMEP 2015).

Terrorism against Coptic Christians has continued as well (Salman and Walsh 2017). On Palm Sunday (April 9, 2017), two suicide bombings at churches, for which the Islamic State sought credit, killed 44 Coptic Christians and injured more than 100. This was the worst violence against Copts in decades. After the attacks, President El-Sisi declared a three-month state of emergency. After this, an attack on a bus near a monastery in the southern Egyptian town of Minya killed 29 people and injured 20 more. The Islamic State claimed credit for the massacre. The Egyptian government blames the Muslim Brotherhood for the majority of these incidents, including being accomplices to the chief prosecutor's assassination (Abdel Hameed 2016).

Egypt has also witnessed the formation of other militant groups, such as Revolutionary Punishment and the Allied Popular Resistance Movement, which have focused on economic and infrastructure targets (Miller 2016a). In January 2014, a newly formed militant group, linked to al-Qaeda, Ajnad Misr ("Egypt's Soldiers"), claimed responsibility for two bomb attacks that targeted a police checkpoint in Giza, Cairo's twin city (TIMEP 2015). Eight people were killed and over 90 were wounded. *Ajnad Misr* has claimed at least 15 attacks in Greater Cairo since then (TIMEP 2015).

Overall, the current scene indicates a difficult path toward the state's monopoly on violence. Violent acts have become more pronounced and more geographically distributed, militants have become organized and selective, new terror groups have emerged, and regional conditions continue to affect the domestic security environment (e.g., some militants pledging allegiance to ISIS). The Egyptian state's institutions – those affiliated with security in particular – also have difficulty generating public credibility and trust.

The Egyptian state's military is closer to monopolizing violence than its bureaucracy is characterized by Weber's rational-legal legitimacy. Egypt is a bureaucratic state, but its bureaucracy desperately needs reform. It is gigantic, partly patronage-based, and dominated by military personnel (El-Houdaiby 2013).

In terms of Weber's third characteristic of modern states, the Egyptian state does not collect sufficient tax revenue to pay for the military, the bureaucracy, and public goods and services. The tax collection apparatus is flawed by the complexity of the system, widespread corruption, and a lack of trust in government institutions (Khalil 2013).

Since the 2000s, successive governments have embarked on modernizing tax laws so that all businesses face the same tax burden, without exemptions for large or foreign businesses, as had previously been the case (Mohamed 2014). Tax reform planners have targeted reducing tax rates, widening the tax base, establishing clear filing rules, and increasing the severity of punishments for noncompliance. Other measures, which have been strengthened and simplified, include tax refund and tax appeal procedures.

Democratic consolidation in Egypt, which became a nation-state nearly 5,000 years ago, could not be derailed by a lack of national unity. As a Weberian state, Egypt has flaws, but it probably had enough of a monopoly over the legitimate use of force, sufficient bureaucratic capacity, and sufficient tax collection capabilities to sustain a democratic transition.

Democratic Consolidation: Socioeconomic Pact

Egypt entered the Arab Spring with massive socioeconomic challenges that contributed to the uprising on January 25, 2011, and to the so-called second revolution on June 30, 2013. The Egyptian socioeconomic context's desperation and volatility at that time has been aptly described by Nader Fergany, lead author of several United Nations Development Programme (UNDP) Arab Human Development Reports (2002–2005):

Egypt's privatization programs have led to a brand of crony capitalism. The operative factor is a very sinister cohabitation of power and capital. The program is helping to reconstruct a kind of society where a small number of people own the lion's share of assets. Privatization in effect has meant replacing the government monopoly with private monopoly. The middle class has been shrinking while there has been an enlargement of the super-rich. State-owned enterprises have been sold to a minority of rich people at below market prices. The record of private sector enterprises creating jobs is very poor. We are not reaping the benefits of an energetic bourgeoisie: what we have is a parasitical, comprador class...The consequences will be no less than catastrophic. This society is a candidate for a difficult period of intense, violent social conflict, and the kind of government we have will not do.[4]

Backed by International Monetary Fund (IMF) and World Bank (WB) loans, economic policymaking since authoritarian breakdown during the Arab Spring in Egypt has been formally based on a market reform strategy that takes advantage of the opportunities for economic growth provided by global markets and a vigorous private sector while avoiding the simpleminded application of market liberalization, privatization, and a minimal state, which has resulted in the crony-capitalist forms of authoritarian rule that characterized the Egyptian political economy under Mubarak (King 2009).

Transforming Egypt's economy – which has been officially making the transition toward a liberal market economy since Sadat's early years in the 1970s – into one actually driven by a vigorous private sector taking advantage of the opportunities provided for economic growth by global markets would take five economic transitions (Amin 2012). Overall, the goal of these five economic transitions would be eliminating elite capture – the shaping of the rules of the game and institutions of the state for the economic benefit of the few.

The first economic transition would involve increasing bureaucratic capacity and forging a developmental state capable of implementing an industrial policy within the framework of a market-oriented model of development. The second would entail private sector actors weaning themselves off of rent-seeking activities to direct all their energy toward production and innovation. The third would be the development of a vigorous and sustainable social policy. The fourth would be more effective regional and global economic engagement, including with the International Financial Institutions (IFIs). The fifth would emphasize the importance of seeking, through national dialogue, consensus and compromise about major social and economic decisions.

Despite committing to the IMF-backed economic strategy and accepting loans from the IFIs, Egypt has made little progress toward the five goals under Morsi and El-Sisi. In fact, for average Egyptians, the Egyptian economy in 2019 under El-Sisi is the same as the Mubarak economy in 2010. In some ways, though, it's worse. The

---

[4] In an interview with the author, October 2006.

military has increased its control of the economy while maintaining its own rules, including walling off its economic assets and enterprises from government policy and oversight. If the military's economic activities are 3% of GDP, or 40%, as some have speculated, it makes little sense to forge a national economic policy without including it.

Although it received some positive reports from the IFIs, Egypt had a troubled economy before the Arab Spring. According to statistics published by the WB prior to the January 25 Revolution, Egypt was showing promise on the economic growth front (WB 2013). After 1998, when GDP per capita was $1,324, Egypt experienced steady economic growth. In 2010, GDP per capita reached $2,804. While economic growth seemed to be booming, poverty was still on the rise and the gap between the rich and the poor widened (WB 2013). The percentage of people under the poverty line increased in the decade prior to the revolution from 16.7% in 2000 to 25.2% in 2011 (Ahram Online 2013).

Given the fury about economic conditions that drove the January 25 Revolution, there is reason to wonder whether the reality under Mubarak was considerably worse than the mixed picture portrayed in the IFIs' statistics. Since the 2011 Revolution, Egypt has struggled to spur economic growth due partly to political instability, which has scared off tourists and foreign investors, both of which are key sources of foreign currency. Indeed, Egypt is currently undergoing its worst economic crisis in decades (Michaelson 2016). Prices are skyrocketing, and there is an import crisis. A video of a rant by a truck driver over the lack of availability of rice recently went viral. A taxi driver in Alexandria set himself on fire to protest rising prices.

These dire socioeconomic conditions exist despite Egypt's receiving of billions of dollars of grants from Qatar and Turkey during Morsi's year in power and billions of dollars of aid from Saudi Arabia and the United Arab Emirates since El-Sisi took over.

Blocked by former regime stalwarts and his party's own decision-making, former President Morsi, in his year in power, did not yield an economic transition that could fully support Egypt's democratic transition. El-Sisi's time in power has been little better. In some areas, it has been worse.

Progress toward weaning the Egyptian private sector off of rent-seeking has been a process of one step forward and two steps back. The January 25 Revolution revealed the extent of corruption in Egypt's neopatrimonial bureaucracy. According to Global Financial Integrity data, Egypt lost an average of $6 billion per year to illicit financial activities and official government corruption in the decade prior to the revolution (Kar and Cartwright-Smith 2008). State assets worth billions more were also lost in crony-capitalist privatization schemes and other economic deals.

A legacy of lack of transparency, accountability, and information from the Egyptian government has made it very difficult to pin down accurate numbers. A credible Egyptian think tank, the Egyptian Initiative for Personal Rights, has estimated that the theft of state funds in Egypt under Mubarak surpassed $132 billion.[5] Moreover, $600 million of the MOI's $14.1 billion annual budget was doled out to the Ministry's top 350 generals and colonels, which works out to more than $1.7 million each per year.

If nothing else, research on state corruption since Mubarak's regime broke down has clarified the 'how it was done question' to a large extent (Diab 2013). Reports assert that profiteering and corruption were legalized under Mubarak. The ruling party controlled both the legislative and executive branches of government. Through this domination, legislation was designed so that the ruling elite could rob state coffers without breaking the law. Tactics included leakages from the balance of payments, trade mispricing, and tax havens. The judicial branch blocked attempts to recover funds through acquittals, claiming that evidence of corruption was not convincing, and leaving cases entangled in the judicial process for long periods of time with no final rulings.

Following the January 25 Revolution, the opposition transitional elites took steps to address the shocking level of predation. A number of Egyptian political icons and financial tycoons were arrested and charged with corruption and profiteering. However, since El-Sisi and other pillars of the Mubarak regime have returned to power, progress in fighting corruption has been reversed.

Ahmed Nazif, the former prime minister, who was charged with profiteering and illegally accumulating wealth, was given one year in jail (which was suspended). He was also assessed a fine of $1.4 million.

---

[5] The following figures and descriptions of corruption are based on Diab (2003). Diab's $132 billion figure is an estimation of illicit outflows from Egypt under Mubarak made by experts from the WB-affiliated Global Financial Integrity think tank.

In February 2015, he was acquitted of that charge. Habib al-Adly, former minister of the interior, who was charged with killing protestors, corruption, and money laundering, was sentenced to life in prison for the killing of protestors, 12 years for money laundering, and 5 years for profiteering. However, he was freed under El-Sisi's rule. In March 2015, a court acquitted him of all charges and he was released.

Youssef Boutros Ghali, the former Minister of Finance, escaped to the United Kingdom before being charged with corruption and illegal accumulation of wealth. He received two 15-year sentences in absentia for wasting public funds, corruption, and abuse of power, as well as another 10 years for profiteering (France 24 2011). The government has asked the United Kingdom for an extradition, but to date he has not been returned to Egypt. Rachid Mohamed Rachid, former minister of trade, was charged with corruption and profiteering and was sentenced in absentia to 5 years in June 2012 and another 15 years in September 2012 (Al-Akhbar 2011). The government has unsuccessfully requested his extradition from Qatar. Hussein Salem, a business tycoon, was charged with fraud, profiteering from a gas deal with Israel, illegal land sales, and corruption (Sharkawy 2014). His retrial was ordered. He is currently in Spain, and the government has requested that he be extradited.

Former minister of housing Ahmed El-Maghrabi, former minister of information Anas El-Fiqi, and former minister of tourism Zuhair Garana were all convicted of corruption and received five, seven, and eight years, respectively. The Court of Cassation rejected the Prosecutor's Office's appeal of El-Maghrabi's acquittal, which in effect meant that he was freed (Shalaby 2015). El-Fiqi was also cleared of the charges (Kamal 2016). Osama El-Sheikh, former Chief of Maspero, was charged with corruption and received five years in prison (Ahram Online 2011). In September 2014, he was cleared of those charges.

Ahmed Ezz, a former NDP official and the one responsible for the monopoly of the steel industry through his Ezz Steel Company, was charged with wasting public funds, money laundering, and operating a monopoly (Sky News Arabic 2012). He received a 37-year prison sentence along with a fine of E£19.5 billion. Ezz's sentence was later overturned (Gamal 2013), and his monopolistic practices fine was reduced from E£100 million to E£10 million (Aboul-Fadl 2014).

Despite these postrevolution efforts to address state corruption (and their reversals), no legal reforms or guarantees of nonrepetition have been implemented. Since the reascent of military power, most believe that state anticorruption momentum has slowed. Initially, after the fall of the Mubarak regime, the government took steps toward enforcing competition legislation; however, with the return of military rule, reports of corruption have rebounded.

The military, which took advantage of privatization to diversify its holdings in the 1990s, has had its personnel obtain top executive posts at public and private firms throughout the country. Businessmen with military connections were passed over during corruption crackdown campaigns in 2011 and 2012 (Shalaby 2015). The Egyptian Competition Authority has not seriously enforced a 2005 competition law and has a history of leniency on repeat offenders such as Ahmed Ezz. In 2015, former president Hosni Mubarak was convicted of using state funds for illegally acquiring property but given a modest three-year sentence (AbdelRazek and Nasr 2016). His two sons were found guilty of the same crime and sentenced to four-year terms (France 24 2016).

Instead of penalties and incentives to wean the private sector off of rent-seeking, then, El-Sisi's government has encouraged impunity. It has also increased the military's role in the economy and brought along private sector cronies as junior partners in huge rent-seeking economic deals (Roll 2015).

The second economic transition, changing Egypt's bureaucracy into a developmental state, was a tall order from the start. After the revolution, the state, through the Central Agency for Organization and Administration (CAOA) and the Ministry of Administrative Development, sought to implement reforms designed to rationalize the state bureaucracy. A major goal has been to end overstaffing and ensure more effective and efficient public services. During the transition, however, strikes and protests by temporary workers in the ministries and public sector have led to the government taking on most as permanent employees. The state has taken on more social welfare burdens, and the number of state employees has increased during the eight-year period since the January 25 Revolution.

The Egyptian bureaucracy has arguably aborted at least three attempts to shift the existing self-interested crony bureaucracy, with its military, security, and civilian components, toward a more rational-legal version. The first was Gamal Mubarak's attempt to succeed his father and reform the Egyptian state's institutions. The second was the 2011 Revolution and the potential it had to combat corruption in state institutions. The third was the rise of the Muslim Brotherhood to power with expectations of some reform (at least to bolster their own rule). In each episode, the bureaucracy withstood forces for change (Adly 2015).

For El-Sisi, the Egyptian bureaucracy is a two-edged sword. As much as it is in dire need of reform, it is also credited for bolstering El-Sisi's regime following the Muslim Brotherhood's removal from power. Yet, Egypt's bureaucracy in its current shape cannot be El-Sisi's vehicle for economic growth led by a vigorous private sector. It is no secret that the bureaucratic apparatus of six million employees has a tarnished reputation when it comes to efficiency, work ethic, transparency, and integrity (Salem 2014). Furthermore, it is creating an unbearable burden on the regime in its own right. Salaries for state employees have increased by 16% annually for the past three years, and they consume a quarter of the annual budget.

Reforming the bureaucracy has proven to be difficult because Egyptian regimes have historically depended on it for providing job security in exchange for political acquiescence. Hiring has seldom improved productivity, and promotions are based on loyalty and seniority rather than on merit. Employee evaluation is haphazard thanks to the existing labor law, which is a major mechanism of bureaucratic malpractice. It shields employees from getting fired and dictates no consequences for those who obstruct projects, investments, decisions, laws, and so on. Furthermore, the constituent ministries, authorities, organizations, and institutions work in isolation, further hurting their usefulness to the plans of a regime and the ambitions of private sector actors (Salem 2014).

Since the 2011 Revolution, Egypt has made some progress toward implementing public administration reforms recommended by the UNDP (Lust et al. 2015). Schools of Government reforms were effectively placed within a broader scheme of decentralization and local development, though a lack of political will has limited the number of attendees that the reforms reach. The improved training of civil servants has been led by the American University in Cairo (AUC) through its School of Global Affairs and Public Policy.

Egyptian leaders have reduced the regulatory burdens for business and investment. The Egyptian Regulatory Reform and Development Activity (ERRADA) initiative has aimed to cut regulatory guidelines by streamlining and cutting administrative burdens through audits, reviews, and standard cost measurement studies. Support for these reforms has wavered during recent periods of political turmoil.

As in Tunisia, decentralization is viewed as a route toward improving shared growth and the bureaucracy. Decentralization reforms started in Egypt in 2007, which in 2010 led to the drafting of the Local Administration Law by the Ministry of Local Development. Reforms stalled in 2012 due to political violence but had resumed by 2014. Local councils' responsibilities were constitutionally expanded so as to allow them to have independent financial budgets based on locally generated tax revenues and nationally allocated resources. Nevertheless, the central government was accorded the right to intervene if it deemed local councils to have overstepped boundaries, which were not clearly delineated.

In July 2015, El-Sisi passed a new civil service law carefully targeting the thorny issue of bureaucratic reform. The law was aimed at creating better managerial practices, transparency, and merit-based hiring, as well as the conduct of regular performance evaluations. To trim the bloated bureaucracy, the new law encouraged early retirement, and it reassigned those who performed poorly to other positions before cutting their salaries and finally terminating their employment while maintaining their pensions. The new law also restructured salaries and bonuses, which had been divorced from performance. However, given the absence of parliamentary or societal debate over the law, in August 2015 state employees began to protest it (Golia 2015). As much as the new law was economically justified – the Egyptian Center for Economic Studies estimated that it would save the government $3 billion (El Wardany and Feteha 2015) – the newly elected Egyptian Parliament soon struck it down. It voted 332 to 150 in January 2016 to repeal the controversial Civil Service Law 18 of 2015 (Ali et al. 2016).

Economic transitions without a vigorous social policy dampen chances of democratic consolidation. Successive governments after the January 25 Revolution in Egypt have promised vigorous social policies: progressive taxation, increased minimum wage, universal health coverage, removal of subsidies for the rich, and redirected spending toward the poor (Kortam 2013). They also promised to invest in infrastructure and encourage tourism to combat unemployment. Since the military coup on July 3, 2013, the government has attempted to make its social justice rhetoric real. To help the poor, increase disposable income and consumption, and stimulate the economy, new tax laws have been developed to exempt people with lower wages from taxation (Kortam 2013). This demonstrates some government intent to benefit the poor and stimulate the economy by increasing disposable income.

The Egyptian state's relationship with the International Financial Institutions has been checkered. Many Egyptians blame the IFIs for validating and supporting the Mubarak regime in the face of rampant corruption and deteriorating governance. Their policies ignored the possibility of state capture. The relationship between the Egyptian government and the IMF does not appear to have changed.

In early 2017, Egypt received the first tranche of a $12 billion IMF loan to rescue it from its economic crisis, which was most obviously manifested in a dollar shortage that had been crippling a range of economic activities (Farid 2016). The loan required unpopular cuts to the country's subsidies program and devaluation of the country's currency at the same time – and at a time when the economic situation is pretty dire. Egyptian civil society was not consulted. A number of political parties, rights organizations, and public figures wrote an open letter to President El-Sisi demanding that the loan be discarded in favor of a national economic reform program designed in a way that makes fundamental changes in the economy through development programs, halting privatization plans, and creating a safety network for the disenfranchised (Farid 2016).

A formalized socioeconomic pact offers the best hope of exiting from the prolonged state of economic crisis that has characterized Egypt under Morsi and El-Sisi. Labor, employers, and the government need to collaborate on economic policymaking (societal corporatism) to avoid the reactive cycle of demand and government commitment, which has kept the economy stagnant and in crisis. Enough of the demands of the politically mobilized have to be met to gain and hold their acceptance while limiting claims that seriously damage efficiency or outrun productive capacity. National dialogue and compromise, a socioeconomic pact, are needed to attain both goals.

On the economy, Morsi and El-Sisi have eschewed national dialogue. Economic policymaking for both has followed an unsustainable cycle of demand and government commitment. Wage and economic policies that met some political demands without overburdening the economy were not established. There has not been any serious effort to dampen   economic   and   political   frustration   by   broadly institutionalizing the economic policymaking process in tripartite agreements among labor, employers, and the government.

Economic disparity and political frustration drove the Egyptian Revolution. The slogan of the January 25 Revolution was "Bread, Freedom, and Social Justice." Bread symbolized putting an end to poverty, securing basic needs, and establishing a just distribution of wealth. However, since Mubarak was ousted, the Egyptian economy has been staggering, growth rates have been decreasing, and unemployment, inflation, and poverty have all been on the rise (El Deen 2013).

Economic growth in Egypt averaged 0.4% in 2011 and 2012 (CAP-MAS 2013). It showed a slight increase in 2013 and 2014 at 2.2%, and a positive performance leaning toward economic recovery in 2015 at 4.2% growth. In 2017–2018, growth increased to 5.3% (WB 2019a).

Unemployment increased during the transition. It was 11.99% in 2011, 12.3% in 2012, 13% in 2013, and reached a peak in 2014 of 13.4%, after which it slightly decreased to 12.8% in 2015. In 2018, the figure dropped to 11.4% (WB 2019b, 2019c). Over 26% of the Egyptian population was officially in poverty in 2013 (Ahram Online 2013). Meanwhile, inflation rates according to the Central Bank of Egypt have also been troubling, registering 10.79% in 2011, 8.6% in 2012, 6.27% at the start of 2013 and then soaring to 12% in December 2013, 8.2% in 2014, and 10.96% in 2015 (Ali 2015).

Feeling the pinch, Egyptians have mobilized for economic reasons since they forced Mubarak out of power (El Deen 2013). There have been frequent labor protests and strikes for better wages and better work conditions. According to a report by the Egyptian Center for Economic and Social Rights (ECESR) in 2012 alone, there were around 1,969 protests and strikes in both the public and private sectors (El-Merghani et al. 2012). Out of this number, 36% demanded better wages, increases in bonuses, and annual raises. Protests about unemployment accounted for 19.3% of the demonstrations. Moreover, 5.5% of the protests were due to mistreatment or unfair termination of employment. Mistreatment by management led to 3.6% of the protests, and the remaining protests were due to various other reasons including the closing of companies and factories leading to the termination of contracts, delays in distributing wages, and corruption. Other mass protests and strikes were held because of poor government performance. Billions of dollars of aid, mostly from Gulf countries, have been used in attempts to demobilize this discontent.

A broad range of groups have participated in these protests and strikes: Metro and taxi drivers, post-office workers, teachers, temporary workers in the Ministry of Health, people with disabilities, women, Coptic Christians, and other groups all demanded their rights and material improvement in their lives (Najjar 2015). The methods of protests have included suicide attempts, marches, gatherings and assemblies, strikes and sit-ins, hunger strikes, stopping roads and railroads, and breaking into offices and governorate buildings. The protests and lack of social and economic stability have also been due to the failure of the government to increase minimum and maximum wage laws and control inflation, as well as to the depreciation of the Egyptian pound. Political mobilization and frustration were driven by increases in the prices of food, fuel, and electricity. Partly because of the increase in expectations fueled by Morsi's electoral promises, protests increased after he assumed power in June 2012.

An interesting source of protests on socioeconomic grounds for El-Sisi's regime ironically came from state employees who had initially been El-Sisi's staunchest supporters. The debate over the new civil service law led 2,000 Tx Authority employees to assemble in August 2015. Importantly, this move was in defiance of the 2013 Protest Law. Tadamon, a group of independent unions, also held another large protest in September 2015 (Najjar 2015). They represented a variety of state employees that included railway operators and physicians.

For good or bad, Egypt's economy is heavily dependent on tourism. The tourism sector includes a variety of options for tourists, including religious, cultural, historical, and beach tourism. The Egyptian government under Mubarak supported the tourism industry. The growing trend of incoming Arab tourists, Egypt's good regional and international relations, its large population, low worker wages, geographic location, and weather all facilitated the industry's growth and development. In 2010, tourism was 13% of GDP and the industry directly or indirectly employed one in seven workers (The Economist 2013).

Political turmoil during the Arab Spring battered Egypt's tourism industry. Islamists in power in 2011 and 2012 considered unpopular (to foreign tourists) bans on alcohol and same-sex beaches only. As discussed, the Sinai Peninsula, historically a tourist destination, has been plagued by political violence. In early 2012, the former minister of tourism Mounir Fakhry Abdel Nour stated that "the number of tourists who came to Egypt in 2011 dropped by more than 33% – to

9.8 million – compared to 14.7 million in 2010. The industry was not expected to return to pre-2011 levels until 2015" (Irish Examiner 2012). This prediction could have been true if no shocks had taken place. After tourism experienced a 41% decline in 2012 and 2013, tourism revenues increased by 27% in 2014. They continued to increase in 2015 until the explosion of the Russian airplane over Sinai that October, after which tourism again began to experience a sharp decline.

An increasing budget deficit and a decrease in foreign currency reserves also contributed to political turmoil in Egypt (Al-Arabiya 2014b). These factors led to the above-discussed $12 billion IMF loan that required cutting public expenditure and reducing or possibly eliminating subsidies on some items. Removing subsidies has had harsh consequences because of the large percentage of the population under the poverty line in Egypt. Heavily subsidized industries and items in Egypt include petroleum products, electricity, and food subsidies. The total amount of subsidies received during the period from July 2012 to April 2013 was E£104,752 million, of which 71% was spent on petroleum products and 20.3% was spent on food subsidies (CAPMAS 2013). In addition, a recent African Development Bank report asserted that "more than 90 percent of gasoline subsidies go to the top 40 percent of the population" (Casey-Baker and Barber 2013). The petroleum market is also facing a rise in prices, a shortage in supply, and an overflow of demand. The black market for petroleum products has increased in size and activity because of the lack of security.

Economically, across the Mubarak, Morsi, and El-Sisi governments one constant has been the military's prominence. Zeinab Abul-Magd states that discussing the military's status in the economy is taboo in Egypt and that researching the topic is difficult (Abul-Magd 2011, 2017). Still, she estimates that the army controls 25%–40% of the economy including many products not connected to national defense. The goods and services that the military provides are held outside channels of transparency and accountability. The military budget is not public or accessible to the government. National economic policies do not impact it directly. The army has avoided decades-long, state-led privatization policies.

Transitions to democracy are enfeebled if economic policies are poor and made by the few. In Egypt, transitional governments did not pursue the institutionalization of socioeconomic dialogues with labor, employers, and other actors. This made it impossible to commit to policies to help the politically mobilized while also using national dialogue to restrain claims that would have kept the economy in crisis and unable to grow. Instead, governments have largely followed a defensive and counterproductive cycle of mobilization and capitulation.

Without a socioeconomic pact after Mubarak's fall from power, economic and political frustrations have mounted in Egypt. Moreover, even if an inclusive national economic policymaking process had been attempted, much of the economy would have been left out, due to the huge chunk of the economy that the military has carved out for itself. In addition, while foreign aid during the Arab Spring has enabled a vigorous social policy, it has been deployed more to stifle protests than to rationally improve the economy. The El-Sisi government has over-turned progress on weaning the private sector off of corruption, and improvements in bureaucratic capacity have been muted. Finally, in regards to Egypt, the IFIs have returned to the policies that distressed the nation enough to fuel a rebellion.

For average Egyptians, the Egyptian economy under El-Sisi is at least as bad as Mubarak's economy. In some respects, it is even worse. Nothing has changed to challenge Arab Human Development Reports' assessment in the 2000s that Egyptian society – due to its economy – is a candidate for a difficult period of intense, violent social conflict. The kind of government it has will not do.[6]

Democratic Consolidation: Transitional Justice, Human Rights, and Rule of Law Pact

Under Mubarak, human rights were not respected. For the most part – instead of protecting human rights and the rule of law – the judiciary and security forces brutally imposed the interests of a narrow corrupt elite.

The January 25 Revolution for "Bread, Dignity, and Freedom" raised Egyptian hopes for transitional justice, human rights, and a dignified life under the rule of law. However, after limited progress during the SCAF-led transition and under former President Morsi, those hopes have been crushed by El-Sisi's coup and a brutal,

---

[6] See n. 4 (Arab Human Development Reports).

military-led reconstruction and deepening of the most reviled aspects of Mubarak's regime:

Since 2013 [Egypt] has experienced the biggest authoritarian crackdown in its modern history, aimed at members of the peaceful opposition, both Islamist and secular. More than 60,000 people have been jailed for political reasons, and hundreds have died in prison. (Hassan 2019)

The crackdown began with assaults on Muslim Brotherhood supporters. El-Sisi marches and rallies were organized across the country; they were characterized by Islamist bashing and defamation of the few secular voices of dissent that rejected the coup:

The results were horrifying. State-sponsored violence was used systematically against Islamist protests; notably, army units and security forces brutally disbanded the Brotherhood's sit-ins in Cairo's Rabaa and Nahda squares on August 14, 2013, killing close to 1,000 citizens. (Dunne and Hamzawy 2017)

El-Sisi's military coup also reversed efforts to reform the judiciary and security sectors. Negative trends are being consolidated by constitutional amendments in 2019 that redraw the Egyptian political system and remove the last pretense of the rule of law, separation of powers, and the subordination of the military to elected governments. Human rights are degraded by military courts that prosecute civilians without due process. Egypt is set to become a military dictatorship in name as well as deed:

The proposed constitutional amendments include provisions that legalize military interventions in politics (Article 200), expand the power of military courts (Article 204), and increase the power of the executive over the judiciary (Articles 185, 190, and 193). These amendments will enshrine the military's position above the state by giving it legal means to intervene against elected governments and enhanced powers to prosecute its political opponents. (Mandour 2019)

Prior to the January 25 Revolution, human rights and freedoms had been partially or fully denied during former President Mubarak's long reign. Egypt's Constitution under Mubarak authorized emergency powers, military courts, and other exceptional powers that overrode constitutional human rights and freedoms. Emergency law had been in place for 30 consecutive years. It was a core piece of authoritarian maintenance. Egyptians could be and were detained without due process, tortured, tried in military courts, and even killed by the state with no protection from the judicial system and the law. This was a frequent strategy against dissidents, and there was little that their families could do about it.

During Mubarak's time in power, limited political debate was allowed as long as it did not cross redlines. The media could cover and debate rising rates in poverty, and well-known cases of torture and other injustices – but only at the regime's discretion. The state's security apparatus controlled protests. Expression was not completely free, and the unfettered right to assembly was denied. The Central Security Forces (CSF) used intimidation to deter protests. Thus, despite a history of labor strikes and other protests, the number of people who came out for the revolution on January 25, 2011 – intentionally and ironically organized for National Police Day – demanding individual rights, freedom, and democracy was unprecedented in Egypt.

The January 25 Revolution represented a pivotal point in the modern history of human rights and freedoms in Egypt. Early on, nearly unfettered debate and freedoms of assembly and press made the democratic transition tangible for all Egyptians. Protests, strikes, and sit-ins outside state security forces' control became a normal part of Egyptian life. Think tanks, journalists, and citizen journalists investigated and publicized infractions by the police, torture, and detentions without due process. Political satire, especially Dr. Bassem Youssef's show, *El-Bernameg* ("The Program"), became a national sensation (Taha 2012).

While the January 25 Revolution was unable to fulfill its hopes for security sector reforms, transitional justice, human rights, and the rule of law, it did – before El-Sisi's military coup – mobilize actions that provided harsh details of Ministry of Interior activities under Mubarak (Ashour 2012). Once it was clear that Mubarak would fall, state security officers had begun destroying files that documented their institutions' corruption and repression, but protestors managed to save and publish some of the incriminating evidence. Torture rooms and equipment were captured on camera. The evidence detailed secret graveyards, medieval dungeons, files of political dissidents, names of judges who fixed elections, and lists of informants including celebrities, religious figures, talk-show hosts, and supposed opposition leaders (Ashour 2012).

Before the El-Sisi crackdown, postrevolution research and interviews also illuminated the depth of the brutality and corruption of Egypt's security institutions under Mubarak:

We arrested this guy [for extremist activity but two officers got into an argument about what to do with him]. They got the information they wanted, but neither wanted the guy. Then [one of the officers] ended the argument. He pushed the guy out of the window. It was Ramadan and he was late for *suhur* meal. The guy died instantly and it was registered as resisting arrest...They laughed about it afterwards. (Ashour 2012)

Security institutions are organized within the MOI in Egypt. Their main components are the police and two sections of the State Security Investigations unit – the domestic intelligence service (SSI later renamed the National Security Apparatus, NSA) and the Central Security Forces (CSF), a paramilitary force whose members served as Mubarak's most thuggish enforcers. During the three decades of Mubarak's rule, all three institutions spied on civilians without cause, repressed them brutally, and rigged electoral results.

Under Mubarak, the SSI was organized internally in an Orwellian fashion (Ashour 2012): the Human Rights Units monitored and suppressed human rights activists. The Arab Activities Group countered the influence of Arab nationalists. The Workers Units sought control over labor. The Sectarian Activity Group dealt with Christian activists. There was also a General Administration for Foreign Activity focused on Europeans and Americans and an Electronic Monitoring Group targeting Internet activists.

Islamists drew the most attention from Egypt's domestic intelligence service under Mubarak. Under the Religious Activism Unit, subunits included Countering Muslim Brotherhood activism, Extremist Organizations, and Prison Security, the latter tasked with countering Islamist political activism in prisons and detention centers. Finally, there was the state-of-the art Counterterrorism Group. All parts of the security apparatus in Egypt have been accused of systematic torture, kidnappings, illegal detentions, and extrajudicial killings before, during, and since the January 25 Revolution (Ashour 2012).

Shortly after the January 25 Revolution, in March of the same year, Egypt's military rulers (SCAF) appointed a revolution-friendly government, including Minister of the Interior Mansour al-Issawi, who was a former general with a clean reputation. However, despite taking some positive steps, General al-Issawi's reforms were viewed as superficial (Ashour 2012). Notably, the reforms, which included renaming the SSI the National Security Agency (NSA), retained the Ministry's involvement in every aspect of political life. Al-Issawi's reforms also did nothing to deter or impede El-Sisi's return to emergency laws, overly broad counterterrorism laws, and constitutional impunity for military and security forces.

President Morsi took power and immediately had to confront reforming a judiciary that had just dismissed an elected parliament and demonstrated little respect for democratic procedures. As soon as Morsi was declared president in mid-2012, Islamists appeared keen on confronting the judiciary (Auf 2014). Morsi's November 2012 constitutional declaration had already triggered frustration among judges. A proposed judicial draft law discussed by the Islamist-dominated Shura Council would have forced senior judges into retirement if it were passed (Auf 2014).

El-Sisi's coup ended any momentum for security and judicial reforms. The 2014 Constitution, 2019 constitutional amendments, and emergency and counterterrorism laws have elevated the military above the law, ensured executive domination of the judicial sector, and shut down Egyptian hopes for respect for human rights, freedom, and the rule of law.

Conclusion

If there is any lesson to be learned from Egypt's democratic consolidation experience, it is that a political pact – a sustained cross-ideological mass uprising demanding democratization – is a necessary condition for its success. Egyptians in general, including Islamists and secularists, rose up against military-backed authoritarian rule in numbers the military was unwilling to violently repress. Mass mobilization forced the military – the most dominant force in Egyptian politics since 1952 – to begin extricating itself from politics enough to give democracy a chance.

However, as soon as Islamist and secularist political parties revealed a reluctance to tolerate each other in an emerging democracy – mere weeks after authoritarian breakdown – the military began to reclaim and deepen its hold on power, with the major blow the coup of July 3,

2013, that "enjoyed" secular support through the National Salvation Front and Tamarod. The military then betrayed secular hopes of installing a democracy without the mobilizational power of the Muslim Brotherhood.

El-Sisi's military authoritarian regime is more autocratic and military-dominated than Mubarak's. The military prevented Egyptians from using their revolution to remake their crony-capitalist economy, eliminate elite capture, and install one based on a vigorous private sector, global exports, and shared economic growth – or any other economic development strategy decided upon within a broad national dialogue. Instead, it used the Egyptian Revolution for "Bread, Dignity, and Freedom" to increase its clandestine share of the Egyptian economy. El-Sisi's economy, at least as bad as Mubarak's for most Egyptians, virtually guarantees instability and possibly a future uprising. El-Sisi's façade of multiparty politics sidelines political parties as he uses patronage-seeking Independents and the military itself as a ruling coalition.

A desire for a dignified life under the rule of law animated the Arab Spring across the region. In Egypt, under El-Sisi, that desire has been buried under the military's brutal reconstruction and deepening of the most autocratic elements of the Mubarak regime. The process has brought a bloody end to Egyptian hopes for transitional justice and human rights.

The military and security forces and their allies in the executive branch have walled themselves off from popular participation (Brown 2018). Constitutional amendments in 2019 placed the military above the law and the Constitution and cemented the executive's subordination of the judicial branch (ICJ 2016). To duplicate the president-for-life model, despised regionwide, the amendments also overrode the presidential term limits set in the 2014 Constitution. El-Sisi's regime appears to accent all the traits that led to Egypt's Arab Spring uprising in the first place.

References

Abdalla, N. 2012. "Social Protests in Egypt before and after the 25 January Revolution: Perspectives on the Evolution of Their Forms and Features." *IEMed Mediterranean Yearbook*: 86–92. www.iemed.org/obser vatori-en/arees-danalisi/arxius-adjunts/anuari/med.2012/abdalla_en.pdf.

AbdelRazek, M. and M. Nasr. 2016. "Final Verdict Sentences Mubarak and His Sons to Three Years in Prison." *Youm7*, January 9.

Aboul-Fadl, S. 2014. "Court of Appeals Reduces the Fine Imposed on Ahmed Ezz and Abu Al-Khair to 10 Million Pounds." *Al-Ahram*, November 25.

Abul-Magd, Z. 2011. "The Army and the Economy in Egypt." *Jadaliyya*, December 23.

  2017. *Militarizing the Nation: The Army, Business, and Revolution in Egypt*. New York: Columbia University Press.

Adly, A. 2015. "Triumph of the Bureaucracy: A Decade of Aborted Social and Political Change in Egypt." *Jadaliyya*, January 31. www.jadaliyya .com/Details/31735/Triumph-of-the-Bureaucracy-A-Decade-of-Aborted-Social-and-Political-Change-in-Egypt.

Ahram. 2013. "Ansar Bayt al-Maqdis Releases a Video of the Attack on Egypt's Minister of Interior." *Al-Ahram*, December 27.

Ahram Online. 2011. "Former Egyptian TV and Radio Union Chairman 'Not Guilty' of Squandering Public Funds." *Ahram Online*, September 8. www.english.ahram.org.eg/NewsContentP/1/20666/Egypt/Former-Egyptian-TV-and-Radio-Union-chairman-not-gu.aspx.

  2012. "Khaled Said: The Face that Launched a Revolution." *Ahram Online*, June 6. www.english.ahram.org.eg/NewsContent/1/64/43995/Egypt/Politics-/Khaled-Said-The-face-that-launched-a-revolution.aspx.

  2013. "Egypt's Poverty Rate Rises to 26% in 2012/13: CAPMAS." *Ahram Online*, November 28. www.english.ahram.org.eg/News Content/3/12/87776/Business/Economy/Egypts-poverty-rate-rises-to-in–CAPMAS.aspx.

  2015. "Updated: Sisi First Egyptian President to Attend Coptic Christmas Mass." *Ahram Online*, January 6. www.english.ahram.org.eg/NewsAF CON/2017/119667.aspx.

  2016. "Egypt's Sisi Attends Coptic Christmas Mass for Second Straight Year." *Ahram Online*, January 7. www.english.ahram.org.eg/NewsCon tentP/1/180296/Egypt/Egypts-Sisi-attends-Coptic-Christmas-mass-for-seco.aspx.

Al-Akhbar. 2011. "Racheed Mohamed: Racheed's Corruption and Abuse of Power." *Al-Akhbar*, March 29.

Al-Arabiya. 2013. "George Ishak: Tamarod Is Another Wave of the Egyptian Revolution." *Al-Arabiya*, May 15.

  2014a. "Ansar Bayt al-Maqdis Releases a Video of an Attack against the Egyptian Army." *Al-Arabiya*, January 27.

  2014b. "Foreign Reserves Fell Sharply after the 2011 Uprising that Ousted President Hosni Mubarak." *Al-Arabiya*, December 7.

www.english.alarabiya.net/en/business/economy/2014/12/07/Egypt-s-foreign-reserves-fall-to-15-88-bln-at-end-Nov.html.

Albrecht, H. and D. Bishara. 2011. "Back on Horseback: The Military and Political Transformation in Egypt." *Middle East Law and Governance*, 3(1–2), 13–23. doi:10.1163/187633711x591396.

Ali, N. et al. 2016. "The Parliament Rejects Civil Service Law." *Parlamany*, January 20.

Ali, R. 2015. "One Year On: Economic Policy under El-Sisi." *Ahram Online*, June 9. www.english.ahram.org.eg/NewsContent/3/12/132189/Busi ness/Economy/One-year-on-Economic-policy-under-ElSisi.aspx.

Alim, T. A. 2011. "National Unity after the Egyptian Revolution." *Ahram Online*, March 23. www.english.ahram.org.eg/~/NewsContentP/4/8367/Opinion/National-unity-after-the-Egyptian-revolution.aspx.

Al-Masry Al-Youm. 2016. "Coptic Church: Too Early to Implement the Personal Status Law." *Al-Masry Al-Youm*, March 11.

Al-Qurashy, K. 2013. "Residents of Kafr Al-Sheikh Form a Campaign to Support El-Sisi and the Egyptian Military." *El-Watan News*, July 19.

Al-Sayyid, M. K. 2003. *The Other Face of the Islamist Movement*. Working Paper. Washington, DC: Carnegie Endowment for International Peace. www.carnegieendowment.org/files/wp33.pdf.

Al-Sudany, M. 2015. "Mahsoub Yakshef Kawalees Jadeeda 'An I'lan Morsi al-Dustoury" [Source reveals behind the scenes of Morsi's constitutional declaration]." *Masr Al-Arabia*, November 30.

Amin, G. 2012. *Egypt in the Era of Hosni Mubarak*. Cairo: American University in Cairo Press.

Ashour, O. 2012. *From Bad Cop to Good Cop: The Challenge of Security Sector Reform in Egypt*. No. 3. Doha: Brookings Doha Center. www.brookings.edu/wp-content/uploads/2016/06/Omar-Ashour-English.pdf.

　2016. "ISIS and Wilayat Sinai: Complex Networks of Insurgency on Egypt's Sinai Peninsula." *DGAGkompakt*, August 15. www.dgap.org/en/think-tank/publications/dgapanalyse-compact/isis-and-wilayat-sinai.

Auf, Y. 2014. "Prospects for Judicial Reform in Egypt." *Atlantic Council*, October 21. www.atlanticcouncil.org/blogs/menasource/prospects-for-judicial-reform-in-egypt/.

Awad, M. 2011. "Egypt To Call March Referendum This Week: Lawyer." *Reuters*, February 27. www.reuters.com/article/us-egypt-referendum/egypt-to-call-march-referendum-this-week-lawyer-idUSTRE71Q11620 110227.

Bayat, A. 2013. "The Arab Spring and Its Surprises." *Development and Change*, 44(3), 587–601. doi:10.1111/dech.12030.

BBC News. 2011. "Egypt Bomb Kills 21 at Alexandria Coptic Church." *BBC News*, January 1. www.bbc.com/news/world-middle-east-1210 1748.

——— 2013. "Multiple Deaths due to Bloody Clashes between Muslims and Copts in Al-Khosoos near Cairo." *BBC News*, April 6.

Brown, N. 2018. *Politics over Doctrine: The Evolution of Sharia-Based State Institutions in Egypt and Saudi Arabia*. Houston: James A. Baker III Institute for Public Policy of Rice University. www.bakerinstitute.org/research/rhetoric-reality-religious-reform/.

Brown, N. and M. Dunne. 2013. "Egypt's Draft Constitution Rewards the Military and Judiciary." *Carnegie Endowment for International Peace*, December 4. www.carnegieendowment.org/2013/12/04/egypt-s-draft-constitution-rewards-military-and-judiciary-pub-53806.

Brown, N. and K. Stilt. 2011. "A Haphazard Constitutional Compromise." *Carnegie Endowment for International Peace*, November 4. www.carnegieendowment.org/2011/04/11/haphazard-constitutional-compromise-pub-43533.

Bumiller, E. 2011. "Egypt Stability Hinges on a Divided Military." *New York Times*, February 5. www.nytimes.com/2011/02/06/world/mid dleeast/06military.html.

Casey-Baker, M. and J. Huber. 2013. "Egypt's Presidency Says Foreign Mediation Efforts Have Failed." *Foreign Policy*, August 7. www.foreign policy.com/2013/08/07/egypts-presidency-says-foreign-mediation-efforts-have-failed/.

Central Authority for Public Mobilization and Statistics (CAPMAS). 2013. *Statistical Information Newsletter*. June. Cairo: Central Authority for Public Mobilization and Statistics.

Diab, O. 2013. *Do We Retrieve Our Stolen Funds? Egypt's Stolen Assets between Reconciliation Deals, Acquittals, and Institutional Corruption*. Cairo: Egyptian Initiative for Personal Rights. www.online.fliphtml5.com/uhie/tbca/.

Dunne, M. 2015. "Egypt's Nationalists Dominate in a Politics-Free Zone." *Carnegie Endowment for International Peace*, April 15. www.carnegieendowment.org/2015/04/15/egypt-s-nationalists-dominate-in-politics-free-zone-pub-59764.

Dunne, M. and A. Hamzawy. 2017. "Egypt's Political Exiles: Going Anywhere but Home." *Carnegie Endowment for Peace*, March 29. www.carnegieendowment.org/2019/03/29/egypt-s-political-exiles-going-anywhere-but-home-pub-78728.

The Economist. 2013. "Arab Spring Break: Turmoil Has Scared off All but the Rugged and the Russians." *The Economist*, May 4.

Ekram, I. 2012a. "Justice Denied: Egypt's Maspero Massacre One Year on."
    Ahram Online, October 9. www.english.ahram.org.eg/NewsContent/1/
    64/54821/Egypt/Politics-/Justice-denied-Egypts-Maspero-massacre-one-
    year-on.aspx.

  2012b. "6th of April 2008: A Workers' Strike Which Fired the Egyptian
    Revolution." *Ahram Online*, April 6. www.english.ahram.org.eg/News
    Content/1/64/38580/Egypt/Politics-/th-of-April–A-workers-strike-which-
    fired-the-Egyp.aspx.

El Deen, W. G. 2013. "Egypt's Economy after the Revolution: Major Crisis
    and Serious Challenges." *BBC Arabic*, January 25.

El-Din, M. S. 2013. "Judicial Committee Proves Military Violations, Presi-
    dency Remains Tightlipped." *Egyptian Independent*, March 11.
    www.egyptindependent.com/judicial-committee-proves-military-violations-
    presidency-remains-tightlipped/.

El-Hadini, W. 2011. "'Islam Is the Solution': A Slogan That Was Extensively
    Criticized by Mubarak." *Egypt Window*, October 8.

El-Houdaiby, I. 2013. "The Bureaucracy Wins." *Middle East Institute*, April
    14. www.mei.edu/publications/bureaucracy-wins.

El-Merghani, E. et al. 2012. *Labor and Protest Movements in 2012*. Cairo:
    Egyptian Center for Economic and Social Rights.

El-Sadek, L. 2012. "Egypt Continues to Make History: Continued Engaged
    Citizenship to Carry Her Revolution." *Huffington Post*, August 28.
    www.actionnews.ca/newstempch.php?article=/entry/egypt-continues-to-
    make-h_b_1628758.html.

El Wardany, S. and A. Feteha. 2015. "El-Sisi Challenge Grows as
    Egypt Bureaucrats Oppose Pay Cuts." *Bloomberg*, August 31.
    www.bloomberg.com/news/articles/2015-08-31/el-sisi-s-challenge-grows-
    as-egypt-mandarins-object-to-lower-pay.

Fahim, K. and M. El-Naggar. 2011. "Violent Clashes Mark Protests against
    Mubarak's Rule." *New York Times*, January 25. www.nytimes.com/
    2011/01/26/world/middleeast/26egypt.html.

Fareg, N. 2011. "Between Piety and Politics: Social Services and the
    Muslim Brotherhood." *PBS.org*, February 22. www.pbs.org/wgbh/
    pages/frontline/revolution-in-cairo/inside-muslim-brotherhood/piety-
    and-politics.html.

Farid, S. 2016. "Egypt's IMF Loan: A Blessing or a Curse?" *Al-Arabiya*,
    November 4. www.english.alarabiya.net/en/2016/09/13/Egypt-s-IMF-
    loan-A-blessing-or-a-curse-.html.

Fawzy, A. et al. 2015. *Commitment to the Party Line: Egyptian and
    International Expriences*. Beirut: Arab Forum for Alternatives.
    www.afalebanon.org/en/publication/4816/commitment-to-the-party-line-
    egyptian-and-international-experiences/.

France 24. 2011. "Former Finance Minister Sentenced to 30 Years in Jail." *France 24*, April 6. www.france24.com/en/20110604-middle-east-egypt-ex-finance-minister-gets-30-years-prison-in-absentia.

2014. "98% of Voters Chose the New Constitution." *France 24*, September 19.

2016. "Court Refuses the Appeal of Mubarak and His Sons." *France 24*, January 9.

Gamal, E. 2013. "Egyptian Court Overturns Steel Tycoon Ahmed Ezz's 37-Year Sentence." *Ahram Online*, December 14. www.english.ahram .org.eg/NewsContent/3/12/89075/Business/Economy/Egyptian-court-overturns-steel-tycoon-Ahmed-Ezzs-y.aspx.

Golia, M. 2015. "Taking on Egypt's Big Bureaucracy." *Middle East Institute*, October 15. www.mei.edu/publications/taking-egypts-big-bureaucracy.

Hassan, B. E.-D. 2019. "Egypt: The Permanent Coup." *The New Arab*, April 15. www.alaraby.co.uk/english/comment/2019/4/15/egypt-the-permanent-coup.

Hauslohner, A. 2014. "Egypt's Military Expands Its Control of the Country's Economy." *Washington Post*, March 16. www.washington post.com/world/middle_east/egyptian-military-expands-its-economic-control/2014/03/16/39508b52-a554-11e3-b865-38b254d92063_story .html.

Hellyer, H. A. 2013. "The Scourge of Sectarianism in Egypt." *Foreign Policy*, June 26. www.foreignpolicy.com/2013/06/26/the-scourge-of-sectarianism-in-egypt/.

Human Rights Watch (HRW). 2011. "Egypt: Human Rights Reform an Urgent Priority." *Human Rights Watch*, June 7. www.hrw.org/news/ 2011/06/07/egypt-human-rights-reform-urgent-priority.

Human Rights Watch (HRW). 2015. "Egypt: Year of Abuses under al-Sisi." *Human Rights Watch*, June 8. www.hrw.org/news/2015/06/08/egypt-year-abuses-under-al-sisi.

2019. "Egypt." *Human Rights Watch*, n. d. www.hrw.org/world-report/ 2019/country-chapters/egypt.

International Commission of Jurists (ICJ). 2016. "Egypt: Authorities Must End Politicization of the Judiciary and Ensure Its Independence and Accountability." *International Commission of Jurists*, October 12. www.icj.org/egypt-authorities-must-end-politicization-of-the-judiciary-and-ensure-its-independence-and-accountability/.

Irish Examiner. 2012. "Egypt's Tourism Revenue Plunges." *Irish Examiner*, January 19. www.irishexaminer.com/breakingnews/world/egypts-tour ism-revenue-plunges-536535.html.

Jumet, K. D. 2017. *Contesting the Repressive State: Why Ordinary Egyptians Protested during the Arab Spring*. New York: Oxford University Press.

Kalin, S. and Y. Saleh. 2014. "Egypt Awards Suez Hub Project to Consortium That Includes Army: Sources." *Reuters*, August 3. www .reuters.com/article/us-egypt-suezcanal/egypt-awards-suez-hub-project-to-consortium-that-includes-army-sources-idUSKBN0G30HY20140803.

Kamal, M. 2016. "Anas El-Fiqi Acquitted of Charges Related to Corruption." *Al-Ahram*, February 11.

Kar, D. and D. Cartwright-Smith. 2008. "Illicit Financial Flows from Developing Countries: 2002–2006." *Global Financial Integrity*, December 14. www.gfintegrity.org/report/global-illicit-flows-report-2008/.

Khalil, H. 2013. *The Tax System and Its Latest Amendments: Same Old Policies and Neglect of Alternatives at Hand*. Cairo: The Egyptian Center for Economic and Social Rights.

King, S. J. 2009. *The New Authoritarianism in the Middle East and North Africa*. Bloomington: Indiana University Press.

Kingsley, P. et al. 2014. "Egyptian Jihadis Pledge Allegiance to ISIS." *The Guardian*, November 10. www.theguardian.com/world/2014/nov/10/egyptian-jihadists-pledge-allegiance-isis.

Kirkpatrick, D. D. 2014. "Prolonged Fight Feared in Egypt after Bombings." *New York Times*, January 24. www.nytimes.com/2014/01/25/world/middleeast/fatal-bomb-attacks-in-egypt.html.

Kortam, H. 2013. "Nearly 5 Million Workers Will Benefit from Minimum Income: Ministry of Finance." *Daily News Egypt*, October 29. www.dailynewssegypt.com/2013/10/29/nearly-5-million-workers-will-benefit-from-minimum-income-ministry-of-finance/.

Lane, G. 2012. "Maspero Massacre: Egypt's Christians Cry for Justice." *CBN News*, January 15. www1.cbn.com/video/maspero-massacre-egypts-christians-cry-for-justice.

Lesch, A. M. 2011. "Egypt's Spring: Causes of the Revolution." *Middle East Policy*, 18(3), 35–48.

Lust, E., E. Rohne, and J. Wichmann. 2015. *The Political Economy of Public Administration: A Study of the Arab Transitions*. New York: United Nations Development Programme. www.undp-aciac.org/publications/ac/2015/f_UNDP_PAR-PoliticalEconomy.pdf.

Mandour, M. 2019. "Egypt's Invisible Executions." *Carnegie Endowment for International Peace*, April 25. www.carnegieendowment.org/sada/78998.

Michaelson, R. 2016. "Sugar Shortage and Soaring Food Prices Fuel Discontent in Egypt." *The Guardian*, October 25. www.theguardian.com/world/2016/oct/25/egypt-sugar-shortage-soaring-food-prices-discontent-abdel-fatah-al-sisi.

Miller, E. 2016a. "Five Years on: Egypt's Minorities." *Atlantic Council*, January 29. www.atlanticcouncil.org/blogs/menasource/five-years-on-egypt-s-minorities/.

2016b. "Five Years on: Security and Economy." *Atlantic Council,* January 28. www.atlanticcouncil.org/blogs/menasource/five-years-on-security-and-economy/.

Mohamed, A. L. 2014. "Towards a Full-Fledged Value-Added Taxation in Egypt." *International Journal of Economics and Finance,* 6(7), 213–225. doi:10.5539/ijef.v6n7p213.

Najjar, D. 2015. "Women's Contributions to Climate Change Adaptation in Egypt's Mubarak Resettlement Scheme through Cactus Cultivation and Adjusted Irrigation." In S. Buechler and A.-M. S. Hanson, ed., *A Political Ecology of Women, Water, and Global Environmental Change.* London: Routledge, pp. 141–161. doi:10.4324/978131579 6208-9.

Nazif, A. 2009. "Gamal Mubarak Could Be a Potential Candidate in Egypt's Future Presidential Elections." *Al Jazeera,* December 27.

O'Donnell, G. and P. C. Schmitter. 1986. *Transitions from Authoritarian Rule: Tentative Conclusions about Uncertain Democracies.* Baltimore: Johns Hopkins University Press.

Oweidat, N. et al. 2008. *The Kefaya Movement: A Case Study of a Grassroots Reform Initiative.* Santa Monica, CA: RAND Corporation. www.rand.org/pubs/monographs/MG778.html.

Tahrir Institute for Middle East Policy (TIMEP). 2015. *Egypt's Rising Security Threat.* Cairo: Tahrir Institute for Middle East Policy. www.timep.org/wp-content/uploads/2015/11/Tahrir_Report_FINAL_WEB.pdf.

Radsch, C. 2012. "Core to Commonplace: The Evolution of Egypt's Blogosphere." *Arab Media and Society,* December 12. www.arabmediasociety.com/core-to-commonplace-the-evolution-of-egypts-blogosphere/.

Roll, S. 2015. "Managing Change: How Egypt's Military Leadership Shaped the Transformation." *Mediterranean Politics,* 21(1), 23–43. doi:10.4324/9781315622279-2.

Saleh, Y. 2014. "Activists Who Backed Mursi's Fall Turn against Military." *Reuters,* February 20. www.reuters.com/article/us-egypt-politics-tamarud/activists-who-backed-mursis-fall-turn-against-military-idUSBREA1J1E420140220.

Salem, M. 2014. "Will Sisi Consider Military Rule over Egypt's Bureaucracy?" *Al-Monitor,* May 22. www.al-monitor.com/pulse/originals/2014/05/sisi-government-military-oversight.html.

Salman, M. and D. Walsh. 2017. "Egypt Declares State of Emergency, as Attacks Undercut Promise of Security." *New York Times,* April 9. www.nytimes.com/2017/04/09/world/middleeast/explosion-egypt-coptic-christian-church.html.

Shaaban, A. B. 2007. *The New Protest Movements in Egypt: Has the Country Lost Patience?* November 11. Paris: Arab Reform Initiative. www.archives.arab-reform.net/en/node/359.

Shalaby, A. 2015. "Court of Appeals Supports the Acquittal of Ahmed El-Maghrabi and Mounir Ghabour." *Al-Masry Al-Youm*, November 10.

Shapiro, S. 2009. "Revolution Facebook-Style." *New York Times*, January 22. www.nytimes.com/2009/01/25/magazine/25bloggers-t.html.

Sharkawy, N. 2014. "Hussein Salem and His Two Sons Sentenced to 10 Years in Prison over Charges Related to Corruption." *Al-Masry Al-Youm*, September 3.

Shehata, S. and J. Stacher. 2006. "The Brotherhood Goes to Parliament." *Middle East Report*, 240. www.merip.org/mer/mer240/brotherhood-goes-parliament. doi:10.2307/25164744.

Sky News Arabic. 2012. "Ahmed Ezz: Falling from the Peak of the Hierarchy." *Sky News Arabic*, September 3.

Springborg, R. 2017. *Egypt*. Malden, MA: Polity Press.

Stepan, A. 2012. "Tunisia's Transition and the Twin Tolerations." *Journal of Democracy*, 23(2), 83–103. doi:10.1353/jod.2012.0034.

Tadros, M. 2011. "Egypt's Bloody Sunday." *Middle East Research and Information Project*, October 13. www.merip.org/2011/10/egypts-bloody-sunday/.

Taha, Y. 2012. "Egypt Political Satire *El-Bernameg* Entertains Millions." *BBC News*, May 25. www.bbc.com/news/world-middle-east-1820 5411.

Taylor, P. 2013. "Two More Dead after Sectarian Clashes in Egypt." *Reuters*, April 8. www.reuters.com/article/us-egypt-clashes-idUSBRE 93503A20130408.

Totten, M. 2016. "Springtime for Morsi?" *New English Review*, November 22. www.newenglishreview.org/blog_direct_link.cfm?blog_id=65379&Springtime%2Dfor%2DMorsi.

Trager, E. 2016. *Arab Fall: How the Muslim Brotherhood Won and Lost Egypt in 891 Days*. Washington, DC: Georgetown University Press.

Tuitel, R. 2014. "The Future of the Sinai Peninsula." *Quarterly Journal*, 13 (2), 79–91. doi:10.11610/Connections.13.2.05.

Utvik, B. O. 2017. "A Question of Faith? Islamists and Secularists Fight over the Post-Mubarak State." *Contemporary Arab Affairs*, 10(1), 93–117. doi:10.1080/17550912.2017.1279384.

World Bank (WB). 2013. *World Bank National Accounts Data*. Washington, DC: World Bank Group.

2019a. "GDP Growth (Annual %)." Washington, DC: World Bank Group.

2019b. "Poverty Headcount Ratio at National Poverty Line (% of Population)." Washington, DC: World Bank Group.

2019c. "Unemployment, Total (% of Total Labor Force)." Washington, DC: World Bank Group.

3 | *Libya*

Libya is on the verge of descending into a civil war which could lead to the permanent division of the country.

–Ghassan Salamé

Libyans initiated a democratic transition in good faith.[1]

Sadly, Libya seems to validate the claim that it is neither plausible nor reasonable to expect that elites whose societies have little semblance of the national unity, bureaucratic capacity, and military power we associate with contemporary statehood would be able to initiate and sustain a democratic transition (Anderson 1999). After breaking down Muammar Qaddafi's dictatorship in a bloody struggle, Libyans hopefully and enthusiastically participated in competitive national elections in 2012 and 2014. Despite that – and, possibly, somewhat *because* of that – since 2014 Libyans have been enduring a low-simmering civil war between two militia coalitions along with mini–civil wars scattered throughout the country. In a country of six million people, since the revolution on February 17, 2011, tens of thousands of Libyans have been killed. The country is on the brink of violently losing tens – if not hundreds – of thousands more.

The breakdown of Qaddafi's autocratic regime revealed that Libya, which was held together by brutal repression, is not fully a nation-state. In Libya, unlike in Tunisia and in Egypt, it cannot be confidently stated that the vast majority of Libyan citizens have no doubt or mental reservations as to which political community they belong to (Rustow 1970). Since Qaddafi's fall, separatist movements have emerged in two of the three former Ottoman provinces – Cyrenaica and Fezzan – that Italians cobbled together during the colonial period (1911–1943). Pro- and anti-Qaddafi tribes have formed militias and fought mini–civil

---

[1] The quote in the epigraph is from May 2019. Salamé, a Lebanse academic, began serving as Special Representative and Head of the United Nations' Support Mission in Libya (UNSMIL) in June of 2017.

wars among themselves. Tubu tribes, of Black African descent, are fighting Arab tribes in southern Libya (Fezzan). Long persecuted, the minority Amazigh (Berber) population has demonstrated its willingness to take up arms and fight for social justice and autonomy. Transnational Salafi and Takfiri Jihadists have taken over towns and declared allegiance to al-Qaeda or the Islamic State (ISIS). Domestic Jihadists – hostile to democracy and Western conceptions of a modern state – continually assert their will to power and control of Libyan territory and resources. City-states and towns – with their own militias, governing councils, and prisons – that emerged from Libya's fragmented armed struggle to overthrow Qaddafi are ambivalent about central authority. Rivalries between towns and vendettas among groups stemming from tensions held in check during Qaddafi's reign have led to violent conflict, the widespread internal displacement of people, and claims of genocide.

Libya under Qaddafi was also not fully a Weberian state. Qaddafi's ideology was hostile to bureaucracy – rational-legal or otherwise – which he viewed as illegitimate in the direct democracy he claimed to have created. Under Qaddafi, Libya's army, security, and police forces monopolized the "legitimate" use of violence and provided stability and safety for most Libyan citizens, but it used brutal repression against all dissidents. To protect his regime, Qaddafi relied on special forces led by relatives and other close allies while he kept the national army weak and supervised by relatives and allies. When Qaddafi's goons fired on peaceful protestors during the country's Arab Spring uprising, many military leaders and ordinary soldiers switched sides.

Transitional leaders in Libya have, to deadly effect, been unable to reproduce national military and security forces capable of monopolizing the legitimate use of violence to provide safety and security for Libyan citizens. In this regard, they certainly took power in 2011 in a difficult situation. Some of the armed groups formed during the uprising were more powerful than the so-called national army of the National Transitional Council (NTC). For that reason, or whatever other reasons, instead of demobilizing, disarming, and reintegrating the revolutionaries that fought Qaddafi into civilian society, transitional leaders in Libya attempted to form a national military and a new Ministry of the Interior (MOI) with security and police forces by incorporating militias as a whole within the state apparatus.

Not disarming the so-called revolutionaries – their numbers increased tenfold "after" Qaddafi's fall – has been a disaster. Instead of being transferred to the state, command, control, and loyalty remain under parochial militia leadership's sway. Militia members of various stripes, including those that joined after the war, have drained the state of resources without providing Libyans with security and peace.

Holding the balance of power, armed groups outside the state's full control have not respected competitive elections' results. They have used force – at times in alliance with politicians who also do not respect elections (when they lose) – to alter electoral outcomes. Pressuring the state apparatus to gain benefits, they have obstructed elected officials' attempts to deliver services and goods to the constituencies they developed during political campaigns.

Instead of contributing to peace, state-building, and national unity, the out-of-control armed groups maintain conflict to continue to siphon resources from the state. These militias – revolutionary, pro-Qaddafi, city-state, tribal, religious, regional, criminal, and as part of national coalitions – are also fighting and sometimes dying for their share of Libya's immense oil wealth.

Since 2014, there have been two rival national governments in Libya, one in Tripoli and one in Tobruk, with a third – in Tripoli as well – recently melting away. Among other issues, the two governments fight over control of the Central Bank (Central Bank of Libya, CBL), the National Oil Corporation (NOC), and the oil wells themselves. The central administration remains weak. In the absence of an effective national police and security sector, and without a national army that monopolizes violence, Libyan society has been managed – remarkably well considering the circumstances – by 113 elected local municipalities (Ahmida 2019).

The overall security situation in Libya is poor and volatile. In addition to taking over Qaddafi's cache of weapons and munitions, militias with varying and conflicting goals have been armed by several Gulf countries, Egypt, and Turkey. The armed groups fight intermittently among themselves and have begun to take over some elected municipalities. Assassinations and kidnappings for criminal or political reasons are rampant. Criminal networks further destabilize the situation.

Taking advantage of Libyans' desperation for stability and security of life and limb, an ambitious general, Khalifa Haftar, has gradually built up popular support in Eastern Libya and in its national government. His so-called Libyan National Army (LNA) recently launched an attack on the military coalition and national government located in Western Libya, and was able to reach Tripoli before being stalled by armed groups on the other side. Haftar promises to eradicate radical Islamists and impose a monopoly over the use of violence in the country to provide physical security for all Libyans. The general, who is supported by the Egyptian government, is likely aiming to impose a military-backed president-for-life political model along the lines of El-Sisi's in Egypt.

Because it had weaker national unity and weaker modern state attributes entering the Arab Spring than Tunisia and Egypt, more background about Libya's shallow history as a nation-state is needed to fully understand why Libya has experienced two civil wars since 2011 and why it is closer to becoming a failed state or a military authoritarian regime than a consolidated democracy.

The History of Libya as a Nation-State

In Libya, the forces of history bequeathed a weak nation-state that has been violently breaking apart as transitional elites attempt to initiate and sustain a democratic transition.

Libya was built around a tribal and regional system that has retained some potency and challenged nation- and state-building throughout its history (Lamma 2017). During the Ottoman era (1511–1911), three distinct administrative divisions or provinces – Cyrenaica, Tripolitania, and Fezzan – covered the territory of contemporary Libya. These divisions are all immense; Cyrenaica is located in the eastern section of the country, Tripolitania is in the Northwest, and Fezzan lies south of Tripolitania.

Ottoman state-building in the last century of its rule and early capitalist development loosened but did completely rupture traditional social organization based on tribes and regions in Libya:

By 1911, when Italian rule of Libya began, the effects of eighty years of Ottoman state formation and the development of European capitalism had unsettled the old tributary social structure and fostered the emergence of more defined class configurations that differed markedly among the country's three regions. Tripolitania had an urban notable class, a peasantry, and tribal confederations, while Fezzan was dominated by tribal confederations, landowning clans, and sharecropping peasants. Cyrenaica had no peasantry, and the formation of the Sanusi state integrated tribal factions into one cohesive force. (Ahmida 2005: 20)

The Ottoman state relied on the integral strength of the tribe to forge a military, raise taxes, and control trade (Lamma 2017). The Ottomans integrated tribal leaders into the state's management structures and depended on them to collect taxes and levy troops from their tribal brethren. Because the Ottoman state's administrative and commercial interests were concentrated on the Mediterranean coast, many Libyan tribes in the interior and south stayed on the fringes and did not live under its control.

The Sanusi (Sufi) Brotherhood has played a particular role in state formation in Libya (Lamma 2017). The politico-religious organization was founded in 1837 by Muhammad ibn As-Sanusi (1787–1859), a claimed descendant of the Prophet. He is known as the Great Sanusi. As a purifying revivalist Islamic movement, the Sanusi Brotherhood sought to remove what it considered to be unacceptable accretions to Islam and to return its adherents to a more pristine, scriptural form of the religion (Khalil 2004).

The Sanussiya established a home in Cyrenaica in Eastern Libya. The tribes in the region were often in conflict, resisted any form of political organization beyond the tribe, and were not under Ottoman control. However, the Great Sanusi and his descendants used their extensive knowledge of Islam to extend their control over the region's tribes (Lamma 2017).

The Sanussiya provided a rudimentary structure of government for the seminomadic tribes of Cyrenaica. This government collected taxes, provided social services, maintained peace between them, and gave them a sense of identification beyond the tribe. Without changing them fundamentally, the Sanussiya amalgamated the Cyrenaican tribes into one cohesive force. In addition to their religious mission, Sanussiya's goal was to mobilize armed resistance to invaders.

By appending itself to Cyrenaica's existing tribal network, the Sanusi Brotherhood played a key role in the military resistance to Italian colonization (1911–1943). Under Italian colonization and due to a United Nations' (UN) resolution in 1951, Libya's three historical provinces became a single state for the first time in its long history. Administratively, though, this European colonial state was comparatively weak (Lamma 2017). Unlike in Tunisia (and in Morocco), where the French contributed to the monopoly on violence, the Italians concentrated on the coast and replaced the Ottoman administration with Italian exclusivity. The local population was excluded from participation in and management of this state, which led them to fall back on the tribe as their central means of organization.

In 1922, the Mussolini government led a military campaign against the Sanusi Brotherhood. It thus became a nationalist movement that allowed Idris al-Sanusi to become a sort of father of the nation, which made him Great Britain's preferred intermediary during World War II (Lamma 2017).

Supported by the British and the UN, King Idris al-Sanusi became Libya's first head of state. The post-Independence Libyan state under King Idris (1951–1969) struggled to make one political community out of Libya's tribes and regions. Its federal structure, based on Libya's three historic regions, was a compromise. The King lacked support outside the Sanusi Brotherhood and supporting tribes in Cyrenaica, and he encountered opposition among the urban population of Tripolitania (Lamma 2017). To govern the country, King Idris relied on the Brotherhood and the tribes in Cyrenaica as a ruling coalition, which received the most state benefits during his rule.

When high-quality oil in large quantities was discovered in 1959, Libya became a full oil-distributive or rentier state. For distribution of this newfound extreme wealth, family ties and tribal links were the most important relationships (Lamma 2017). Instead of forging national unity and the commitment of all Libyans to the European-implanted Sanusi Monarchy, King Idris's rule pitted region against region and tribe against tribe.

In addition to neglecting nation-building –and like his counterparts in Gulf oil-exporting monarchies – for economic reasons, King Idris used oil revenues to avoid building a modern state with a rational-legal bureaucracy and administrative reach throughout the country (Vandewalle 2006). The construction of a modern state would have fully incorporated citizens and tied them to impersonal institutions while potentially awakening their demands for the accountable and broadly shared use of oil revenues beyond the minimal distribution necessary for political passivity. In place of dedicated efforts at modern state-building, King Idris sustained an earlier form of political community based on family and tribe that circumvented the country's more formal state institutions and rules that had been constructed to manage its emerging oil export economy (Vandewalle 2006).

Advances in the traits of a nation-state and Weberian state in Libya did not occur under the rule of Muammar Qaddafi (1969–2011) either. Qaddafi viscerally disliked centralized authority, and this was perhaps due to his Bedouin heritage (Davis 1987). In his stateless vision, bureaucrats and political party operatives were the enemies of direct (real) democracy. He initially denounced primordial tribal and family ties as antiquated and unsuitable for his *Jamahiriya*, but then increasingly relied on them for his physical survival when his revolution faltered.

For Wolfram Lacher, tribal loyalties remained potent in Libya despite urbanization and the transformation of Libyan society after the influx of oil revenues in the early 1960s (Lacher 2011). He asserts that under King Idris tribal leaders played a leading political role. Urbanization patterns saw communities in cities settle according to kinship ties as districts in major cities came to be dominated by specific tribes.

Qaddafi initially curbed tribal notables' power by redrawing administrative units to transcend tribal fiefdoms, but he then increasingly used tribal divisions and loyalties as instruments of power. Qaddafi formalized tribes' roles in the 1990s through the establishment of Popular Social Committees.

In addition, the stateless *Jamahiriya* made political mobilization through parties or civil society organizations impossible, leaving tribal mobilization as a default.

Qaddafi's *Jamahiriya* (State of the Masses)

Libya's transformation from autocratic Arab socialism to a crony-capitalist form of authoritarian rule differed from its Arab-socialist counterparts: Libyan Arab socialism had a pronounced personalist and idiosyncratic dimension in its crafting by Muammar Qaddafi, the "Brotherly Leader" of the Great Socialist People's Libyan Arab *Jamahiriya*. Libya is also an oil- and natural-gas-rich rentier state with repressive and distributive attributes along with the neotraditional social arrangements common to those states.

Qaddafi came to power in 1969 as the leader of a military coup executed by the Free Officers Movement against the Libyan Constitutional Monarchy. He then dismantled the hierarchy of institutions –

Parliament, political parties, the bureaucratic administration – that in his view prevented the masses from governing themselves directly without the negative impact of intermediaries (Anderson 1986).

In contrast to Arab socialism in Tunisia and Egypt, Qaddafi's *Jamahiriya* was intentionally stateless and in theory a form of direct democracy and economic populism. However, in practice it was neither (Joffé 2013). On the political side, the new system was built upon Basic People's Congresses (BPCs) through which the population's views on local, national, and international policy matters were translated into policy in political, economic, and social spheres. Every Libyan citizen was nominally required to participate in the BPCs. Officially, during the path from popular views to policy, the Libyan population's preferences were expressed through mandated delegates from the BPCs at regional congresses and then in the General People's Congress (GPC), which acted as Libya's Parliament. The GPC, in turn, elected the members of the General Popular Committee, Libya's equivalent of a ministerial cabinet, which was charged with formulating policy in accordance with principles passed on to it by the GPC. A bureaucracy created by and accountable to the BPCs transmitted and implemented these policies.

In practice, Qaddafi's *Jamahiriya* was not a direct democracy in which Libyans ruled themselves. To begin with, Qaddafi held more power in the *Jamahiriya* than anyone else. Sharing power to a lesser extent were other military figures in the Revolutionary Command Council (RCC) formed from the Free Officers Movement to govern Libya after they executed the military coup that removed the Sanusi Monarchy. These reserved powers became starker in the late 1970s, when Qaddafi resigned from the Secretariat of the General People's Congress, named himself "Brother Leader," and disingenuously claimed to no longer have any official role or power in the political system he dominated.

In addition, only a year into his political experiment, which began in 1977, Qaddafi created a separate system that was more powerful than the BPC system: the Revolutionary Committee Movement. Revolutionary Committees (RCs) were charged with monitoring, guiding (into a continuous revolutionary fervor), and repressing (through the use of arbitrary "people's tribunals") participants in the formal political structures that made up the *Jamahiriya*. Low participation rates in the BPCs and the GPC along with rising dissent spurred the creation of the RCs.

Formed largely of Qaddafi's family and tribe, the Qaddahfa, and under the direct control of Colonel Qaddafi himself and his closest collaborators, RCs held a great deal of power, which meant that, instead of a direct popular democracy in Libya, Qaddafi and his inner circle made all key decisions. They were in charge of everything from foreign policy to the budget to the delegation of powers in the GPC. Informal institutions and relationships mattered more than formal institutions did. Virtually from the start, Qaddafi's Libya was closer to a personalist authoritarian regime than a direct democracy:

Within a year of the establishment of his *Jamahiriya*, Qaddafi had effectively rendered its formal political institutions impotent, turning them into little more than a façade. Now, unfettered by the constraints of the cumbersome political system he had created, Qaddafi became a behind-the-scenes grand chess master, cannily moving the pieces around his board. (Joffé 2013: 96)

In addition to the gap between theory and practice in the BPC system, Libya's stateless society did not in reality replace impartial institutions – a bureaucratic organization as an instrument of governing – with direct democratic action to prevent the modern state from usurping the people's authority. Instead, Qaddafi manipulated the stateless system to keep adversaries off balance, turning Libya into one of the most dysfunctional places on earth (Vandewalle 2006).

The judicial, military, intelligence, and security systems also fell far short of direct democracy ideals. The judiciary did not protect the rule of law. The December 1969 Law on the Protection of the Revolution, the Penal Code, and Law No. 71 of 1972 rendered even mundane unauthorized political activity and comments punishable by imprisonment and potentially by death (Joffé 2013).

To protect the regime, Qaddafi often appointed only close relations to crucial posts within the military and intelligence services (Haddadt 2011). While there was compulsory military service for all Libyans under Qaddafi, he marginalized the armed forces and kept their leaders outside his innermost circle. To do this, Qaddafi abolished traditional military ranks and promoted the creation of quasi-military structures led by close family members or by members of his tribe and other core supporters.

The regime was closely defended by the elite 32 Brigade headed by Qaddafi's son, Khamis. Other security bodies were headed by his two other sons, Mu'tasim-Billah and Saadi. The Revolutionary Guard Corps and the Islamic Pan-African Legion – a group of mercenaries from various parts of Africa – were also created to counterbalance the regular armed forces. Qaddafi appointed family members and members of his tribe to leadership roles in the regular army as well.

In theory, but not in practice, based on Qaddafi's Green Book, Libya's economy was subject to populist controls through a popular committee system that was designed to eliminate the private sector and the exploitation of wage laborers. In place of the wage system, Qaddafi put forward the principle of "self-government in the economy."

In the new system, enterprises were transferred to the collective management (popular committees) of those who worked there. With the principle "partners not employees," workers and employees under the leadership of Basic People's Committees took over the management of businesses and institutions in production, trade, and services. The former owners received compensation and the opportunity to participate in the economic BPCs but in equal partnership with producers.

In addition, with the slogan "real estate property for its inhabitants," Qaddafi turned tenants of rental apartments and houses into the properties' owners. Qaddafi's economic prescriptions attacked the accumulation of surplus by any individual, ordering that in his stateless society all citizens should be allowed to share in and profit equally from the country's wealth.

The gap between theory and practice under Qaddafi was perhaps greatest in the economic realm. In practice, his policies did not amount to a form of economic populism in which all Libyan citizens shared equally in the country's wealth – far from it. Tribal affiliation either facilitated, in the case of tribes close to Qaddafi, or hindered the attainment of jobs, career advancement, and other economic privileges (Mokhefi 2011). In terms of defending the regime from internal opposition, Qaddafi used the tribal system to implement a carrot-and-stick policy: Libyans found themselves reliant on tribal connections to exercise their rights, attain protection, or even to secure positions for themselves within state institutions. On the other hand, tribal opposition was met with severe repression (Mokhefi 2011).

Qaddafi's manipulation of the tribal system produced a political economy in which virtually all of Eastern Libya – Cyrenaica, including its center in and around Benghazi – felt disadvantaged, targeted, and even hated by the Qaddafi regime. Moreover, the most important oil resources, which made the Libyan state wealthy, are located in the eastern part of Libya, where the most marginalized tribes under Qaddafi are located.

In a further affront to Qaddafi's proclaimed economic populism, Qaddafi's closest family members took full advantage of the wealth that poured into state coffers from Africa's largest exporter of oil. Even during the period beginning in the late 1980s, when Libya gradually implemented economic reforms – including an attempt to privatize 360 state enterprises between 2003 and 2006 – hardworking, intelligent, entrepreneurial, and capable Libyans were not encouraged or rewarded for these virtues (St. John 2013). Instead, family, clan, and tribe were rewarded through nepotism and cronyism:

Graft and corruption were pervasive...Qadhafi's family dominated the most lucrative sectors, and although most Libyans suspected the extent of their activities, the release of Wikileaks cables at the end of 2010 revealed the horrific extent of nepotism for all to see. Qadhafi's eldest son from his first wife, Muhammad, was chairman of the General Post and Telecommunications Company; Qadhafi's third son, Sa'adi, was head of a construction company involved in most of the major construction projects across the country; his fifth son, Hannibal, was the first marine consultant to the management committee of the General National Transport Company with a near monopoly on the transport of Libyan oil and natural gas; and his second son, Saif-al-Islam, was chairman of a diverse portfolio of companies known as the One Nine Group. Therefore, it became increasingly difficult to pursue any commercial opportunity in the country without first getting one or more of Qadhafi's children involved. (St. John 2013: 93)

Theoretically, Qaddafi's *Jamahiriya*, with its Basic People's Congresses, was designed to end tribalism in Libya. However, as noted above, tribal solidarity continued to play an important role in Libyan politics under Qaddafi's rule. The Cyrenaican tribes faced harsh repression. They were the most integrated into the Sanusi Sufi Order of King Idris – the Al-Awagir, Al-Abaydat, Drasa, Al-Barasa, Al-Zuwayya, and the Al-Majabra. Given their location and social connections, these tribes formed the core social base of the Sanusi Monarchy that Qaddafi overthrew (Charkow 2011).

The 1969 coup reversed the tribal hierarchy (Lacher 2013b) and placed the Qaddahfa tribes of Tripolitania in the political driver's seat.

Along with Qaddafi's own Qaddahfa tribe located in Sirte, the Warfalla with their stronghold in Bani Walid near Tripoli, and the Magarha from Fezzan formed the backbone of the regime. This was especially the case in the military, quasi-military, intelligence, and security apparatuses. Among other tribes, the Al-Hutman, Al-Hassawna, Toubou, and Tuareg are based in Fezzan. The Tuareg largely backed Qaddafi's regime while the Toubou opposed it.

In Libya's "direct democracy," then, Qaddafi and his kin, tribe, and core clients dominated the formal political structures, the informal structures that subverted them, the state's military and quasi-military organizations, the security sector, and all intelligence activities.

Challenging Qaddafi

Some Libyans challenged Qaddafi's rule from its inception. RCC members, troubled by Qaddafi's haphazard allocation of state resources and hostile to his *Jamahiriya* project, led a failed coup. In the aftermath of the 1975 coup attempt, Qaddafi eliminated the RCC as a substantive political institution and consolidated one-man rule supported by the Revolutionary Committees and an influx of his tribe and family into sensitive security and intelligence positions. Nevertheless, numerous plots and coup attempts by the military continued through the 1980s and 1990s. In 1984, an abortive coup attempt led by Libyan exiles with internal support led to a sharp government crackdown in which thousands were imprisoned, interrogated, and executed (eight in public). Underneath these coup attempts were battles to determine how Libya's oil wealth would be used, what role the state should play, how extensive its intervention should be in economic affairs, and how much private property should be abolished in favor of centralized planning (Vandewalle 2006).

Beyond military coup plotters, an Islamist opposition against Qaddafi and the RCC emerged at the latter's inception.[2] Despite claiming an Islamic basis for the revolution, the RCC encountered opposition from various Islamist factions. Upon taking power, the RCC banned alcohol, gambling, and prostitution – all of which had been legal under King Idris. Qaddafi declared a plan to replace all existing laws with

---

[2] On Islamist challenges to Qaddafi, see Global Security (2014); Benotman et al. (2013); Ashour (2012); and Metz (1989).

Sharia, though he arrogated to himself the role of the most authoritative interpreter of the religious law of Islam (*mujtahid*). Most controversially, he swept aside the entire body of Islamic commentary and learning, including the Hadith (the Prophet Muhammad's normative sayings and actions).

The *Jamahiriya*'s "Islamic" dimensions were opposed by the country's traditional religious hierarchy, including the Ulema (which viewed Qaddafi's idiosyncratic religious beliefs as heretical innovations). In 1975, Qaddafi banned Libya's Ulema from commenting on politics and he abolished the position of Grand Mufti to eliminate political threats from Libya's traditional religious establishment and to present himself as an Islamic leader. In 1980, an outspoken imam of a prominent mosque in Tripoli, Shaykh al-Bishti, was arrested in his mosque and then murdered.

In 1978, after failing in an attempt to foment a military coup by radicalizing high-ranking military officers, Hizb al-Tahrir (HT), a small rebel group with the goal of creating an Islamic Caliphate in Libya, met face-to-face with Qaddafi to deliver a comprehensive critique of the Green Book and emerging *Jamahiriya*. It called for him to turn over power to legitimate Islamic rulers. In response to the ideological and political threat, Qaddafi had members of HT hanged on their university campuses, and ordered the assassination of others abroad. This removed HT as a viable threat within Libya while teaching other Islamist movements to avoid directly confronting the regime before gradually building up broad social and military support.

The Libyan branch of the Muslim Brotherhood dates back to 1949, when a number of Egyptian Brotherhood members fled a crackdown in Cairo and took refuge in Benghazi, where they were hosted by Sanusi Brotherhood leader, Idris al-Sanusi. The group's spread among Libyans was accelerating in 1969, when the coup brought Colonel Qaddafi to power. In reaction to the coup, the group froze most of its activities to avoid repression. Their caution was warranted: Qaddafi also viewed the Muslim Brotherhood as a key ideological and political threat. Qaddafi spoke out against the Libyan Muslim Brotherhood directly and ordered security operations that eliminated many of its top leaders.

Libyan Jihadists who had traveled to Afghanistan to fight against the Soviet occupation of an Islamic country formed the Libyan Islamic

Fighting Group (LIFG), a secretive and exclusively paramilitary organization aimed at toppling the regime by force to establish an Islamic state. The LIFG was based in the eastern part of the country (Cyrenaica), the area traditionally opposed to Qaddafi. A cell of the clandestine organization in Benghazi was randomly discovered in 1995. In retaliation, the regime brutally repressed all of Cyrenaica, leading to a low-scale guerrilla war throughout the region between the LIFG and Libyan military and security forces. During the three-year conflict, there was an attempt to assassinate Qaddafi, and a number of senior security officials were killed. The regime bombed LIFG hideouts and unleashed the Revolutionary Committee Movement to engage in collective punishment against the towns from where the LIFG fighters came.

The origin of Salafi trends in Libya goes back to the 1960s. Due to its ideology and connections with conservative Saudi Arabia and Wahhabism, Qaddafi viewed the Salafi movement in Libya as a threat to his domestic and international ambitions. To combat Salafi inroads in Libya, mainly on the cultural level of dress and public behavior, Qaddafi launched campaigns against beards and hijabs. These, in his view, symbolized Saudi influence and the rejection of his modernizing ideology.

In 1986, a Revolutionary Committee member was assassinated in Benghazi by the hitherto unknown Hisballah ("Party of God"). This led to the closure of 48 Islamic institutions. In 1987, nine members of a group called Holy War were executed for allegedly plotting to assassinate Soviet advisers.

Outside Libya, dissident exiles formed the Libyan National Salvation Front (LNSF) and the Libyan National Army (LNA), the latter composed of former Libyan prisoners of war (POWs) in Chad (Global Security 2014). The head of the POWs in Chad, Khalifa Haftar, has played a major role militarily since the 2011 Revolution began. The LNSF was led by Mohamed al-Magarief, a former Libyan ambassador to India, who became an important opposition political leader during and after the war against Qaddafi. The LNSF reportedly received the active support of the United States Central Intelligence Agency and likely led, with internal support, the 1984 coup attempt that failed and spurred a reign of terror within Libya. To deal with external opposition, Qaddafi's regime followed a policy of physical liquidation of opponents, wherever they could be found. Between 1980 and 2011, 20 anti-Qaddafi Libyans – "stray dogs" in the regime's rhetoric – were assassinated abroad.

Students were probably the most visible source of opposition to Qaddafi's regime.[3] Several students, who were protesting at the University of Benghazi, were reportedly killed in the 1970s, a claim the regime denied. The incident led to the temporary closure of the university, which was renamed Al Fatah University when it reopened. In 1984, two students at Al-Fatah University were publicly hanged on campus.

Many political prisoners – coup plotters, university dissidents, Islamist opposition figures, and others – were housed at Abu Salim prison in Tripoli. The international Non-governmental Organization (NGO) Human Rights Watch (HRW 2006) has claimed that 1,200 prisoners were killed or disappeared from the political prison on June 29, 1996, in a likely mass killing. Years prior to the 2011 Arab Spring uprisings, families of the missing and dead from Abu Salim prison formed an organization and held regular protests in Benghazi. A lawyer and human rights activist, Fathi Terbil (who lost four family members in the prison massacre), had represented them over the years.

The arrest of Fathi Terbil in February 2011 sparked a demonstration in Benghazi by relatives of deceased prisoners on February 15, 2011 (Memri 2011). That demonstration marked the start of the Arab Spring in Libya.

Authoritarian Breakdown

Nation-state and Weberian-state attributes – which were historically weak in Libya – collapsed as the Arab Spring uprising quickly turned into a civil war. On February 15, 2011, Fathi Terbil was arrested for leading protests against the Abu Salim prison massacre. In a context of mass antiregime uprisings in neighboring Egypt and Tunisia (the Tunisian president, Zine El Abidine Ben Ali, had already fled the

---

[3] In the 1970s, Qaddafi ordered his RCs to persecute university students suspected of opposing his regime. See "Qaddafi Crimes since 1969: A Working and Partial List," a collaborative list developed by an academic with the handle @Ms. Entropy. At the time of writing this volume, it can be seen at www.docs.google.com/file/d/0B-B_2d4pgCD9YWQ5YTNhOTgtNzcyYy 00NjY4LTkyZDUtYWJhNjBlZjYxZmRj/edit?hl=en&authkey=COiSmpUN.

country), his arrest triggered a riot and antigovernment protests demanding regime overthrow.

People in Cyrenaica, the region most maligned by Qaddafi, began the Libyan Revolution on February, 17, 2011 (Al Jazeera 2011; Rashad 2011). After two days of protests in the region's capital, Benghazi, security forces opened fire on protesters, killing 14. The next day, February 18, a funeral procession for one of those killed passed by the Katiba, Benghazi's sprawling military compound for the Qaddafi regime. A fight broke out between soldiers within the Katiba and mourners. Another 24 protestors were killed. This led to the hanging of two policemen accused of shooting the protestors.

Overwhelmed by the number of protestors, police and army personnel in Benghazi, outside of a core group within the Katiba, withdrew from the city. On February 20, 2011, opposition fighters, led by a suicide car bomber, Mohammed Zeyo, and aided by reinforcements from nearby towns (Bayda and Derna), who had raided local army compounds for weapons stormed the Katiba (Rashad 2011). That same day, Qaddafi sent special forces led by Libyan Major General and Interior Minister Abdul Fattah Younis to wipe out the uprising in Benghazi and rescue his cornered troops within the Katiba. However, once Younis arrived in Benghazi, he and his battalions defected to the opposition, while the remainder of Qaddafi's troops fled. Thus, after only three days of conflict, on February 20, 2011, Benghazi became free from Qaddafi's control (Stephen 2011).

Post-Qaddafi nation- and state-building began after the defection of General Younis in Benghazi. When he defected, he declared that the Libyan army should join the people and respond to their legitimate demands (Tripoli Post 2011). In response, opposition rebels declared him commander-in-chief of its armed forces.

In addition to efforts to build a national army out of the uprisings, which had expanded throughout the country, the opposition began developing other aspects of a modern state and democratic government. Rebels formed a National Transitional Council (NTC) to act as the political face of the revolution and the country's administrative center domestically and internationally (Pack and Barfi 2012). Members of the newly formed NTC chose Qaddafi's former Minister of Justice, Mustafa Abdul Jalil, as their Chairman. As a judge, Jalil had earned a reputation for ruling consistently against the regime and seeking to protect human rights, including publicly demanding the release of political prisoners (Clotter 2010). He had defected to the opposition (along with Abdul Fattah Younis, the first senior Qaddafi figures to do so) on February 21, 2011, after being sent to Benghazi to negotiate the release of the Katiba's trapped soldiers (Reuters 2011).

The NTC, based in Benghazi, attempted to create a nationwide body by selecting representatives from each region, including those still under Qaddafi's control. However, it was clear early on that the NTC's state-building initiative would struggle: the NTC and the new "national army" could offer little to support local uprisings outside Benghazi when Qaddafi unleashed all of his military and security forces to suppress them. In addition, leaders of many local rebellions distrusted the NTC, which was populated by former Qaddafi figures and returning political dissidents (Pack et al. 2014).

In addition to seeking to represent Libya as a whole, the NTC in Benghazi focused on obtaining international recognition as the new Libyan state and legitimate representative of the Libyan people, which they received from the United Nations General Assembly in September 2011 (UN 2011). It also pursued access, which it gradually secured, to an estimated $150 billion of Libyan assets – largely from oil exports – held in foreign accounts that the United Nations Security Council froze on February 26, 2011, shortly after the war began (Cadigan and Prieston 2011).

As the region where the revolution erupted and the city where the opposition established its seat of power, Cyrenaica and Benghazi initially became the focus of Qaddafi's policy of ruthlessly eradicating the uprisings. By the middle of March 2011, Qaddafi's forces had reached Benghazi and pounded the city with artillery and tank shells, punching through the outskirts of the city to engage in fierce street fighting (Lucas 2011). However, international intervention saved the city. After suffering severe setbacks along the Mediterranean coast between Tripoli and Benghazi, the NTC, backed by the Arab League, called for and received international intervention (Mezran and Eljarh 2014).

France, Lebanon, and the United Kingdom officially proposed enacting the United Nations Security Council Resolution (1973) that was adopted on March 17, 2011 (UN 2011). The resolution buttressed international military intervention in the Libyan Civil War. It demanded an immediate ceasefire and authorized the international community's right to establish a no-fly zone and to use all means necessary (short of foreign occupation) to protect civilians (Roth 2011). The United States and a coalition of European and Middle Eastern states participated in the military action against Qaddafi's regime, which began on March 19 and prevented pro-Qaddafi forces from capturing Benghazi (Al Jazeera 2011). Thus, Cyrenaica rapidly became free from the threat of Qaddafi's forces.

Despite the NTC's early success in Cyrenaica, Islamist militias within the region fighting against Qaddafi but not loyal to the NTC also emerged (Terrorism Research and Analysis Consortium 2012). The strength of Islamist forces within Cyrenaica that were not loyal to the NTC foreshadowed stiff post-Qaddafi challenges to democracy and nation-state building. Jihadi Salafis tied to al-Qaeda, Abd al-Hakim and Sufyan bin Qumu, formed the Abu Salim Martyrs' Brigade. Another militant, Abd al-Basit Azuz, reportedly had been sent to Libya by al-Qaeda's Ayman al-Zawahiri in the wake of the 2011 revolts to establish an al-Qaeda foothold in Derna. Jihadi Salafis who rejected NTC initiatives also formed Ansar al-Sharia ("Partisans of Islamic Law") militias in Benghazi and Derna, both having ties to al-Qaeda's central command and its branch in the Maghreb, AQIM (Terrorism Research and Analysis Consortium 2012).

Outside Cyrenaica, towns, cities, and tribes opposed to Qaddafi faced ferocious attacks from the regime. Without the assistance of the new "national military" based in Cyrenaica, they had to rise up and form neighborhood brigades and town militias to survive. For the most part, they were also not afforded the foreign-led no-fly zone that protected Cyrenaica. These militias fought the brunt of the civil war against Qaddafi's loyal forces. When they won, they gained widespread legitimacy as the true "revolutionaries" who killed Qaddafi and ended his 40-plus years of tyranny. These local militias and the local governing and judicial arms they also developed have never been fully absorbed into the post-Qaddafi state and governments.

In Northwest Libya (Tripolitania), militias from Misrata and Zintan became the most powerful ones in Libya during the revolution – and the most difficult to control and assimilate into the central state afterward (Elmaazi 2013).

Located southeast of Tripoli, Misrata is Libya's third largest city after Tripoli and Benghazi, with approximately 300,000 people. The uprising in Misrata began on February 19, 2011, when Qaddafi's security forces attempted to derail a planned protest scheduled to begin inside the city's central mosque. Misrata turned into the bloodiest battle of the war against Qaddafi. The siege of the city lasted seven weeks before rebel forces, with the eventual aid of NATO air strikes, forced Qaddafi's troops out. More than 2,000 rebels and civilians were killed in the battle for Misrata, and at least 900 were injured, making it one of the bloodiest of the war.

During the revolution Qaddafi viewed Benghazi, Misrata, and the Nafusa mountain region (especially Zintan) southwest of Tripoli as rebel strongholds. He acted accordingly with his most ferocious use of force against them. The Nafusa Mountains shelter most of Libya's Amazigh (Berber) population, who suffered intense persecution and repression of their culture and language under Qaddafi's rule (Smith 2011). Berbers were frightened to use their language outside their home, and Qaddafi insisted on publicly calling them Arabs (Daragahi 2011). Little state funds were spent in Amazigh towns.

Zintan was an important city for Qaddafi in the Nafusa Mountains (Elmaazi 2013). It is populated mainly by Arabs. Over the years, Qaddafi had tried to use Arabs to dominate the region's Berbers. He favored Arab Zintanis in state patronage and arms and fomented mutual suspicions through his deputies in the region. Despite his patronage, Arab Zintanis were among the first to rise up against Qaddafi in the February 17 Revolution (Pack and Barfi 2012). Many former Qaddafi military officers led them. Reportedly, resentment against Qaddafi ran high in Zintan because it was the hometown of many detained army officers who took part in the failed coup in 1993 (3News 2011). Zintanis, who made notable contributions to the fight against Italian occupation, come from a region known for its fighters; they also tended to be critical of Qaddafi's idiosyncratic *Jamahiriya* state project (Terrorism Research and Analysis Consortium 2011).

When the Arabs in Zintan rose up against Qaddafi, the Nafusa Mountain Berbers moved past historical tensions and joined them in their revolt (Daragahi 2011). Rebellions occurred in the Nafusa Mountain towns of Kikla, Gharyan, Yafran, and Nalut as well (Amnesty International 2011). Qaddafi's forces surrounded the region and attacked it with armored vehicles and rocket launchers that killed many – men, women, and children, rebels, and nonrebels. Thousands fled to neighboring Tunisia.

Under siege for months, the Nafusa Mountain rebellion began to receive support from NATO aircraft strikes against Qaddafi's forces in

April 2011. Rebel militias in the region also began to coordinate their efforts and offer mutual support. In November 2011, the Al-Zintan Revolutionaries' Military Council was formed as an umbrella for 23 militias in Zintan and the Nafusa Mountains (divided into five brigades including the Martyr Muhammad al-Madani Brigade, with 4,000 fighters) (Terrorism Research and Analysis Consortium 2011).

While Cyrenaica briefly and Tripolitania especially bore the brunt of the war against Qaddafi's regime, there were anti-Qaddafi uprisings in Fezzan as well. The relatively sparse population in arid southern Libya is dominated by Toubou tribes (Murray 2012). Their territory stretches from Sabha in Fezzan to Kufra in southern Cyrenaica, which is 560 miles east of Sabha. The seminomadic Toubou's home territory also crosses the border into Chad, Niger, and Northern Sudan. Ethnic Toubou are predominantly Muslim, but they speak Tebu and are darker than most Libyans. The Toubou experienced heavy discrimination under Qaddafi (Murray 2012). In 2007, Toubou Libyans were stripped of their citizenship, with the Qaddafi regime claiming that they were Chadians, not Libyans. They were denied access to education, health care, skilled jobs, and decent housing. Forced evictions from their homes led to charges that the Libyan government was responsible for a deliberate policy of ethnic cleansing in Kufra.

The Toubou sided with anti-Qaddafi forces during the revolution. On the other hand, Qaddafi established Fezzan as part of his regime's stronghold by using the region's Arab tribes as a primary recruitment base for the regime's security forces and intelligence services (Lacher 2014). Overall, Qaddafi's patterns of security recruitment, his Arabization campaign, and divide-and-rule tactics favoring the South's Arab communities (including the Zwai, Awlad Suleiman, and Warfalla tribes) helped the regime control the South until the end of the war.

The Toubou uprising in the South, in Sabha and Kufra, attracted some NTC recognition (Murray 2012). During the Libyan Revolution, the NTC assigned a Toubou militia a key role in monitoring the South's porous border. The Toubou also activated their tribal ties across Libya's border with Sudan, Chad, and Niger to aid the rebels' battle against Qaddafi throughout the country.

Since the collapse of Qaddafi's regime, former members of government forces have also held on to parts of their weapon stockpiles and organized themselves into militias along tribal lines (Lacher 2014).

Qaddafi's End

The international intervention of NATO forces, which began on March 19, 2011, turned the war decisively in the rebels' favor. Six months into the war, the battle over Tripoli began on August 20, 2011 (Al-Manar 2011). Rebel militias and brigades had been underground since their initial uprising was crushed by Qaddafi loyalists early in the conflict. An uprising within the city was coordinated with attacks from outside. In a pincer move, the largest militias from Zintan and Misrata among others converged on the city. Within a week, Tripoli fell to the rebels and the National Transitional Council took control of the capital. The war in Libya against Qaddafi was almost over.

Qaddafi's fate was decided on October 20, 2011, when a militia from Misrata killed Muammar Qaddafi and his son Mutassim in their hometown of Sirte, one of the last three cities to fall to the rebels (Al Riyadh 2011). A militia from Zintan captured Qaddafi's son Saif al-Islam as he was trying to flee the country across the Sahara to Niger on November 18, 2011. The NTC declared the liberation of Libya and the official end of the revolution on October 23, 2011. The NTC moved to Tripoli from Benghazi to face daunting democratic transition and consolidation challenges.

Notably, when the NTC moved to Tripoli to establish central state authority, the militias organized along local and ideological lines were more powerful than the National Liberation Army, which had been formed in Cyrenaica early in the uprising (McQuinn 2012). For the most part, the war was waged outside Cyrenaica. Misrata's militia alone, with 40,000 men, is one of the largest and most powerful in the country. It projected its strength to other areas of the country during and after the war. The Zintan militia was powerful as well. In most of the towns and cities over which they gained control during the revolution, local militias set up autonomous mini-states with governing and judicial bodies (including their own prisons). Radical Islamists did the same in the towns and parts of cities that they controlled. Tribes and regions also became armed actors and potential state-builders.

Due to historical factors and the nature of Libya's February 17 Revolution, then, elites who led Libya's transition were immediately confronted with steep nation- and state-building challenges that they had to address while also attempting to implement democratic institutions.

Democratic Transition

Libya's National Transitional Council produced a roadmap for the country's democratic transition. Plans for founding elections were spelled out in a Temporary Constitutional Declaration (TCD) enacted by the NTC on August 3, 2011 (Al Riyadh 2011). The constitutional declaration called for the NTC to organize elections for a 200-member General National Congress (GNC) within 240 days after the end of the war. The NTC appointed Abdurrahim El-Keib as interim prime minister (November 2011–November 2012) on the understanding that he would be replaced after the GNC was elected and took power.

From the start, transitional authorities in Libya seeking to consolidate democracy had to struggle against or work with militia bosses with revolutionary legitimacy based on armed conflict. The challenge was insurmountable. By 2014, the democratic transition, as it was conceived in 2011 by the National Transitional Council, had completely broken down.

Since 2014, the competition for power in Libya has largely taken place outside the formal institutional framework (ECFR 2014). Direct armed control of the ground and its resources has become the crucial stake.

Electoral politics dominated the first two years of the Libyan transition. The GNC was designed to replace the NTC as a governing body, and to appoint and oversee a constituent assembly charged with writing the country's new constitution. After ratification of this new constitution, the GNC would oversee a general election for yet another government to replace itself. The TCD also passed election, political party, and constituency laws, and it appointed the High National Election Commission to implement the electoral process.

After bargaining among various social groups about electoral rules, founding elections took place on July 7, 2012. The final electoral law ordained that 80 of the 200 seats would go to party lists while the majority, 120 seats, would go to Independents, many with ties to political parties. The National Forces Alliance (NFA), led by ex-interim Prime Minister Mahmoud Jibril, won 39 out of the 80 political party seats and formed a ruling coalition with associated Independents. The Justice and Construction Party (JCP), the political arm of the Muslim Brotherhood in Libya, won 17 party seats. Here are the results:

- National Forces Alliance: 39
- Justice and Construction: 17
- National Front Party: 17
- Wadi al-Hiya Alliance: 2
- Union for the Homeland: 2
- National Centrist Party: 2
- Libyan National Democratic Party: 1
- The Message: 1
- The Foundation: 1
- National Party for Development and Welfare: 1
- Nation and Prosperity: 1
- Authenticity and Renewal: 1
- Moderate Umma Assembly: 1
- Libik Watani: 1
- National Gathering of Wadi al-Shati: 1
- Moderate Youth Party: 1
- Libyan List for Freedom and Development: 1
- National Coalition of Parties: 1
- Libya the Hope: 1
- Wisdom Party: 1

While most foreign observers reported the results of the election of July 7, 2012, as a victory for secularists over Islamists, the NFA was more of a broad centrist coalition that included both self-identified Islamists and non-Islamists (Grant 2012).

Defensiveness by "secularists" led to concessions early in the transition that could hamper democracy and the equal citizenship rights expected of it. Angered by the Muslim Brotherhood's exclusive claims to the mantle of Islam and leery of charges of being secularists in a conservative environment, NFA leaders stressed that they were nationalists and Muslims while differentiating their party by advancing a practical national economic reform program (Grant 2012). They also advocated for *Sharia* to be considered a main source of legislation along with popular rule. NFA deputies opposed remaking Libya into a secular state. To pad their Islamist credentials, they adopted key Islamist demands that legalized polygamy and instituted Islamic banking.

Based on the election results, GNC members had to form an interim government to steer the country until new elections took place based on a new constitution. After squabbles over cabinet positions doomed other candidates, Ali Zeidan of the NFA, a human rights lawyer who defected in 1980 while serving as a Libyan diplomat in India, emerged as the prime minister entrusted to form the GNC's government. After the Congress approved his cabinet nominees, Zeidan took office on November 14, 2012. On August 9, 2012, GNC members had voted Mohamed Yousef al-Magariaf, leader of the secular liberal National Front Party (NFP), president of the GNC with 113 out of 200 votes.

Democratic Consolidation: Nation-State and Weberian-State Pacts

In their efforts to govern and institutionalize political democracy, the El Keib and Zeidan governments faced overwhelming challenges. They did not have a viable Weberian state at their disposal. The military of the state they took over was weaker than many of the militias that had prevailed over Qaddafi. Due to the nature of the February 17 Revolution, there were competing mini-states seeking allegiance based on region, town, village, tribe, and religion. Nearly all of them had military, judicial, and governing arms.

While oil wealth largely vitiated the need for a tax collection apparatus for the El Keib (November 24, 2011–November 14, 2012) and Zeidan governments (November 14, 2012–March 11, 2014), Qaddafi had bequeathed both a stunted and grossly dysfunctional bureaucracy. Their governments did not monopolize the use of violence – far from it. Reflecting on the challenges that his government faced, Ali Zeidan stated:

Libya [has] lived through 42 years of systematic destruction...the government has no army or security forces to control the Libyan street...armed Islamic groups [are] spreading radical new ideas...and the [country's] administration is weak and small. (Najm 2013)

Starting from such weak foundations, nation- and state-building under El-Keib and Zeidan understandably did not go well. During their time in power, the militias with their own commanders, not the fledgling national army, possessed most of Qaddafi's army's weapons and military hardware. In addition, with relatively weak armed forces under its control the NTC/GNC dissipated what authority it had by repeatedly accommodating the demands of armed groups that represented the reemergence of local and tribal structures as independent loci of political and military power (Pack and Cook 2015).

The Faustian bargain that Libya's transitional governments made with revolutionary brigades and militias produced a hybrid security sector, near anarchy, and the massive leaching of Libya's oil wealth by so-called revolutionary militias, whose memberships increased tenfold from the numbers who actually fought Qaddafi once people smelled the money and state weakness.

The damage was done almost systematically. One, Eastern militias pushed for and received greater power than militias from other regions. Two, the powerful Zintan militia forced its leader into the role of Minister of Defense and then created a parallel army under his control. Three, the powerful Misrata militia pressured the provisional government into making their leader Minister of Interior and then created a parallel national police and security force under his control. Four, Misratan and Zintani armed groups engaged in turf wars, fighting for control of ministries and strategic sites like airports. Five, Islamist militias either pressured the provisional government to impose *Sharia* or operated completely outside of state authority. They also destroyed the Sufi shrines of Libya's customary Islam. Six, federalist militias from Cyrenaica, which harbors most of Libya's oil, became territorial over the country's oil supply. Seven, vendettas between towns and political assassinations along with the emergence of criminal militias made the country's security vacuum painfully obvious for most Libyans. Eight, General Haftar began his machinations as future strongman, seeking to duplicate Egyptian President Abdel Fattah El-Sisi's emerging military authoritarian regime.

Virtually all of these militias, by the force of arms, had their ever-expanding membership placed on the public payroll. The first sign of the central state's impotence came quickly.[4] In the run-up to the July 2012 vote, a powerful militia shut down roads in order to press its demand that Eastern Libya (Cyrenaica) have a greater say than other regions when the incoming Parliament drafted a constitution (Shane and Becker 2016). Contradicting the TCD, the authorities capitulated, leaving the writing of the Constitution for a second elected assembly with more votes from the East.

---

[4] On the development of Libya's post–Qaddafi hybrid military and security sector, see Wehrey (2014).

In a second sign of localized armed forces dominating the emerging political transition, under pressure from "the revolutionaries" the El-Keib government appointed Osama al-Juwali, head of the powerful Zintan militia, interim Minister of Defense.[5] Fawzi abdel A'al, head of the powerful Misrata militia, was appointed interim Interior Minister. More tellingly, the NTC/GNC integrated the revolutionary militias and brigades into the National Army and Ministry of Interior as whole units. By doing so, they created a hybrid security sector in which the armed groups' cohesion and parochial outlook were preserved, albeit under the cover of the state (Wehrey 2014). This decision impeded hopes for the efficient disarmament, demobilization, and reintegration of the militias and brigades that emerged during and after the revolution and impeded efforts to build up regular army and police.

From the start, the national army and the revolutionary militias still largely operated along two parallel tracks with different command and control structures. While there were a few instances of truly mixed units in which the members of the revolutionary militias were fully integrated in the regular armed forces and national police, in most cases the relationship between the two sides was marked by ambivalence, hostility, and a lack of coordination.

The NTC/GNC governments never attained authority over the country's fragmented armed groups. Powerful commanders of the revolutionary militias launched the Libya Shield Force as a way to resist full incorporation into the regular Libyan army. The El-Keib government deployed the Libya Shield Force to quell ethnic and tribal fighting across the country. Though formally commanded by a regular Libyan army officer, the commanders of the militias whose men comprised the Shield divisions called the shots. Within a couple of years, the Libya Shield Force had developed into a shadow army that eclipsed the regular forces' power.

The Libya Shield Force's divisions across the country were composed of the young men of the towns and provinces where they were garrisoned, and they reflected those areas' parochial agendas and outlooks. For example, there was a strong Islamist and tribal hue to the Benghazi-based Libya Shield Force division. In Misrata, the Libya Shield Force division emphasized its town's autonomous outlook.

---

[5] On the development of Libya's post-Qaddafi hybrid military and security sector, see Wehrey (2014).

The Libya Shield Force also preserved the structure and cohesion of the armed groups that developed during their uprising against Qaddafi. The most damning effect of this system is that heads of the individual armed groups comprising the Libya Shield Force were free to pursue their own agendas – whether ideological, regional, or criminal – while using the official writ of the government as cover (Wehrey 2014). Partially incorporated into the state apparatus, senior army officers regarded the Libya Shield Force as a poorly disciplined, highly politicized Islamist group. Meanwhile, from the Libya Shield Force's point of view, the regular army was hollow and corrupt, tainted by its connection to Qaddafi.

Within the MOI, a similar relationship of distrust and parallel tracks with revolutionary militias emerged under the El-Keib government (Pusztai 2012). Under the umbrella of the MOI, the NTC created the Supreme Security Council (SSC) with 17 subordinated SSCs in major cities. The SSCs were built from small revolutionary militias willing to cooperate with the MOI. The SSCs were authorized to support the Libyan police. However, the police saw the SSCs as unruly, ideological, and criminal; the SSCs viewed the police as incompetent and tainted by the legacy of affiliation with the Qaddafi regime (Wehrey 2014). Just as the Libya Shield Force was more powerful than the national army, so too the SSC was more powerful than the national police.

Beyond the Libya Shield Force's usurpation of a national army role and the Supreme Security Council (and its subordinate SSCs) having units more powerful than police units, other revolutionary militias based on town, region, and ideology maintained their arms and claimed legitimacy based on some affiliation with competing organs of the weak and fragmented post-Qaddafi Libyan state: "Islamist, Misratan, Zintani, and Federalist militias all used force or the threat of force to pressure the country's elected institutions, or to seize strategic assets like border checkpoints, oil facilities, armories, ports, and airports" (Wehrey 2014).

Misratan and Zintani armed groups engaged in turf wars, fighting for control of ministries and strategic sites like airports (Wehrey 2014). The Qaqa Brigade, composed largely of Zintani members, was based in Tripoli and affiliated with the army's chief of staff. It provided border security along the country's porous southwest frontier and guarded oil installations in southern fields. It was also known for predatory and mafia-like activities in Tripoli. The Qaqa Brigade also acted as the armed wing of the party of former prime ministers Mahmoud Jibril and Ali Zeidan, the National Forces Alliance (NFA).

Various Islamist militias from the East rose up against Qaddafi in the early days of the revolution (Wehrey 2014). They included the February 17 Revolutionary Martyrs' Brigade, the Rafallah al-Sahati Companies, The Zawiya Martyrs' Brigade, the Martyr Omar Al-Mukhtar Brigade, the Abu Salim Martyrs' Brigade, and the Free Libyan Martyrs' Brigade. Many of their members refused to surrender arms, demobilize, and integrate into the formal security apparatus until the regular security forces were cleansed of Qaddafi-era personnel (Wehrey 2014).

On a moral plane, Islamists decried state institutions as irreparably tainted by ethically bankrupt supporters of the former regime, womanizers, and drug addicts. Prior to surrendering arms, they also demanded a constitution based on *Sharia* law. Other Islamists operated entirely beyond the pale of state authority. Among them were the militant Salafist group and al-Qaeda affiliate, Ansar al-Sharia, which prohibited participation in elections.

The Eastern city of Derna, which was under the control of supporters of Ansar al-Sharia during the revolution, transferred its allegiance to the Islamic State of Iraq and al-Sham (ISIS) in 2014 (Middle East Eye 2016). After the al-Qaeda-affiliated AQIM regrouped and drove them out of Derna, ISIS's Libyan branch moved to Sirte and to other former Qaddafi strongholds including Bani Walid and Tarhouna. Neighboring Tunisia has supplied a large number of ISIS recruits in Libya. ISIS in Libya has been potent because of a willingness of Libyan regions that lost power in the postrevolutionary era to support ISIS and because of the availability of a steady stream of Jihadis from Tunisia (Middle East Eye 2016).

Post-Qaddafi, federalists claimed a militia with more than 17,000 fighters under their command in oil-rich Cyrenaica (Wehrey 2014). In 2012, the El-Keib government set up a Petroleum Facilities Guard (PFG), specifically to protect Libya's vital oil installations. However, the PFG leader, Ibrahim Jadhran, affiliated himself with the federalist movement and began implementing policies that overruled government directives.

General Khalifa Haftar, who took part in the coup that brought Qaddafi to power and who defected to the United States after leading a disastrous war in Chad in the 1980s, returned to command ground forces in the revolution against Qaddafi. He has since commanded armed groups with varying ties to the Libyan transitional national governments. At one point, he announced a coup that never occurred and called for Libyans to rise up against the elected GNC government, which they never did. In the chaotic post-Qaddafi environment, Haftar eventually emerged as the leader of a military campaign against all flavors of Islamists in Libya, from the Muslim Brotherhood to extremist groups.[6] He and the armed groups he commands have been the main armed forces of the Tobruk government elected in 2014.

At times, Libya's disparate armed groups have impinged, in dramatic ways, on elected leaders' ability to rule (Lacher and al-Idrissi 2018). After accused terrorist Abu Anas al-Libi was captured by US special forces in 2013, the Libya Shield Force kidnapped Prime Minister Ali Zeidan. The kidnappers blamed the weak Zeidan government for allowing the kidnapping of a Libyan citizen by a foreign power. Pro-Zeidan armed groups freed the prime minister, who was unharmed. Following that incident, Zeidan moved into a compound controlled by the Zintan militia to protect himself, thereby clearly associating the elected government with one faction in an armed struggle (Lacher and al-Idrissi 2018). That same year, various armed groups forced their way into Zeidan's office and pressured him into paying $1.5 billion to newly established state-sanctioned militias (Lacher and al-Idrissi 2018).

In addition, in March 2014 the GNC ousted Zeidan from power in a no-confidence vote when his government was unable to prevent a rebel militia, which had declared itself an autonomous government, from selling oil without the authorization of the state-owned Libyan National Oil Corporation. (See below for a fuller discussion of the political motivations.) Ultimately, US Navy Seals thwarted the sale. Fearing for his life, Zeidan fled the country.

In another indication of transitional governments lacking the monopoly of violence, the post-Qaddafi era has also been marked by a wave of political assassinations, which have been primarily targeted at those perceived to be Qaddafi loyalists (HRW 2013). Most have taken place in Benghazi and Derna in volatile Eastern Libya. More than 50 political assassinations have occurred without anyone being held accountable. Fearing they will be next, a number of Libyan political, administrative, and business elites have fled the country.

---

[6] One group of Saudi-influenced quietist Salafis have rallied to Haftar's side.

Post-Qaddafi, powerful militias flexed their muscles. After Qaddafi was killed by Misratans in his hometown of Sirte, his body was taken to Misrata, where he was put on display for tourists in a refrigerated meat store (Netto 2011). The Misratan militia had more say in the handling of his body than the interim government.

Similarly, Qaddafi's son and assumed successor, Saif al-Islam Qaddafi, was captured by the Zintan militia and held in its hometown. Claiming that Qaddafi remnants in the judiciary might try to declare him innocent, Zintan militia commanders refused requests to hand him over to the central government (Freeman 2013). He was reportedly freed in 2017.

For Americans, the clearest signal that the Libyan transition would be marked by steep challenges due to civilian leaders' inability to control armed actors occurred on September 11, 2012, when a local Salafi brigade, Ansar al-Sharia, purportedly working in conjunction with al-Qaeda in the Islamic Maghreb (AQIM), stormed the US diplomatic outpost in Benghazi, killing Ambassador Christopher Stevens and three of his colleagues. The tragic event has had a seismic effect on Libya's relations with the outside power most responsible for its liberation, the United States. Less well known is that the event had a powerful effect on Libyan society, which was beginning to reel from postrevolution militia violence and its threat to their revolution's goals of peace, security, democracy, human rights, and socioeconomic justice.

Libyans took to the streets to protest the murder of the idealistic American supporter of their revolution and temporarily pushed Ansar al-Sharia out of Benghazi. They also began to actively protest militias' power and demanded the presence of the regular army and national police:

The attack [on the US Diplomatic outpost] came on the heels of a wave of violence over the summer: the assassination of Qadhafi-era officials in the east, vendettas between rival towns like Misrata and Beni Walid, Zintan and Mashashiya...and rampages by armed Salafists against the country's Sufi Shrines. For Libyan citizens, the assault was the final straw. It was a wake-up call that the Faustian bargain the country's provisional government had made with the revolutionary brigades was no longer tenable. It was time for the government to rein in the numerous armed groups that had filled the security vacuum left by the collapsed national army and anemic police. (Haraf and Al-Khalidi 2012)

Ultimately, in the post-Qaddafi environment, Libya was unable to quickly construct a Weberian state capable of monopolizing the use of violence. This alone dramatically dimmed democratic prospects. Post-Qaddafi, Libya also fell apart as a nation-state – a single political community. Vendettas between rebel towns, and tribes versus perceived pro-Qaddafi towns and tribes, have contributed to the security crisis that post-Qaddafi governments have been unable to adequately address.

Bani Walid was one of the last pro-Qaddafi towns to fall to the rebels. Bani Walid had a historic rivalry with the city of Misrata, one of the first cities to rise up against Qaddafi (Bloomberg 2012). Fearing arrest and execution if they surrendered, many former Qaddafi top figures fled to Bani Walid after Qaddafi's fall. In 2012, local fighters in Bani Walid took control of the town and expelled the new government. In an act of revenge, they also captured, tortured, and killed one of the young Libyan rebels credited with capturing Qaddafi, Omran Shaaban (Reuters 2012). Shabaan was a native of Misrata. In late 2012, Libyan government forces (in the form of Libyan Shield Brigades) and allied militias from Misrata attacked Bani Walid to regain control and avenge Shabaan's murder. After roughly a month of fighting, pro-government forces retook Bani Walid.

Other groups viewed as supporters of Qaddafi, namely, the Warfalla, Magarha, and Qaddahfa tribes, have faced violence and have been largely excluded from the political process on the pretext that they worked with the former regime. Bani Walid is a Warfalla-dominated town. Many of the Magarha and Warfalla fled to the safety of the desert after Qaddafi's fall to oppose the NTC. The Islamic State built its base in Sirte, Qaddafi's hometown, partly based on the alienation of Sirte residents from the post-Qaddafi governments that viewed them with suspicion.

Post-Qaddafi, historic hostility between the Zintani and the Mashashiya also erupted into violence that the NTC/GNC governments could not control (Von Rohr 2011; Bassiouni 2013). According to Zintani tribal elders, in the 1970s Qaddafi gave the Mashashiya land belonging to the Zintani and other tribes in the Nafusa Mountain region, which led to Mashashiya support for Qaddafi during the February 17 Revolution (a charge many Mashashiya have denied). As a result of the war, most Mashashiya were forced to flee the Nafusa Mountain region and settle in refugee camps throughout the country. Zintani militias forced the entire village of Awaniyya to leave their homes. Other Mashashiya towns were looted, and their property was burned. Mashashiya detainees were tortured. Mashashiya who have attempted to return to their homes have been beaten and turned away. Given the power of the Zintani militia, the NTC/GNC governments did little to improve the post-Qaddafi fate of the Mashashiya.

The Qaddafi regime politically and culturally marginalized the Black African Toubou tribe, who are indigenous to southern Libya, Chad, and Niger. Since the end of the revolution, serious armed clashes have taken place between Arabs/Berbers and the Toubou in both Sabha and Kufra (Abdel-Meguid 2014). Militias, primarily from Misrata, sent to quell hostilities by the NTC/GNC government, have sided with Arab–Berber communities and worsened the conflict. The NTC/GNC also delegated security of much of Libya's southern border to the Toubou, who have used that power to engage in the lucrative smuggling of arms, people, and illicit goods.

In another sign of the anarchic conditions and national unity challenges in post-Qaddafi Libya, armed Salafi groups demolished Sufi teaching centers, shrines, mosques, and mausoleums in Tripoli, Misrata, and Zliten (Wehrey 2012). As with other violent Salafi activism, post-Qaddafi governments have not had the will or the capacity to quell Salafi violence toward Sufis (Cherstich 2012).

In Benghazi, an armed uprising by its residents, in coordination with army units and an air force loyal to General Haftar, have battled extremist Islamists groups (Ansar Al-Sharia and its allies) for much of the transition period (Eljarh 2014). As noted, Derna was once completely brought under the control of a mesh of extremist Islamists. Mostly loyal to al-Qaeda, some of them have pledged allegiance to the leader of ISIS in Iraq and Syria, Abu Bakr al-Baghdadi.

The people of Derna and Tobruk have claimed that, without Haftar's forces, no one else – including the Libyan state – would act to protect them from Islamic extremists. Seeing that the Libyan state and the international community had not even attempted to enter their city militarily and return Derna to government control, residents turned to Haftar for help. When UN Secretary General Ban Ki Moon demanded that Haftar halt his campaign against Islamists in Benghazi and elsewhere because they were not under the Libyan state's authority, one Benghazi resident responded: "To whom does Ban Ki Moon plan on leaving us? And what is his alternative to counter the [Islamic] terrorist groups in Benghazi?" (Eljarh 2014).

Democratic Consolidation: Political Pact

National unity and state capacity issues severely compromised hopes for sustaining a political pact or democratic bargain in Libya. After founding elections, Ali Zeidan of the "relatively" secular-oriented National Forces Alliance (NFA) formed a government (October 14, 2012–March 14, 2014). In an effort to forge the twin tolerations and quell Islamic–secular polarization, the NFA reached out to the Muslim Brotherhood's Justice and Construction Party (JCP) to form a unity government. It was rebuffed. Instead, the JCP turned to allied militias, which used force and intimidation to alter electoral results and help the Muslim Brotherhood take over the General National Congress (GNC).

In addition to Islamist–secular polarization in Libya, there is also a core conflict between local political actors and central authority. For democracy's sake, organized political forces in Libya have had to manage tribal, regional, and local cleavages that challenge the making of national and ideological parties in a country that had banned political parties for the previous 40 years.

Finally, as an added challenge to hopes for political parties striking a democratic bargain in Libya, a national rift has developed between revolutionaries, who did most of the fighting against Qaddafi and who fared worse under his rule, and groups that revolutionaries view as having benefited from Qaddafi's time in power and as being reluctant to make revolutionary changes in the country's political economy. The stakes in the oil-rich country are high enough to convince – up to 200,000 people after 20,000 actually engaged in combat – to join militias after the fact (Ahmida 2019).

The Ali Zeidan government and other political elites in Libya, then, have attempted – unsuccessfully to date and against stiff odds – to institutionalize political democracy in a country with major fissures: Islamist–secular, local–national (and regional), and revolutionary versus the status quo. At the same time, transitional elites in Libya have fared poorly in meeting the national unity and state capacity challenges that they were forced to address as soon as they took power.

Transitional elites in Libya took power without a modern state. To forge a military, security, and police apparatus capable of monopolizing violence, they appeased and attempted to integrate militias into the state apparatus. This created the worst of both worlds. The state and elected governments never gained control over the militias, and the militias – along with the national army and the MOI they penetrated – were unable to provide Libyans with peace, safety, and security. Instead, the militias have bled the state of its resources.

Bureaucratic capacity post-Qaddafi has remained weak:

At present, Libyan institutions mainly advance individual and city interests rather than the public good, and attempts to establish stable control over these government structures have so far failed. (Al-Shaheedi and Ezzedine 2019: 1)

In terms of national unity, Libyan transitional governments have also fared poorly. It is difficult to see serious effort to stich Libya together as a single political community when the state uses militias with vested interests as intermediaries in communal conflicts. Instead, communal conflicts have been weaponized. Armed brigades and militias target people of Tawergha, Mashashiya, and Black African origin. Amazighs are armed and determined to no longer be marginalized. Tribal supporters of Qaddafi – Qaddadhfa, Warfalla, and Magarha – have been politically marginalized and physically targeted by rival tribes. Regional interests – especially in Cyrenaica – have been appeased by transitional elites without due consideration of national political community.

By the end of 2014, rampant and rampaging armed groups paired with national disunity and a weak state ended serious progress toward a Libyan political pact in support of a democratic transition. Political parties and Independents, especially Islamist, had turned to militias to alter electoral outcomes and state policies. The competition for power began to take place outside the institutional framework. Armed groups began to fight over control of the ground and its resources: "Islamist, Misratan, Zintani, and federalist militias all used force or the threat of force to pressure the country's elected institutions, or to seize assets like border checkpoints, oil facilities, armories, ports, and airports" (Wehrey 2014).

By the end of 2014, two governments and two national military coalitions had emerged. Since then, a UN-led effort to unite the nation has faltered. A low-simmering conflict between the two armed coalitions is on the brink of a full-scale civil war. Many Libyans are pinning their hopes on a new national dialogue to peacefully manage a transition to a new political economy that can revive Arab Spring hopes for democracy, human rights, and socioeconomic justice. Others feel that strongman General Khalifa Haftar can at least deliver peace and stability, and are resigning themselves to the emergence of a military authoritarian regime.

Growing Islamist–Secularist Polarization

While political parties' inability to compromise and agree on a variety of conflicts has led to the failure of political pact-making in Libya, deficiencies in the development of the twin tolerations between Islamists and secularists has been as important a factor as any. Moderate and radical Islamist politicians, who used their associated brigades and militias to change policy and electoral results, carry most of the blame for this failure (Al-Sheikh 2015).

Despite the NFA's concerns about being labeled secularist and the steps it took to avoid the label (including appointing an inclusive cabinet), during Ali Zeidan's tenure as prime minister, Libya's Muslim Brotherhood party, the JCP, repeatedly attempted to remove Zeidan through a vote of no-confidence (finally succeeding in March of 2014). Eventually, the party's five ministers resigned from the Zeidan cabinet (Reuters 2014).

The JCP made alliances with Islamic extremists hostile to democracy and supported antigovernment militias, which interfered in the political process (Benotman et al. 2013). Instead of advancing the twin tolerations, Islamist militias and their supporters in the GNC forced through the Political Isolation Law (PIL), which effectively disqualified anyone involved in Qaddafi's regime from government, administration, and the armed forces. The law was passed while armed militias held the GNC under a military siege, blocked a number of other ministerial buildings in Tripoli, and actively intimidated individual members of the GNC (Mzioudet 2013). The net result and likely intention of the PIL was to achieve Islamist domination of the GNC, the exact opposite of the results of the July 2012 elections.

By the time subsequent elections were held in 2014, Islamist–secularist splits had largely aligned with the formation of rival governments in Tripoli (Islamists) and Tobruk (secularists). The Political Isolation Law forced many elected NFA members out of the GNC, including its president, Mohamed al-Magarief, and four ministers. As a result, the Muslim Brotherhood's JCP and its more extreme ally, the Islamist Loyalty to the Blood of the Martyr's bloc, which was led by Abdel Wahab al-Qayed (the brother of al-Qaeda's second-in-command, Abu Yahya al-Libi) increased their relative numbers within the GNC (Najm 2013). They voted in, as president, Nouri Abusahmain, a figure who was sympathetic to their Islamist agenda.

Once in control of the GNC, Islamists refused to relinquish power. According to the timeline established by the Temporary Constitutional Declaration, the General National Congress was supposed to step down on February 7, 2014 (Eljarh 2014). Instead, the Islamist-dominated GNC ratified a decision to extend its mandate to December 2014, despite the opposition of a large segment of the Libyan population critical of its inability to halt Libya's slide into chaos and lawlessness (News 24 2014). GNC members who supported the change argued that, because the country had not yet drafted a new constitution, there would be no legislative body to replace it (Eljarh 2014). Those who opposed the mandate extension argued that the GNC completely failed to meet milestones and deadlines, and that the legislature was unjustifiably clinging to power despite a poor record in leading and uniting the country through its transition.

As the standoff dragged on and Libya marked the third anniversary of the start of the February 17 Revolution that toppled Qaddafi, militias originating from Zintan, backed the NFA, took up a position against Islamists by calling on Parliament to hand over power by 9:00 p.m. local time on February 7. They said that legislators who refused to do so would be considered "usurpers" and would be detained (Trabzouni 2014).

Ultimately, by appealing to the Zintani militias' commanders to give political dialogue a chance and to allow new general elections to be held as soon as possible, UN special representative to Libya Tarek Mitri helped diffuse the conflict between Islamist and non-Islamist blocs in the GNC over the deadline of February 7, 2014 (Trend News Agency 2014).

Still, the Muslim Brotherhood called the militias' warnings a blatant use of force to impose a certain political point of view. Others simply called it a coup attempt. In support of Islamists, the powerful Misrata militias vowed to protect the GNC beyond the February 7 deadline (News 24 2014). NFA founder Mahmoud Jibril rejected the show of force, but he viewed it as a result of the GNC and the government's failure to fulfill their missions, adding that it was urgent for all sides to reach an agreement and hand over power to an elected body (Trend News Agency 2014).

In the midst of the standoff between Islamist and non-Islamist blocs over the dates of the GNC's mandate, Islamists successfully removed Prime Minister Zeidan from power through a no-confidence vote on March 11, 2014. Success finally came after the embarrassment of a cargo of oil being sold by Cyrenaican federalists without Zeidan's or the Libyan National Oil Corporation's authority.

Three days later, and despite a travel ban imposed due to corruption investigations, Ali Zeidan fled the country. After Zeidan's departure, the GNC struggled to identify a replacement capable of attaining the 120 GNC votes necessary to elect a new prime minister. On May 5, 2014, a televised vote took place for a prime minister candidate backed by the Islamist bloc, Ahmed Maetig (Al Jazeera 2014). Maetig, a businessman relatively unknown to the public, obtained 113 votes, at which point television service nationwide was interrupted. When it returned one hour later, Maetig had the 120 necessary votes. There were widespread protests from the NFA and the general public, but GNC President Nouri Abusahmain, a member of the Islamist bloc, approved the vote and declared Maetiq prime minister (HuffPost Maghreb 2014).

Rejecting the power move by Islamists, GNC Vice-President Ezzeddine Al-Awami and other members of the secular–liberal bloc declared the vote null and void and formally asked Abdallah al-Thinni, who had temporarily taken over the office after Zeidan's vote of no-confidence, to stay in power as prime minister until new elections for a new parliament could be held (HuffPost Maghreb 2014).

The vote to replace Zeidan with Maetig as prime minister essentially meant that Libya had two prime ministers, one for the Islamist and one for the non-Islamist bloc in the GNC. Associated militias once again thrust themselves into the standoff between Islamists and secularists, resulting in opposing militia coalitions, roughly parallel to the Islamist and secular–liberal blocs in Parliament, with Misrata supporting Islamists and Zintan supporting secularists.

On May 16, 2014, retired general Khalifa Haftar launched what he called Operation Dignity to dissolve the Islamist-dominated GNC (Al Jazeera 2014). He was joined by most of Libya's small army and air force, which had accused the GNC of diverting funds from regular forces to Islamist militias as well as to federalist forces in the east. The powerful Zintan militia also joined Haftar's coalition. They attacked the GNC, which made the Libyan International Airport in Tripoli – under their control since Qaddafi's fall in 2011 – a target of attacks by GNC supporters.

To battle Haftar's Operation Dignity, Islamist militias backing the GNC created the Libya Dawn coalition. To form Libya Dawn, a militia linked to the Muslim Brotherhood, the Libya Revolutionaries Operations Room (LROR), was joined by the hardline Islamist Ansar al-Sharia and most members of the Misrata-based militias that represented the most powerful single force in Libya (Al Jazeera 2014).

While Ansar al-Sharia has battled Operation Dignity, unlike the LROR they have dismissed democracy as a rhetorical goal, seeing their participation in armed force against NFA-supported militias as a necessary step to establish a *Sharia*-based political system.

As the opposing militia coalitions – Operation Dignity versus Libya Dawn – stood on the brink of an outright civil war, the GNC continued its struggle for a political pact. On May 25, 2014, the GNC set June 25, 2014, as the date for elections to replace itself with a new parliament, the House of Representatives (Reuters 2014). To reduce tensions, all candidates contested the election as individuals or Independents instead of running on party lists, though the results were tied to either secular or Islamist factions.

Secular forces won decisively, with Islamists winning only 30 seats. The GNC's Islamist bloc refused to accept the results. Misrata's militia took over Tripoli, drove the Zintan militia out of the airport, and forced the newly elected Parliament to leave Tripoli and set up government in a five-star hotel in Tobruk in Eastern Libya near the Egyptian border (Laessing 2014). Temporary Prime Minister Abdallah al-Thinni became the first Prime Minister of the House of Representatives, though the Tobruk lawmakers and their government can do little to enforce anything outside their limited enclave (Al-Arabiya 2014).

Notably, some close Libya observers do not view the Libya Dawn and Operation Dignity coalitions as primarily representative of a conflict between Islamists and secularists. Instead, they see a conflict between elites under Qaddafi (Operation Dignity) versus new elites that emerged during the revolution (Libya Dawn):

The new Libya is deeply divided. Two opposing camps are emerging from a fragmented political landscape, each including a wide range of interests. Representatives of forces presenting themselves as revolutionary seek root-and-branch renewal of the political and business elite to their advantage. They face a heterogeneous camp of established, moderate, and conservative forces that aim to draw a line under the period of upheaval and fear further loss of influence to the revolutionaries. (Lacher 2013a: 6)

The governments in Tobruk and Tripoli have dealt with each other much like independent countries, with the Tobruk government requiring special entry permits for its area on top of the normal Libyan visa (Laessing 2014). The Tobruk government has ceded a lot of power to ambitious General Haftar, accepting his Operation Dignity forces as the core of the new Libyan National Army. Western and central Libya are dominated by Operation Libya Dawn. Benghazi, lying between Tripoli and Tobruk, is being fought over by the two governments. The impoverished and neglected south is largely left alone, and is ruled by tribal, ethnic, and racial groups that fight among themselves. The militia coalitions from Operation Dignity and Operation Libya Dawn threaten each other and stand perched on the brink of full-scale civil war while UN-led negotiations continue.

In terms of the competition for real power in Libya, the UN reentered the political fray after the late 2014 shift, when militias, armed struggle, and direct control over parts of Libyan territory and its resources had largely replaced political power based on election results. Even the two main militia coalitions had their own Central Bank – where oil money is paid and government money is disbursed – and their own National Oil Corporation.

The international community initially backed the elected Tobruk government in Eastern Libya over the Government of National Salvation, a vestige of the General National Congress reimposed in Tripoli by the Islamist and Misratan forces of Libya Dawn. In 2015, under the auspices of the UN, representatives from throughout Libya met in Skhirat, Morocco. The Libyan Political Agreement (LPA) was signed on December 17, 2015.

The LPA's roadmap was based on the idea that a caretaker government accommodating the two parliaments and their allies could establish political stability, distribute fairly the benefits of the oil-based economy, and reintegrate militias under Libyan state control:

When, in January 2015, the UN launched the negotiations that would produce a Libyan Political Agreement by year's end, its aim was a power-sharing deal to surmount institutional and military fractures precipitated by a mid-2014 governmental crisis. The process…envisioned the creation of a unity government and eventually a new constitution and elections. A legitimate, sovereign government could restart oil production and exports, right the economy, begin demobilizing and reintegrating armed groups and call on the international community to root the Islamic State (IS) out of Sirte. (ICG 2016)

The LPA established a Presidency Council with members representing different political and geographical constituencies to serve as Libya's executive until the appointment of a Government of National Accord (GNA). Faiez al-Serraj, a member of the Tobruk House of Representatives (HOR) representing Tripoli, became Council president. Serraj was to become prime minister once the HOR ratified the LPA and approved a cabinet. The governments linked to the Tripoli and Tobruk parliaments were to be dissolved, and the HOR would stay as the legitimate parliament, while most members of the Tripoli-based GNC would be integrated into the consultative High State Council, a new body with a say in appointing top state posts (ICG 2016).

Nearly five years on, the Libyan Political Agreement has been a failure. Despite signing the agreement, the Tobruk-based HOR has not shifted loyalty from their "own" government to Serraj's "unity" Government of National Accord in Tripoli. They refuse to approve a cabinet that would make Serraj prime minister and limit Libya to one government. Haftar and his so-called national army have been especially hostile to the UN initiative.

However, the UN-backed Government of National Accord has done little better. It has failed in basic governance and is beholden to militia barons who have carved the capital into fiefdoms and plundered the state's coffers (Wehrey 2019). Instead of beginning the process of disarming militias and forming a true national army as envisioned in the LPA, the powerful Misrata militia, Tripoli militias, and some Islamist militias became the backbone of Serraj's GNA in Tripoli.

In essence, the conflict between rival parliaments in Tobruk and Tripoli and their associated governments has gradually become a stagnant conflict between LPA supporters and opponents, each heavily armed and both suspect in terms of their commitment to the greater good.

Haftar has been moving to end the stalemate. He and his Eastern-based NLA have taken control of the South and attacked Tripoli in an assault to take control of the West. However, that aggression has remobilized, in defense of the capital, Misrata and Islamist militias that served as part of Libya Dawn. There are no easy answers militarily. A full-scale civil war would be bloody and unpredictable. Haftar's momentum has been blocked, and most see the need for a new national dialogue – accepting the failure of the LPA – that includes armed groups.

Democratic Consolidation: Socioeconomic Pact

Libya has a rentier economy that is highly dependent on oil revenues. In rentier economies, oil revenues are controlled by the select few who control the state apparatus. The rest of society uses state revenues distributed by the state without any participation in the production of the revenue (Beblawi 1990). Shrewd, autocratic rulers in rentier states buy off dissent while also collecting the largest cut of petro-dollars. However, Qaddafi's rentier economy produced high unemployment and failed to modernize the economy and fully include the Eastern region of Cyrenaica in economic distribution (Mezran and Elarjh 2014). For that, Qaddafi paid a price.

Because it has a rentier economy that is heavily dependent on hydrocarbon exports, economic transitions that support democracy in Libya begin with the fair distribution of oil and natural gas wealth to all Libyans. Based on postconflict engagement between the International Financial Institutions (IFIs) and Libyan officials, economic transitions that will aid democratization also include the development of the private sector and a market economy able to produce inclusive growth and create employment.

There has been little room for economic development strategies. Since late 2014, violent conflict over Libya's immense oil wealth has structured political life more than efforts to consolidate political democracy. Haftar possibly attacked Tripoli to gain control over the Central Bank and the National Oil Corporation (ICG 2019). Militias and militia coalitions have rapaciously drained state coffers and viciously taken direct control of the ground and its resources.

Still, the economic challenges in Libya stretch beyond the oil economy. Rentier economies have weak agricultural and industrial sectors. Rulers of rentier economies are under pressure to diversify before their countries' hydrocarbon wealth runs out. In addition to distributing petro-dollars fairly, Libya's economy also needs to diversify and produce more jobs to change the socioeconomic conditions that contributed to the Arab Spring uprising. The International Monetary Fund (IMF) and the World Bank (WB) are engaging with Libya to meet the second goal by encouraging their leaders to implement a private-sector-driven market-based approach that produces inclusive growth, diversifies the economy, creates jobs, and (presumably) avoids the elite capture and crony capitalism that was emerging in Libya at the end of Qaddafi's rule:

A longer-term goal is to help develop the framework and institutions for a more diversified market-based economy, broadening the economic base beyond the oil and gas sector. The Bank's post-conflict engagement includes creating a more vibrant and competitive economy with a level playing field for the private sector to create sustainable jobs and wealth. It also includes transforming the management of oil revenues to ensure they are used in the best interests of the country and to the benefit of all citizens equally. (WB 2019)

Oil revenues in Libya are definitely not being used in the country's best interests and to the equal benefit of all citizens.

The management and division of oil revenue is the source of most conflicts in contemporary Libya. Armed groups are claiming their stakes all over the place partly to be in the strongest position possible when peace and security is restored and a national dialogue on the division and management of the country's oil wealth can take place. The status quo is characterized by resource competition in a context of delayed resolution of political strife and the persistence of internal division and inoperative institutions (WB 2019). The fragile situation is worsened by recurring clashes around oil terminals and in large cities, most of which aim to gain control over oil wealth (WB 2019).

Effective management of Libya's oil wealth begins with increasing productive capacity. In Libya, under Qaddafi, oil sector revenues constituted 65% of Gross Domestic Product (GDP), 96% of total exports, and 97% of government revenue. Daily oil production averaged 1.6 million barrels per day (bpd). However, due to political and military rivalries and the poor security situation in Libya, post-Qaddafi governments have found it difficult to manage to produce even 1 million bpd (WB 2019).

The devastating impact of Libya's multifactional conflict over oil production can be illustrated by the case of Ibrahim Jadhran, the commander of the Petroleum Facilities Guard (PFG) (Reed 2013). In 2013 Jadhran, a federalist that flirts with secession, shut down Libyan oil terminals and attempted to sell oil on behalf of Cyrenaica in Eastern Libya. He was turned away by the Libyan navy. In 2014, he was more successful until a tanker he had commandeered was intercepted by US Navy Seals. That event precipitated Prime Minister Ali Zeidan's ouster. In 2013, Jadhran's militia took over some terminals and suspended oil exports from them until 2016, reportedly costing Libya more than $100 billion, including repairing damage to oil infrastructure (Fetouri 2018). He was finally ousted by Khalifa Haftar and his LNA, another faction in the country's armed conflicts, who took over the oil ports.

In another political incident involving oil, an Amazigh (Berber) militia west of Tripoli shut down an important pipeline linking Libya to Sicily (Morabito 2013). The leader of the Berber militia, Adel al-Falu, explained: "We are stopping gas exports to the European Union to urge the General National Congress to recognize the Amazigh language."

In addition to political instability reducing oil production, the division of the country into two governments in 2014 has contributed to the poor management of oil revenues. The UN-backed Government of National Accord moved to Tripoli in 2015 without an army to protect it. Tripoli, Islamist, and Misratan militias took on that role. Those militias have increasingly taken over the "national" administration in Tripoli and have used their power to dramatically enrich themselves from it (Lacher and al-Idrissi 2018).

Institutional fragmentation has also harmed the efficient management of oil revenues. In 2014, after the government split, the Central Bank in Libya also split into two branches – one in Tripoli and one in Benghazi for the Eastern government. The branch in Tripoli, which is associated with the al-Serraj UN-backed Government of National Accord (GNA), has exclusive access to state funds accruing from oil sales (ICG 2019). However, the House of Representatives government in the East and Haftar's Libyan National Army (LNA) control most of the country's oil fields and export terminals (which are mostly located in the East). This is a stalemate in which the GNA and the Central Bank in Tripoli could squeeze the East and cut off funding to Haftar's troops. Yet, if backed into a corner, the LNA could take over the oil itself, possibly precipitating the partition of the country (ICG 2019).

Haftar and the HOR government in the East have also created their own National Oil Corporation (NOC), from which they have exported small amounts of oil, though international agreement to only buy from the Tripoli NOC has limited that initiative.

To pay for most of its administration and military, the Haftar-backed government in the East has drained commercial banks in the region, printed money, and manipulated exchange rates. They also have turned to foreign backers – Egypt, Saudi Arabia, and the UAE. The Central Bank in Tripoli also continues to pay for civil servants in the East and even Haftar's militias, though it has threatened to stop these practices.

Haftar possibly attacked Tripoli in April 2019 to take control of the Tripoli Central Bank and its NOC (ICG 2019). The persistence of armed conflict in general has limited the efficient use of oil revenues in Libya. In addition to concerns about using the public payroll to pay for militias that are not under state control, the public payroll is used as a stabilizing instrument – by increasing salaries and the state hiring more – in a context of multifactional conflict (WB 2019).

Obviously, the Libyan economy would benefit from unifying the central banks and NOCs. Doing so implies a political, military, and security settlement that would also enable the recovery of the oil sector and a return to exporting 1.6 million bpd.

Presumably, the cease-fire and national dialogue that everyone is calling for will include the economy and discussions of both the management of oil revenues for the benefit of all Libyans and the implementation of a private-sector-driven market-based approach to grow and diversify the economy while avoiding elite capture.

Democratic Consolidation: Transitional Justice, Human Rights, and Rule of Law Pact

Libya desperately needs an end to armed conflict, the disarmament of militias, the establishment of a national army and police, and a national dialogue to address challenges to its democratic transition. The UN's intervention is likely needed to mediate among armed groups, to facilitate disarmament, and to support the development of new military and security institutions (Ahmida 2019).

For the sake of democratic consolidation, Libya also requires transitional justice, national reconciliation, a greater respect for human rights, and the establishment of the rule of law, including judicial and security sectors that respect democratic norms.

During his four-plus decades in power, Qaddafi and his senior government and military and security officials committed heinous crimes and human rights abuses and absconded with hundreds of billions of dollars of state funds from oil exports. Recall that, in one day alone, over 1,200 imprisoned political dissidents were executed (HRW 2009). The victims and their families deserve justice, truth, and reparations through punishing individuals who perpetrated crimes against humanity and war crimes against them.

The country also needs national reconciliation. Post-Qaddafi, the enmity between the revolutionary groups and the pro-Qaddafi tribes and armed forces is probably Libya's greatest transitional justice and national reconciliation challenge. Among the revolutionary groups, there is a perpetual urge to avenge the physical and emotional damage inflicted under Qaddafi including extreme forms of torture, killing, and rape (Abrahams 2013). The Libyan government(s)'s lack of control over these militant groups who seek revenge indicates the difficulty of an effective reconciliation to end Libya's current stalemate. To establish the rule of law and respect for human rights, Libya needs judicial reforms. In Libya's difficult transition, the state's judiciary has been as weak and hollow as the army and the police. Under Qaddafi, Libya's justice system was characterized by corruption, political influence, weak judicial education, and the creation of parallel People's Courts staffed by regime loyalists charged with quashing political dissent (Mangan et al. 2014).

During and after the uprising against Qaddafi, court functions and state provision of justice were suspended then built up again at a glacial pace, leaving a vacuum partly filled by local militias and their councils, courts, and jails: "Independent armed groups assumed state functions, arresting, detaining and kidnapping individuals without oversight or accountability" (ICG 2013: 18). They also exercised informal supervision over local police stations tasked with conducting preliminary investigations, recording witness statements, and carrying out arrests to control crime (ICG 2013). In the absence of state courts, communities also turned to traditional mechanisms to resolve disputes – tribal leaders, wise men, and religious leaders.

The armed groups' interventions into Libya's justice system have been marred by arbitrary detentions, unauthorized interrogations, coerced confessions, torture, and other forms of ill treatment, including deaths in custody (Amnesty International 2012). A UN report in late 2013 declared that around 8,000 detainees were held in militia prisons two years after the formal end of the February 17 Revolution (All Africa 2013).

Armed brigades especially target people of Tawergha, Mashashiya, and Sub-Saharan African origin. After Qaddafi's fall, the whole population of Tawergha, estimated at 30,000, was driven out by Misrata militias; most were forced into poorly resourced camps in Tripoli and Benghazi (Amnesty International 2012). The Mashashiya community from the Nafusa Mountains faced a similar plight at the hands of Zintani militias. Foreign nationals from Sub-Saharan Africa face widespread abuse – if not arrested on a large scale on suspicion of being foreign mercenaries for Qaddafi, they are routinely rounded up from their homes by armed militias and accused of remaining in the country illegally.

The once popular *thuwars* ("revolutionaries") have also been accused of engaging in crimes themselves by a public hungry for the rule of law and a competent state police. Overall, the judicial sector in Libya since the revolution has left Libyans weak in the belief that a nominally democratizing regime can provide for their most basic concerns – the security of their family members and the provision of justice and dispute resolution. Petty crimes, rape, and assassinations are widespread eight years after the end of the revolution. In late December 2014, a keen Libya observer declared that "Libya [still] has no functioning courts, the militias run its prisons, and torture is widespread" (Wehrey 2014).

Libya's Political Isolation Law (PIL) also indicates a lack of balance in holding Qaddafi-era officials accountable while respecting due process and advancing national reconciliation. Libya's expansive PIL was implemented in part to provide an advantage for Islamists within the General National Congress. As discussed, militias aligned with the Muslim Brotherhood's Justice and Construction Party, and Misratan militias, stormed the GNC and ministries to make sure the law would be passed.

Libya's PIL also infringes on human rights including, obviously, the right to vote. By eliminating elected representatives from the GNC, it invalidated citizens' active right to vote and to be represented by a particular deputy, as well as the deputy's right to hold elected positions (Mzioudet 2013).

For all Libyans, the democratic promise of individual rights to life, due process, association, speech, and press have not been protected in a lawless context dominated by militias organized along ideological, religious, political, ethnic, tribal, racial, and sometimes purely criminal lines.

References

3News. 2011. "Libya: Zintan Withdrawal Rare Success for Rebels." *3News*, March 24. www.3news.co.nz/Libya-Zintan-withdrawal-rare-success-for-rebels/tabid/417/articleID/203851/Default.aspx.

Abdel-Meguid, A. 2014. "Tebu Tribe: Zidan Is Trying to Frame Us for the Country's Problems." *Al-Sharq Al-Awsat*, January 20. www.aawsat.com/home/article/20571.

Abrahams, F. 2013. "Why Have We Forgotten about Libya?" *Global Public Square*, March 25. www.globalpublicsquare.blogs.cnn.com/2013/03/25/why-have-we-forgotten-about-libya/.

Ahmida, A. A. 2005. *Forgotten Voices: Power and Agency in Colonial and Postcolonial Libya*. London: Routledge.

2019. "Social and External Origins of State Collapse, the Crisis of Transition, and Strategies for Political and Institutional Reconstruction in Libya." In S. J. King and A. M. Maghraoui, ed., *The Lure of Authoritarianism: The Maghreb after the Arab Spring*. Bloomington: Indiana University Press, pp. 236–263. doi:10.2307/j.ctvfc54tb.13.

Al-Arabiya. 2014. "Libya Torn between Two Parliaments." *Al-Arabiya*, August 25. www.english.alarabiya.net/en/News/middle-east/2014/08/25/Egypt-hosts-diplomats-at-Libya-conference-.html.

Al Jazeera. 2011 "The Martyr Who Settled the Battle of Benghazi." *Al Jazeera*, March 1.

2014. "Ahmed Maetig: The Youngest Prime Minister in Libya since the Revolution." *Al Jazeera*, June 5. www.aljazeera.com/news/middleeast/2014/06/libya-new-pm-promises-tackle-violence-2014636355949462.htm.

All Africa. 2013. "Libya: Thousands Detained in Libya Outside State Control." *All Africa*, September 24. www.allafrica.com/stories/201309241066.html.

Al-Manar. 2011. "Rebels in Tripoli under the NATO's Air Support." *Al-Manar*. August 22.

Al Riyadh. 2011. "The Death of Qaddafi: Libya Starts a New Era." *Al Riyadh*, October 21.

Al-Shaheedi, A. H. and N. Ezzedine. 2019. *Libyan Tribes in the Shadow of War and Peace*. Policy brief. The Hague: Clingendael Magazine, February 18. www.clingendael.org/publication/libyan-tribes-shadow-war-and-peace.

Al-Sheikh, M. 2015. "Libya: Strangled between the Presence of Violent Groups and an Unfinished Democracy." *Arab Future Journal*, 124–136.

Amnesty International. 2011. *Libya: Disappearances in the Besieged Nafusa Mountain as Thousands Seek Safety in Tunisia*. London: Amnesty International, May 27. www.amnesty.org/en/documents/MDE19/020/2011/en/.

2012. *Militias Threaten Hopes for New Libya*. London: Amnesty International, December. www.amnesty.nl/content/uploads/2016/12/libya_i_report_i_militias_threaten_hopes_for_new_libya_-_no_pic.pdf?x65391.

Anderson, L. 1986. *The State and Social Transformation in Tunisia and Libya, 1830–1980*. Princeton, NJ: Princeton University Press.

1999. "Introduction." In L. Anderson, ed., *Transitions to Democracy*, New York: Columbia University Press, pp. 1–13.

Ashour, O. 2012. "Libyan Islamists Unpacked: Rise, Transformation, and Future." *The Brookings Institution*, May 2. www.brookings.edu/research/libyan-islamists-unpacked-rise-transformation-and-future/.

Bassiouni, M. C. 2013. *Libya: From Repression to Revolution: A Record of Armed Conflict and International Law Violations, 2011–2013*. Leiden: Martinus Nijhoff Publishers.

Beblawi, H. 1990. "The Rentier State in the Arab World." In G. Luciani, ed., *The Arab State*. Los Angeles: University of California Press, pp. 85–98.

Benotman, N. et al. 2013. "Islamists." In J. Pack, ed., *The 2011 Libyan Uprisings and the Struggle for the Post-Qaddafi Future*. Basingstoke, UK: Palgrave MacMillan, pp. 191–228. doi:10.1057/9781137308092_8.

Bloomberg. 2012 "Libya Army in Heavy Fighting with Militias in Beni-Walid." *Bloomberg*. December 18. www.bloomberg.com/news/articles/2012-10-18/libya-army-in-heavy-fighting-with-militias-in-beni-walid.

Cadigan, L. T. and L. C. Prieston. 2011. "Returning Libya's Wealth." *SovereigNet*, n. d. www.sites.tufts.edu/sovereignet/returning-libyas-wealth/.

Charkow, R. 2011. "The Role of Tribalism in Libya's History." *CBC News*, March 1. www.cbc.ca/news/world/the-role-of-tribalism-in-libya-s-history-1.1045638.

Cherstich, I. 2012. "Persecution of Sufis in Libya Is a Relic of Qaddafi's Stratagem." *The National*, December 5. www.thenational.ae/persecution-of-sufis-in-libya-is-a-relic-of-qaddafi-s-stratagem-1.598646.

Clotter, P. 2010. "Rights Researcher Calls for Expanded Libyan Prisoner Compensation." *VOA News*, August 7. www.voanews.com/africa/rights-researcher-calls-expanded-libyan-prisoner-compensation.

Daragahi, B. 2011. "Joint Fight with Arabs against Kadafi Spurs Berber Hopes of Equality in Libya." *Los Angeles Times*, July 16. www.latimes.com/world/middleeast/la-xpm-2011-jul-16-la-fg-libya-berbers-20110717-story.html.

Davis, J. 1987. *Libyan Politics: Tribe and Revolution*. Berkeley: University of California Press.

Eljarh, M. 2014. "Libya: The Lesser of Two Evils." *Atlantic Council*, October 22. www.atlanticcouncil.org/blogs/menasource/libya-the-lesser-of-two-evils/.

Elmaazi, A. 2013. "Libyan Society Held Hostage to Trauma." *Al-Akhbar*, May 22. www.english.al-akhbar.com/content/libyan-society-held-hostage-trauma.

European Council on Foreign Relations (ECFR). 2014. "A Quick Guide to Libya's Main Players." *European Council on Foreign Relations*, n. d. www.ecfr.eu/mena/mapping_libya_conflict.

Fetouri, M. 2018. "What Can We Expect from Italy's Conference on Libya?" *Middle East Monitor*, November 8. www.middleeastmonitor.com/20181108-what-can-we-expect-from-italys-conference-on-libya/.

Freeman, C. 2013. "Saif Gaddafi Asks for Trial to Be Heard in Zintan rather than Tripoli." *The Telegraph*, September 19. www.telegraph.co.uk/news/worldnews/africaandindianocean/libya/10321188/Saif-Gaddafi-asks-for-trial-to-be-heard-in-Zintan-rather-than-Tripoli.html.

Global Security. 2014. "Qadhafi Era Opposition." *Global Security*, n. d. www.globalsecurity.org/military/world/libya/opposition.htm.

Grant, G. 2012. "Party Profile: The National Forces Alliance." *Libya Herald*, July 1. www.libyaherald.com/2012/07/01/party-profile-the-national-forces-alliance/#axzz61mhTugxr.

Haddadt, S. 2011. *The Role of the Libyan Army in the Revolt against Qadafi's Regime*. Doha: Al Jazeera Centre for Studies, March 16.

Haraf, B. and S. Al-Khalidi. 2012. "Bitar Haraf and Sulaiman Al Khaldi, 'Libya Tantafidu Didd 'Ansar Al Sharī'a Al 'Islāmiya Al Libiyah'." [Libya rises up against Ansar al-Sharia in Libya] *Libya Al-Mostakba*, n. d. www.libya-al-mostakbal.org/news/clicked/26359.

HuffPost Maghreb. 2014 "Libya: Two Ministers." *HuffPost Maghreb*, May 5.

Humans Rights Watch (HRW). 2006. "Libya: June 1996 Killings at Abu Salim Prison." *Human Rights Watch*. June 27. www.hrw.org/news/ 2006/06/27/libya-june-1996-killings-abu-salim-prison.

Human Rights Watch (HRW). 2009. "Libya: Free All Unjustly Detained Prisoners." *Human Rights Watch*, October 16. www.hrw.org/news/ 2009/10/16/libya-free-all-unjustly-detained-prisoners.

2013. "Libya: Wave of Political Assassinations." *Human Rights Watch*, August 8. www.hrw.org/news/2013/08/08/libya-wave-political-assassinations.

International Crisis Group (ICG). 2013. *Trial by Error: Justice in Post-Qadhafi Libya*. Report No. 140. Brussels: International Crisis Group, April 17. www.crisisgroup.org/middle-east-north-africa/north-africa/ libya/trial-error-justice-post-qadhafi-libya.

2016. *The Libyan Political Agreement: Time for a Reset*. Report No. 170. Brussels: International Crisis Group, November 4. www.crisisgroup .org/middle-east-north-africa/north-africa/libya/libyan-political-agreement-time-reset.

2019. *Of Tanks and Banks – Stopping a Dangerous Escalation in Libya*." Report No. 201. Brussels: International Crisis Group, May 20. www.crisisgroup.org/middle-east-north-africa/north-africa/ libya/201-tanks-and-banks-stopping-dangerous-escalation-libya.

Joffé, G. 2013. "Civil Activism and the Roots of the 2011 Uprisings." In J. Pack, ed.,*The 2011 Libyan Uprisings and the Struggle for the Post-Qadhafi Future*. Basingstoke, UK: Palgrave Macmillan, pp. 23–51. doi:10.1057/9781137308092_2.

Khalil, M. 2004. "Renaissance in North Africa: The Sanusiyyah Movement." In M. M. Sharif, ed., *A History of Muslim Philosophy*, Vol. 2. Delhi: LP Publications, pp. 1456–1480.

Lacher, W. 2011. "Families, Tribes and Cities in the Libyan Revolution." *Middle East Policy Council, Middle East Policy*, 18(4), 142–150. doi:10.1111/j.1475-4967.2011.00516.x.

2013a. *Fault Lines of the Revolution: Political Actors, Camps and Conflicts in the New Libya*. Berlin: German Institute for International and Security Affairs. www.css.ethz.ch/en/services/digital-library/publica tions/publication.html/164123.

2013b. "The Rise of Tribal Politics." In J. Pack, ed., *The 2011 Libyan Uprisings and the Struggle for the Post-Qadhafi Future*. Basingstoke, UK: Palgrave Macmillan, pp. 152–168. doi:10.1057/ 9781137308092_6.

2014. *Libya's Fractious South and Regional Instability*. Geneva: Small Arms Survey. www.smallarmssurvey.org/fileadmin/docs/R-SANA/ SANA-Dispatch3-Libyas-Fractuous-South.pdf.

Lacher, W. and A. al-Idrissi. 2018. *Capital of Militias: Tripoli's Armed Groups Capture the Libyan State*. Geneva: International Security Sector Advisory Team (ISSAT). June. www.issat.dcaf.ch/Learn/Resource-Library2/Policy-and-Research-Papers/Capital-of-Militias-Tripoli-s-Armed-Groups-Capture-the-Libyan-State.

Laessing, U. 2014. "Libya's Runaway Parliament Seeks Refuge in Tobruk Bubble." *Reuters*, October 2. www.reuters.com/article/us-libya-security-insight/libyas-runaway-parliament-seeks-refuge-in-tobruk-bubble-idUSK CN0HR1GO20141002.

Lamma, M. B. 2017. *The Tribal Structure in Libya: Factor for Fragmentation or Cohesion?* Paris: Fondation pour la Recherche Stratégique. www.frstrategie.org/web/documents/programmes/observatoire-du-monde-arabo-musulman-et-du-sahel/publications/en/14.pdf.

Lucas, R. 2011. "Libyan Rebel Stronghold Benghazi Rejoices after NATO Air Attack Zaps Gadhafi Forces." *Associated Press*, March 20. www .cleveland.com/world/2011/03/libyan_rebel_stronghold_bengha.html.

Mangan, F. et al. 2014. *Security and Justice in Post-Revolution Libya: Where to Turn?* Washington, DC: United States Institute of Peace, September 17. www.css.ethz.ch/en/services/digital-library/publications/publication.html/184173.

McQuinn, B. 2012. *Armed Groups in Libya: Typology and Roles*. Geneva: Small Arms Survey.

Memri. 2011. "Libyan Lawyer and Human Rights Activist Fathi Terbil: The People Who Succeeded in Toppling Al-Qadhafi's Regime Will Not Allow Others to Hijack the Revolution." *Memri*, March 14. www.memri.org/reports/libyan-lawyer-and-human-rights-activist-fathi-terbil-people-who-succeeded-toppling-al.

Metz, H. C. 1989. *Libya: A Country Study*. Washington, DC: Department of the Army.

Mezran, K. and M. Eljarh. 2014. *The Case for a New Federalism in Libya*. Washington, DC: The Atlantic Council, December 23. www.atlantic council.org/in-depth-research-reports/issue-brief/the-case-for-a-new-fed eralism-in-libya/.

Middle East Eye. 2016. "Islamic State in Libya: The Power of Propaganda." *Middle East Eye*, January 10. www.middleeasteye.net/news/islamic-state-libya-power-propaganda.

Mokhefi, M. 2011. *Gaddafi's Regime in Relation to the Libyan Tribes*. Doha: Al Jazeera Center for Studies. March 20.

Morabito, G. 2013. "Libya: A Great Economic and Political Opportunity for the Global Community." *Medea*, November 27.

Murray, R. 2012. "Libya's Tebu Tribe Hopes for Lasting Peace." *Al Jazeera English*, December 3. www.aljazeera.com/indepth/features/2012/11/20121118115735549354.html.

Mzioudet, H. 2013. "Failed Candidate for GNC Presidency Resigns His Seat." *Libya Herald*, June 26. www.libyaherald.com/2013/06/26/failed-candidate-for-gnc-presidency-resigns-his-seat/.

Najm, M. A. 2013. "Ali Zeidan on Libya's Struggles." *Al-Sharq Al-Awsat*, December 10. www.eng-archive.aawsat.com/michelabunajm/interviews/ali-zeidan-on-libyas-struggle.

Netto, A. 2011. "Muammar Gaddafi's 'Trophy' Body on Show in Misrata Meat Store." *The Guardian*, October 22. www.theguardian.com/world/2011/oct/21/muammar-gaddafi-body-misrata-meat-store.

News 24. 2014. "New Dispute Brewing in Unrest-Riddled Libya." *News 24*, February 6. www.news24.com/Africa/News/New-dispute-brewing-in-unrest-riddled-Libya-20140206.

Pack, J. and B. Barfi. 2012. *In War's Wale: The Struggle for Post-Gaddafi Libya*. Washington, DC: The Washington Institute for Near East Policy, February.

Pack, J. and H. Cook. 2015. "The July 2012 Libyan Election and the Origin of Post-Qadhafi Appeasement." *The Middle East Journal*, 69(2): 174–182. doi:10.3751/69.2.11.

Pack, J. et al. 2014. *Libya's Faustian Bargains*. Washington, DC: Atlantic Council, May 5. www.atlanticcouncil.org/in-depth-research-reports/report/libya-s-faustian-bargains-breaking-the-appeasement-cycle/.

Pusztai, W. 2012. "Libya – Perspectives for the Security Situation after the Elections." *Istituto per gli Studi di Politica Internazionale*, July 10. www.ispionline.it/it/pubblicazione/libya-perspectives-security-situation-after-elections-6693.

Rashad, M. 2011. "Libya Today: Omar Al-Mokhtar's Son Joins the Libyan Protestors in Benghazi." *Youm7*, February 21.

Reed, M. 2013. "No End in Sight for Libya's Oil Drama." *Atlantic Council*, September 11. www.atlanticcouncil.org/blogs/menasource/no-end-in-sight-for-libya-s-oil-drama/.

Reuters. 2011. "Libyan Minister Quits over Crackdown – Report." *Reuters*, February 21. www.reuters.com/article/libya-protests-resignation-idAFLDE71K1PJ20110221.

2014. "Libyan Islamist Party's Ministers Resign from Zeidan Government." *Reuters*, January 21.

Roth, R. 2011. "UN Security Council Approves No-Fly Zone in Libya." *CNN*, March 18. www.cnn.com/2011/WORLD/africa/03/17/libya.civil.war/index.html.

Rustow, D. 1970. "Transitions to Democracy: Toward a Dynamic Model." *Comparative Politics*, 2(3), 337–363. doi:10.2307/421307.

Shane, S. and J. Becker. 2016. "A New Libya, with 'Very Little Time Left.'" *New York Times*, February 27. www.nytimes.com/2016/02/28/us/politics/libya-isis-hillary-clinton.html.

Smith, G. 2011. "Small Rebel Victory Big Moment for Persecuted Berber Tribes." *The Globe and Mail*, April 21. www.theglobeandmail.com/ news/world/small-rebel-victory-big-moment-for-persecuted-berber-tribes/ article577334/.

Stephen, C. 2011. "Abdel Fatah Younis: From Gaddafi's Right-Hand Man to Libya's Rebel Leader." *The Guardian*, July 28. www.theguardian.com/world/2011/jul/28/abdul-fatah-younes-profile.

St. John, R. B. 2013. "The Post-Qadhafi Economy." In J. Pack, ed., *The 2011 Libyan Uprisings and the Struggle for the Post-Qadhafi Future*. Basingstoke, UK: Palgrave MacMillan, pp. 85–111. doi:10.1057/ 9781137308092_4.

Terrorism Research and Analysis Consortium. 2011. "Al-Zintan Revolutionaries' Military Council (ZMC)." *Trackingterrorism.org*, n. d. www.trackingterrorism.org/group/al-zintan-revolutionaries-military-council-zmc.

2012. "Ansar al-Sharia in Libya (ASL)." *Trackingterrorism.org*, n. d. www.trackingterrorism.org/group/ansar-al-sharia-libya-asl.

Trabzouni, A.-A. 2014. "Al-Qaqa and Al Sawa'k in Libya: Two Highly Skilled and Well-Equipped Militant Groups." *Al-Arabiya*, February 19.

Trend News Agency. 2014. "Libyans Vote for Constitutional Body amid Tension." *Trend News Agency*, February 20. www.en.trend.az/world/ arab/2244187.html.

Tripoli Post. 2011. "Nations' Feedback on Libyan Uprising." *Tripoli Post*. February 23.

United Nations (UN). 2011. "After Much Wrangling, General Assembly Seats National Transitional Council of Libya as Country's Representative for Sixty-Sixth Session." *United Nations*, September 16. www.un.org/press/en/2011/ga11137.doc.htm.

Vandewalle, D. 2006. *A History of Modern Libya*. Cambridge: Cambridge University Press.

Von Rohr, M. 2011. "Settling Old Scores: Tribal Rivalries Complicate Libyan War." *Spiegel Online*, July 26. www.spiegel.de/international/ world/settling-old-scores-tribal-rivalries-complicate-libyan-war-a-7766 95.html.

Wehrey, F. 2012. "The Wrath of Libya's Salafis." *Carnegie Endowment for International Peace*, September 12. www.carnegieendowment.org/sada/ 49364.

2014. "Ending Libya's Civil War: Reconciling Politics, Rebuilding Security." *Carnegie Endowment for International Peace*, September 24. www.carnegieendowment.org/2014/09/24/ending-libya-s-civil-war-rec onciling-politics-rebuilding-security-pub-56741.

2019. "A Minister, a General, and the Militias: Libya's Shifting Balance of Power." *New York Review of Books.* March 19. www.carnegieendowment.org/2019/03/19/minister-general-and-militias-libya-s-shifting-balance-of-power-pub-78632.

World Bank (WB). 2019. "Country Overview: Libya." *World Bank*, n. d., www.worldbank.org/en/country/libya/overview.

4 | Yemen

During the Arab Spring, Yemenis rose up to end President Ali Abdullah Saleh's decades-long – and despised – crony-capitalist authoritarian regime. Their demands for democracy, dignity, respect for human rights, and socioeconomic justice were inspiring. A Yemeni woman, Tawakkol Karman, shared the Nobel Peace Prize in 2011.

Aware of the challenges of democratic consolidation, Yemenis organized a National Dialogue Conference (NDC) at the outset of their transition with committees assigned to address major challenges that could derail their hopes for democratic transformation including:

- A national unity and state-building pact: (especially establishing the state's monopoly of legitimate violence);
- A national pact extricating the military from politics;
- A political pact or democratic bargain among political parties representing all of the country's major factions;
- A new socioeconomic pact; and
- A pact establishing transitional justice, human rights, and the rule of law.

Ultimately, the will of the people, idealism, and negotiated national efforts to address fundamental challenges were not enough to prevent the derailment of Yemen's democratic transition. Instead, episodic violence during the transition turned into a civil war – with Saudi Arabia, and to an extent Iran, backing either side. During the war, the Houthis, leaders of a Zaydi branch of Shia Islam, may be attempting to use force to reestablish their Imamate (897–1962). Southern Yemenis, for their part, seem committed to secession.

In recent months, a United Nations (UN)-backed peace process has reduced some but not all armed conflict in Yemen. However, after four years of war, Yemenis are still enduring the world's worst humanitarian crisis (UN 2019). Seventy thousand Yemenis have died in their civil war (Al Jazeera 2019). Yemen is the poorest country in the Arab world. Its economy is on the verge of collapse, having contracted about 50% since conflict began in 2015. The country is on the brink of famine. Eighty percent of the population – of 27 million people – need humanitarian assistance, including 14.3 million who are in acute need. More than 20 million Yemenis are food insecure, including 10 million that are starving, while war disrupts the provision of humanitarian assistance.

Most Yemenis are deprived of sanitation, clean water, and health care, as the death toll from preventable diseases mounts. Over three million people are displaced. Due to bombings, the infrastructure – hospitals, roads, clinics, universities, factories, and homes – is in ruins. Radical Islamists have flourished. Daily, Yemenis face serious risks to their safety, well-being, and basic rights, including indiscriminate aerial attacks and artillery shelling of civilians. Law and order is a dream.

How did things go so wrong?

Yemen entered the Arab Spring with more challenges to democratic consolidation than most autocratic countries would face. First, more than anything, nation-state issues derailed Yemen's democratic transition. Second, an unusually large number of sharp conflicts made it difficult for political parties to forge a democratic bargain or political pact among all of the country's major factions. Third, Yemen is the poorest country in the Arab world, making it difficult to forge a new socioeconomic pact. Fourth, Yemen's military had dominated politics prior to the Arab Spring, making its extrication more difficult than for militaries in more civilian-led regimes. Fifth, the path to establishing the rule of law, transitional justice, and respect for human rights in Yemen was exceptionally difficult.

The deficits were too steep to be successfully addressed by committees during the National Dialogue Conference. Instead, the transition – which took place without the state's monopoly of violence – sparked violence. Armed groups sought to improve their bargaining positions, dictate the new political rules of the game, and prepare for the possibility of "plan B" if negotiations failed (Longley-Alley 2013), which they did in March 2015, when the Houthi armed movement and its allies marched south and conquered the capital. This forced the interim government's president, Abdrabbuh Mansur Hadi, to flee. In response, a coalition led by Saudia Arabia launched military operations to restore the "Yemeni" government.

Fully understanding the poor outcomes of Yemen's democratic transition begins with taking into account that until recently there were two Yemens and that the southern separatist movement is now gathering steam.

North Yemen

A single nation-state within the borders of what is now the Republic of Yemen (ROY) had never existed before 1990 (Lackner 2014). A traditional Imamate led by a descendant of the Prophet Muhammad intermittently ruled North Yemen for more than a thousand years, at times extending their control across South Yemen as well.[1] The Imamate was based on Zaydi Islam, a subset of Shia Islam that is considered closest to Sunni orthodoxy. The Yemeni state of Zaydis was founded in 893.[2] In 1962, a military coup ended the Imamate. This was followed by a period of foreign intervention and a bloody civil war that culminated in the rise of a series of military rulers, including Ali Abdullah Saleh, who took power in 1978 and held on to it until February 27, 2012.

State-builders in North Yemen have had to confront and accommodate the Arabian Peninsula's tribal system. Historically, the tribe has served as the central sociopolitical unit and basis for individual and collective identity in the absence or weakness of the state. A modern state has never been fully developed. Instead, it has been argued that the various states in the history of what is now the Republic of Yemen should be viewed as "political fields" (i.e., arenas in which diverse actors compete for influence and resources) (Rabi 2015).

In North Yemen, the first political field or state beyond tribes was centered on the learned Zaydi Imams, who claimed descent from the Prophet Muhammad through his son-in-law and daughter, Ali and Fatima, respectively. Zaydi Imams arbitrated among tribes, collected taxes, and claimed dominion over wide swaths of territory that crossed tribal lines.

According to Paul Dresch's account, in 893 certain Yemeni tribes invited Yahya b. al-Husayn al Rassi, a *sayyid* (descendant of the

---

[1] There were periods of Ottoman rule as well. On nation-state building in Nort Yemen's Imamate, see Dresch (1989); Rabi (2015); and Brehony (2015).
[2] Uzi Rabi (2015: 284) provides the date 897.

Prophet) to intervene in their affairs as an arbitrator (Dresch 1989, 158). Upper Yemen at that date was tribal, and two families were particularly prominent: the al-Du'am of Bakil and the al-Dahhak of Hashid. The tribal confederations around these two families were named the Bakil Confederation and the Hashid Confederation. Those names have been retained for over a millennium. The Bakil Confederation is the largest tribal confederation in contemporary Yemen; the Hashid Confederation is the second largest and the most influential.

Zaydi Imams over the centuries ruled with the Bakil and Hashid confederations' support, along with that of various other lesser tribes and tribal groups. Based in a mountainous region that has served as a natural defensive barrier, the Bakil and Hashid have never been completely subjugated to any supratribal authority. It has been inconceivable for any ruler to control Yemen for extended periods without the support of the heads of these two tribal confederations (Rabi 2015).

From the outset, the Zaydi Imamate was a tribal state that sprawled across a broad territory. However, this was not Weberian state or a full nation-state. Talking about the Imamate and confederations in Yemen, Uzi Rab maintains the following:

In most cases, these states had limited resources and a simple system of administration based on personal relations. These states were mainly concerned with the application of religious law and tax collecting; and thus their control was nominal. Tribes enjoyed a discernible degree of autonomy in their own affairs and maintained tribal militias. (Rabi 2015: 358)

At times in Yemen's history, tribal or tribal confederation heads (*sheikhs*) have administered and taxed regions outside their home territory, thereby vying with imams as state-builders. The most prominent *sheikh*, historically speaking, was Ali Qasim al-Ahmar of the Hashid Confederation (Dresch 1989).

In addition, various *sadah* (other claimed descendants of the Prophet) have competed with each other for the role of Imam in North Yemen. In 1889, the modern Zaydi Imamate – the Mutawakkilite Kingdom of Yemen – was established by the Hamid al-Din family, which had been dominant in Yemeni politics for over a thousand years (Rabi 2015). The dynasty lasted until a coup in 1962 and had survived struggles for power against the Ottomans, the British, other *sadah*, and insubordinate tribes (including the historically loyal Hashid confederation at times). The Hamid al-Din Imams bargained with the tribes as much as they ruled them (Rabi 2015). They took advantage of intra-tribal conflicts, using coercion, kidnapping, bribery, and the cultivation of religious affinity to assert their power. Their nominal rule outside the sedentary tribes around Sanaa was dependent upon the loyalty of *sheikhs* and the *sadah*.

Initially, the imams created military units that were based on tribes instead of building a modern army. However, in 1943 Imam Yahya bin Husayn bin Muhammad (in power from 1904 to 1948) took on the role of state-builder. He abolished the old army in favor of a standing army – some members of which were trained in Iraq for this purpose – that could better serve him in establishing control over the state and the tribes (Willis 2018). He also improved the state bureaucracy by expanding the scope of administrative functions and by appointing his sons as governors and supervisors of old and new institutions.

To improve coercive state powers, Imam Yahya created a unit of career soldiers, the Victorious Regular Royal Army. They were directly subordinate to him personally. Most of those who enlisted were Hashid and Bakil tribesmen. He also established a special unit of the royal army to serve as his personal guard. The new armed forces also engaged in law enforcement, tax collection, and security functions, which were aimed at extending the Imam's authority over the tribes. Still, tribes throughout the country maintained arms and the capacity to act as militias.

When it existed, the tribes' subordination to central rule under Imam Yahya was evident from the payment of taxes. In principle, tribal heads collected taxes for central rule and saw the Imam as a spiritual and political leader as long as he ruled in accordance with Islamic morals and values. In addition, the Imam served as a mediator between rival groups.

Before his efforts to create a modern state, Imam Yahya attempted to preserve the Zaydi Imamate's traditional tribal Islamic character. He sought to preserve the status quo against the forces of change and modernization that were occurring throughout the Arab world.

Inevitably, however, modernizing influences penetrated North Yemen. An Arab Cold War between revolutionary republics and conservative monarchies engulfed the region. Yemeni students in Egypt were exposed to Nasserist secular and socialist Arab nationalism, which inspired the formation of the Free Yemenites movement

(Al-Abdin 1979). Yemenis were also attracted to the teachings of the Muslim Brotherhood. At one point, Yemen's branch of the Muslim Brotherhood conspired with the Free Yemenites to overthrow the Imamate (Al-Abdin 1979). In addition, some army officers sent to Iraq for training as part of Yahya's decision to establish a standing army returned with revolutionary ideas of their own.

Imam Yahya was assassinated in 1948. Ahmad Bin Yahya, his first-born son, was appointed successor. Imam Ahmad faced two coup attempts that he narrowly averted with the support of northern tribes. Despite their support for Imam Ahmad in the 1948 and 1955 coup attempts, the northern Zaydi tribes had reservations about his rule (Orkaby 2017). While they preferred the Imam to the reformist opposition, they resented Ahmad's effort to reduce their autonomy. Their conflicts came out into the open when Ahmad fell ill in 1959 and went to Italy for treatment, leaving his first-born son, Muhammad al-Badr, to rule in his place (Orkaby 2017).

The Hashid and Bakil tribes immediately challenged al-Badr's rule. To appease them, al-Badr allocated large financial royalties to the tribal heads of the two confederations. Military officers also demanded "their share," but a sudden return from Italy by Ahmad led to the suppression of the revolts.

During his reign, Imam Ahmad took defensive state-building measures (Rabi 2015). In 1960, he created a national army of 20,000 men as a counterweight to hostile tribes who had come to view him as a symbol of central rule that sought to restrict their power. To combat revolutionary Arab nationalist ideology that cast his Imamate as an anachronism and hindrance to the Arab revolution, he strategically joined the United Arab Republic that unified Egypt and Syria from 1958 to 1961.

Still, diverse tribal opposition signaled the oncoming end of the rule of the Hamid al-Din family (Rabi 2015). Hashid tribesmen turned against Imam Ahmad. In this revolutionary atmosphere, Yemen dissolved into tribal warfare. A tribal bloc coalesced in opposition to the *al-sadah* notables and proposed an imam from their own ranks. Urban officers and the educated middle class supported a different tribal bloc, which was also seeking to depose Imam Ahmad.

The end came quietly but peacefully for Imam Ahmad. He died in his sleep on September 19, 1962. His eldest son, Muhammad al-Badr, was proclaimed Imam and King in his place. However, only a week into his reign the coup that ended the Hamid al-Din family dynasty was executed. Coup leader and former head of the Imam's palace guard, Abdullah al-Sallal, declared the former Imamate in North Yemen a republic under his presidency.

The Civil War

After the coup, continuing conflicts between Royalists and Republicans led to a civil war (1962–1970) in the newly formed Yemen Arab Republic (Rabi 2015). Deposed Imam Muhammad al-Badr rallied northern Shia tribes in an attempt to retake power. These Zaydi tribes recognized that the Republican regime sought to create a new order that would relegate them to the sidelines of Yemen's political arena. The new rulers had proclaimed their desire to implement wide-ranging social and administrative reforms that threatened the tribes. While a small number of tribesmen and tribal groups – including the leading *sheikh* of the Hashid Confederation, Sheikh 'Abdullah al-Ahmar – joined the Republicans, the civil war largely ended the estrangement between the northern tribes and the Imamate.

The Yemeni civil war that developed after the 1962 coup became a critical component of the Arab Cold War between monarchies and emerging Arab socialist republics (Orkaby 2017). Jordan, Saudi Arabia, and Britain supported the Royalist side. The Egyptian president, Gamal Abdel Nasser, supported the Republicans with as many as 70,000 Egyptian troops. The war officially ended with the Compromise of 1970, a political agreement between the Republican and Royalist factions. The agreement led to a Republican government that incorporated members from the Royalist faction, but not the royal family.

Like the imams, Abdullah al-Sallal and the other officers who took part in the coup struggled to create a state that extended sovereignty over the entire country and provided security and services. To do so, they were forced to seek northern tribes' support and to promise them that their privileges would not be violated (Orkaby 2017).

In 1967, Abdullah al-Sallal was deposed in a military coup. Between 1967 and 1978, Presidential Council members (judges mostly) and military coup leaders alternated in power (Orkaby 2017). The tension between Royalists and Republicans and between attempts to maintain a tribal Islamic state and attempts to build a modern state continued.

On July 17, 1978, after the assassination of his mentor General Ahmad bin Hussein al-Ghashmi, Major Ali Abdullah Saleh was appointed as the new president of the Yemen Arab Republic, a position that he would hold for more than 30 years. A Zaydi, Saleh hailed from the Sanhan tribe, a minor tribe in the Hashid Confederation that had traditionally provided the Imam's army with soldiers, though Saleh himself had fought valiantly in the civil war on the side of the Republicans (Rabi 2015).

Ali Abdullah Saleh came to power based on a 1978 "power-sharing" agreement with leading tribal and military figures (Global Security 2019). Sheikh Abdullah al-Ahmar, who headed the Hashid Confederation, and Brigadier General Ali Mohsen, Commander of the Northeastern Military District – and reputedly the most powerful military man in the land – were guaranteed great influence over presidential decision-making, including the naming of Saleh's successor from among their ranks (Rabi 2015). Beyond the covenant with General Mohsen and the Sheikh, Saleh also ruled by putting his relatives and confidants in the most important military and administrative institutions.

To broaden his support beyond the military, Saleh undertook several initiatives (Rabi 2015). He issued a national charter, which called for the expansion of political participation. In conjunction with the charter he established a Committee for National Dialogue. In 1982, he held elections for a newly established General People's Congress (GPC). The GPC was composed of 75 members and was headed by President Saleh. Its members stood for elections every four years. Although the GPC was not initially founded and presented as a political party, in effect it became the ruling party of the Yemen Arab Republic.

South Yemen

Tribes in the south are smaller and less cohesive than the tribes in the north of Yemen and were never dominated by powerful tribal confederations like the Hashid and Bakil (Rabi 2015). The southern population is also predominantly Sunni-Shafi, not Shia-Zaydi. Throughout most of Yemen's history, the Shia-Zaydi imams of Northwest Yemen ruled over the Sunni-Shafi population. Where their power held sway, the Shafis recognized the Imam's right to rule but did not accept his religious authority. However, by the time the British arrived in the nineteenth century, the tribes of what became South Yemen were organized in independent sultanates, emirates, and sheikhdoms (Brehony 2015).

British rule in South Yemen began in 1839, when they established a military base in the strategic seaport of Aden, which was subsequently put under the direct control of the government of British India (Rabi 2015). The goal was to stop pirate attacks against British shipping to India. At the time, Aden was surrounded by a hinterland in which *sadah* and *sheikhs* ruled small polities. The British attempted to organize these small polities in a manner similar to what would, a decade later, become the United Arab Emirates (UAE). The Federation of Arab Emirates of the South was established in 1959. By 1962, there were 15 states in the federation and the name was changed to the Federation of South Arabia.

As the British attempted to establish the Federation of South Arabia in the 1960s, fighting from the North Yemen civil war spilled over into the South. Gamal Abdel Nasser and his Egyptian and Yemeni nationalist supporters attacked the British hold on the South (Rabi 2015). As pan-Arabism and Arab socialism spread into South Yemen, the British and traditional Emirs feared losing power and control over the region.

The battle against the British and supporting *sadah* and *sheikhs* in South Yemen was defined in terms of first a decolonization struggle and then a class struggle, both with tribal undertones (Rabi 2015). The Yemeni nationalists in the South had high expectations and grand visions that did not include the perpetuation of traditional statelets linked to British power. Explicitly political movements emerged in Aden from trade-union-related activities and the influence of Arab nationalism.

Two separate groups, who ultimately failed to overcome their differences, became the dominant organizations combating British rule in South Yemen. (Brehony 2015). The Front for the Liberation of Occupied South Yemen (FLOSY) was the descendant of the Aden trade union movement and was closely allied with Nasserist Arab nationalism and socialism. The National Liberation Front (NLF), a Marxist paramilitary faction of Arab nationalism, was led by rural young people. The NLF won the battle against its rival and is the main ancestor of the Yemeni Socialist Party (YSP), which took over after British departure.

Beginning in 1963, the NLF and FLOSY joined the armed struggle against the British. The NLF's strength in rural areas, and its defeat of FLOSY in battles in Aden, persuaded the British to hand over power to the NLF when it departed the country in 1967 (Lackner 2015). Within two years of independence, the NLF/YSP set up the only socialist state in the Arab world, renaming the country the People's Democratic Republic of Yemen (PDRY). Supported by the Soviet Union and China, the PDRY had difficult relations with its neighbors on the Arabian Peninsula.

Within 23 years of its founding, the PDRY would unite with the Yemen Arab Republic to form the Republic of Yemen.

The Republic of Yemen

In 1990, the leaders of the Yemen Arab Republic (North Yemen) and the People's Democratic Republic of Yemen (South Yemen) merged the two states into the Republic of Yemen (ROY). Ali Abdullah Saleh and other GPC leaders in the North had been facing a growing Islamist current and initially sought in the YSP a more secular-oriented ally (BTI 2014). The YSP, led by Ali Salim al-Beidh, looked to unification partly because it had literally gone bankrupt without the support of the Soviet Union, which collapsed in 1989. In addition, there was broad popular support for unification in both North and South Yemen (Lackner 2015).

The ROY under Saleh fashioned its own form of crony-capitalist rule. It was an authoritarian regime with a façade of multiparty politics, a narrow ruling coalition, and a progressively corrupt, patronage-based economic system. Politically, while opposition parties could not realistically expect to win power, the authoritarian regimes of North and South Yemen sought to advance their varying interests after unification via multiparty political institutions that made the Republic of Yemen the most pluralistic regime on the Arabian Peninsula in the early 1990s (BTI 2014).

The Yemen Unity Constitution was ratified in 1991. It introduced new democratic elements such as multiparty parliamentary elections, an unprecedented level of press freedom, and a Presidential Council (BTI 2014). Parliamentary elections were held in 1993. This was the resulting parliament:

- GPC: 143
- YSP: 69
- Islah/Yemeni Congregation for Reform (YCR): 63
- Bathists: 6
- Nasserists Unionist People's Party: 3
- al Haq: 2
- Independents: 15

Islah's strong showing was particularly surprising and changed the dynamics of unification (BTI 2014). The newly formed conservative Islamist party was led by Yemen's most influential tribal figure, Sheikh Abdullah al-Ahmar, as a religious alternative to the secular GPC and YSP. Election results produced a coalition government of the GPC, the YSP, and the newly formed Islah (YCR).

Major conflicts between North and South Yemen, which would lead to a brief civil war in 1994, began shortly after unification (BTI 2014). South Yemen contained at most 30% of the population, but the YSP had hoped for a 50–50 sharing of power with the GPC after unification. From the YSP's point of view, other issues also contributed to unification regrets. The exploitation of oil reserves on former PDRY territory and other political decisions that seemed to favor the North intensified distribution conflicts among the political elite.

In May 1994, leaders of the GPC and YSP entered into open warfare. Ali Abdullah Saleh and the Northern leadership used its own military and militias made up from Northern tribesmen and militant Islamists to defeat the South in July 1994.

The 1994 war led to a postwar coalition government of the GPC and YCR (Islah). The two parties amended the Constitution. The Presidential Council was abolished, increasing Saleh's power. *Sharia* was made the sole source of legislation, an act along with others that set back the progress that women had made in South Yemen (Lackner 2015). Press freedom was restricted. Political parties and nongovernmental organizations (NGOs) faced repression, and the regime silenced critical voices by labeling them separatists.

In 1997, parliamentary elections were held, but the YSP boycotted them because its assets had been confiscated in 1994. Yemen's first direct presidential elections were held in 1999. Having boycotted the 1997 parliamentary elections, the YSP was barred from nominating a candidate and Islah (YCR) supported the incumbent president, Saleh, who won 96.2% of the vote. Constitutional amendments in 2001, accepted by referendum, extended the terms of the president and the Parliament. But these also weakened the Parliament's position vis-à-vis the executive. Parliamentary elections were held a third time in 2003. Saleh's GPC won 229 of 301 seats.

Overall, the period from the end of the 1994 civil war until the eruption of the Arab Spring in 2011 was characterized by a gradual restriction of pluralism, a narrowing of political freedoms, and the increasing concentration of wealth (Lackner 2015). President Saleh began to monopolize political control with a small group of supporters composed of a shrinking tribal base, relatives, and close associates mostly from his hometown of Sanhan (Lackner 2015).

To limit Saleh's and the GPC's increasing dominance, in the 2000s the Yemeni Socialist Party (YSP) and Islah, along with some smaller parties, built a common platform of opposition, the Joint Meeting Parties (JMP) (BTI 2014).

The JMP supported Faisal Bin Shamlan against Saleh in the 2006 presidential elections. Shamlan officially won 20% of the vote. Between 2006 and 2011, the government and opposition, under pressure from external actors, opened up negotiations on political reforms, but they did not produce any positive results. Parliamentary elections had not been held since 2003 when the Arab Spring erupted.

The Yemen economy under Saleh before the Arab Spring had been distressing for the majority in a number of ways.[3] In a country of 27 million people with a per capita GDP of US$1,394 in 2010, the country was one of the poorest in the Arab world. The World Food Programme estimated unemployment at 35%. Half the population lived in poverty, and half the country's children suffered from chronic malnutrition. One-third of the population as a whole suffered from acute hunger. Water scarcity was a source of major disputes and conflicts. The country's renewable water supply was being mined at an unsustainable rate. The people's hopes of Yemen's economy becoming an oil- or gas-wealthy rentier economy, like those of the GCC (Gulf Cooperation Council) countries surrounding them, were dashed by the relatively small amounts available to be produced per day in the country (although the export of oil and, to a lesser degree, natural gas was the main source of state income).

---

[3] On the Yemeni economy under Saleh, see Lackner (2014: 15–18).

Industry and services developed slowly under Saleh. The industrial sector was small, consisting mainly of the processing of imported food concentrates, while services – including the military – accounted for 50% of GDP. The potential income from tourism, especially cultural tourism, had been inhibited by security concerns. Fifty-five percent of the labor force was engaged in agriculturally related activities, but they produced only 8% of GDP. Micro-landholdings, low livestock supplies, and weak rainfall levels in a sector dominated by rain-fed crops kept much of the country's predominantly rural population struggling to attain incomes capable of maintaining typically large Yemeni households.

Rural households' main income derived from the wages earned by young men who traveled to towns and cities, where they worked as casual unskilled laborers in jobs ranging from building work to hocking secondhand goods on the street.

Yemen's dire objective economic conditions – high unemployment, ongoing drought, low educational standards (39% illiteracy for those over 15 and 70% for women), limited quantities of oil and gas to export, inadequate infrastructure, and declining income from remittances (Yemeni workers sending money back from Saudi Arabia and other GCC countries) – were compounded by recurring political crises and patronage politics, which allotted most of the benefits of the economy to the wealthy and powerful few (Longley-Alley 2010). The country has been following a neoliberal economic development model that had failed to reduce poverty, inequality, or corruption.

Outside the income from remittances sent or brought home by Yemeni workers in other countries, Yemen's economy under Saleh has been described as an economy based on networks of patronage with identifiable rules of inclusion, exclusion, rewards, and punishments (Longley-Alley 2010). Upon taking power, Saleh immediately placed his close relatives and members of his Sanhan tribe in powerful and high-paying military and security positions. Saleh also incorporated influential social elites, particularly tribal *sheikhs*, into networks of patronage through the distribution of government posts, preferential access to private sector opportunities, and direct payments. Over the course of his rule, Saleh also manipulated access to import licenses so as to favor certain *sheikhs*, who used them to emerge as tribal business elite or sold them to traditional businessmen for a profit.

Similar to Egypt, the military became a major economic actor under Saleh. The Yemen Economic Corporation (YEC, formerly the Yemen Military Economic Corporation, or YMCO), a state-run organization originally established to provide subsidized goods to soldiers, expanded dramatically under Saleh (Longley-Alley 2010). After he came to power, he used it to compete with civilian businesses without any transparency, auditing, or accountability (Noman and Sorenson 2013).

Under Saleh's instruction, the "state" took over the ownership of most profitable public companies and most fertile land (Longley-Alley 2010). It took over thousands of hectares in different agricultural areas, including most landholdings from Imamate times. It then expanded from farming to retailing, packing, and refrigeration. Saleh used the Yemen Economic Corporation's (YEC) money tap to fund the country's most thuggish militias, including the ones he ordered to confront the 2011 uprising. Also, similar to Egypt, security sector budgets lacked transparency and civilian oversight. There was a constitutional article that banned the monitoring of defense and security budgets; the Ministry of Defense monitored the defense budget and the Ministry of the Interior controlled intelligence and internal security funds.

The president's networks of patronage were also anchored by oil production and diesel subsidies (Longley-Alley 2010). Oil revenues under Saleh comprised 90% of the country's export revenue and approximately 75% of the central government's budget. Saleh used the energy sector as his major source of patronage distribution. It paid the lion's share of salaries for civil servants and the military. The president also distributed the rights to sell the Yemeni government's share of extracted crude oil to prominent clients.

Saleh made the GPC an important component of the patronage system (Longley-Alley 2010). GPC membership became a sign of loyalty to the regime and an expected part of reciprocity if one intended to be included in the president's patronage networks. GPC membership was a prerequisite for political and civil service appointments.

Saleh's patronage system included elites from a variety of overlapping groups: tribal elites, religious leaders, traditional merchants, military officials, and technocrats (Longley-Alley 2010). Religious leaders included prominent *sadah* and religious leaders associated with the Muslim Brotherhood or the Salafi movement. Technocrats who possessed the skills necessary to manage the modern parts of the state and the economy were included as well. Military and security officers probably benefited the most from the system. Over time, the categories became fluid; most *sheikhs*, for example, became businessmen as well. The average Yemeni citizen under Saleh was excluded from the benefits of the patronage system.

To garner broad elite commitment to the status quo, Saleh included all prominent elites in the patronage system, even those from the formal opposition. As time passed under Saleh's rule, elites began to view networks of patronage around the president as the main source of political and economic competition (Longley-Alley 2010).

Eventually, however, a shrinking resource base (declining oil revenues) made ecumenical distribution more difficult. In addition, Saleh exacerbated the problem by deciding to narrow patronage distribution around his family, especially his sons and nephews (Longley-Alley 2010). Moreover, according to a Global Security (2017) report, based on a UN sanctions panel study, Saleh alone netted $60 billion from his corrupt patronage system, which would have made him the world's fifth richest person.

Challenges to Saleh's Regime

The Republic of Yemen's political economy under Saleh faced four major challenges (Lackner 2015): (a) the Houthi wars; (b) the Southern Movement; (c) Jihadi Salafis; (d) elite challenges to the increasing concentration of wealth and power in the hands of Saleh and his relatives.

The progressively deteriorating relationship between the regime and the Zaydi Shia elite in the northwestern Saada Governorate erupted in a series of six wars, the Houthi wars. The Houthis are Zaydi Shia revivalists who were originally motivated by what they interpreted as the betrayal of Zaydi values by the Saleh regime that had enabled the intrusion of Wahhabism / Sunni Salafism into their homeland in the Saada Governorate (Brehony 2015). Institutionally, the conflict began as a rivalry between Houthi summer camps and a Saudi-financed Salafi institute in the historically Zaydi town of Dammaj (Yadav and Carapico 2016).

The Houthi movement originated in the early 1990s in an organization set up by Hussein Badr al-Din al-Houthi called the Believing

Youth (Brehony 2015). In addition to explicitly religious concerns, they also bitterly contested the economic and social marginalization of Saada and the corruption of the Saleh regime. Zaydi revivalism and socioeconomic resentment collided with anti-imperialism when Hussein al-Houthi attacked Ali Abdullah Saleh's alliance with the Bush administration during the 2003 invasion of Iraq. Saleh responded to the provocation with violence and a manhunt for Hussein. As repression against Zaydism progressed, Hussein militarized the movement, urging members to purchase weapons to defend themselves against armed allies of Saleh's regime.

Hussein al-Houthi was killed at the end of the first war in 2004. Hussein's father, Badr al-Din al-Houthi, and his brother, Abd Malik al-Houthi, assumed leadership of the Houthi movement. Five more wars ensued. In 2010, the Houthi movement had to survive the onslaught of both the Saudi and Yemeni militaries.

The wars transformed the Houthi movement from comprising student activists seeking religious revival to one comprising seasoned insurgents (Brehony 2015). The Houthi base of support also expanded from Zaydi university students to all Yemenis aggrieved by Saleh's policies in the North. Countering Saleh's claims that the Houthis wanted a return of the Imamate, the Houthis asserted that they wanted a republican system and things that all Yemenis crave: government accountability, the end of corruption, regular utilities, fair fuel prices, job opportunities for ordinary Yemenis, and the end of Western influence (Newsweek 2015).

Beyond the Houthi movement, Zaydi *sadah* took diverse political positions in reaction to the removal of the Imamate in 1962 (Lackner 2015). Searching for a new place in the ROY, some formed a political party, Hizb al-Haqq. However, the party performed poorly in parliamentary elections. Some even joined the ruling party, which did not stop them from being universally attacked as agents of the ancient regime.

The Southern Movement (Hirak) formed the second major challenge to Saleh's regime. The pre-unification tensions between former North Yemen and South Yemen never completely disappeared, resulting in an ongoing secessionist movement in some areas and general hostility toward the regime everywhere in the South.

Throughout the former PDRY, there was a perception of oppression by the North. Actions taken by Saleh's regime bolstered this impression

(Lackner 2015). In 1994, he forcibly retired many Southern military and security officers and paid their pensions irregularly (or not at all). Powerful Northerners took Southern land and were appointed to top military and security positions in the South. Southern areas received less state investment than the North, and most Southerners believed that the government sought to develop the North while doing little to nothing to alleviate their bleak socioeconomic conditions.

Hirak was initially led by the Southern military officers that were "retired" by Saleh (Lackner 2015). They sought reinstatement and full payment of their pensions. However, by 2010 the Southern Movement had spread its influence to the point that Aden and other parts of the South were "effectively low-level war zones, where the state's army was retrenched behind sandbags in fortified positions fearing attacks from local insurgents, and where flags of the former PDRY flew openly and were painted all over the place" (Lackner 2015: 11).

In addition to the Houthi conflicts and the Southern Movement, Jihadi Salafis were the third major challenge to Saleh's regime. Saleh was challenged by armed Islamist militants operating in the name of al-Qaeda in the Arabian Peninsula (AQAP) and insurgents from its local franchise Ansar al-Sharia. AQAP became active enough for the United States to deem them to be an important threat to Saleh and to American security. US drone strikes targeted the militants but sometimes hit civilians. This generated Yemeni hostility toward Saleh's regime, which permitted the bombings over Yemeni air space.

The fourth challenge to Saleh came from regime elites who had become discontent due to his practice of increasingly concentrating wealth and power in his and his closest relatives' hands (Longley-Alley 2013). After ruling Yemen for years through a complex web of tribal and regional patronage – broad inclusion had been key to the regime's overall stability – Saleh alienated his own partners by resolving to place his son as his successor. This alienated long-time allies.

In addition to the four prominent and outright challenges to Saleh's regime, constant insecurity in parts of Yemen was caused by small and large incidents of community-level, intertribal conflict, as well as by conflicts between tribes and state forces (Lackner 2015). The incidents reflected struggles over access to scarce water and land, the continuation of feuds, or other issues. The conflicts flourished because the regime did nothing to enforce state power through modern judicial or policing methods, sometimes even encouraging the conflicts (Lackner 2015).

Authoritarian Breakdown

Just prior to the Arab Spring, worsening frustration and anger at Yemen's political economy had made the country a prime candidate for violent social conflict aimed at removing a regime that appeared to be in terminal decline.[4] In early 2011, successful uprisings and the overthrow of dictatorships in Tunisia and Egypt transformed the broad and deep discontent within Yemen into a mass popular and tribal uprising that demanded the removal of President Ali Abdullah Saleh and his family from power. The revolt, led by the young, met sharp repression. The ensuing conflict lasted more than 10 months and created a security vacuum.

The tipping point to authoritarian breakdown came on March 18, 2011, when the regime fired on unarmed protesters, killing more than 50 people (Longley-Alley 2013). The brutal crackdown precipitated a split among regime insiders. General Ali Mohsen and the army units he commanded were the most prominent defectors from Saleh's regime during the Arab Spring uprisings. Other defectors included the Ahmars, the traditional *sheikhs* of the Hashed Confederation, and tribal militias associated with Islah and the JMP. When the Bakil Confederation publicly backed the protestors, the opposition could mobilize more than 100,000 protestors once or even twice a week (Longley-Alley 2013).

The defections confirmed resentment about Saleh's abandonment of the power-sharing agreement that he had made with General Mohsen and the Ahmars at the start of his ascent to the presidency (Longley-Alley 2013). His partners most egregiously resented his choice to anoint his son as successor when they had been promised the right to make that decision. They also had become accustomed to a wide berth to run their affairs with informal armies, courts, and economic empires, privileges that seemed threatened by Saleh's narrowing of patronage to close family and clan members (Longley-Alley 2013).

Saleh loyalists during the Arab Spring uprising in Yemen included the Republican Guard, modeled after Saddam Hussein's force of the

---

[4] On the Arab Spring and authoritarian breakdown in Yemen, see Lackner (2014); Transfeld (2016); Longley-Alley (2013); and Knights (2013).

same name, which was commanded by President Saleh's half-brother Ali Saleh. He also maintained support from other areas: artillery brigades controlled by officers from the president's village; the United Yemeni Air Force led by the president's half-brother Mohammed Saleh Abdullah; and the Yemeni Special Operations Forces commanded by the president's son, Ahmed Ali (Longley-Alley 2013).

In addition to the backing of the parallel armies he had created within the Ministry of Defense, President Saleh could largely count on a 50,000-strong paramilitary force under the Ministry of the Interior (MOI) known as the Central Security Organization (CSO) (Longley-Alley 2013). The CSO was led by the president's nephew, Yahya Abdullah Saleh. The organization functioned as public order troops and was employed as a first line of defense during protests. Saleh also had at his disposal a parallel intelligence agency, the National Security Bureau (NSB), which was run by Ammar Mohammed Abdullah, the president's (other) nephew. Finally, President Saleh had overtaken the Ministry of Defense's chain of command by creating the Office of the Commander-in-Chief, which was led by his half-brother Ali Saleh. While all these forces largely remained loyal to Saleh, just prior to his decision to resign the presidency, even some Republican Guard and CSO members had defected (Longley-Alley 2013).

Neither side felt certain of victory when Saleh's regime split during Yemen's Arab Spring. Regional and international actors feared a devastating civil war on a scale of the unfolding conflict in Syria. To end the political crisis, a GCC initiative backed by the United Nations Security Council and the European Union was put forth (Transfeld 2016).

The GCC Initiative, signed in November 2011, had the parties agree to a peaceful transfer of power, with Saleh handing over all presidential powers to his vice-president, Abdrabbuh Mansur Hadi, on February 27, 2012.

Democratic Transition

After the elections in 2012, in which he stood unopposed, Abdrabbuh Mansur Hadi was sworn in as the president of Yemen for a two-year term. He formed an interim government of national unity composed equally of General People's Congress (GPC) members and members from the main opposition, the Joint Meeting Parties (JMP). In exchange for signing the GCC Initiative, Saleh received immunity for himself and officials who had served under him. He remained active in politics as chairman of the GPC.

Under the GCC Initiative, President Hadi and the government of national unity convened a comprehensive "Conference for National Dialogue for all forces and political actors, including youth, the Southern Movement, the Houthis, other political parties, civil society representatives and women."[5] Then–UN Special Envoy for Yemen Jamal Benomar declared that the National Dialogue Conference (NDC) would open a new page in the history of Yemen, breaking from the past and paving the way for democratic governance founded on the rule of law, human rights, and equal citizenship (BBC News 2014).

The national dialogue process covered all five areas relevant to democratic consolidation. Among other issues, thematic working groups within the NDC mandate attempted to forge military, political, socioeconomic, nation-state, and transitional justice, human rights, and rule of law pacts.

Overall, the NDC structure aimed to draw up blueprints for state-building and a new constitution (Fattah 2014).

Unfortunately, Yemen's democratic transition derailed and morphed into a civil war in late 2014 largely due to overwhelming nation-state issues. In power, the Hadi government struggled to deal with a variety of problems, including a revolt in the North, a separatist movement in the South, power and territory aggrandizement from al-Qaeda's strongest branch (al-Qaeda in the Arabian Peninsula, AQAP) and the Islamic State, and the continuing loyalty of many military officers to Saleh, as well as corruption, unemployment, and food insecurity (BBC News 2019).

Two years into Hadi's rule, the Shia (Zaydi) movement led by the Houthi family took advantage of the new president's weaknesses by militarily taking control of their Northern heartland, including the country's capital, Sanaa.

Armed forces still loyal to Saleh, and the former president himself, formed an alliance with the Houthis. (This was opportunistic – as a route to regain power – since Saleh was Yemen's leader during the first six Houthi Wars.) Disillusioned with the transition, many ordinary

---

[5] GCC (2011).

Yemenis – including Sunnis – supported the Houthis' move against Hadi's government (BBC News 2019). On March 25, 2015, President Hadi was forced to flee to Saudi Arabia.

Abdullah Hamidaddin interprets the Yemeni civil war of 2014 as the seventh Houthi war with a pronounced intervention by Saudi Arabia and the lesser participation of Iran (Hamidaddin 2015). For Hamidaddin, all seven Houthi wars took place within the same political structure. Structurally, the seven Houthi wars are bound by a weak Yemeni state that is neither Weberian or Westphalian (Hamidaddin 2015). For Hamidaddin, in the absence of an effective state that monopolizes violence and protects citizens, the population functions through tribal structures that protect people enough to avoid a Hobbesian world. In his view, whatever state exists in Yemen is predatory, controlled by one power among many within Yemen. It sustains itself through divide-and-rule tactics. He treats the state itself as a tribe in that it does not have the legitimacy to govern other tribes.

The Yemeni state is also weak in terms of sovereignty. Hamiddadin emphasizes the importance of the role that Saudi Arabia has played in Yemen in recent decades. In an attempt to shape Yemen's political identity after the Imamate's abolishment, Saudis have been co-opting tribal powers in its southern neighbor since the mid-1960s. Many Yemeni elites have overt ties with Saudi Arabia and receive financial support from the Saudi government. Tens of thousands of Yemenis, directly or indirectly, receive Saudi aid.

During the Houthi wars, Saudi senior officials regularly met with Yemeni *sheikhs* to advance Saudi interests, including their hostility toward the Houthis and Zaydi Shiism. Their main ally in Yemen has been the Hashid Confederation, which has mobilized tribal militias against the Houthis.

The National Dialogue Conference attempted to resolve the Houthi conflict and reconcile Houthis with the Yemeni state and restore hopes for democratic transformation. However, with the Hadi government struggling to address socioeconomic demands and corruption, the sense of persecution of Shia Zaydis by the state and Saudi-sponsored Salafism was revived. Within that context, remember, the Houthis made their military move south that forced President Hadi to flee the country.

In 2015, Saudi Arabia and a coalition of other Arab nations began bombing the Houthi rebels to try to degrade their forces and restore

President Hadi to power (Hubbard 2016). The United States has provided the Saudi-led coalition with targeted intelligence and offered other support including the refueling of planes (New York Times 2016). While the claims appear to be exaggerated, many assert that the (Shia) Houthis are being aided militarily by Iran, a majority Shia nation.

Saudis (and Hadi) consider the fight against the Houthis as part of a larger regional sectarian struggle between Sunnis led by Saudi Arabia and Shias led by Iran. Saudis argue that the Houthis are seeking to overthrow the Yemeni government and bring it under Iranian influence. The Houthis and Iran deny a close relationship and downplay levels of support from Tehran.

After four years of war, the Saudis still publicly claim that they are intervening in Yemen to restore Hadi's "legitimate" government. In the meantime, their near indiscriminate bombings are taking a bloody toll on Yemeni lives. At this point, returning to a National Dialogue Conference under Hadi, and expecting it to consolidate a Yemeni democracy – if that is indeed the Saudis' goal – seems like a pipe dream.

Democratic Consolidation: Nation-State and Weberian-State Pacts

The National Dialogue Conference attempted unsuccessfully to address Yemeni weaknesses in attributes of Weberian modern states and national unity. In terms of a Weberian state, in the GCC Initiative President Abdrabbuh Mansur Hadi's interim government was charged with unifying and professionalizing the military under a central command structure that elected elites could control (Transfeld 2016).

State-building challenges in this area were steep. The Yemeni state was largely absent in many parts of the country, and state institutions were unable to counter lawlessness and social disorder in many "ungoverned dark spaces" (Fattah 2012). In those spaces, armed tribes and Jihadi actors partly filled institutional gaps. In addition, since Yemen's military itself was composed mainly of tribesmen, the feelings of tribal allegiance inside Yemen's military were as strong or stronger than feelings of military allegiance (Longley-Alley 2015).

Under Saleh, Yemeni political elites had attempted to monopolize violence by dividing the armed forces into five military districts corresponding to geographical regions of the country.[6] The commanders of each district – all generals – oversaw several brigades and military camps and were high up in the military chain of command. Due to Yemen's weak central state, the five regions were really para-states. The generals transferred funds for development to residents, or they withheld funds to punish disloyal citizens. The generals also orchestrated the ghost soldiers' scam. Up to one-third of Yemen's soldiers were actually ghost soldiers: they showed up only on the rolls of the commanders, who pocketed their salaries and sold their equipment.

Four of the five commanders were replaced during the transition, all except the powerful defector, General Ali Mohsen of the Northwestern District.

The Southern Military District was the most turbulent and insecure of the five. There, during the transition, AQAP's insurgent arm, Ansar al-Sharia, seized territory and attacked military bases. AQAP also took advantage of state military and security forces' withdrawal from some rural areas as they faced-off in the capital. For a year, the Abyan Governorate and some areas of the Shabwa Governorate were ruled by Ansar al-Sharia. Since 2012, al-Qaeda has launched a sustained campaign of assassinations of Yemeni military and security personnel and appears to control significant parts of the Hadramawt Governorate. Claiming to want to disrupt drone command centers in Yemen, al-Qaeda has also launched bold raids against military bases, including the Ministry of Defense in downtown Sanaa. ISIS has also sought to take advantage of Yemen's instability.

Armed tribes also mobilized during the transition (Knights 2013). The Al Saad tribe was formed in 2012 to counter Ansar al-Sharia in Abyan. As the general security situation deteriorated, renegade tribesmen in the East attacked power transmission lines and oil and gas pipelines. Their goal was to either exact payments from the government in exchange for security or to demand the reinstatement of tribal subsidies. Some blamed their attacks on Saleh, asserting that he was backing tribal attacks to undermine the transitional government.

---

[6] On military and security organization under Saleh and during the transition, see www.criticalthreats.org/yemen/gordon-military-command-graphic-april-12-2012 and Knights (2013).

The Alliance of Yemeni Tribes was formed in 2011 to oppose the Saleh government. Perhaps most damaging to state monopoly of the legitimate use of violence, the powerful al-Ahmar clan has maintained its control over the armies of the Hashid Confederation.

To rise to the challenge of establishing civilian control over the Yemeni military, Hadi formed a Military Affairs Committee to prevent narrow clan power bases from forming in the future (Knights 2013). He also removed 20 military officials from command posts, including several of Saleh's relatives (Knights 2013). After his ouster, former Air Force Commander Mohammed Saleh threatened to shoot down planes landing at Sanaa's international airport unless he was reinstated. Hadi also created a new force, the Presidential Protective Security Forces, to replace several armed units previously led by former President Saleh's relatives, including important subunits of the Republican Guard (Knights 2013). Beyond that, Hadi restructured military fields into seven geographical regions and formed "Reserve Forces" out of six brigades to be deployed only by the decision of the president (Noman and Sorenson 2013).

The measures President Hadi took to establish civilian control over the military achieved little. The Southern Movement maintained their armed forces. Obviously, Houthi armed forces were more powerful than the "national" armed forces Hadi controlled, as they forced him to flee the country and regroup in Saudi Arabia.

Prior to Hadi's forced departure from Yemen, former President Saleh's relatives still commanded a weaker version of the Republican Guard, Yemen's special forces, and the Central Security Organization (CSO). Saleh and the forces he continued to control, which also included tribal forces, made a temporary alliance with the Houthis against Hadi's government of national unity.

In any future transition in Yemen, there will almost certainly be a power struggle between the military command and civilian leadership. Given the power of armed tribal forces in the country, their autonomous power would have to be confronted elected civilian control over the armed forces would have to be established.

The tribal Hashidi solution to the threat of the military and government acting contrary to their informal power and interests has been to colonize their ranks with tribal leaders and constituents who do not subscribe to the corporate identity of a professional military (Noman and Sorenson 2013). Thus, efforts to professionalize the military would have to be undertaken to overcome those tactics. The military subcommittee of the National Dialogue Conference asserted in its conclusions that the military should be professionalized and depoliticized and that only the state should form armed groups; however, they did not provide clear instructions about how to achieve that goal (Schmitz 2014b). Some have recommended bringing at least some nonstate armed groups into the national military, with a focus on the Houthi and Southern Movement forces (Noman and Sorenson 2013).

Notably, even if Hadi and the unity government had removed all of Saleh's relatives from the military, which in practical terms is what Hadi's military restructuring amounted to (Transfeld 2016), Hashidi officers in the military could still dominate the government (Knights 2013). Civilian leadership would still be vulnerable to the armies of Hashid Confederation tribal *sheikhs* (e.g., the Ahmars). Insiders continue to doubt that any non-Hashid elected president could attain the loyalty of the armed forces and the biggest armed tribes, baldly stating the challenge: "How then will they be able to impose their authority?" (Knights 2013).

In addition to monopolizing the use of force to provide security and enable the provision of public goods, new democracies gain legitimacy if their elected governments have an efficient bureaucracy at their disposal that is capable of implementing laws and policies rationally and legally. By contrast, under Saleh the Yemeni national administration was part of the country's patronage politics (Longley-Alley 2010).

Beyond the estimated $60 billion that found its way into former President Saleh's private bank accounts, public payrolls for the military also included double-dippers and ghost workers receiving millions of dollars each year (Al-Batati 2014). In 2010, Transparency International ranked Yemen near the bottom in control of corruption – 154th out of 168 countries.[7] A 2010 Global Integrity Report described Yemen's performance in combating corruption as very weak and deteriorating.

Yemen's National Dialogue Conference included "Good Governance" as one of the nine issues assigned to committees. Several of their recommendations touched on improving the quality of the state bureaucracy, though implementation mechanisms were vague and little

---

[7] See www.transparency.org/cpi2010/results.

had been done before the Houthis forced the transitional government from power.

In terms of national unity, alarmingly, federalism, for Yemen-specific reasons, seems like an unlikely solution to national disunity.

Katherine Zimmerman (2014) argues that the conditions for successful federalism do not exist in Yemen for two reasons. First, it will be difficult to create strong local governments that can challenge traditional centers of power. The federalist map would have to be drawn over a volatile tribal, religious, and regional basis. Mayors of towns, villages, and cities have to be vested with greater powers than tribal *sheikhs* and possess more influence over decision-making. Furthermore, local elected officials have to have control over local budgets. Second, scarce resources are not distributed equally in different regions and local areas. Some of the governorates within Yemen have no natural resources, no access to the sea, and no active human capital. Thus, federalism would have to manage sharp conflicts over "who gets what, when, where, and how" in Yemen.

In addition to the reasons cited by Katherine Zimmerman, federalism will be difficult because of the strong secessionist feelings in the former South Yemen. Displaying displeasure about the direction of the national dialogue, mass demonstrations in the South renounced it and called for secession. The UN and the group of 10 Gulf countries backing the NDC attempted to appease the South in a variety of ways (Sandig and Granzow 2018). A committee was formed to address the pensions and employment of those in the Southern military and bureaucracy who were dismissed after the 1994 war. Another committee was created to resolve the issue of land and property in the South. With a $350 million donation from Qatar, President Hadi announced the creation of a trust to fund efforts to resolve issues and compensate those hurt in the South during the last two decades of Saleh's rule. Finally, to address stalled negotiations, a special high-level committee within the NDC was created outside the framework of the Southern issue subcommittee.

None of these efforts were compelling enough to overcome the secessionist sentiment in the South, and secession was still very much on the table when the Houthis overran Sanaa in September 2014. It has increased since then.

Like neutralizing the Southern Movement, NDC efforts to diffuse the Houthi conflict obviously failed as well. Recall that one of the nine major issues that were to be addressed at the National Dialogue

Conference was how to alleviate the grievances of the Houthi in Saada (Schmitz 2014a). Nevertheless, the Houthi movement had no representation in the Hadi-led transitional government. Witnessing a transitional government of political parties established during Saleh's rule, the Houthis viewed the government as no different from the regime that conducted wars against them.

Attempting to capitalize on widespread resentment against the transitional government (seen by many as a continuation of the corrupt regime under Saleh), the Houthis have characterized their occupation of Sanaa as a continuation of the popular revolt that overthrew Saleh in 2011 (Schmitz 2014a). They present themselves as legitimate brokers of a credible, nonpolitical, technocratic government capable of solving Yemen's urgent problems.

Ultimately, the Houthis gained widespread support for their overthrow of the transitional government. Despite US and GCC support for Hadi's transitional government, it had lost its legitimacy in Yemen. Most Yemenis support the Houthis' accusation that the United States and Saudi Arabia have imperial interests in the country.

However, Houthis face opposition as well. Liberal Yemenis worry about Houthi violence against their enemies. The Houthi movement today seems split between wanting to press ahead militarily – thereby taking the country deeper into civil war – and choosing to use its considerable political capital to form a wider, more inclusive, and legitimate government in Yemen that can address the country's serious problems (Schmitz 2014a).

Democratic Consolidation: Political Pact

In one sense, the goal of a political pact – getting all parties to agree to compete according to the rules of political democracy – was largely achieved during the transition in Yemen. The two most established parties, Saleh's GPC and the Joint Meetings Parties (JMP), committed to the National Dialogue Conference. The parties had histories conducive to the twin tolerations between secularists and Islamists within a democratic framework.

In 2002, remember, an Islamist party, the Yemeni Congregation for Reform (YCR, Islah), and a secular-socialist party, the Yemen Socialist Party (YSP), merged with smaller parties in an opposition alliance to form the Joint Meetings Parties (JMP). From the outset, the JMP pushed for democratic change in Saleh's Yemen (Durac 2011). In addition, as Vincent Durac (2011: XXX) writes, "the sustained existence of the JMP points to the possibility of mutual learning and respect on the part of very diverse political actors in Yemen and seems to suggest that cross-ideological cooperation between [secularists] and Islamists is feasible." While not changing worldviews, the JMP increased toleration of different ideological standpoints and the adoption of democratic norms within the structures and processes of both Islamist and secular-oriented political parties (Durac 2015).

However, working against a political pact, the establishment parties were not able to include the Houthi and Southern movements in a democratic bargain. The established parties also did not overcome their association with elites, many of whom had benefited greatly from Saleh's patronage politics. Ministerial posts in Hadi's transition government were split 50–50 between Saleh's GPC and the JMP. Transitional terms favored conservative Salafi currents within Islah and Saleh's ruling GPC (Yadav and Carapico 2014). Saleh was even allowed to continue on as the leader of the GPC.

Feeling unrepresented, fearful of the return of the prior regime, and enduring an atmosphere dominated by the transitional government's failure to manage economic, corruption, and security crises, many Yemenis became open to a countermobilization – which became violent – to oppose the GCC and NDC's transition roadmap.

By the time the Houthis took over power in Sanaa, most Yemenis had rejected the Saudi- and UN-backed National Dialogue Conference and shared the Houthi claim that the GCC-led transition retained too much of the status quo dominated by Saleh, his family, the GPC, the Hashid Confederation, the Northern security apparatus, the entrenched corrupt bureaucracy, and the elite within the Joint Meetings Parties, especially Islahi conservatives (Yadav and Carapico 2014).

Democratic Consolidation: Socioeconomic Pact

Socioeconomic development was addressed in Yemen's National Dialogue Conference. Based on consultations with local and international experts, the NDC's Sustainable Development Working Group recommended the same market reform model advocated across the Arab Spring: a market reform model that eliminates elite capture and takes advantage of the opportunity for economic growth provided by a vigorous private sector and global markets.

However, close Yemen observers noted that the GCC agreement gave holdover elites from the Saleh regime and traditional parties vast influence over the transition, which they judged would perpetuate patronage and corruption centered in Sanaa regardless of the economic prescriptions that emerged from the NDC process (Longley-Alley 2013).

Yemen's poverty adds to the need for inclusive policymaking to help consolidate democratic rule once the war ends. The NDC's Sustainable Development Working Group called for reinforcing the societal role in setting and executing development plans with an emphasis on civil society organizations and "independent" youth.[8] More importantly, it moved toward inclusive policymaking by stipulating the creation of a socioeconomic council as an institutional framework that coordinates the joint efforts between the government, the private sector, and civil society across the Yemeni republic.

The NDC's Sustainable Development Working Group envisioned an active social policy (NDC 2013). Its recommendations aimed to create jobs and alleviate poverty by increasing the funds, outreach, and functions of the Social Fund for Development, the Public Work Project, and the Small Industries Fund. Wage policies were mentioned vaguely. The working group advocated for legislation to oblige the public, private, and mixed sectors to protect workers' rights so that the latter may receive fair and adequate compensation for their labor. Income protection was addressed in a number of proposals. Without discussing figures and financing, it advocated for adequate unemployment insurance and retraining programs as joint public and private ventures.

The working group supported various poverty programs and favored joint projects with civil society organizations. It advised a clear national strategy and policy for food security and combating malnutrition with contributions from the private sector, charitable organizations, and civil society. It also emphasized increasing the capital of banks such as Bank of Hope and Bank of the Poor, which helps those in financial need. It envisioned partnerships between microfinance institutions, public banks, and the private sector.

[8] The official website for the National Dialogue Conference: www.ndc.ye/default.aspx.

Most of the social policy recommendations included some emphasis on improving opportunities for the young, including access to education and educational reforms linked to job opportunities. The working group asserted that the state should spend more on education than on defense and security.

The Yemeni Economy and GCC Membership

Full integration into a regional block, the GCC, is probably Yemen's best hope economically (Spencer 2015). For the last 45 years, the Gulf Cooperation Council (GCC) has tried to manage its Yemen problem – an unstable poor neighbor without much oil and a large population – with half-measures short of full integration (Spencer 2015). Most member states' attitude has been fond but standoffish. The Gulf states have been fairly generous in providing aid and funding projects. However, the populous country is kept at arm's length for demographic and ideological reasons, the latter being fear of Marxism and republicanism. Prior to the Arab Spring, Saudi Arabia tried to maintain Yemen's elite-dominated status quo through the disbursement of billions to both Yemeni government officials and tribal leaders. This strategy has weakened the state.

Yemen was in negotiations for GCC membership prior to the Arab Spring. It had gained membership in GCC councils for education, health, social affairs, sports, industry, and metrology. Since the Arab Spring, GCC states have stalled Yemen's full membership request and its potential for mutual benefit (Spencer 2015). Among other issues, they fear that the Zaydi Houthis are a fifth column for Iran. Were Yemen admitted to the GCC, the modernization process of the Yemeni state would benefit from military, security, and national administration interactions. The GCC would gain a supply of cheap labor, and the remittances would help Yemenis while increasing the consumer base for GCC goods and services (Spencer 2015).

Transitional Justice, Human Rights, and Rule of Law Pact

Yemen's National Dialogue Conference included a working group that addressed transitional justice and national reconciliation.[9] Based on

---

[9] The official website for the National Dialogue Conference: www.ndc.ye/default.aspx.

comparative experiences of foreign countries and conducted in consultation with local and international experts, the working group's recommendations followed international best practices to achieve transitional justice.

The greatest weakness in the Yemeni approach was the lack of balance on the ground between transitional justice and national reconciliation. The working group included the core elites who were most responsible for the human rights violations that it was assigned to address, and they sabotaged the process from within and without (Manea 2014).

Former President Saleh and all those who worked with him were pardoned by the GCC Initiative, and any recommendations made by the NDC's Transitional Justice Working Group were viewed as subordinate to the GCC's immunity deal (Gaston and Al-Dawsari 2014). During the transition, core elites maintained an important role in the Yemeni political system. Saleh, in his role as GPC head, controlled half the transition government; in contrast the ruling party under Ben Ali was banned during Tunisia's transition. Incumbents also continued to hold key security positions during Yemen's transition.

Influenced by Saleh, the working group's interpretation of transitional justice entailed measures that led to reconciliation and peace rather than accountability, vetting, and truth-seeking (Manea 2014). Ultimately, Yemen's transitional justice process under Hadi fell far short of satisfactory for a country with a long history of political violence and human rights abuses, both before it became a unified state in 1990 and since, including the 1994 civil war, the Houthi wars, the Southern conflict, and the 2011 youth uprising (Manea 2014).

In addition, American drone strikes in the long-running US campaign against al-Qaeda in Yemen has likely killed more civilians than terrorists (Manea 2014). Several hundred Yemeni civilians have died in those strikes and other covert US missions.

Making any future transitional justice process even more difficult, since the transition slid into a civil war, thousands of Yemeni civilians have been killed by Houthi groups and the Saudi-Arabia-led coalition strikes to counter them (with ground support from troops from Qatar and Sudan). Additional violence against the innocent has been perpetrated by al-Qaeda, ISIS, and Sunni and tribal militias.

Protecting human rights and establishing the rule of law in Yemen will require major reforms in the judicial and security sectors. President

Hadi started the process. Under former President Saleh, the security sector was oriented toward protecting his autocratic regime and providing patronage to close allies (Sorenson 2013). Saleh politicized the security sector, with rent payments and plum positions for relatives and other allies (Sorenson 2013). Special units got privileged access to housing, the best sporting clubs, and the best hospitals. He also exercised security sector control by issuing unconstitutional laws and decrees granting him the power to control the security services.

To support democratic consolidation, Yemen's security sector needs to be depoliticized and reconstructed as a professional and publicly accountable body dedicated to protecting citizens' inalienable human rights and safety. The internal security services require a transformation from regime defenders dependent on rent payments to a professional service.

Instead of being the cornerstone of the rule of law, Yemen's judiciary under Saleh was used to maintain his power. The executive dominated the judicial branch as much as he dominated the legislative branch. Serious judicial reforms in Yemen that support the rule of law and equal citizenship rights would require major changes. They would need to transform the country's current legal culture into one embodying universal rules that apply to all citizens and that are uniformly enforced by the state.[10]

Yemen's formal legal system incorporates elements from *Sharia*, customary/tribal laws, excerpts from Egyptian and other Arab laws, and international principles (Al-Zwaini 2012). These various elements can be seen in Yemen's Constitution, Personal Status Code, Criminal Code, and its Arbitration Code. Through informal mediation and arbitration procedures, tribal justice continues to solve the majority of conflicts and other legal matters throughout the country (such as homicide, family matters, and traffic accidents), despite state-issued laws to limit and regulate the use of tribal customary norms (Al-Zwaini 2012).

In practice, Yemen's Arbitration Code, which covers the procedural relationship between formal and informal law, condones tribal dispute settlements (Al-Zwaini 2012). It also favors noncodified *Sharia* rules over codified state laws as the ultimate legal reference for all arbitrations, formal and informal. Considering that almost 80% of Yemenis

---

[10] On judicial reforms in Yemen, see Al-Zwaini (2012).

are not within reach of official courts, state law is not the supreme law in Yemen either effectively or in the perception of most Yemenis (Al-Zwaini 2012).

The Yemeni judicial situation holds out little prospect for rapid reform. When Hadi came to power, courts and legal structures did not even exist in many districts and in several governorates (Al-Zwaini 2012). The following will continue to hold sway: tribal justice manned by local notables and guided by customs and traditions; religious law and symbolic acts designed to contain dispute, compensate for damages, and reconcile disputants; and the maintenance of honor.

While most Yemenis perceive the nonstate justice system as more legitimate, fair, participatory, efficient, and effective than formal state procedures, human rights organizations report that the former discriminates against women and those coming from weak tribes, and indigent people who do not have any tribal affiliation or support (Al-Zwaini 2012). Since informal justice is primarily committed to maintaining stability and hierarchies and since it holds the collectivity as its primary focus, it is incompatible with contemporary Western conceptions of human rights, which are focused on individuals' equal rights.

The informal system is also at odds with the concepts of the centralization of power and state monopoly over the rule of law (Al-Zwaini 2012). These are fundamental challenges that will have to be addressed to link the two legal spheres and establish the rule of law with equal citizenship rights. Also, despite tribal justice and stability mechanisms, tribal conflicts such as kidnappings, blood feuds, and other violent acts persist and have been brought into cities, including the foothold of state power, Sanaa (Al-Zwaini 2012).

In addition to tradition and conservative interpretations of *Sharia* that lead to widespread discrimination against women, Yemen has a caste system that would have to be challenged for the country to use a democratic transition to bolster human rights (Lackner 2015). The lowest social strata are occupied by darker-skinned people who are manual laborers who carry out various activities in different parts of the country, including farming – although they are distinguished from tribal farmers, who own land. Most view this stratum to consist if the descendants of slaves, and it is difficult for them to rise in the social hierarchy, though it is possible through education and the accumulation of wealth. The Akhdam, or "servants" (or, less derogatorily, to use the self-adopted term, the Muhamasheen or "marginalized"), are mostly urban. Their occupations focus on the "unclean" activities such as street-cleaning and, in former times, collecting human waste (Lackner 2015). Some are beggars, and some higher-status Yemenis do not consider them to be Yemenis.

While the status of racial minorities has remained distressingly static, Yemen's Arab Spring led to the emergence of women as a social and political force. They had strong representation and a positive role in the National Dialogue Conference. Tawakkol Karman, a Yemeni journalist and senior member of the Islah political party, was a co-recipient of the Nobel Peace Prize in 2011 in recognition for her work on women's safety and their right to full participation in Yemeni peace-building.

Conclusion: A Return to National Dialogue?

Yemen's National Dialogue Conference (NDC) mirrored our perspective on democratic consolidation. The various working groups at the conference sought negotiated compromises, or pacts, to address all conflicts that could derail the country's democratic transition. It was, in the views of some, the only negotiated and most inclusive attempt at democratic transition in the history of the Arab world (Jadallah 2014).

Despite laudable recommendations, the NDC was unable to contribute significantly to the consolidation of Yemen's democratic transition. A youth delegate to the conference observed that instead of national consensus to resolve all of the country's conflicts, the only consensus reached was that all delegates should receive jobs in the government (Transfeld 2014).

Cynicism about Yemen's National Dialogue Conference is only partly warranted. The challenges were steep. Compared to many countries, including Tunisia and Egypt, Yemen was much less of a nation-state and a Weberian state when the Arab Spring – and its hopes for democracy, dignity, and socioeconomic justice in the region – erupted. Nation- and state-building while attempting to institutionalize political democracy in a poor country was, to say the least, a major undertaking. Despite the NDC, transitional elites in Yemen also seemed on a path to recreating a political economy dominated by a narrow ruling elite.

It's not too surprising, then, that while Yemen's National Dialogue Conference was taking place, political violence was on the rise. The civil war that began in 2015, when the Houthis marched south and toppled the Hadi government, continues. The Saudi-led invasion has stymied forward progress by the Houthis but has been unable to reinstate the Hadi government. The Houthi armed groups were able to grow strong partly by building a coalition with armed groups still under the control of former President Saleh. When Saleh reached out to the Saudis in a bid to switch sides, he was killed by the Houthis.

During the conflict so far, armed Southern separatists of the Hirak movement have benefited from support from the United Arab Emirates, who have sought their participation in the Saudi-led counterattack against the Houthis (Al-Araby 2018). However, the alliance may break if Hirak continues to demand secession and possibly a revived socialist republic, both of which would be counter to the UAE's interests.

In December 2018, a UN-backed peace process to end Yemen's civil war took place in Sweden. The main warring parties agreed to de-escalate the war's fiercest battle – over Al Hodeidah, a port city responsible for both supplying the Houthis with weapons and delivering over 80% of food and other aid to Yemenis undergoing the world's worst humanitarian crisis. The ceasefire in Al Hodeidah is envisioned as the start of the process to hopefully end the fighting nationwide (UN 2019).

The Hodeidah Agreement has slowed, but not stopped, armed conflict in Yemen.

References

Al-Abdin, A. Z. 1979. "The Free Yemeni Movement (1940–1948) and Its Ideas of Reform." *Middle Eastern Studies*, 15(1), 36–48. www.jstor .org/stable/4282728.

Al-Araby. 2018. "What's behind Crumbling Saudi Support in Yemen's South?" *Al-Araby*, September 13. www.alaraby.co.uk/english/comment/ 2018/9/13/whats-behind-crumbling-saudi-support-in-yemens-south.

Al-Batati, S. 2014. "Yemen Reforms Corruption-Ridden Public Payroll." *Gulf News*, August 14. www.gulfnews.com/world/gulf/yemen/yemen- reforms-corruption-ridden-public-payroll-1.1372192.

Al Jazeera. 2019. "More than 70,000 Killed in Yemen's Civil War: ACLED." *Al Jazeera*, April 19. www.aljazeera.com/news/2019/04/ yemen-war-death-toll-reaches-70000-report-190419120508897.html.

Al-Zwaini, L. 2012. *Rule of Law Quick Scan Yemen*. The Hague: The Hague Institute for Innovation of Law, September. www.hiil.org/projects/rule-of-law-quick-scan-yemen/.

BBC News. 2014. "Yemen's National Dialogue Conference Concludes with Agreement." *BBC News*, January 21. www.bbc.com/news/world-middle-east-25835721.

2019. "Yemen Crisis: Why Is There a War?" *BBC News*, March 21. www.bbc.com/news/world-middle-east-29319423.

Bertelsmann Stiftung (BTI). 2014. *Yemen Country Report*. Transformation Index BTI. Berlin: Bertelsmann Stiftung. www.bti-project.org/en/reports/country-reports/detail/itc/YEM/.

Brehony, N. 2015. "Yemen and the Houthis: Genesis of the 2015 Crisis." *Asian Affairs*, 46(2), 232–250. doi:10.1080/03068374.2015.1037162.

Douglas, J. Leigh. 1987. *The Free Yemeni Movement, 1935–1962*. Beirut: American University of Beirut.

Dresch, P. 1989. *Tribes, Government, and History in Yemen*. Oxford: Oxford University Press.

Durac, V. 2011. "The Joint Meeting Parties and the Politics of Opposition in Yemen." *British Journal of Middle Eastern Studies*, 38(3), 343–365. doi:10.1080/13530194.2011.621697.

2015. "Social Movements, Protest Movements and Cross-Ideological Coalitions – The Arab uprisings Re-appraised." *Mediterranean Politics*, 22(2), 238–258. doi.org/10.1080/13510347.2015.1010809.

Fattah, K. 2012. "Ensuring the Success of Yemen's Military Reforms." *Carnegie Middle East Center*, December 13. www.carnegie.ru/2012/12/13/ensuring-success-of-yemen-s-military-reforms-pub-50349.

2014. "Yemen's Insecurity Dilemma." *Carnegie Middle East Center*, February 11. www.carnegie-mec.org/2014/02/11/yemen-s-insecurity-dilemma-pub-54657.

Gaston, E. and N. Al-Dawsari. 2014. *Dispute Resolution and Justice Provision in Yemen's Transition*. Washington, DC: United States Institute of Peace, April. www.usip.org/sites/default/files/SR345_Dispute-Resolution-and-Justice-Provision-in-Yemen%E2%80%99s-Transition.pdf.

Global Integrity. 2010. *Global Integrity Report 2010: Corruption Notebook: Yemen*. Washington, DC: Global Integrity. www.globalintegrity.org/resource/gir-2010-yemen/.

Global Security. 2017. "Ali Abdullah Saleh." *Global Security*, n. d. www.globalsecurity.org/military/world/yemen/saleh.htm.

2019. "North Yemen Civil War (1962–1970)." *Global Security*, n. d. www.globalsecurity.org/military/world/war/yemen.htm.

Gulf Cooperation Council (GCC). 2011. *Agreement on the Implementation Mechanism for the Transition Process in Yemen in Accordance with the*

Initiative of the Gulf Cooperation Council. UN Translation. May 12. www.peacemaker.un.org/yemen-transition-mechanism2011.

Hamidaddin, A. 2015. "Yemen: Negotiations with Tribes, States, and Memories." In I. W. Zartman, ed., *Arab Spring: Negotiations in the Shadow of the Intifadat.* Athens: University of Georgia Press, pp. 116–144.

Hubbard, B. 2016. "Airstrikes Kill Dozens in Western Yemen." *New York Times,* October 31. www.nytimes.com/2016/10/31/world/middleeast/airstrikes-kill-dozens-in-western-yemen.html.

Jadallah, A. 2014. "The Yemeni National Dialogue: Setting a Standard for Other Arab Countries." *S-CAR News,* 8(3), 1, 7–8. www.activity.scar.gmu.edu/newsletter-article/yemeni-national-dialogue-setting-standard-other-arab-countries.

Knights, M. 2013. "The Military Role in Yemen's Protests: Civil Military Relations in the Tribal Republic." *Journal of Strategic Studies,* 36(2), 261–288. doi:10.1080/01402390.2012.740660.

Lackner, H. 2014. *Why Yemen Matters: A Society in Transition.* London: Saqi Press.

2015. "The War in Yemen." *OpenDemocracy,* April 6. www.opendemocracy.net/en/north-africa-west-asia/war-in-yemen/.

Longley-Alley, A. 2010. "The Rules of the Game: Unpacking Patronage Politics in Yemen." *Middle East Journal,* 64 (3), 385–409. doi:10.1353/mej.2010.0016.

2013. "Yemen Changes Everything and Nothing." *Journal of Democracy,* 24(4), 74–85. doi:10.1353/jod.2013.0070.

2015. "Nobody Will Win the War in Yemen." *Al Jazeera,* April 8. www.aljazeera.com/indepth/opinion/2015/04/win-war-yemen-150407082542371.html.

Manea, E. 2014. "Yemen's Contentious Transitional Justice and Fragile Peace." *Middle East Institute,* February 24. www.mei.edu/publications/yemens-contentious-transitional-justice-and-fragile-peace.

National Dialogue Conference (NDC). 2013. *Sustainable Development Working Group Final Report (Translated from Arabic).* July–September. www.ndc.ye/ar-page.aspx?show=106.

Newsweek. 2015. "Rise of the Houthis." *Newsweek,* September 2.

New York Times. 2016. "How the US Became More Involved in the War in Yemen." *New York Times,* October 14. www.nytimes.com/interactive/2016/10/14/world/middleeast/yemen-saudi-arabia-us-airstrikes.html.

Noman, M. and D. S. Sorenson. 2013. *Reforming the Yemen Security Sector.* Working Paper No. 137. Stanford, CA: Center for Democracy, Development, and the Rule of Law (CDDRL), June. www.cddrl.fsi.stanford.edu/arabreform/publications/reforming_the_yemen_security_sector.

Orkaby, A. 2017. "Yemen's Humanitarian Nightmare: The Real Roots of the Conflict." *Foreign Affairs*, November/December. www.foreignaffairs.com/articles/yemen/2017-10-16/yemens-humanitarian-nightmare.

Rabi, U. 2015. *Yemen: Revolution, Civil War, and Unification.* London: I. B. Tauris. www.newsweek.com/photo-essay-rise-houthis-305511.

Sandig, J. and T. Granzow. 2018. "Aligning with the UN: Nonviolent Self-Determination Movement in the Global South." *Journal of Global Security Studies*, 3(3), 322–338. doi:10.1093/jogss/ogy019.

Schmitz, C. 2014a. "The Huthi Ascent to Power." *Middle East Institute*, September 15. www.mei.edu/publications/huthi-ascent-power.

2014b. *Yemen's National Dialogue.* Washington, DC: Middle East Institute, March 10. Policy Paper. www.mei.edu/publications/yemens-national-dialogue.

Schwedler, Jillian. 2006. *Faith in Moderation: Islamist Parties in Jordan and Yemen.* Cambridge: Cambridge University Press.

Sorenson, D. S. 2013. *An Introduction to the Modern Middle East: History, Religion, Political Economy, Politics.* Boulder, CO: Westview Press.

Spencer, J. 2015. "The GCC Needs a Successful Strategy for Yemen, Not Failed Tactics." *Middle East Research and Informative Project*, September 11. www.merip.org/2015/09/the-gcc-needs-a-successful-strategy-for-yemen/.

Transfeld, M. 2014. *Yemen: GCC Roadmap to Nowhere: Elite Bargaining and Political Infighting Block a Meaningful Transition.* Berlin: German Institute for International and Security Affairs, May. www.swp-berlin.org/fileadmin/contents/products/comments/2014C20_tfd.pdf.

2016. "Political Bargaining and Violent Conflict: Shifting Elite Alliances as the Decisive Factor in Yemen's Transformation." *Mediterranean Politics*, 21(1), 150–169. doi:10.1080/13629395.2015.1081454.

United Nations (UN). 2019. *Agreement on the Implementation Mechanism for the Transition Process in Yemen in Accordance with the Initiative of the Gulf Cooperation Council (GCC).* New York: United Nations Security Council, May 12. www.peacemaker.un.org/yemen-transition-mechanism2011.

Willis, J. M. 2018. "Yemen in Crisis: Autocracy, Neo-Liberalism and the Disintegration of a State by Helen Lackner (review)." *The Middle East Journal* 72(4): 709–710.

Yadav, S. P. and S. Carapico. 2014. "The Breakdown of the GCC Initiative." *Middle East Research and Information Project*, 273. www.merip.org/2014/12/the-breakdown-of-the-gcc-initiative/.

Zimmerman, K. 2014. "Yemen's Pivotal Moment." *Critical Threats*, February 12. www.criticalthreats.org/analysis/yemens-pivotal-moment.

5 | Broken States
Iraq, Syria, and ISIS

The puzzle is how do you glue these states [Iraq and Syria] back together again? They're gone. They're gone into a million pieces.

—Fawaz Gerges

The harrowing developments in post–Saddam Hussein Iraq, as well as in Syria, Libya, and Yemen – all countries in which the forces of history bequeathed relatively weak national unity, military power, and bureaucratic capacity – suggest that democratic consolidation is much more likely if nation-state and Weberian-state pacts precede attempts to institutionalize political democracy (political pacts). Attempting democratization, including implementing competitive elections, without those attributes can completely break countries apart.[1]

Iraq was a relatively weak nation-state and Weberian state when a US-led military coalition uprooted Saddam Hussein's brutal autocratic regime and imposed competitive elections. However, US policy – through De-Baathification of the military and state bureaucracy – weakened the national unity and state capacities needed to sustain and consolidate democracy.

The outcome was an insurgency, a civil war, and a partial state collapse resulting in the Islamic State capture of Iraqi territory. Currently, Iraqi elites are desperately nation-building and state-building while they continue to hold competitive elections. Democratic prospects in the country depend on the success of these efforts.

In terms of national unity and state capacity, Syria was also a relatively weak nation-state and Weberian state when the Arab Spring erupted. In Syria, a mass uprising for democratic transformation led to a vicious civil war and the spread of radical Islam. With the military

---

[1] The quote in the epigraph is from Fawaz Gerges, a professor at the London School of Economics. He is cited in Sly (2015).

help of Russia, Iran, and Hisballah, Bashar al-Assad, has survived the Arab Spring. He survived through violence, authoritarian repression, a series of short-term fixes, and heavy reliance on foreign allies (Samaha 2019). Only the Idlib province and areas controlled by Kurds remain as rebel strongholds, and they are coming under attack. Close observers concede that Assad has won, that his regime is here to stay, and that he will dictate the postconflict political order (Samaha 2019).

Assad is committed to remaining in power and recapturing all Syrian territories at any cost – there have already been over 500,000 war-related Syrian deaths since the Arab Spring began. He rejects federalism and any form of autonomous administration, even when a decentralized state offers the best hope for ending the Syrian bloodbath (Kupchan and Ülgen 2019). Instead, he is returning Syria to a society in which a brutal state – controlled by a minority – uses extreme violence to remain in power.

Prior to the Arab Spring, Syria under Assad was a bunker state, which is defined as a state in a potential war with the society it rules (Henry and Springborg 2010); feeding a bunker mentality, the underlying conflict in Syria was that a minority Alawite Shia population ruled the Sunni majority. Currently, Assad seems singularly focused on regaining his government's monopoly of violence and reimposing minority rule, with little effort to forge national reconciliation and unity and certainly no effort to transition to democracy:

Damascus has done little to pursue post-conflict reconciliation or address high levels of mistrust between Syria's communities . . . nothing is being done to heal the rifts within society. Beyond the amnesties and putting opposition fighters in with the army, the government has not done anything to fix the mistrust and animosity amongst the people. There needs to be serious mechanisms and initiatives that focus on bringing the people back together. (Samaha 2019)

The Islamic State took advantage of the upheavals in Iraq and Syria to carve out their own territorial state (Caliphate). In doing so, they created many powerful enemies, both from within and beyond the region. It was only a matter of time before armies from Arab countries and the West defeated ISIS as a territorial state. Since that time, ISIS has returned to guerrilla warfare and insurgency in Iraq and Syria, sought territory elsewhere, and made more attacks against their "far enemies" in the West.

Iraq, Syria, and the Islamic State are all broken states with uncertain futures. Instead of the possibility of democratic transformation in Iraq and Syria, a more pertinent consideration may be whether or not they can continue to exist at all. This chapter explores how Iraq, Syria, and ISIS became broken states and how their governments have attempted to put them back together again.

Iraq

Iraq's borders reflect foreign influences that increased nation- and state-building challenges by enclosing people that were divided along religious, sectarian, and ethnic lines. European colonialism created Iraq. The European defeat of the Ottoman Empire led to the 1916 Sykes-Picot Agreement, which divided the Middle East into separate spheres of British and French influence. To form Iraq, the British united the three Ottoman provinces of Baghdad, Mosul, and Basra into one nation-state. Within Iraq, Shia Arabs became the majority in a tribal Iraqi population that included Sunni Arabs, Kurds, Sunni Arab–Kurd mix, Shia Arab–Sunni Arab mix, Sunni Turkmen, and a small number of Christians and Persians.

Despite the heterogeneity of the Iraqi population, strides were made toward building national unity and attributes of a modern state in Iraq post-European colonization (Cook and Leheta 2016). Unfortunately, the US-led mission in Iraq (Operation Iraqi Freedom) that took down Saddam Hussein's autocratic regime also implemented policies that "reduced" built-up national unity and bureaucratic capacities that were needed to help consolidate the democracy that their mission had attempted to impose.

The US presence in Iraq has resulted in a horrific civil war, the birth of ISIS (a Takfiri-Jihadi group that took over one-third of Iraqi territory and focused its blood-letting on other Muslims), and competitive elections that alienated the large Sunni minority from the Iraqi state, making them excellent recruits for ISIS.

Competitive elections continue in Iraq, but so does a degree of intercommunal violence, with many accelerants still around and a demand for secession by Iraqi Kurds. Efforts to rebuild the Iraqi nation-state now focus on creating an Iraqi military and security force that is capable of monopolizing violence and resisting Kurdish independence. This requires meeting the steep challenge of bringing all armed groups under the command and control of the Iraqi state and elected governments. Improved bureaucratic capacity is desperately needed to better implement public policy and meet a major corruption challenge that is draining the democracy of its meaning. With a legacy of violent conflict between Sunnis and Shias, national unity challenges in Iraq stretch far beyond the Kurdish issue.

While weak national unity and modern-state capacities are the biggest challenge to consolidating democracy in Iraq, it is not that Iraq never began to develop national unity and the attributes of modern states. Iraq sits upon the world's fifth largest proven oil reserves. The country's oil wealth contributed to building national unity and state bureaucratic capacities in the relatively young country (Cook and Leheta 2016). Iraq's oil wealth provided the resources for a large welfare state that provided jobs and services such as education, law enforcement, electricity, and running water. As citizens' day-to-day lives became more dependent on state institutions, they came to see a bureaucratic state as a necessity. Growing state capacities created significant dependence on and loyalty to the new Iraqi state.

The Baathists, secular pan-Arab and socialist, in some ways made the bureaucracy rational, but in other ways they did the opposite. Bureaucratic capacity was built up and hollowed out by internal and external pressures. Rulers could largely avoid taxing the population due to the country's oil reserves, which paid for Iraq's military, bureaucracy, and extensive social welfare policies. Under the Baathists, Iraqis sometimes received state benefits that built attachments to the state; at other times, the regime favored its Sunni base.

Saddam Hussein damaged the bureaucracy when he took control in 1979. He created a large, centralized, corrupt bureaucracy with the president at the apex (Sassoon 2012). After becoming president, Hussein created a shadow state in the form of the presidential *diwan* (administration), with ultimate power and large staffs that competed with official ministries and ministers: Every bureaucratic measure, intelligence report, and ministry update "flowed upward to the *diwan*." Most, rules, regulations, and policies emanated from verbal presidential orders with scant discussions or consultations. With real decision-making concentrated in the presidential *diwan*, "all other

state organs were reduced to conduits of information and resources"
(Sassoon 2012: 228–229, 236)

Iraq's bureaucratic capacities were tested when circumstances produced a change in economic policy (Sassoon 2012). The 1980s were dominated by the eight-year war against Iran and sharp drops in oil prices; this forced the regime to launch liberalization and privatization policies. These efforts were mostly unsuccessful, mainly due to the long Baathist legacy of centralized state control and a bloated, overstaffed bureaucracy that was unable to meet the challenges posed by implementing such reforms. Feeling the financial crunch, Saddam Hussein believed that invading Kuwait and taking possession of its oil reserves offered a solution (Sassoon 2012).

Hussein invaded Kuwait on August 2, 1990. Iraqis paid a steep price for the invasion. Iraq's foreign-held assets were frozen, and the United Nations (UN) imposed an embargo on its oil exports. The sanctions lasted until Hussein was overthrown in 2003, and they affected the country in many fundamental ways (Sassoon 2012). Food became scarce, leading to rationing. There was a brain drain, with Iraqi hospitals losing around 75% of their staff. The distribution system upon which rentier and personalist regimes like Saddam Hussein's Iraq depends was put under pressure. With fewer resources, what effective action the inept bureaucracy was capable of was entirely directed toward one goal: ensuring the survival of the regime (Al-Sallami 2014).

State Monopoly of Violence under Saddam Hussein

While the Iraqi bureaucracy under Saddam Hussein and the Baathist state was only partly rational, his government fully – though brutally – monopolized the use of violence.

Hussein's military and security forces provided a degree of law and order – mostly order in a country without the rule of law – and security in Iraq, and communal conflicts cooled after the vicious handling of Shia and Kurdish uprisings. That stability, for whatever it was worth, was ended by the 2003 US-led invasion.

George W. Bush's Operation Iraqi Freedom broke down Saddam Hussein's monopoly of the use of force in Iraq and tragically failed to replace it. Iraq's military and security capabilities under Hussein have been ably described (Otterman 2005). Iraq had around 400,000 members in their armed forces. Its military was led by Saddam Hussein and was divided geographically into four regional commands. Saddam Hussein was regularly concerned with military coups, and he protected his regime by developing better equipped and trained special forces manned by relatives, tribal members, and Sunnis in general who contained threats from within the military. The regular army had between 300,000–350,000 men organized into 16 divisions.

The Republican Guard had between 60,000 and 70,000 men. Compared with the regular troops, it was an elite force with better equipment, training, and compensation. The Republican Guard and other special forces fell directly under the control of Saddam's son Qusay. The elite Special Republican Guard had 15,000 men drawn from the most loyal of the regime's supporters (Otterman 2005). The Special Guard was responsible for protecting the president, his family, and other VIPs. It had its own air defense command unit and was the only part of the army permitted within central Baghdad.

Saddam Hussein utilized the Iraqi security apparatus to maintain regime control – and stability – through surveillance and fear (Otterman 2005). He controlled his regime through a complex and interlocking network of security and secret police that answered directly to his son Qusay and other top officials. These 100,000+ agents generated fear of and loyalty to the regime. A Special Security Organization (SSO), composed of 2,000–5,000 men, played a major role in surveilling the other security services. Controlled by Qusay, the SSO had its own military brigade that was independent of the military establishment. At least a dozen other overlapping security forces existed in Iraq under Saddam Hussein. On the local level, agents from the General Security Services (GSS) monitored daily life in every town and village. The GSS had countless local informants and its own paramilitary wing.

Why was there a need for so much brutalization of the population and ruthless intelligence-gathering in "The Republic of Fear" that Saddam Hussein erected in Iraq? (Al-Khalil 1989). Obviously, Hussein feared that the benefits of a petrol-state and Baathist secular ideology (which focused on socialism and social progress to unite the country's various ethno-religious groups) were not enough to build a single national political community in Iraq. The manipulation of foundational myths and nationalist imagery was also not enough (Cook and Leheta 2016).

National Unity under Saddam Hussein

The repercussions of the 1979 Iranian Revolution and the subsequent Iran–Iraq War (1980–1988) played a role in Saddam Hussein's brutality. The emergence of a Shia theocracy in neighboring Iran mobilized the majority Shia community in Iraq. It did the same for Iraq's oppressed Kurds. Saddam went to war to beat back challenges by Shias and Kurds. After suppressing communal conflict, Iraq was stabile for about a decade until the US-led invasion in 2003 once again unleashed pent-up violent conflicts and national disunity.

The violent challenges to the Iraqi state under Saddam Hussein were partly linked to the heterogeneity of a population in which a dictator from the Sunni minority (32%–37% of the population) ruled over a Shia-majority country (60%–65% of the population) through the use and threat of violence.

The Sunni–Shia conflict in Iraq has long been linked to Iran (Hadhari 1981). Just prior to the start of the Iran–Iraq War (1980–1988), Iraqi Shias in the militant Islamist Dawa Party under Mullah Baqir Al Sadr declared a *fatwa* against Saddam Hussein and the Baathist government. This was at the instigation of Ayatollah Khomeini, who had been urging Muslims in Iraq to rise up against the secular Baathist Sunni-dominated regime. Shia militias killed Iraqi government officials, detonated bombs, and targeted Iraqi embassies around the world. Najaf, a Shrine city of Shia Islam, was practically in open rebellion during the Iran–Iraq War.

The Ayatollah's hope for a Shia uprising in Iraq never materialized. Saddam Hussein's secret security forces executed several Dawa Party members, affiliates, and relatives, including the revered Baqir Al Sadr and some of his family members (Norton 2007). Iraqi Shias worshiped Al Sadr, who was practically an Ayatollah in his own right. But no groundswell of Shia rebellion came – Saddam had cowed them into submission. The greatest single threat within Iraq to Baathist control, to date, was neutralized (Shadid 2005).

Tensions between Kurds and the Baathist Party in Iraq, which predated Saddam Hussein's presidency, also led to challenges to the state's monopoly of violence. Kurds in Iraq, as well as in neighboring Syria, Iran, and Turkey, have long sought an autonomous homeland. In 1970, the Baathist Party, anxious to secure its precarious hold on power, created the Autonomous Kurdistan Region in the northern governorates of Erbil, Sulaymaniyah, and Dohuk (HRW 1993).

Sharp conflicts between Kurds and the Sunni-controlled Iraqi state dominated the 1970s and 1980s (HRW 1993). While the Autonomous Region covered only half of the territory that the Kurds considered rightfully theirs, and carefully excluded the vast oil wealth that lay beneath the fringes of Kurdish land, it provided a measure of self-rule. However, the autonomy decree was followed by the "Arabization" of the oil-producing areas of Kirkuk, Khanaqin, and other parts of the North, evicting Kurdish farmers and replacing them with poor Arab tribesmen from the South (HRW 1993).

Led by Mullah Mustapha Barzani and his Kurdistan Democratic Party (KDP), the long-simmering Kurdish revolt flared up in 1974 (HRW 1993). It was crushed in 1975, leading to the forced removal of tens of thousands of Kurds into the desert in the south of Iraq. In the late 1970s, the regime moved against the Kurds again, destroying their villages and forcibly evacuating at least a quarter of a million people from Iraq's borders with Iran and Turkey (HRW 1993).

Kurdish nationalists mobilized after the start of the Iran–Iraq war in 1980 (HRW 1993). Many government garrisons in Kurdistan had been abandoned. In the vacuum that was left by Iraqi troops, the Kurdish *Peshmerga* – "those who face death" – began to thrive. In 1983, the KDP, led by one of Barzani's son's, Masoud, aided Iranian troops in their capture of a border town. In retaliation, Iraqi troops abducted between 5,000 and 8,000 Kurdish males aged 12 or over and killed them after imprisonment.

For the remainder of the Iran–Iraq War, the Iraqi regime's authority in the North was largely limited to the cities, while the mountains and countryside of Iraqi Kurdistan were effectively liberated territory (HRW 1993).

At the end of the Iran–Iraq War, Kurds paid a heavy price for assuming this independence. In 1988, the Iraqi government committed genocide against Kurdish Iraqis (HRW 1993). Another name for it is *Anfal*, the "Spoils," after the eighth *sura* ("chapter") of the Koran. This is a name given by the Iraqis to a series of military actions, which lasted from February 23 until September 6, 1988. The end of the Iran–Iraq War provided an opportunity for Saddam Hussein's regime to bring Kurds to heel (HRW 1993). Hussein granted special powers in Kurdish areas to a cousin, Ali Hassan al-Majid. Ali *"Anfal,"* or

"Chemical" Ali utilized chemical weapons and the integrated resources of Iraq's entire military, security, and civilian apparatus to, in his words, "solve the Kurdish problem and slaughter the saboteurs" (HRW 1993). At least 50,000 noncombatant Kurds were killed or disappeared during the campaign, including young children and entire families.

The *Anfal* mass murders against Kurds resembled a Nazi-style genocide campaign. Kurds were shipped to camps and prisons. There were mass gravesites:

While the camp system is evocative of one dimension of the Nazi genocide, the range of execution methods described by Kurdish survivors is uncannily reminiscent of another – the activities of the *Einsatzkommandos*, or mobile killing units, in the Nazi-occupied lands of Eastern Europe. Each of the standard operating techniques used by the *Einsatzkommandos* is documented in the Kurdish case. Some groups of prisoners were lined up, shot from the front and dragged into pre-dug mass graves; others were shoved roughly into trenches and machine gunned where they stood; others were made to lie down in pairs, sardine-style, next to mounds of fresh corpses, before being killed; others were tied together, made to stand on the lip of the pit, and shot in the back so that they would fall forward into it–a method that was presumably more efficient from the point of view of the killers. Bulldozers then pushed earth or sand loosely over the heaps of corpses. Some of the gravesites contained dozens of separate pits, and obviously contained the bodies of thousands of victims. Circumstantial evidence suggests that the executioners were uniformed members of the Ba'ath Party, or perhaps of Iraq's General Security Directorate (*Amn*). (HRW 1993)

The United States became actively involved in Iraqi communal conflicts in the early 1990s. In the 1990–1991 Gulf War, as a response to Iraq's annexation of Kuwait, the United States led a coalition force from 34 nations against Baathist Iraq. The war led to renewed uprisings by both Shias and Kurds.

Saddam Hussein's rapid defeat in Kuwait had created the perception that he was vulnerable to regime change. In addition, as American-led forces were driving Saddam's troops out of Kuwait, President George H. W. Bush repeatedly broadcast a call for the people of Iraq to rise up and overthrow the dictator, with the implication that US troops would join the uprising (Lando 2007). Eager to end decades of repression, the Kurds rose up in the North, and Shias revolted against Hussein in the South, quickly capturing major cities.

Unfortunately for the rebels, the 1991 uprising against Hussein never received the expected support from the allied forces, which were still on the ground in southern Iraq (Johns 2006). When American support did not arrive – belatedly, Bush had decided that the Shias and Kurds were backed by Iranian Islamists and should not be supported – Saddam Hussein responded viciously to end the uprising (Lando 2007). The Iraqi military dropped aerial bombs filled with sarin, a binary nerve agent, and CS, a very potent teargas, to put down the revolts in Kurdish and Shia areas. Iraqi army helicopters poured kerosene on rebels and civilians fleeing from Iraqi troops and set them on fire. People were shot in the street and left to rot or be eaten by dogs. Women were raped. The onslaught was broadcast by Iraqi television to send a message to other Iraqis.

Thus, after the departure of Western forces in 1991, Saddam Hussein's armed forces once again monopolized the use of violence within Iraq. Steep national unity challenges were buried under brutal repression.

Following the First Gulf war, international sanctions challenged the Iraqi state and nation. The United States and her allies imposed debilitating sanctions that harmed all Iraqis. Ironically, the sanctions probably expanded the role of the Iraqi state and the commitment to it by Iraqis of all backgrounds (Cohen and Driscoll 2003). Just prior to the 2003 invasion, 13 years of harsh sanctions had increased public support and empathy for the Baathist Party and the Iraqi state (Sassoon 2012).

Remarkably, Saddam Hussein's cynical and violent rule – and European-imposed borders – did not destroy the possibility of Iraqi national unity. Opinion polls taken in the years following Saddam's removal in 2003 showed that the Iraqi population had a strong commitment to a unified state and were bound to it by a vibrant nationalism (Dodge 2014). The 2003 Oxford Research International polls indicated that 79% of Iraqis preferred one unified Iraq with a central government in Baghdad. Only 12% of Kurds and 3.8% of all Iraqis called for the country to be broken up into separate states (cited in Dodge and Wasser 2014).

The invasion and occupation of Iraq by the George W. Bush administration, and the elected Iraqi governments that followed it, broke down Iraqi national unity and the Iraqi state in dramatic fashion. In 2003, the United States claimed that Saddam Hussein harbored weapons of mass destruction and religious terrorists. This resulted in their return to Iraq. The invasion was followed by the implementation of competitive elections that enabled the Shia Arab majority to claim power for the first time in Iraqi history while cementing special rights and protections for Kurds.

However, foreign occupation in Iraq also gave rise to a fierce Sunni insurgency that targeted US troops, new Shia-dominated governments, and even ordinary Shia civilians; this led to a sectarian war that peaked between 2006 and 2008 (Brands and Feaver 2019).

As we shall see, implementing competitive elections in Iraq beginning in 2003 would have fared better for the US-led coalition if it had not degraded Iraqi national unity and state capacities at the same time.

The US-Led Invasion, the Coalition Provisional Authority, and Abu Musab al-Zarqawi

It's the Pottery Barn rule: You break it, you own it. 'You are going to be the proud owner of 25 million people,' he told the president. "You will own all their hopes, aspirations, and problems. You'll own it all."

Abu Musab al-Zarqawi, a Jordanian Jihadist, was an al-Qaeda leader in Afghanistan when the United States attacked Osama Bin Laden and his followers in retaliation for the terrorist assaults on US territory on September 11, 2001.[2] Zarqawi was wounded in the US bombings in Afghanistan and fled to the mountains of Northeastern Iraq to once again recruit, train, and unleash al-Qaeda operatives (Warrick 2015).

In 2003, the United States invaded and occupied Iraq. Great Britain was their main coalition partner; there was little other international support. During the occupation, Zarqawi and other small Jihadist groups initially operated in a Kurdish area outside of Iraq's control due to a US no-fly zone (Warrick 2015).

The Bush administration's claim that Saddam Hussein's Iraq harbored terrorists and possessed weapons of mass destruction proved faulty. Al-Qaeda's leaders hated Iraq's secular regime, and Saddam Hussein had persecuted and killed Islamic extremists (Warrick 2015).

---

[2] According to Bob Woodward of the *Washington Post*, US Secretary of State Colin Powell cited the rule in the summer of 2002 when warning President George W. Bush of the consequences of his planned military action in Iraq. See Woodward (2004).

Despite US claims, there had been no weapons of mass destruction in Iraq or cooperation between al-Qaeda and the Iraqi government. The Bush administration expected to be welcomed for removing a despised tyrant. Though many Iraqis were grateful, most wanted the removal of Saddam Hussein without any subsequent US occupation. The Bush administration was also optimistic about its goal to help establish an Iraqi democracy. Little apparent consideration was given to the impact that the US invasion and occupation would have on the Iraqi state and nation.

Sensing the chance provided by the US-led invasion and occupation to create a future state for his emerging al-Qaeda affiliate, Zarqawi took steps to ensure the violent rupture of the Iraqi state and Iraqi society. Zarqawi attempted to turn Iraqi ethnosectarian tensions into a civil war by coordinating a strategic campaign of car bombs and suicide attacks that directly targeted mosques and marketplaces in Baghdad and elsewhere (Warrick 2015). He zeroed in on Shias with the goal of destabilizing Iraq and eliminating what he deemed as a historic Shia apostasy. The biggest blow came in the summer of 2003 (ICG 2006). As a crowd exited the Imam Ali Mosque in Najaf, a car bomb staged by Zarqawi exploded, killing 85 worshipers, including Ayatollah Muhammad Baqir al-Hakim, a powerful and charismatic leader of one of Iraq's largest political parties.

After that, a civil war emerged in Iraq with civilians dying at a rate of more than 50 a day (Stern and Berger 2015). It became a bloody conflict pitting Sunni against Shiite, Shiite against Sunni, in which the most radical elements on each side set the agenda (ICG 2006). Attacks on Shia crowds by suicide bombers were countered by violent sweeps through predominantly Sunni towns and neighborhoods by Shia militias.

Foreign Jihadists flocked to Zarqawi's campaign (Warrick 2015). Armed enclaves based on sect emerged in an Iraq where Sunnis and Shias had often attended schools and universities together, lived side by side in mixed neighborhoods, and intermarried (Warrick 2015). The killing of innocent Muslim civilians caused a break with al-Qaeda leaders. Osama Bin Laden and Ayman al-Zawahiri became concerned about losing the hearts and minds of the Muslim community and did not consider Shias to be apostates.

To sum up, foreign-influenced state borders from the colonial era set up steep challenges to political community within Iraq. The cynical, divisive, and violent policies of autocratic leaders from the minority Sunni population strained national politics and decades of state-building. War and economic sanctions cut deeply. The terrorist attacks led by the organization that would become ISIS contributed heavily to the start of a sectarian war between Sunni and Shia communities within Iraq.

Finally, to fully understand the breakdown of the Iraqi nation-state and how it has hindered democratic consolidation, consideration must also be given to the ways in which most of the governments that have ruled Iraq since 2003 have systematically undermined each pillar of the state's sustainability.

At the same time as it was imposing democracy (competitive elections) in Iraq, the US occupation was harming Iraqi national unity and state capacities in several ways. One, it disbanded the Iraqi military and police without replacing them with different institutions that monopolized the use of violence and provided security for Iraqi citizens. Two, it disbanded the Iraqi bureaucracy without replacing it. Three, it formed Iraqi governments in a manner that weakened national political community by increasing ethnosectarian tensions and conflicts. Four, it shepherded a constitution seemingly designed to break down ethnosectarian harmony. And five, its administrative practices fostered a great deal of corruption.

After defeating Saddam Hussein's regime, the United States put in place the Coalition Provisional Authority (CPA) and the Iraqi Governing Council (IGC), an advisory body to the CPA. Saddam Hussein's Baathist government had ruled Iraq for 35 years when the CPA, led by US Ambassador Paul Bremer, replaced it. In power, the Bremer administration focused on elections. At the same time, it misguidedly weakened the attributes of a modern nation-state that had survived Hussein's time in power.

Issued by Bremer, Order Number 1 (De-Baathification) gutted the Sunni-dominated bureaucracy. It banned the Baathist Party and removed its members from positions in Iraq's administration. The broad order went beyond the state's senior structure (Cordesman 2006). It stretched down to lower levels and across various areas, creating a climate where people could be expelled from roles as innocuous as university or grade-school teachers. The capacity to provide public goods was deeply compromised. The courts and local governance collapsed. Businesspeople faced extortion and increased corruption. By removing the secular core from the administration and government, at both the central and local levels, the CPA also crippled the Iraqi economy (Cordesman 2006).

Order Number 2 disbanded Saddam Hussein's military, security, and intelligence infrastructure. This ended the state's monopoly of violence. Order Number 2 meant that Iraqis could no longer count on the state to provide safety and security for their families. In addition, the Sunni men who were jettisoned from the military and security services were left with caches of weapons, military and intelligence training, and few employment prospects. The De-Baathification process left 750,000 Iraqis, mainly Sunnis, unemployed and hostile to the emerging state and government (Ozerdem 2010).

The CPA's plan in 2003 to create a new Iraqi military and police that would monopolize legitimate violence; be professional, nonpolitical, representatives of all Iraqis; and remain under the control of elected civilian authorities developed slowly and ultimately failed. While the Iraqi internal security apparatus under Saddam Hussein was brutal and repressive, its abrupt dissolution fostered lawlessness, sectarian violence, and the development of various types of militias. In 2019, at the time of the writing of this volume, many of the militias are still outside the control of the state.

Taken together, Order Number 1 and Order Number 2 overwhelmed Iraq's tenuous national unity. Political community – widespread commitment to the state – depends partly on the state's ability to provide public goods. The CPA regressed in the provision of public goods from the status quo under Saddam Hussein. In addition, the CPA's De-Baathification policies left many Sunnis feeling that they did not have a part in the new order, including an emerging democracy dominated by the Shia majority and the Kurds. Sunnis also feared retaliation by Shias for their role in Saddam Hussein's brutalization of Shias and Kurds.

Upon taking power, the CPA also discouraged national unity by officially designating the Kurdish regional government, which had had some autonomy since the 1991 Gulf War, as an official autonomous region in Iraq (Mansour 2016).

Before transferring power to a sovereign Iraqi government, the Coalition Provisional Authority created the Iraqi Governing Council (IGC, July 13, 2003–June 1, 2004). Instead of encouraging national unity, the IGC was composed in a manner that fostered ethnosectarian politics (Mansour 2016). It consisted of various Iraqi political and tribal leaders who were appointed by the CPA to provide advice and leadership. The council included 13 Shias, 5 Sunnis, 5 Kurds (also Sunnis), 1 Turkmen, and 1 Assyrian.

Working against national unity, the CPA's decision to compose the IGC based on Iraq's sectarian and ethnic demographics, rather than on national political platforms, made communal politics the fundamental organizing principle of government for the first time in Iraq's history (Alkadiri and Toensing 2003).

Iraqis had diverse views of the IGC. Some thought of it as a first step toward indigenous governance. Others viewed it as an illegitimate body made up disproportionately of formerly exiled groups, with few constituents within Iraq. However, Shias viewed the IGC more favorably than Sunnis.

Politically, the IGC was dominated by two prewar opposition parties led by men in exile with a professed commitment to secular democracy: The Iraqi National Congress founded by Ahmed Chalabi, which had been long supported by the Central Intelligence Agency (CIA), and the Iraqi National Accord, headed by Iyad Alawi, a one-time ally of Saddam Hussein turned opponent, which had been supported by both the CIA and Britain's MI6 (Alkadiri and Toensing 2003). In addition, the IGC was heavily represented by two Shia religious parties: The Supreme Council for Islamic Revolution in Iraq (SCIRI) and the al-Dawa Party, both of which had links to Iran. Kurds were represented in the IGC by the Kurdish Democratic Party and the Patriotic Union of Kurdistan.

In what amounts to a summary of the negative impact of the US occupation, the constitution it shepherded weakened Iraq as both a nation-state and a Weberian state (Jawad 2013). The Constitution enshrined the De-Baathification law that gutted the bureaucracy of trained civil servants. At the expense of national unity, the Constitution made excessive concessions to the Kurds on the issues of federalism and natural resources in Kirkuk, an oil-rich province in which the majority are not Kurds. More generally, due to US influence, the Constitution ignored the history of the Iraqi state and Iraqi identity, reducing the Iraqi state to a collection of Shias, Sunnis, Kurds, and other minorities: "The US aimed to create not a nation-state but a civic nation with an identity based on the combination of Arab Shia, Arab Sunni, and Kurdish religious and secular populations that had been held together by a succession of authoritarian states" (Jawad 2013).

Instead of building on the history of Iraq as a nation-state, the parties and groups that the US helped put in power adopted their more sectarian view of Iraqi society (Jawad 2013). For instance, the new Iraqi Constitution emphasized sectarian differences much more than the general Iraqi population did, and the new powerholders began acting in more sectarian ways than they did prior to the US occupation (Jawad 2013).

The new Iraqi Constitution also weakened central government and strengthened provinces (Jawad 2013). In the new federal system, federal entities gained powers that superseded those of the central government, including overriding efforts by the central government to achieve greater equality in the distribution of oil wealth.

Finally, the Iraqi Constitution was also flawed in terms of fostering the monopoly of violence by the military (Jawad 2013). It did not empower or require the state to establish one unified military, and in practice the Ministry of Defense had no authority over ethnic and religious-based militias, including the Kurdish *Peshmerga*, which is officially regarded as part of the Iraqi military and is financed by the central government.

Based on the new constitution, competitive elections from the outset harmed national unity. Due to low participation by Sunnis, Shia and Kurdish blocs ended up being overrepresented in the new assembly, which wrote the new Iraqi Constitution that was biased against Sunnis (Jabar 2007). Sunni underrepresentation strengthened the rejectionist and militant groups among the Sunni Arab community and reinforced the logic of using force to respond to perceived institutional injustices (Jabar 2007). During this period, the insurgency took an increasingly large toll on coalition troops, Iraqi government personnel and institutions, and civilians (Allawi 2008). The Sunni–Shia civil war that resulted in the Islamic State ignited as well.

Similar to the US occupation, most post–Saddam Hussein Iraqi governments weakened Iraqi national unity and modern state capabilities in several ways as the country began to conduct competitive elections. One, new Iraqi elites adopted the more ethnosectarian view of Iraqi politics held by the United States (Alkadiri and Toensing 2003). Two, the elected Shia-dominated Nouri al-Maliki governments (2006–2014) discriminated against Sunnis enough for them to join an insurgency and the ranks of ISIS. Three, instead of rationalizing the bureaucracy, Maliki also entrenched governing based on the ethnosectarian divisions of Iraq's oil wealth and corruption. Four, the Kurdish regional government has been unable to contain secessionist sentiments. Five, no Iraqi government has been able to rein in militias and establish the state's monopoly of violence.

The Iraqi Governing Council did little to prevent the breakdown of the Iraqi state (Alkadiri and Toensing 2003). Its federal structure, reflecting the demographic strength of Shia Arab, Sunni Arab, and Kurdish populations, pulled against national unity. Little progress was made in providing public goods. Most Iraqis felt that the IGC failed to address their personal and economic needs for security, electricity, and jobs. Overall, the IGC confirmed a fundamental alteration of the political balance of power in Iraq to favor Shias and Kurds over Sunni Arabs (Alkadiri and Toensing 2003). IGC policies equated all Sunnis as Baathists and Saddam loyalists, making reconciliation difficult and perpetuating a Sunni-dominated insurgency.

Instead of supporting pluralism, democracy, the rule of law, and national reconciliation and unity, the elected Nouri al-Maliki governments' (2006–2014) drew their legitimacy almost purely from a divisive ethnosectarian agenda (Khedery 2015). Maliki, a Shia dissident under Saddam Hussein's regime, rose to prominence after he fled a death sentence in 1979 and spent decades abroad, mainly in Iran. Abroad, he became a senior leader of the Islamic Dawa Party and sought Iranian and Syrian help to overthrow Saddam Hussein. In 2006, Maliki was elected prime minister of Iraq.

Maliki proved to be a poor partner to the United States in dealing with the insurgency that emerged almost as soon as the latter and Great Britain occupied Iraq. His policies fed the insurgency and ISIS by alienating Sunnis. His unwillingness to foster reconciliation dissipated the gains of the US surge and rapprochement with Iraqi Sunnis.

The Insurgency

A stunned Sunni Arab community rejected the US-led regime change that brought the Shias and Kurds to power in Baghdad (Hashim 2006). Dominated by alienated Iraqi Sunnis, the insurgency contained elements of ex-Baathists, Iraqi nationalists, Sunni tribal forces, secular Sunni partisans, and domestic Jihadists. Some followed a *fatwa* by the head of the Association of Muslim Scholars, Harith al-Dhari, calling for a national insurgency against US occupation (Hashim

2006). The insurgency took a large toll on coalition troops, Iraqi government personnel and institutions, and civilians. The complex and mutating insurgency against US occupation and Shia-dominant governments was initially composed of 20 or so loose, decentralized armed groups, which were all motivated to fight what they viewed as foreign occupation and foreign-imposed rule.[3]

There were several Sunni-dominated, secular nationalist or tribal groups that took part in the insurgency (Hashim 2006). The General Command of the Armed Forces, Resistance, and Liberation in Iraq was composed of former Iraqi military personnel. The Popular Resistance for the Liberation of Iraq accused Arab and Muslim leaders of turning themselves into local policemen for the United States; they issued a call on June 26, 2003, to all in the Arab and Islamic worlds to come and attack the United States in Iraq.

Sunni militias that incorporated nationalist and religious elements included the Higher Command of the Mujahideen (Holy Warriors) in Iraq (Hashim 2006). More explicitly religious Sunni groups that battled the US and British occupation included Jaish Ansar al-Sunna (Hashim 2006). The Army of the Followers of the Teachings of the Prophet was one of the largest and deadliest militias in Iraq. The Sunni-dominated, conservative, and religious town of Fallujah produced the Armed Islamic Movement of Al-Qaeda Organization. The fanatical Islamic Army of Iraq, IAI, had ties to Osama Bin Laden and Zarqawi. A large militia with up to 17,000 members, it attacked all Westerners and Iraqis that it deemed to be Western collaborators (Hashim 2006).

Notably, the US invasion and occupation also produced enemies within the Iraqi Shia community that it had helped put in power (Hashim 2006). Muqtada al-Sadr, the scion of an influential clerical family, led a rebellion against the CPA, which he viewed as a foreign occupier led by a foe that he considered a greater enemy than Saddam Hussein (Japan Times 2016). Sadr commanded a political movement and the Mahdi Army militia that fought fierce battles against American and Iraqi government forces. He found his strongest support in poor Shia neighborhoods such as the Sadr City area of Baghdad and in his family base in southern Iraq around Najaf and Qom.

---

[3] For a comprehensive survey, see Hashim (2006).

Sectarian Civil War

Prodded by Zarqawi, forces of the Sunni insurgency also attacked Shia-dominated governments and civilians. This led to the formation of Shia militias outside of the state. Shias facing Sunni insurgents and Zarqawi's Jihadists – who targeted Shia civilians, mosques, markets, and religious festivals with lethal force using including car bombs, improvised explosive devices (IEDs), and suicide bombers – formed their own religious and tribally organized militias to defend themselves. These Shia militias, some of whom operated under government auspices, often retaliated with indiscriminate violence against Sunnis (Ozerdem 2010).

In addition to informal Shia militias, the two most important Shia religious parties, SCIRI and al-Dawa, developed well-armed militias with ties to Iran (Hahsim 2006). Heavily armed militias fighting during the rule of the CPA also included the battle-hardened Kurdish *Peshmerga*, which numbered at least 50,000 fighters (Diamond 2004).

The Sunni-dominated insurgency and Sunni–Shia sectarian conflicts were at their height from 2005 until early 2007. US military leaders in Iraq were unable to counter the lethal insurgency, and Sunni–Shia violence approached the intensity of a full-scale civil war. However, by mid-2008 there was a dramatic reduction in both the insurgency and sectarian violence. In addition, al-Qaeda in Iraq was all but destroyed, with remnants fleeing to desert areas and into Syria (Warrick and Mekhennet 2016).

The Surge and the Sunni Anbar Awakening

Part of the reduction in bloodshed can be explained by a "surge" in the numbers of US forces ordered by President George W. Bush in January 2007 (Wilbanks and Karsh 2010).

More of it can be explained by (1) the development of an alliance between US forces and many Sunni tribal militias who, at least temporarily, turned against their former al-Qaeda allies and (2) changed paths from violent resistance to cautious integration into the Shia-dominated political economy that had replaced Saddam Hussein's Sunni-dominated regime (McCary 2009).

Signs of the factors that would diminish bloodshed in Iraq became noticeable in late 2006 due to developments in the majority-Sunni areas of the country (McCary 2009). Most of the Sunni population in Iraq resides in the "Sunni Triangle" – a vast area between Baghdad in the South, Mosul in the North, and Rutba in the East. Inhabitants of the Sunni Triangle shifted to a greater reliance on tribal formations to organize sociopolitical life and provide benefits such as jobs and social welfare in the wake of exclusion from the new Shia state structure (Long 2008).

Initially, many Sunnis were also receptive to an insurgency led by al-Qaeda's Iraqi branch under the leadership of Zarqawi. However, by late 2006, it appeared that al-Qaeda had worn out its welcome (McCary 2009). At the start of the US occupation, Sunni tribal *sheikhs* had feared that both the new state structures and the imposition of democratic processes dramatically shifted power to the Shia community. That threat had led to the insurgency and an alliance with al-Qaeda in Iraq. However, eventually, Sunni tribal leaders in the region realized that al-Qaeda posed an even greater threat, as it took over all forms of power in the region from violence and politics to finance (McCary 2009). Al-Qaeda asserted territorial control in Sunni areas through money and violence (kidnappings, assassinations, torture, and grotesque murders of tribal leaders and their family members, including beheadings and public dismemberment), in addition to usurping economic enterprises, including by smuggling and using extortion, upon which the Sunni tribes had relied for decades.

Realizing the threat of international Jihadists, Sunni tribal groupings in Anbar began seeking an alliance with the United States and the central government of Iraq to fight al-Qaeda in Iraq (McCary 2009). The US alliance with this group, the Anbar Salvation Council (ASC), became known as the Anbar Awakening. Essentially, the Awakening refers to Sunni tribal militias in Anbar and other Sunni-majority provinces breaking their alliance with foreign Sunni al-Qaeda in Iraq fighters that had been formed to wage an insurgency against the US occupation of a Muslim land.

The Awakening tribes formed a new alliance with the US military and, more hesitantly, with the Shia-dominated central government of Iraq (McCary 2009). Al-Qaeda's violent coercion within Sunni areas and the improved efficacy of the US military after the arrival of the surge brigades led to the new US military–Sunni tribal alliance. As the US alliance with Sunni tribes spread, the insurgency greatly weakened and Sunni areas became relatively peaceful. By changing its approach to the Anbar region – from declaring it politically and militarily lost and hostile to actively courting Sunni tribal *sheikhs* – the US military became the alternative to al-Qaeda aggression.

During the Anbar Awakening, US military leaders changed their reconstruction and security policies in the province. Instead of relying on the Iraqi central government, the United States began directly authorizing, funding (giving cash to Sunni *sheikhs*), and arming Sunni tribal militias, which overtook al-Qaeda and the insurgency and began providing local security (McCary 2009). The United States also used the new alliance to press for better Sunni–Shia relations (McCary 2009). It pushed the Iraqi central government to convert Sunni tribal militias to state-run security forces and to more actively extend the state's economic largesse into majority Sunni areas.

For their part, leaders of the Sunni Awakening movement changed it from an armed movement to a political movement seeking to pursue their interests through the new Iraqi socioeconomic political order (McCary 2009). However, sectarian tensions remained. Sunni tribal leaders retained their suspicions of the Shia-led central government and its perceived association with Iran; the central government saw the increasing power and independence of tribes in the Sunni Triangle as a threat to its control.

Nouri al-Maliki and the Islamic State

The nation-building promises of the surge, which had nevertheless conceded militia formations outside the control of the state and elected governments, were dashed by the elected governments of Nouri al-Maliki (2006–2014) and by the withdrawal of most US troops, which led to an increase in sectarian politics that corroded the Iraqi military's cohesion and confidence (Broder 2015).

Maliki weakened the state bureaucracy through corruption and instigated a pattern of ethnocentric rule that contributed to national disunity. Maliki made little effort to mollify alienated Sunnis, including the tens of thousands that had lost livelihoods in the De-Baathification of the military and administration.

Before they withdrew most of their armed forces, the Americans had largely failed to convince Maliki's government to incorporate the

Sunni tribal militias from the Sunni Awakening Councils into newly established Iraqi security and state structures, or to include them more fully in the state's economic largesse (Wilbanks and Karsh 2010). Sunnis did not attain the amount of government positions they expected from their cooperation in the Awakening Movement. Those that did often were not paid (Byman 2016).

Maliki's government formally accepted the Awakening Councils under the name of the Sons of Iraq (SOI) but repressed the leaders and numbers of SOIs, insisting that the prime minister's office vet all members (Stansfield 2016). Maliki's sectarianism was so bad that Human Rights Watch (HRW 2013) charged his governments with engaging in a campaign of violence and harassment of Iraq's Sunni population characterized by torture, air strikes, and extrajudicial killings.

In addition to being an especially poor nation-builder, Maliki was a poor state-builder as well. Granted, it was initially the fault of the US invasion and occupation that the Iraqi state lacked a basic bureaucracy and a military and police that monopolized the use of violence. Still, instead of an all-out effort to forge these modern state attributes, Maliki combined new state-built armed forces with the armed militias of the former Shia opposition parties (Stansfield 2016). Instead of a professional military, the result of the combination was a mainly ragtag force characterized by barbarism (state terrorism), incompetence, volatile sectarian and ethnic allegiances, and unstable hierarchical chains of command.

The military and security apparatuses were not insulated from political, partisan, and sectarian influence (McCary 2009). The post–Saddam Hussein regular army divisions, 12 of them comprising approximately 300,000 soldiers and officers, were distributed according to region, sect, and ethnicity (McCary 2009). There were Shia, Kurdish, and Sunni divisions, and divisions associated with political parties, which mitigated the development of a unified patriotic army. In the security sector and intelligence service, the Ministry of the Interior mostly followed the orders of the Iraqi Shia Islamist political party (the Supreme Council for Islamic Revolution). The Ministry of National Security was aligned with the Shia Islamic Dawa Party. Factional, partisan politics infiltrated the national intelligence service.

ISIS Makes Its Move against Maliki's Rag-Tag Force

In January 2014, ISIS took over Raqqa in civil-war-torn Syria and made it its capital. Crossing into Iraq, in three stunning days in June 2014, ISIS swept through much of Northern and Central Iraq, seized control of most of the Sunni Triangle – Mosul, Tikrit, Fallujah – and threatened Kirkuk and Baghdad as four divisions of the Iraqi army shed their uniforms and fled (Chulov 2014).

After the military debacle, Nouri al-Maliki's government, which had made many Sunni Arabs feel that ISIS was the lesser of two evils, was removed from power and replaced by the Haider al-Abadi government (2014–2018). US officials pressured for the change and demanded greater inclusion of the Sunni minority in the Iraqi formal political economy.

After the Iraqi military's collapse against ISIS, the US military began training several Iraqi brigades to launch a counteroffensive against ISIS (Broder 2015). However, their early retaliatory campaigns against ISIS failed, though their performance improved over time. Early attempts to recapture Tikrit as a preparatory phase to retaking Mosul, ISIS's de facto capital in Iraq, were not successful.

The continuing poor record of Iraq's military forces prompted several of Iraq's Iranian-supported Shia militias (armed, funded, and equipped by Iran along with Iranian military advisors) to take the lead on dislodging ISIS militants (Broder 2015). The Shia militias and Kurdish militias, some nominally part of the Iraqi state but fighting under the command of their sectarian militia leaders, have performed better than the formal Iraqi military in the battle against ISIS in Iraq.

While strongly motivated to battle ISIS, which has dubbed Shias apostates and therefore targets for death, the presence of Shia fighters in the predominantly Sunni areas conquered by ISIS provokes questions for postconflict state-building (Broder 2015). Shortly after ISIS's early victories, the Iraqi government formed the Popular Mobilization Force (PMF) as the governmental umbrella for the armed factions against ISIS (Al-Salhy 2015). The Popular Mobilization Force consisted of Shia militias already linked to the state and new Shia armed formations that developed after the ISIS offensive (Broder 2015). A minority of Sunni battalions also emerged to join the Popular Mobilization Force and battle ISIS, and a few developed ties with Shia groups to form multisectarian armed forces (Al-Salhy 2015). Building on Maliki's efforts, the Abadi model for the Popular Mobilization Force was to assist the Iraqi army at ridding the country of ISIS through the creation of a new government-financed and supervised paramilitary force in each province (The Economist 2014).

Ultimately, assaults by the Iraqi army, the Popular Mobilization Force, Iran's Quds Force officers on the ground, and American, British, and French air forces recaptured all of Iraq's conquered territories from the Islamic State. In terms of the state-rebuilding process, a core challenge for Prime Minister Abadi (2014–2018) and his successor, Adil Abdul-Mahdi (2018–present), has been how to incorporate and professionalize all armed groups under the authority and control of the state and elected governments. Unfortunately, neither have made any real progress in this regard, which means that the country is virtually always on the precipice of renewed civil war.

State- and Nation-Building after Maliki: The Monopoly of Legitimate Violence

In terms of Iraqi governments forging the monopoly of the use of violence, the biggest problem is the Popular Mobilization Force. The PMF is seeking to establish a formal institutional presence and play a role in politics and the economy (Mansour 2018). The Popular Mobilization Force, dominated by Shia with close ties to Iran and ambiguous ties to the Iraqi state, has resisted incorporation under the auspices of the Ministry of Defense or the Ministry of the Interior. It also continues to hold territory in areas they liberated from ISIS in places like Mosul and Kirkuk. It engages in economic activities and some criminal activities while playing the role of state armed forces.

The PMF has proposed themselves as Iraq's de facto National Guard – an independent security body protecting the political system, like a praetorian guard for the state under the auspices of the prime minister (Mansour 2018). By not integrating into the army or police, the militias retain their names, flags, and leaders. The PMF also gained direct political power by forming a political organization, Fatah Alliance, to run in the 2018 elections. The Fatah Alliance won 48 out of 329 seats, making it the second largest group in Parliament. The PMF also holds formal and informal economic power by rebuilding roads,

health facilities, and infrastructure, and by collecting taxes and facilitating trade in areas under its control. It engages in mafia-like coercive,
wealth-gaining activities as well.

In sum, The Popular Mobilization Force has become institutionalized as part of the state but retains the autonomy of a nonstate actor
(Mansour 2018). It challenges the state's and the government's command structure and monopoly over legitimate violence. Its electoral
strength, as the second largest group in Parliament, also challenges the
government's authority. Thus, the Iraqi central state apparatus and
governments have allowed militias to institutionalize their role as part
of the state while maintaining autonomy as independent security,
political, and economic actors. Informal or nonstate powers have
allowed militia leaders to compete against the state for power and
capacity (Mansour 2018).

Current Prime Minister Mahdi (2018–present) recently issued an
executive order with a plan to rein in the militias, including ending
any economic ventures, shedding individual militia names, and pulling
the PMF out of Sunni-only areas. However, it is not clear whether the
plan will reduce militias or dangerously consolidate their power: it all
depends on how it is implemented (Knights 2019). Certainly, many
militias continue to operate outside of state control.

If the Popular Mobilization Force challenges the Iraqi state's monopoly of violence and territory, then the Kurds do so even more.
Kurdish regions in Northern Iraq exercise a high degree of autonomy, with their own government (Kurdistan Regional Government,
KRG), parliament, and security forces. Kurdish-controlled areas are
rich in oil, and the KRG and Iraqi state fight over profits from oil
exports. In passing, the same can be said about federalist calls from
oil-rich Shia regions in the South. The Sunni provinces in the Northwest, of course, are also ambivalent about Shia-dominant governments in Baghdad. In 2018, Iraqi Kurds held a referendum in which
well over 90% of Kurds voted for full independence. The Baghdad
government and allies, including the United States, had advised
Kurds against it. After the referendum, the Iraqi government in
Baghdad sent state forces to successfully seize control of the city of
Kirkuk and its surrounding oil fields (Manfreda 2019). Kurds are
dispirited, turning to apathy and weighing a full break with Baghdad
(Manfreda 2019).

Unifying the Nation and Rationalizing the Bureaucracy

Along with ending the military's ability to monopolize the use of violence without replacing it, steep challenges in national administration and national unity have been poorly addressed by post–Saddam Hussein Iraqi governments. Post–Saddam Hussein Iraqi governments have largely done the opposite of rationalizing the country's bureaucracy. Political elites, operating within a disintegrating state and in a country suddenly flush with massive sums of cash, have taken advantage of an anticorruption framework full of loopholes to enrich themselves, while generalized corruption has spread throughout the bureaucracy.[4]

Under Saddam Hussein, corruption had been largely limited to his family and close associates, who utilized state funds for their personal use and enjoyment (Al-Ali 2014).

However, after the Coalition Provisional Authority was established, Iraq witnessed an alarming rise in corruption (Borger 2006). Proceeds from Iraq's massive oil wealth were transferred to a newly created Development Fund for Iraq (DFI) to be used at the CPA's discretion. The CPA built a national administration rife with corruption. Procurement rules did not follow Iraqi or American standards. Large non-competitive contracts, usually paid in cash and without proper instructions and planning, were distributed to nine US corporations. The contracts produced poor-quality public goods, if any at all. Audits established year after year that over 90% of DFI funds – billions of dollars targeted for Iraqi reconstruction – could not be accounted for. Auditing rarely led to punishment for malfeasance. In a Wild West atmosphere, during the occupation US officials also distributed billions of dollars in cash to placate potential enemies. Graft was so out of control that Iraqi government officials and the US special inspector general for Iraq reconstruction, Stuart Bowen, referred to corruption as a second insurgency, which threatened the viability of the Iraqi state (Borger 2006).

The post–Saddam Hussein Iraqi governments have not enacted effective anticorruption reforms (Jabar 2007). Many Iraqis who took

---

[4] This discussion of corruption in Iraq is based primarily on Al-Ali (2014), especially pp. 189–218.

over the state apparatus continued to siphon off billions of dollars in state funds. The Allawi, al-Jaafari, and al-Maliki administrations continued the legacy of the CPA by not cracking down on corruption through legal reforms and stringent enforcement mechanisms (Jabar 2007). From 2003 to 2011, a law in the Criminal Procedure Code, Article 136B, stated that an investigative judge could not prosecute a state official without the relevant minister's prior permission, which meant that ministers could unilaterally grant their staff immunity. The provision became universally regarded as an invitation to steal, until Parliament repealed it in 2011 (Al-Ali 2014).

Governments themselves have also created opportunities for corruption (Al-Ali 2014). Governments instituted a corrupting sectarian quota system, where instead of staffing ministries based on competence and experience, political blocs and militias have divvied up ministries and treated them as their fiefdoms, stuffing them with their cadres and emptying state coffers with ghost projects and ghost workers. Governments have also used intimidation to bury accusations of corrupt practices. Under Maliki, the government seized control of the Integrity Commission and Board of Supreme Audit. Corrupt senior officials were untouchable (Al-Ali 2014).

Corruption and administrative incompetence in Iraq since 2003 has been aggravated by corrupt and incompetent international assistance (Al-Ali 2014). The practices of the CPA were partly continued by the US embassy and the swarms of international organizations that entered the crisis-ridden country. There was a lot of money to spread around. Salaries were high, though few had the cultural experience to effectively implement development projects in Iraq. The uninformed became responsible for multi-million-dollar projects. Some engaged in corruption. The average Iraqi received little benefit from international assistance.

The Maliki governments (2006–2014) were especially egregious when it came to corruption and irrational bureaucratic practices. They also increased national disunity through ethnosectarian politics and, as the ISIS blitz through the country demonstrated, weakened the state and the government's monopoly of the use of violence.

In response, Prime Minister Haider al-Abadi (2014–2018) was put in power by internal and external supporters to improve nation-state building. He declared four main goals but achieved little (Al-Qarawee 2016):

- Rationalize the bureaucracy;
- Improve ethnosectarian relations;
- Rein in militias and forge the state's monopoly of the use of force; and
- Change from Nouri al-Maliki-style personal rule to collective rule.

Abadi ultimately failed to achieve any of the four goals. He lacked the leverage to establish the political consensus needed to legislate and implement major reforms. In order to reform the state, improve relations between ethnosectarian communities, and set-forth a clear vision of a post-ISIS Iraq, Abadi needed a broad and committed constituency behind him, which he did not have (Al-Qarawee 2016). Under Abadi, the political parties were too invested in ethnosectarian power-sharing arrangements to extend this support.

The 2018 parliamentary elections in Iraq were dominated by campaigns against corruption. Muqtada al-Sadr and his Sairoon bloc were the clear winners. Sadr played kingmaker for Prime Minister Adil Abdul-Mahdi. In order to end the corrupt sectarian patronage system, Sadr has proposed that independent technocrats, rather than politicians, run government ministries (Manfreda 2019).

After once being part of the insurgency, the sometimes-militant cleric Muqtada al-Sadr has pledged to work with anyone, and he has called for both US and Iranian troops to leave Iraq. Sadr's largely Shia Sairoon bloc includes a minority of Sunnis. It is unlikely that Sadr will be able to clean up corruption, rationalize the bureaucracy, and rein in the country's diverse militias. It is hard to imagine that Sadr will be able to forge national unity in Iraq.

In sum, post–Saddam Hussein Iraqi governments, beginning with the US and British invasion and occupation, have performed poorly at building a nation-state and a Weberian state within Iraq. National administration, national unity, and the state's ability to monopolize the use of violence have all been weaker since Hussein's fall. Weaknesses in state capacities and political community have hindered the development of democracy.

Some argue that, despite the rocky path, Iraq has become a consolidated democracy and that most Iraqis would not want to return to the time before the US-led invasion (Brands and Feaver 2019). If so, the costs have been cruelly high. The post-invasion Iraqi civil war has claimed at least 60,000 Iraqi lives (Caryl 2013). Between 2003 and

2012, 4,486 US military personnel lost their lives in Iraq as well. The United States has spent at least $800 billion in the Iraqi conflict in addition to up to $2 trillion in war-related expenditures (Caryl 2013).

Yes, there are competitive elections in Iraq to choose the country's most powerful decision-makers, but is it a democracy under these conditions? Militias outside of state control compete with elected governments' security, economic, and governing capacities, including ruling territory. As a result, citizens are not provided with law and order, the rule of law, or security. Post–Saddam Hussein, the bureaucracy has been irrational. The elections largely serve to divide up oil profits along ethnosectarian lines, with elites receiving far greater benefits than their communal brethren. One-third of the country has voted to secede. There is enough secessionist sentiment all over Iraq to raise the possibility of dividing it into three countries – majority Sunni, Shia, and Kurd. This means that many Iraqis do not want to be part of Iraq, regardless of how democratic it becomes.

Imposing competitive elections in Iraq from the outside by the United States and Great Britain, when "every" political faction – including political parties – has an armed wing, has created a volatile situation. Doing so in a country emerging from communal violence and Takfiri Jihadism, and with significant oil profits at stake, almost ensures that electoral losers will turn to violence to change negative electoral results. Ultimately, it will take "better" nation- and state-building to consolidate Iraq's democracy and put it back together again.

The Islamic State (ISIS, ISIL)

Introducing competitive elections in Iraq, paired with what amounted to the opposite of nation- and state-building, prepared the ground for what became the Islamic State on Iraqi and Syrian territory.[5]

The Islamic State, or ISIS, wants to eliminate (kill) infidels (Christians) and apostates, including inauthentic Muslims (by its definition), impose *Sharia* law (its own interpretation of Islamic law) worldwide, and hasten the arrival of the Mahdi, a man from the Prophet's family,

---

[5] ISIS refers to the Islamic State of Iraq and al-Sham (Syria). ISIL refers to the same group of people, the Islamic State of Iraq and the Levant. By self-proclamation, the same people now refer to themselves as the Islamic State.

"The Rightly Guided One," who, according to Islamic State prophecy, will appear during the End of Days to lead the final battle against the infidels, supposedly in Dabiq, Syria (Walt 2015).

Unlike al-Qaeda, the Islamic State has had immediate ambitions to control territory and build a state on it. With astonishing cruelty, the Islamic State's foot soldiers have pursued their organization's goals. They took advantage of the Arab Spring uprising in Syria and the nation-state vulnerabilities created by the US-led invasion and occupation of Iraq to create the rudiments of a genuine state in large parts of Iraq and Syria.

The Islamic State no longer controls territory. It was broken into pieces by a range of enemies. Iraqis and Syrians, and their allies, regrouped to battle the Islamic State. The organization's radical interpretation of Islam and *Sharia* law, and its Takfiri ways – murdering fellow Muslims on charges of ideological impurity – alienated many Arabs, Kurds, and Christians in Iraq, Syria, and adjoining countries, all of whom attacked ISIS. Even al-Qaeda's leadership condemned killing fellow Muslims, including declaring Shias apostates.

Western powers have engaged their declared enemy as well. Thus, ISIS's enemies that have been willing to use force to destroy them include the Syrian and Iraqi governments, the Syrian opposition, Iraqi Shia militias, Iraqi and Syrian Kurdish militias, Iran, al-Qaeda/Jabhat al-Nusra, Saudi Arabia and other Arab League countries, Turkey, Israel, Russia, the United States, and European Union countries.

The build-up and inevitable breakdown of the territorial Islamic State provides some clues as to how the radical Islamists plan to regroup and put their "state" back together again. Beginning in the summer of 2014, ISIS used ruthless violence, including suicide missions that displayed a fearlessness to its enemies, to capture territory, eliminate or intimidate rivals, and demonstrate their power to the wider world (Walt 2015). The Sunni extremist group attracted foreigners to its territorial state through its ideology and propaganda that declared the Islamic State as the only place in the world in which Muslims can live in an Islamic empire according to Islamic law – the first time this has been the case since the fall of the Ottoman Empire in the 1920s.

In its sweep across Syria and Iraq to gain territory and monopolize the use of violence within it, ISIS committed unfathomable atrocities against civilians. It conducted horrible massacres, perpetrating genocide against Yazidis, Christians, and Shias (Westcott 2016). Ethnic and sectarian cleansing forced a mass exodus of peaceful families lucky enough to survive the onslaught. ISIS fighters raped women and young girls multiple times a day (Benotman and Malik 2016). It required military service for tribes that surrendered to them (Lewis 2014). Within conquered areas, ISIS engaged in public executions with an emphasis on beheadings, torture and mutilation, and extremist interpretations of *Sharia* law, including severe public beatings and the enslavement of women (sexual slavery with a focus on the Yazidi minority) and children (UN 2014). Severed heads or crucified bodies were prominently displayed in crowded public places. Political prisoners were burned alive. ISIS recruited and indoctrinated some children into their radical ideology, and it killed and maimed others (UN 2014). To desensitize children and create militants, ISIS forced them to play soccer with decapitated heads (Benotman and Malik 2016). Children, many kidnapped, were utilized as suicide bombers and executioners (UN 2014). Suspected gay men and boys were raped and thrown off rooftops (Newton 2016). ISIS destroyed private property, cultural sites, and places of worship. ISIS or the Islamic State's propensity for violence and intimidation in order to subdue internal resistance and attract media attention to its rule cannot be overstated.

ISIS was no less brutal on the battlefield. ISIS's leadership, including some of Saddam Hussein's former military, security, and intelligence officers, delighted in battle and slaughter (UN 2014). Its militants leveraged multiple military styles in Iraq, including terrorism, guerrilla warfare, and conventional warfare, often in combination (DeAtkine 2015). Industrial-scale use of suicide bombers and small swarms of militants intimidated the Iraqi army. Enemy commanders were decapitated to instill fear in enemy soldiers (Byman 2016). Videos of executions, massacres, and assassination squads were distributed widely (Hashim 2014). Stephan Rosiny described ISIS's savage "shock and awe" tactics as its militants took over Iraq's Sunni heartland:

The militia attacked with some suicide bombers, then broke through front lines on pick-ups and looted Humvees and started a guerrilla war while sleeper cells in the hinterlands simultaneously carried out bomb attacks. They separated border guards, police and soldiers according to their sectarian affiliation: Sunnis were "forgiven" if they joined ISIS; Shiites and members of other minorities were murdered by the thousands. Propaganda videos on the Internet showed the brutal mass execution of captives by mass shooting and sadistically slow beheadings. (Rosiny 2015: 99)

ISIS's military operations in 2014 swiftly led to the seizure of Mosul, Fallujah, Ramadi, and other Northwestern Iraqi cities (Edwards 2015). With between 3,000 and 5,000 fighters, along with about the same number of allied Iraqi Sunni forces, ISIS quickly overwhelmed all four Iraqi army divisions, an estimated 30,000 troops, stationed in the area (Terrill 2014). The divisions fled, leaving behind their weapons, equipment, and supplies, including artillery, tanks, and a variety of other military vehicles.

As government troops deserted, Prime Minister Maliki offered to arm any citizens willing to battle ISIS in Mosul and other cities (Al-Arabiya 2014). Ultimately, ISIS's alliances with the alienated Sunni population and its savagery terrorized unmotivated government troops (mainly Shia who were reluctant to defend local Sunnis or Sunnis reluctant to fight on behalf of the Shia-dominated Iraqi government), who fled largely without fighting (Al-Arabiya 2014).

States have to pay for their armies and bureaucracies. To fund their Caliphate, ISIS militants primarily relied on oil sales via smuggling networks from the oil fields under its control in Iraq and Syria (UN 2014). While air strikes progressively limited oil revenue, in 2014 ISIS's estimated revenue from crude oil ranged from $846,000 per day to $1,645,000 per day (UN 2014). Other revenue streams came from extorting local businesses, "taxing" businesses and individuals, theft, and kidnapping for ransom (UN 2014). ISIS also took over banks in its conquered territories. In Mosul alone, ISIS seized up to $480 million from the city's banks (Chulov et al. 2014). It has also received limited donations and traffics women and children (Chulov et al. 2014).

To maintain power and control within its territory, ISIS did not rely solely on intimidation and violence. Ideology and the state's ability to provide essential state functions – such as public goods and services – were utilized to build political community. ISIS soldiers were provided with a salary, a house, food, and, in many cases, a wife, who was either a sex slave or a coerced local woman, or a domestic or foreign female Jihadist eager to marry militants and raise families (Callimachi 2016). The official Islamic State al-Hayat Media Office projected an image of the Islamic State as a utopia free from the immorality of the West (Benotman and Malik 2016). There were all-female and all-male morality police (Moaveni 2015). To tempt people – skilled professionals, fighters, religious figures, ordinary citizens – to make *hijra* ("migration") to the Caliphate, ISIS's media emphasized pictures and videos that showed modern infrastructure, schools, health services, outreach, and state administrative works (Benotman and Malik 2016).

For the 10 million people that lived within its territory, ISIS controlled access to electricity and water, provided medical assistance and traditional Islamic education, built markets, ran soup kitchens and provided other food aid, installed new power lines, initiated public transport, enforced price controls, minted coins, and created a consumer protection bureau (Zelin 2014). It provided traffic officers, police forces, and draconian courts; started vaccination programs; fixed potholes; created orphanages; and even organized fairs for children, which were complete with ice cream and inflatable slides (Zelin 2014). While the quality of these services were poor, even limited services are valuable in war zones (Byman 2016).

Over time, the gap between ISIS's propaganda and reality increased for the inhabitants of its rule. In addition to the provision of public services to build political community, and of "security" by monopolizing the use of violence, ISIS has relied on its ideology, an extreme form of Jihadi Salafism, which has appealed to some disaffected Muslims in the region and in the West (Moghadam 2008).

From ISIS's point of view, the Muslim world is in crisis. Islam is in a constant state of decline in religious, political, military, economic, and cultural terms due to the persistent attacks and humiliations of Muslims on the part of an anti-Islamic alliance of "Crusaders," Zionists, and apostates (Moghadam 2008).

ISIS has a distinctive view of the Islamic concept of *takfir*. ISIS conceptualizes *takfir* in an extreme way, more extreme than other violent Jihadi Salafi groups (Sorenson 2014). For ISIS, saintly worship ("Sufism"), the Christian Trinity, and Shia belief (due to the Shia elevation of their imams to partnership status with God) all violate *tawhid* ("monotheism"), making their adherents apostates. ISIS condones mass murder to rid Islamic society, and eventually the world, of these deviants. *Takfir* doctrine as practiced by ISIS is so extreme and expansive that some al-Qaeda leaders and theorists have questioned its legitimacy.

To defeat the Crusaders, Zionists, and apostates, and reverse the tide of history, ISIS calls for *jihad*, though it understands the act in military as opposed to spiritual terms and even elevates violent *jihad* to a sixth pillar of Islam, second only to the profession of faith, *shahada*

(Moghadam 2008). Martyrdom is extolled as the ultimate way in which *jihad* can be waged – hence ISIS's prolific use of suicide attacks.

Ideologically, ISIS has had an appeal to a minority of mostly young Muslims searching for an identity amid difficult socioeconomic and spiritual times (Moghadam 2008). It promises an immediate "pure" life under a resurrected, invincible, Islamic Caliphate that strictly replicates their interpretation of the times of Islam's pious ancestors: the first three generations of Muslims, *al-salaf al-salih*. To those who are disoriented, ISIS provides a new self-definition based on a supranational entity in which the only identity that truly matters is that of membership in the global Islamic community, *umma*, that bestows comfort, dignity, security, and honor among downtrodden Muslims (Moghadam 2008).

More prosaically, ISIS promises to disaffected, young, angry, violent men the following: adventure, money, sexual access to women, loot, membership in a warrior brotherhood, escape from a sense of powerlessness, respect, glory, and eternal salvation.

Like in Christianity and in Judaism, apocalyptic views and a belief that this world will end with catastrophic battles pitting the forces of good against the forces of evil – battles that will cleanse and purify a corrupt and sinful world – are found in Islam. A tenet of ISIS's Jihadi Salafism identifies portents of the apocalypse in recent events in the Middle East. The US-led invasion of Iraq in 2003 led to an insurgency against an occupying Crusader power and a civil war. The Arab Spring uprisings for democracy, dignity, and socioeconomic justice, which began in late 2010, added more civil wars, chaos, and bloodshed to the lives of people living in the Islamic world, especially in Syria.

Instead of seeing these events as failed democratic transitions, ISIS framed the current turbulent and bloody times in the Muslim world as the coming apocalypse (Stansfield 2016). A controversial *hadith* – a report describing the words, actions, or habits of the Prophet Muhammad – names Dabiq in Syria as the site of the end-of-times battle. For ISIS, the great battle against infidels and apostates (Crusaders, Romans, Europeans, Zionists, Americans, apostates, unbelievers) will take place in the immediate future in Dabiq as the final conflict preceding the Day of Judgment and a new golden age of Islam (Warrick 2015). As a first step on the road to the final confrontation with the armies of the Crusaders, Abu Bakr al-Baghdadi, the Caliph of the Islamic State, declared the formation of a Caliphate on the first day of Ramadan, June 29, 2014, and with some success exhorted Muslims around the world to travel to the lands then controlled by ISIS to fight in the final battles of the apocalypse (Palmer 2015). Baghdadi's rule superseded that of all other Muslim leaders because he was the Caliph.

Before Baghdadi, Abu Musab al-Zarqawi had also underlined the apocalypse in the *hadith*: "Black flags will come from the East, led by mighty men, with long hair and beards, their surnames taken from their home town. These black-clad soldiers will reclaim ancient Muslim lands and instigate the final cataclysmic struggle ending in the destruction of the West's great armies, in northern Syria" (Warrick 2015: 8). These declarations have attracted tens of thousands of foreign fighters dressed in black and carrying black flags to the Caliphate. For the moment, that dream has been crushed by the Arab, Kurdish, and Western-armed might that retook Iraqi and Syrian territory from the Islamic State.

To put their Caliphate back together again, the Islamic State has gone underground into sleeper cells in Iraq and Syria and reverted to guerrilla attacks (McCabe, 2017), and a renewed insurgency. This has allowed the group to begin to reconstitute itself in isolated areas in both countries (Brown 2019).

The Takfiri Jihadis have also formed mini–Islamic States or provinces anywhere that state and nation vulnerabilities allow Islamic State-affiliated cells to capture territory, including Sirte and Derna in Libya and Egypt's Sinai Peninsula. In addition, the Islamic State has also become more like al-Qaeda by targeting the far enemy in the West with terrorist attacks and by returning to traditional recruitment practices based on face-to-face interaction, preexisting bonds, and a shared radical milieu (Brzuszkiewicz 2019).

To render ISIS an unthinkable alternative, the challenge post-ISIS will be to build true modern states in the region that monopolize legitimate violence, that provide security and public services, and that command the allegiance of the vast majority of people within the countries' territorial boundaries. Finally, it should be noted that surveys of support for ISIS within the Muslim world generally fall in the single digits.

Syria

Syrians have paid the highest price during the Arab Spring and its aftermath for mobilizing and attempting to transform their brutal autocratic regime into one characterized by respect for human dignity, democracy, and socioeconomic justice. Their government, ruled by a minority, responded to their humanity in the most vicious way possible. It waged a long and brutal military campaign against opposition groups and civilians alike – a campaign that resulted in the deaths of hundreds of thousands of civilians, the detention of tens of thousands more in government prisons, and an unknown fate for thousands of others (Samaha 2019).

In addition, after the mass uprising brought the people to the precipice of removing Bashar al-Assad's blood-soaked regime, Syria's foreign allies – primarily Iran and Russia – provided unwavering financial, political, and military support that led to Assad's victory. Syria's civil war is more or less over. The regime will soon recapture the last opposition enclave in the Idlib province and probably retake the territory held by Kurdish forces. For a while, the opposition had been dominated by religious extremists, as others who rose up against Assad accepted that there will be no political transition; they are more focused on survival and getting on with their daily lives as best they can (Samaha 2019).

Assad's plans to put Syria back together again are horrific (Samaha 2019). He categorically rejects any foreign-imposed constitutional or political process. He rejects any form of federalism or local political autonomy, and he pledges to win back all Syrian territory, by any means, and at any cost, for the Syrian people. He is propelling the country toward a Republic of Fear more brutal than the one erected by Saddam Hussein in Iraq, or by any of his predecessors in Syria.

The path to the most horrific civil war of the Arab Spring began with the shallow history of Syria as a nation-state.

The History of Syria as a Nation-State and Weberian State

As in Iraq, by replacing historic communal boundaries with borders suitable to French and British interests, European colonialism set the stage for ethnosectarian and religious challenges to the development of a modern state in Syria.

In the late nineteenth and early twentieth centuries, under the Ottoman Empire there was a geographical entity generally known as Greater Syria (Tekdal 2011). Greater Syria comprised the area that is currently occupied by Jordan, Israel/Palestine, Lebanon, and Syria. In their dismemberment of the Ottoman Empire, France and Britain arbitrarily and artificially divided the population of Greater Syria and delineated new communal boundaries. The Sykes-Picot Agreement assigned Syria and Lebanon to France. To create a pro-French, Christian-dominated state, France formed Lebanon from the Christian mountainous region (Mount Lebanon), Beirut, and the predominantly Muslim coastal cities of Tripoli, Sidon, Tyre, and their administrative hinterlands. The population was evenly split between Christians and Muslims.

After the removal of Lebanon, the state of Syria included the main towns of Aleppo, Hama, Homs, and Damascus (Tekdal 2011). Ninety percent of Syria's pre–Arab Spring population of 22 million people were Arabs. Two-thirds were Sunni Muslims, while another 16% were Arab members of various offshoots of Shia Islam, Alawites, Druze, and Ismaili. Alawites dominated the numbers of non-Sunni Muslims, with 11%–12% of the overall population. Kurds, Sunni Muslims for the most part, constituted 8% of the population, and Christians roughly 11%–12%.

Postcolonial Rule

In Syria, as in Iraq, a Baathist political party officially committed to Pan-Arabism and socialism dominated the post-independence state apparatus. In the Syrian version, minority Shia Alawites, historically poor and discriminated against, rose to power by becoming Baathists and rising to top ranks in the military, while Sunni Baathists, accustomed to privilege, shied away from military service.

After independence in 1946, the Baathist Party gradually rose to power in a country that oscillated between multiparty politics and military coups, until the Baathists agreed to disband in 1958 in order to form the United Arab Republic (UAR) and implement Arab socialism under the leadership of Gamal Abdel Nasser of Egypt.

Nasser implemented land reforms and nationalized many privately owned enterprises in order to create a populist base of support and to break the grip on power held by Syria's traditional elite, which was composed primarily of Sunni landowners, merchants, businesspeople, and religious notables.

The traditional oligarchy staged a secessionist counter coup against the UAR in 1961. A 1963 coup brought the Baathists to power free from Egyptian dominance. From 1963 to 1970, Syria took steps to eliminate the threat of the traditional oligarchy for good (Heydemann 1999).

In 1970, Hafez al-Assad staged a coup to moderate the socialist orientation of the Baathist Party-state and to make it more inclusive (Hinnebusch 2001). After his death in 2000, his son, Bashar al-Assad, took his place in power.

To build political community, the Baathist Party-state provided public goods and distributed benefits to various constituencies. Peasants gained access to landownership and greater political power. Labor received employment in new state-owned enterprises, regulation of working hours, and protection against firing. To improve the purchasing power of workers and peasants, the state established an extensive subsidy system and price-control regime.

As mentioned above, there was a sectarian dimension to Baathist populist authoritarian rule. In the Syrian case, the minority Alawite offshoot of Shia Islam attained a pronounced presence within the state power structure. Under Syria's traditional Sunni oligarchy, Alawite living conditions had lagged far behind those of the majority Sunni population. They moved into power by ardently joining the military and security apparatus as the Baathist Party rose to power.

While Syria is often characterized as a country in which a minority Shia Alawite population rules over majority Sunnis, scholars have hotly debated the degree of sectarianism during the populist phase of authoritarian rule. The weight of the evidence points to an Alawite military and security base and less sectarianism and more class warfare in terms of state policy in other areas.

Nikolaos Van Dam argued that in the late 1960s non-Alawite officers were swept from their top military positions, leaving Alawites to dominate the state. These officers pursued policies that greatly favored their communal group and, to an extent, other non-Sunni minorities (Van Dam 1996). In contrast, Raymond Hinnebusch and Volker Perthes (Van Dam 1996) suggested that Baathist policies favored certain classes and rural interests over urban interests and did not purely focus on primordial ties. Hanna Batatu (1999), while confirming the rural and Alawite identity of Syria's ruling elite, downplayed the extent to which it was motivated by sectarianism. He argued that class background and rural social origin influenced their political behavior more than sectarianism.

In addition to national unity challenges, the Baathist state's bureaucracy was weak just prior to the Arab Spring. Socialism was gradually being supplanted by marketization and privatization policies that were implemented in a manner that led to regime elites and crony capitalists overriding the rule of law in order to seize state assets and greatly enrich themselves (King 2009). In addition, the broad coalitions of the socialist era had left a legacy of "side payments" to coalition allies that consumed resources and weakened the ability of the state to rationally pursue economic development and industrialization (Waldner 2001).

The Baathist Syrian bureaucracy was characterized more by generalized corruption than by rationality and legalism. To fund the bureaucracy and military, the state relied more on fluctuating oil exports from their limited oil fields than on taxation. At the expense of state capacities, patronage and minority rule became the prevailing mode of political organization under Hafez al-Assad (Sadowski 1987).

Notably, in some areas sectarianism played a smaller role than in others (Sadowski 1987). State investment in social services, infrastructure, and the public sector was distributed to promote the national economy rather than sectarian interests. Assad utilized patronage to include many Sunnis in his inner circle as well. When he took power in 1970, Assad sought to broaden the popular base and moderate one of the most radical governments in the Arab world. He reached out to Sunnis. He encouraged private entrepreneurship and utilized state patronage to tie the reemerging private sector to the regime. His policies helped create rich peasants. Under his son, Bashar al-Assad, privatization of land and state-owned enterprises accelerated and led to an even greater merger of the old Sunni elite and the Alawite-dominated state elite.

Prior to the Arab Spring uprising in Syria, the Baathist state met challenges to its monopoly of violence with a brutality that set the tone for fierce state–society relations in much of the post-independence Arab world (Friedman 1989). Often, the state's repressive apparatus operated in a manner that, at a minimum, strained political community. In this vein, the conflict between the secular Baathist regime dominated by Alawites and the Muslim Brotherhood (MB) of the Sunni majority is one of the most notorious.

While Hafez al-Assad reached out to Sunnis in his "corrective movement," strong tensions remained (Friedman 1989). Syria's Muslim Brotherhood was dominated by Sunni traditional notables and religious leaders. In the 1960s, as Baathists sought to consolidate their rule, MB militants organized armed resistance to the regime. Their activities were met with violent state repression. In 1964, national guards killed scores of MB members. In the 1970s and early 1980s, the conflict between the regime and the Muslim Brotherhood accelerated. Muslim Brothers engaged in assassinations and mounted urban demonstrations with a focus on Alawites, Baathists, military and police figures, and some civilians. The conflict reached its apex in Hama, an important base for the Muslim Brotherhood and the most visible symbol of the overturning of power and wealth between Sunni absentee landlords and the Alawite rural poor that the Baathist revolution represented. In 1982, the regime attacked the Muslim Brotherhood stronghold in Hama. Some 12,000 government troops killed between 5,000 and 10,000 people, effectively ending the MB's uprising that had gone on for nearly two decades.

Despite challenges to political community based on colonial heritage and Alawite dominance over a majority Sunni population, an emphasis on sectarianism in Syrian politics at the dawn of the Arab Spring can be exaggerated. Prior to the Arab Spring uprising, Syrians of diverse backgrounds lived together and intermarried; communal cohesion and homogeneity did not exist. While the Baathists adopted some policies favoring Alawites that aggravated subnational identities, they implemented other policies with a broad impact and claimed to rule in the name of Syrians as a national community.

Syrian President Bashar al-Assad's decision to kill as many Syrians as necessary to stay in power, armed or civilian, has destroyed Syria's national political community.

The Arab Spring and Civil War in Syria

Syria's harrowing civil war began with impulsive acts by children during the Arab Spring. In February 2011, shortly after Tunisian President Ben Ali and Egyptian President Mubarak had been forced out of office by public protests, schoolboys in a border town near

Jordan named Daraa utilized red paint to scrawl on their school's walls and the town's grain silos slogans that included "Your turn, doctor" (Bashar al-Assad is an ophthalmologist by training) and the slogan of the Arab Spring as a whole: "The people want the fall of the regime."[6]

The children's act of defiance catapulted Syria into the frontline of the Arab popular revolts (Macleod 2011). The secret police arrested 15 boys between the ages of 10 and 15 for painting the slogans, interrogated them, and tortured them. They were beaten and bloodied by grown men. They were burned and had their fingernails pulled out. Family members marched to the governor's house to demand their release. In response, the security services opened fire and prevented ambulances from ferrying the injured to hospitals.

While the boys were in prison protests grew in size and frequency (Macleod 2011). In addition to demanding the release of the children, protesters called for freedom, democracy, an end to corruption, and finally an all-out ouster of Assad. After two weeks in jail, the 15 children were released. However, the protests and brutal repression continued, and a vicious cycle began – funerals turned into rallies against the regime, which led to gunfire by the security forces, and more funerals, rallies, and deaths at the hands of security operatives. Assad tried to stem the spread of protests by issuing a decree to cut taxes and raise state salaries, to which protesters responded: "We don't want your bread, we want dignity (Macleod 2011)."

The Syrian president blamed the Daraa uprising on a foreign plot or on the acts of Islamist extremists, while promising the town's leaders that he was personally committed to bringing justice to those who had opened fire (Macleod 2011). From Daraa, a largely peaceful and decentralized protest movement with national goals spread across the country (Phillips 2015). The opposition spoke for "the people" and for "Syria" rather than for any ethnosectarian group. The regime responded to the protests by emphasizing inclusiveness and its nationalist credentials. However, over time both the regime and opposition took advantage of politicized sectarian identities that had existed before the conflict and deployed them to achieve their goals in what became a bloody ethnosectarian civil war (Phillips 2015).

---

[6] Reports vary on exactly what was painted and where. See Macleod (2011). See also Asher-Schapiro (2016).

Syria's civil war has taken dramatic twists and turns. At the start, a secular-dominated opposition – the Free Syrian Army (FSA) – led by regime defectors seemed to be mounting an effective broad opposition without sectarian overtones. However, that effort floundered, partly due to the lack of Western support. A more fragmented opposition took its place. At one point, the fragmented opposition gained the upper hand, and the country seemed to be self-dividing into four smaller states, with the possibility of a federalized solution to the conflict after Assad was removed from power. Instead, Russia, Iran, and Hisballah intervened to turn the tide militarily in favor of the Assad regime.

Before foreign intervention, it seemed like Assad and his regime would not survive. The peaceful mass uprising was massive. Militarization of the uprising began in June 2011, when army defectors formed brigades under the banners of the Free Syrian Army (FSA). The main armed opposition grew under the FSA umbrella and spread throughout the country with units and brigades emerging in both major cities and rural areas. However, without external support, the FSA failed in its attempt to topple the regime in order to implement democratic politics and other goals of the uprising.

The FSA's failure led to the proliferation of armed groups with different and conflicting agendas and strategies, including ISIS, the Syrian al-Qaeda affiliate, Jabhat al-Nusra, the Islamic Front, the Army of Islam, and the Kurdish People's Protection Units (YPG).

Simultaneously, the Assad regime's military, the Syrian Arab Army (SAA), withered, and the regime was forced to rely on homegrown militias such as the National Defense Forces (NDF) and the *shabiha* (thugs or civilians who support and are armed by the regime). In addition, Russia, and regional groups such as Lebanon's Hisballah and Iraqi and Iranian militias intervened to help the SAA achieve its military objectives and keep Assad in power.

The diffused violence in Syria led to the territorial fragmentation of the country. Regional conglomerations of brigades created fronts or networks of violence that attempted to defend areas, hold territory, and establish some semblance of administration (Abboud 2016). By 2017, Syria was slowly fragmenting into four regions with different rulers: (1) the Assad government; (2) the Free Syrian Army; (3) the Kurdish YPG; and (4) al-Qaeda's Jabhat al-Nusra.

Violent sectarianism ripped apart Syria's political community (Abboud 2016). All armed groups – in the regime and in the opposition – began a process of communal cleansing. Kidnapping, looting, and rape became sectarian acts. Foreign actors with sectarian agendas – Iraq, Saudi Arabia, Qatar, Turkey, and Iran – gave further meaning to the sectarian logic of the war. Sectarianism became a facet of everyday life during the conflict and began to shape relationships on a personal level. Many Syrians experienced violence and displacement as an outcome of their own sectarian affiliation. Despite many minorities supporting the opposition and many Sunnis supporting the regime, sectarian identities were politicized and mobilized. Syrian identities retreated into narrow allegiances to sect.

In sum, Syria as a nation-state was replaced by a patchwork of administrative authorities backed up by violent networks. After unfathomable bloodshed, in a conflict that took on sectarian dimensions, four identifiable territories emerged in the place of postcolonial Syria, each with their own social base and institutional structures.

Arguably, the fragmentation of Syria into four smaller states should have been the basis for a federalized solution to the civil war (Abboud 2016). After forcibly removing radical Islamists, the four regions could have been institutionalized and the state decentralized without threatening the sovereign state.

Ultimately, the imminent possibility of a federalized solution ended when Russia and Iran intervened in support of Assad. Their military, financial, and political might turned the tide and allowed Assad to begin dictating the postconflict order. Militarily, Assad has subdued everything but the Idlib province and areas controlled by Kurdish forces. In all likelihood, he will be in control of all Syrian territories soon.

Assad's Plan to Reconstitute Syria

Assad's regime is here to stay, and he is reconstituting centralized authority and constructing a grim future for most Syrians (Samaha 2019). The security situation in most government-held territories is relatively stable. Assad's government believes in what it calls the "long breath" – the process of enduring until they have retaken all Syrian territory (either through reconciliation, negotiation, or through military offensives). Assad is also hostile to Syria's obvious need for decentralization and federalism. While he implemented a law (107) that transferred some administrative and bureaucratic powers to the local councils that emerged during the civil war, Assad has stopped short of providing them with political rights and has rejected all aspirations for federalism or any form of autonomous administration among Kurds and other groups (Samaha 2019). If maintained, that stance guarantees a brutally repressive future for Syria.

In the last two years – aware that it has helped Assad win the war and in an effort to help him win the peace – Russia has brokered a series of reconciliation initiatives to reestablish government control in opposition-held areas (Samaha 2019). Through this process, Assad has granted amnesties and actively worked to integrate both progovernment militias and former opposition groups into a more official military infrastructure, largely through the creation of the 5th and 6th Corps. Integrating militias has also served as a desperately needed employment program for the war-damaged economy. In addition to offering state benefits for supporters who never abandoned him during the eight-year conflict, Assad is also reconstituting the varying networks of privilege that he presided over to fortify his rule before the Arab Spring (Heydemann 2004). He is bringing business oligarchs, some Sunni and religiously conservative, back into the fold through religious reforms and by offering government partnership and support for their return to commercial activities.

Assad's overall plan for displaced Syrians, half the prewar population, is more hesitant. He is aware that a large influx of returnees would increase the economic strain on the state, as it would be forced to provide employment, housing, infrastructure, and basic services to them (Samaha 2019). Unsurprisingly, Assad has been vindictive in this regard. He has passed a series of laws designed to permanently displace Syrians who opposed the regime and take over their properties and businesses. Assad's plans for Syria's postconflict political order seem indifferent to Western sanctions, which they have countered by doing business with foreign allies beyond Russia and Iran, including China and Arab countries that are interested in making profits in a country with devastating reconstruction needs.

Assad also only seems interested in peace plans on his own terms. The Astana Talks – after the Geneva Talks – were held in Kazakhstan at the end of April 2019 (Semenov 2019). Russia, Iran, and Turkey served as guarantor states. There was also a UN representative and representation from the Syrian government and the Syrian opposition. During the talks, Syria and its Iranian backers focused on peacefully facilitating Assad's recapture of the opposition enclave in Idlib. The opposition requested autonomy for the Kurdish-held areas that the regime continues to categorically reject.

In sum, for Syrians, the Arab Spring rapidly turned into the Arab Winter, especially after the West chose not to support them with a no-fly zone and a protective enclave for the opposition, as they had done in Libya. Assad's monstrous plan to put Syria back together again – brutally repressing rather than building a single national political community and supporting national reconciliation through some regional autonomy – will be built upon a monstrous legacy.

During the Arab Spring, thousands of Syrians were murdered each month mainly by the Assad regime (Abboud 2016). More than 500,000 Syrians, half of whom are believed to have been civilians, have died in the conflict that started when President Bashar al-Assad brutally cracked down on a peaceful Arab Spring uprising. Nearly 18,000 Syrians, more than 300 a month, have been tortured and killed while in custody for opposing the Assad regime (Amnesty International 2016). One half of Syria's prewar population of 22 million people have fled or been displaced internally, creating more than 11 million refugees (Jenkins 2014). Refugees have risked their lives on the way to Europe or have attempted to make new homes in neighboring countries that struggle to accommodate them. Inside Syria, families are struggling to survive. In addition to the 500,000 violent deaths, another 70,000 Syrians have died from the lack of adequate food, clean water, health services, medicine, sanitation, and proper housing (SCPR 2015). To fend off starvation, residents have been forced to eat grass, tree leaves, dogs, and cats (Porter 2016). The youngest – most no longer able to attend school – are confused, scared, and scarred by their experiences (Agha 2016).

References

Abboud, S. 2016. *Syria: Hotspot in Global Politics*. Cambridge: Polity Press.
Agha, S. 2016. "Quick Facts: What You Need to Know about the Syria Crisis." *Mercy Corps*, June 16. www.mercycorps.org/articles/iraq-jordan-lebanon-syria-turkey/quick-facts-what-you-need-know-about-syria-crisis.

Al-Ali, Z. 2014. *The Struggle for Iraq's Future: How Corruption, Incompetence and Sectarianism Have Undermined Democracy.* New Haven, CT: Yale University Press.

Al-Arabiya. 2014. "Maliki Offers to Arm Citizens Willing to Fight ISIS." *Al-Arabiya*, June 10. www.english.alarabiya.net/en/News/middle-east/2014/06/10/Iraq-insurgents-overrun-Mosul-govt-HQ.html.

Alkadiri, R. and C. Toensing. 2003. "The Iraqi Governing Council's Sectarian Hue." *Middle East Research and Information Project*, August 20. www.merip.org/2003/08/the-iraqi-governing-councils-sectarian-hue/.

Al-Khalil, S. 1989. *Republic of Fear: The Politics of Modern Iraq.* Berkeley: University of California Press.

Allawi, A. 2008. *Occupation of Iraq: Winning the War, Losing the Peace.* New Haven, CT: Yale University Press.

Al-Qarawee, H. H. 2016. *From Maliki to Abadi: The Challenge of Being Iraq's Prime Minister.* Middle East Brief. Waltham, MA: Crown Center for Middle East Studies, Brandeis University.

Al-Salhy, S. 2015. "Iraqi Sunnis Join Shia Militias to Fight IS Militants." *Middle East Eye*, June 15. www.middleeasteye.net/news/iraqi-sunnis-join-shia-militias-fight-militants.

Al-Sallami, W. 2014. "I Grew Up in Iraq during Saddam's Worst Days – Here's What Life Was Like." *Business Insider*, July 2. www.businessinsider.com/heres-what-life-in-iraq-was-like-under-saddam-hussein-2014-7.

Amnesty International. 2016. "18,000 People Die in Syrian Custody since 2011." *BBC News*, August 18. www.bbc.com/news/av/world-middle-east-37115626/18000-people-die-in-syrian-custody-says-amnesty-international.

Asher-Schapiro, A. 2016. "The Young Men Who Started Syria's Revolution Speak about Daraa, Where It All Began." *Vice News Middle East*, March 15. www.vice.com/en_us/article/qv5eqb/the-young-men-who-started-syrias-revolution-speak-about-daraa-where-it-all-began.

Batatu, H. 1999. *Syria's Peasantry: The Descendants of Its Lesser Rural Notables and Their Politics.* Princeton, NJ: Princeton University Press.

Benotman, N. and N. Malik. 2016. *The Children of the Islamic State.* London: Quilliam Foundation.

Borger, J. 2006. "Corruption: The 'Second Insurgency' Costing $4bn a Year." *The Guardian*, December 2. www.theguardian.com/world/2006/dec/02/usa.iraq.

Broder, J. 2015. "A Bloody Disaster: The Iraqi Army's Fight against Isis." *Newsweek*, March 7. www.newsweek.com/iraqi-army-fight-against-isis-312105.

Brands, H. and P. Feaver. 2019. "Lessons from the Iraq War." *National Review*, July 8. www.nationalreview.com/magazine/2019/07/08/lessons-from-the-iraq-war/.

Brown, F. 2019. "Can the US Fully Defeat the Islamic State? Here's What Can Help." *Carnegie Endowment for International Peace*, May 21. www.carnegieendowment.org/2019/05/21/can-u.s.-fully-defeat-islamic-state-here-s-what-can-help-pub-79171.

Brzuszkiewicz, S. 2019. "An Interview with Daniel Koehler." *European Eye on Radicalization*, January 2. www.eeradicalization.com/an-interview-with-daniel-koehler-german-institute-on-radicalization-and-de-radical ization-studies/.

Byman, D. 2016. "Understanding the Islamic State." *International Security*, 40(4), 127–165. doi:10.1162/ISEC_r_00235.

Callimachi, R. 2016. "To Maintain Supply of Sex Slaves, ISIS Pushes Birth Control." *New York Times*, March 12. www.nytimes.com/2016/03/13/world/middleeast/to-maintain-supply-of-sex-slaves-isis-pushes-birth-control.html.

Caryl, C. 2013. "The Democracy Boondoggle in Iraq." *Foreign Policy*, March 6. www.foreignpolicy.com/2013/03/06/the-democracy-boondog gle-in-iraq/.

Chulov, M. 2014. "How an Arrest in Iraq Revealed Isis's $2bn Jihadist Network." *The Guardian*, June 15. www.theguardian.com/world/2014/jun/15/iraq-isis-arrest-jihadists-wealth-power.

et al. 2014. "Iraq Army Capitulates to ISIS Militants in Four Cities." *The Guardian*, June 11. www.theguardian.com/world/2014/jun/11/mosul-isis-gunmen-middle-east-states.

Cohen, A. and G. Driscoll. 2003. "The Road to Economic Prosperity for a Post-Saddam Iraq." *Heritage Organization*, March 5. www.heritage .org/middle-east/report/the-road-economic-prosperity-post-saddam-iraq.

Cook, S. A. and A. T. Leheta. 2016. "Don't Blame Sykes-Picot for the Middle East Mess." *Foreign Policy*, 13 May. www.foreignpolicy.com/2016/05/13/sykes-picot-isnt-whats-wrong-with-the-modern-middle-east-100-years/.

Cordesman, A. 2006. "The Lost Year in Iraq." *Frontline*, July 18. www.pbs.org/wgbh/pages/frontline/yeariniraq/interviews/cordesman.html.

DeAtkine, N. B. 2015. "Muhammad Taught US How to Fight: The Islamic State and Early Islamic Warfare Tradition." *Middle East Review of International Affairs*, 19(3). www.questia.com/library/jour nal/1P3-4026842231/muhammad-taught-us-how-to-fight-the-islamic-state.

Diamond, L. 2004. "What Went Wrong in Iraq." *Foreign Affairs*, 83(5), 35–56. doi:10.2307/20034066.

Dodge, T. 2014. *Seeking to Explain the Rise Of Sectarianism in the Middle East: The Case Study of Iraq.* Washington, DC: Project on Middle East Political Science (POMEPS), March 9. www.pomeps.org/seeking-to-explain-the-rise-of-sectarianism-in-the-middle-east-the-case-study-of-iraq.

Dodge, T. and B. Wasser. 2014. "The Crisis of the Iraqi State." *Adelphi Series,* 54(447), 13–38. doi:10.1080/19445571.2014.995936.

The Economist. 2014. "Confronting the Islamic State: The Next War against Global Jihadism." *The Economist.* September 13. www.economist.com/middle-east-and-africa/2014/09/15/the-next-war-against-global-jihadism.

Edwards, A. 2015. "ISIS and the Challenge of Islamist Extremism." *Political Insight,* 6(1), 12–15. doi:10.1111/2041-9066.12081.

Friedman, T. 1989. *From Beirut to Jerusalem.* New York: Farrar Straus, and Giroux.

Hadhari, M. 1981. *Istishhad al-Imam Muhammad Baqir al-Sadr* [The martyrdom of Imam Muhammad Baqir al-Sadr] Beirut: Hizb al-Da'a-wah al-Islamiyyah.

Hashim, A. S. 2006. *Insurgency and Counter-Insurgency in Iraq.* Ithaca, NY: Cornell University Press.

2014. "The Islamic State: From Al-Qaeda Affiliate to Caliphate." *Middle East Policy,* 21(4), 61–83. doi: 10.1111/mepo12096.

Henry, C. M. and R. Springborg. 2010. *Globalization and the Politics of Development in the Middle East.* Cambridge: Cambridge University Press.

Heydemann, S. 1999. *Authoritarianism in Syria: Institutions and Social Conflict, 1946–1970.* Ithaca, NY: Cornell University Press.

2004. *Networks of Privilege in the Middle East.* Basingstoke, UK: Palgrave Macmillan.

Hinnebusch, R. 2001. *Syria: Revolution from Above.* London: Routledge.

Human Rights Watch (HRW). 1993. *Genocide in Iraq: The Anfal Campaign against the Kurds.* New York: Human Rights Watch, July. www.hrw.org/reports/1993/iraqanfal/.

2013. "Iraq: A Broken Justice System." *Human Rights Watch,* January 31. www.hrw.org/news/2013/01/31/iraq-broken-justice-system.

International Crisis Group (ICG). 2006. "The Next Iraqi War? Sectarianism and Civil Conflict." *International Crisis Group,* February 27. www.crisisgroup.org/middle-east-north-africa/gulf-and-arabian-peninsula/iraq/next-iraqi-war-sectarianism-and-civil-conflict.

Jabar, F. A. 2007. *Iraq Four Years after the US-Led Invasion: Assessing the Crisis and Searching for a Way Forward.* Washington, DC: Carnegie Endowment for International Peace, July. www.carnegieendowment.org/2007/07/09/iraq-four-years-after-u.s.-led-invasion-assessing-crisis-and-searching-for-way-forward-pub-19420.

Japan Times. 2016. "Muqtada al-Sadr, Iraq's powerful and unpredictable Shiite Cleric, Reinvents Himself as a Reform Champion." *Japan Times*, 1 May. www.dailydigitalnews.com/single-article-view.php?article=76660.

Jawad, S. N. 2013. "The Iraqi Constitution: Structural Flaws and Political Implications." *London School of Economics Middle East Centre Paper Series*, 1, 1–24. www.eprints.lse.ac.uk/54927/.

Jenkins, B. M. 2014. *The Dynamics of Syria's Civil War*. Santa Monica, CA: Rand Corporation, n. d. www.rand.org/pubs/perspectives/PE115.html.

Johns, D. 2006. "The Crimes of Saddam Hussein." *PBS*, January 24. www.pbs.org/frontlineworld/stories/iraq501/events_index.html.

Khedery, A. 2015. "Iraq in Pieces." *Foreign Affairs*, November/December. www.foreignaffairs.com/articles/iraq/2015-09-22/iraq-pieces.

King, S. J. 2009. *The New Authoritarianism in the Middle East and North Africa*. Bloomington: Indiana University Press.

Knights, M. 2019. "Iraq's Popular Mobilization Force Reform: Reintegration or Consolidation of Militia Power?" *The Defense Post*, July 3. www.thedefensepost.com/2019/07/03/iraq-popular-mobilization-units-reform-opinion/.

Kupchan, C. and S. Ülgen. 2019. "The US Is Still Needed in Syria." *Project Syndicate*, July 2. www.project-syndicate.org/commentary/trump-syria-premature-withdrawal-by-charles-a-kupchan-and-sinan-ulgen-2019-07? barrier=accesspaylog.

Lando, B. 2007. "How George H. W. Bush Helped Saddam Hussein Prevent an Iraqi Uprising." *Alternet*, March 27. www.democraticunder ground.com/discuss/duboard.php?az=view_all&address=103x271807.

Lewis, J. D. 2014. *The Islamic State: A Counter-Strategy for a Counter-State*. Middle East Security Report. Washington, DC: Institute for the Study of War, July. www.understandingwar.org/report/islamic-state-counter-strategy-counter-state.

Long, A. 2008. "The Anbar Awakening." *Survival: Global Politics and Strategy*, 50(2), 67–94. doi:10.1080/00396330802034283.

Macleod, H. 2011. "Syria: How It All Began." *Public Radio International*, April 23. www.pri.org/stories/2011-04-23/syria-how-it-all-began.

Manfreda, P. 2019. "Impacts of the Iraq War on The Middle East." *Thoughtco*, February 4. www.thoughtco.com/iraq-war-effect-on-middle-east-2353056.

Mansour, R. 2016. *The Sunni Predicament in Iraq*. Washington, DC: Carnegie Middle East Center, March. www.carnegieendowment.org/files/CMEC_59_Mansour_Sunni_Final.pdf.

2018. "The Popular Mobilisation Forces and the Balancing of Formal and Informal Power." *LSE Middle East Centre Blog*. March 15. www.blogs.lse.ac.uk/mec/2018/03/15/the-popular-mobilisation-forces-and-the-balancing-of-formal-and-informal-power/.

McCary, J. A. 2009. "The Anbar Awakening: An Alliance of Incentives." *Washington Quarterly*, 32(1), 43–59. doi:10.1080/01636600802 544905.

Moaveni, A. 2015. "ISIS and Enforcers in Syria Recount Collaboration, Anguish and Escape." *New York Times*, November 21. www.nytimes .com/2015/11/22/world/middleeast/isis-wives-and-enforcers-in-syria-recount-collaboration-anguish-and-escape.html.

Moghadam, A. 2008. "The Salafi-Jihad as a Religious Ideology, Combating Terrorism Center at West Point." *Combating Terrorism Center Sentinel*, 1(3). www.ctc.usma.edu/the-salafi-jihad-as-a-religious-ideology/.

Newton, J. 2016. "A Split Second from Death: Gay Man Plummets to the Ground after ISIS Murderers Throw Him from a Roof in Iraq." *Daily Mail*, August 11. www.dailymail.co.uk/news/article-3734616/A-split-second-death-Gay-man-plummets-ground-ISIS-murderers-throw-roof-Iraq.html.

Ozerdem, A. 2010. "Insurgency, Militias and DDR as Part of Security Sector Reconstruction in Iraq: How to Not Do It." *Disasters*, 34 (Suppl. 1), S40–S59. www.ncbi.nlm.nih.gov/pubmed/19459905.

Norton, A. R. 2007. *Hezbollah: A Short History*. Princeton, NJ: Princeton University Press.

Otterman, S. 2005. "Iraq's Prewar Military Capabilities." *Council on Foreign Relations*, February 3. www.cfr.org/backgrounder/iraq-iraqs-prewar-military-capabilities.

Palmer, R. 2015. "Radical Islam's New Top Target: Rome." *The Trumpet*, July 17. www.thetrumpet.com/11921-radical-islams-new-top-target-rome.

Phillips, C. 2015. "Sectarianism and Conflict in Syria." *Third World Quarterly*, 36(2), 357–376. doi:10.1080/01436597.2015.10157.

Porter, T. "2016. "Residents of Besieged Syrian Towns Forced to Eat Grass, Dogs and Cats to Fend Off Starvation." *International Business Times*, January 6. www.ibtimes.co.uk/residents-besieged-syrian-towns-forced-eat-grass-dogs-cats-fend-off-starvation-1536413.

Rosiny, S. 2015. "The Rise and Demise of the IS Caliphate." *Middle East Policy Council*, 22(2), 94–107. www.mepc.org/rise-and-demise-caliphate.

Sadowski, Y. M. 1987. "Patronage and the Ba'th: Corruption and Control in Contemporary Syria." *Arab Studies Quarterly*, 9(4), 442–461. www.jstor.org/stable/41857946.

Samaha, N. 2019. "Can Assad Win The Peace?" *European Council on Foreign Relations*, May 15. www.ecfr.eu/publications/summary/can_assad_win_the_peace_syria.

Sassoon, J. 2012. *Saddam Hussein's Ba'th Party: Inside an Authoritarian Regime*. Cambridge: Cambridge University Press.

Semenov, K. 2019. "New Name, Same Old Problems: Syria Talks Kick Off in Kazakh Capital." *Al-Monitor*, April 30. www.al-monitor.com/pulse/originals/2019/04/russia-turkey-iran-nursultan-astana-talks.html.

Shadid, A. 2005. *Night Draws Near: Iraq's People in the Shadow of America's War*. New York: Holt.

Sly, L. 2015. "How the Battle against the Islamic State Is Redrawing the Map of the Middle East," *Washington Post*, January 1. www.washingtonpost.com/world/on-the-front-lines-of-the-war-against-the-islamic-state-a-tangled-web/2015/12/30/d944925a-9244-11e5-befa-99ceebcbb272_story.html.

Sorenson, D. 2014. "Priming Strategic Communications: Countering the Appeal of ISIS." *Parameters*, 44(3), 25–36. www.semanticscholar.org/paper/Priming-Strategic-Communications%3A-Countering-the-of-Sorenson/006ff61e6054a8707be5c6577410030eb0002c4d.

Stansfield, G. 2016. "Explaining the Aims, Rise, and Impact of the Islamic State in Iraq and al-Sham."*Middle East Journal*, 40(1), 146–151. www.muse.jhu.edu/article/607730/pdf.

Stern, J. and J. M. Berger. 2015. *ISIS: The State of Terror*. New York: HarperCollins.

Syrian Center for Policy Research. 2015. *Alienation and Violence Report*. Damascus: Syrian Center for Policy Research, March 30. www.scpr-syria.org/scpr-alienation-and-violence-report-2014-2/.

Tekdal, A. 2011. "The Troubles in Syria: Spawned by French Divide and Rule." *Middle East Policy*, 18(4). www.mepc.org/troubles-syria-spawned-french-divide-and-rule.

Terrill, A. W. 2014. "Understanding the Strengths and Vulnerabilities of ISIS." *Parameters*, 44(3), 13–23. www.questia.com/library/journal/1G1-397579199/understanding-the-strengths-and-vulnerabilities-of.

United Nations (UN). 2014. *United Nations Security Council Report from the Chair of the Security Council Committee pursuant to resolutions 1267 and 1989*, November 13. Geneva: United Nations.

Van Dam, N. 1996. *The Struggle for Power and Society under Assad and the Ba'th Party*. London: I. B. Tauris.

Waldner, D. 2001. *State Building and Late Development*. Cambridge: Cambridge University Press.

Walt, S. 2015. "ISIS as Revolutionary State: New Twist on an Old Story." *Foreign Affairs*, November/December. www.foreignaffairs.com/articles/middle-east/isis-revolutionary-state.

Warrick, J. 2015. *Black Flags: The Rise of ISIS*. New York: Doubleday.

Warrick, J. and S. Mekhennet. 2016. "ISIS Readies for Fall of Caliphate." *Breaking 911*, July 13. www.breaking911.com/isis-readies-for-fall-of-caliphate/.

Westcott, L. 2016. "ISIS Is Committing Genocide against Yazidis, Christians, and Shiites: John Kerry." *Newsweek*, March 17. www .newsweek.com/isis-genocide-kerry-yazidis-christians-shia-437944.

Wilbanks, M. and E. Karsh. 2010. "How the Sons of Iraq Stabilized Iraq." *Middle East Quarterly*, 17(4), 57–70. www.academia.edu/11230859/ How_the_Sons_of_Iraq_Stabilized_Postwar_Iraq.

Woodward, B. 2004. *Plan of Attack*. New York: Simon & Schuster.

Zelin, A. 2014. "The Islamic State of Syria and Iraq Has a Consumer Protection Office," *The Atlantic*, June 6. www.theatlantic.com/inter national/archive/2014/06/the-isis-guide-to-building-an-islamic-state/ 372769/.

6 | *The Arab Winter*
Summary and Conclusions

The Arab Spring demonstrated that the vast majority of Arabs yearn for democracy, respect for human rights, and socioeconomic justice. Across the region, millions were killed, injured, or displaced while striving for those goals.

The Arab Winter concludes that the poor to harrowing results – beyond Tunisia – of the Arab Spring can be largely explained by democratic transitions that failed to overcome very difficult democratic consolidation challenges.

To summarize, Tunisia entered the Arab Spring with comparative advantages in attributes of modern states and as a nation-state. Leaders of Tunisia's democratic transition did not have to – desperately – nation-build and state-build at the same time as they were implementing competitive elections for the first time in the country's history. Tunisian leaders, due to a history of an apolitical and professional military, also did not have to attempt to extricate a powerful military from politics and the economy as they engineered Tunisia's democratic transition. In addition, Tunisia was exceptionally blessed with Islamists and secularists willing to negotiate and compromise in support of democracy. Success at – or the absence of a need to address – nation-state, military, and political pacts established considerable democratic consolidation in Tunisia. Tunisian elites, however, have fared poorly at establishing a new socioeconomic pact and the rule of law, which threatens the country's democracy as a whole.

Egyptian transitional elites had the same relative advantages in national unity and modern state capacities as their counterparts in Tunisia. However, Islamist–secularist polarization was greater in Egypt, and the country's Islamist and secularist political parties were too distrustful to tolerate each other in a new democracy. The Egyptian military, accustomed to dominance in the economy and politics, utilized the failure of political parties to establish the twin tolerations during the transition to stage a coup and reestablish a military authoritarian regime.

Libya entered the Arab Spring, with comparative disadvantages in attributes of modern states and as a nation-state. Due to those factors, the introduction of competitive elections contributed to a civil war. Political parties contributed as well, as Islamists turned to allied militias to overturn the outcome of democratic elections. Secularists in Libya were more willing to tolerate Islamists in a new democratic political pact.

Most prominently, Libya's democratic transition illustrates the absolute necessity, for democratic outcomes, of the state and transitional governments having the monopoly of the use of violence.

The state's inability to establish the monopoly of force contributed to Yemen's descent into civil war during the country's democratic transition. Historically bequeathed, fragile national unity and modern state deficits did as well. Paradoxically, political parties in Yemen established the twin tolerations, but were too elitist to represent a population that ultimately rejected the country's national dialogue process. National parties in Yemen also failed at consummating a political pact by not sustaining the support of the Zaydi Shia Houthi movement and Southern secessionists in the national effort to establish democracy.

Iraq's shallow and violent history as a nation-state made it a poor candidate for a democracy imposed by Western powers, especially when Western powers – the United States and Great Britain – attempted to do so after doing grave damage to the fragile national unity and limited state capacities that existed in the country prior to the American invasion. The result was an insurgency and sectarian civil war.

Syria's Arab Spring uprising had promise and was heading in the democratic opposition's favor until foreign intervention by Russia, Iran, and Hisballah allowed the Assad regime to win the civil war that had started when the country's president decided to kill as many Syrians as necessary – armed opposition and civilians alike – in order to stay in power. Assad is currently reconstructing an autocratic, minority-based, bunker regime in Syria that will be more brutal and repressive than the one that sparked the Arab Spring uprising in the first place.

The emergence of ISIS, The Islamic State of Iraq and al-Sham/Syria, or simply the Islamic State, may be the most disheartening outcome of the Arab Spring. Radical Islamists were put on the defensive during the Arab Spring. Why use violence to attain power when mainstream Islamists were taking advantage of their realization that electoral democracy provides them with the chance to gain social and political power? However, as democratic consolidation challenges led to civil wars, authoritarian reversals, and state collapse, Jihadi and Takfiri Salafis took advantage of the new circumstances to spread radical ideas and establish, at least temporarily, their versions of an Islamic Caliphate.

And their versions of an Islamic Caliphate are horrific. This is especially true when it comes to Takfiri Salafis like Islamic State adherents, who revel in killing fellow Muslims.

Democratic Consolidation: Nation-State and Weberian-State Pacts

Modern States: Rationalizing the Bureaucracy, Monopolizing Violence, and Tax-Collecting

The Arab Winter demonstrates the desirability of examining the contours and trajectory of state formation for analysis of democratization. Libya entered the Arab Spring with comparative deficits as a modern state. Qaddafi's regime monopolized the use of violence, but his armed forces split, with some siding with the opposition, during the Arab Spring uprising. Post-Qaddafi provisional and elected governments failed in their efforts to reestablish the state's monopoly of violence. Instead of insisting on disarming, demobilizing, and reintegrating "civilian" militias and brigades that contributed to the country's revolution on February 17, 2011, Libyan elites made a Faustian bargain with the revolutionary fighters (*thuwwar*).

Post-Qaddafi governments co-opted and appeased the militias by bringing them under the auspices of the state to serve roles in the national army, the security sector including the police and Ministry of the Interior, and the Petroleum Facilities Guard. Militia members remained loyal only to their unit commanders, not to the ministries or governments that paid their salaries. The *thuwwars* actively ignored the official chain of command. Their commanders insisted on state payments to all their members, who increased tenfold *after the revolution*, once the National Transitional Council began handing out checks for participation in the uprising against Qaddafi. The overall result has been the leeching of state resources and the rise of armed groups outside of state and government control that are more powerful than the national army and national police, which means that the state cannot keep Libyans safe in the streets.

Without the state's monopoly of violence, Libya's transition toward electoral democracy derailed and a second civil war began. By mid-2014, militias' armed struggles for direct control over parts of Libyan territory, infrastructure, and oil profits had replaced political power based on election results. Two militia coalitions emerged for the armed struggle for resources. If the two militia coalitions continue to all-out war, then the tens of thousands of Libyans who lost their lives in the battle against Qaddafi could turn into tens – if not hundreds – of thousands more. Want-to-be strongman General Haftar has made a viable push for power by capitalizing on fears and promising security throughout the country.

In addition to not having a national army that monopolized the use of violence, Libyan history did not bequeath a rational-legal bureaucracy for the use of transitional leaders. The Italian colonization stunted bureaucratic development. King Idris's oil economy did the same. Qaddafi's ideology was exceptionally hostile toward the development of a rational-legal bureaucracy. As a result, the first elected government in Libyan history had an administration that was small and weak. The feeble administration could not provide public services and implement policies well enough to help validate an emerging democracy.

Finally – and this is something in the country's favour – Libyan oil and natural gas reserves will provide the country with resources to pay for a national military and modern bureaucratic apparatus once the violence ends.

The trajectory of state formation in Yemen is similar to the one in Libya, if not worse, for democratic prospects. Tribal militias in Yemen's long history have prevented the development of the state's monopoly of the use of violence. The Arab Spring uprising, which led to military defections to the opposition, decreased the state's monopoly of violence that much more. The provisional government failed to rein in militias, including of course the Houthi armed groups that defeated its army during Yemen's democratic transition and forced its leader into exile, prompting an armed intervention by Saudi Arabia. Democracy and a return to a transition toward it is almost beside the point in a civil war in which more than 80% of the Yemeni population risks starvation because violent conflict has prevented the delivery of humanitarian assistance.

Instead of a rational-legal bureaucracy, Yemen entered the Arab Spring with a state administration that acted as a political field of resources colonized for patronage by various social forces. Fear of a return to corrupt patronage politics alienated participants in Yemen's Arab Spring uprising. Yemen is also a poor country, with an underdeveloped tax collection apparatus to pay for a national military and modern bureaucracy.

Prior to the Arab Spring, Iraq's military and security forces brutally monopolized the use of violence. Its administration limited corruption among the masses. The US and British invasion and occupation led to the end of the Iraqi state's monopoly of violence and a drastic weakening of rational-legal aspects of the state administration. An insurgency and civil war were the results of foreign-imposed democratic elections in a country in which the state lacked bureaucratic capacity and the monopoly of violence. The Iraqi government has been unable to rein in militias, leading to the leaching of resources and to competitive elections in which every political party has an armed wing and there is the potential for violence to alter electoral results.

In contrast to Libya and Yemen, Tunisia and Egypt entered the Arab Spring stronger in attributes of modern states. Their states and governments monopolized violence during the countries' democratic transitions. There was enough bureaucratic capacity to prevent derailment of their transitions. The tax collection apparatus in both countries provided enough resources to pay for the military and bureaucracy.

Of course, Egypt's military staged a coup against an elected government during the country's democratic transition. Still, Egypt and Tunisia's more modern states partly explains why there was less violence and bloodshed during their countries' tumultuous transitions than what occurred in Libya and Yemen.

In conclusion, it is desirable to examine the contours and trajectory of state formation for analysis of democratization because they contribute to understanding how and why democratic transitions turn violent and become civil wars. In that light, there was an opportunity in Libya for international actors to help disarm militias and establish the monopoly of the use of violence for elected Libyan governments. The Libyan opposition and the Arab League had invited international intervention. It's hard not to think about how much good would have been done if the United States, France, Britain, the United Nations (UN) and others who answered the call of distressed Libyans had made the effort to remove the guns from militias' hands before leaving the country.

The same argument could be made for Iraq. How many lives would have been saved if Ambassador Bremer and the CPA had maintained the state's monopoly of violence by forging a new one that could have maintained security during de-Baathification and the dissolution of Saddam Hussein's military and security forces? Who can rein in the militias at this point?

In Yemen, the National Dialogue Conference recognized the need to establish the state's monopoly of violence but seemed impotent at making a dent in changing centuries of armed tribes and the recent formation of various types of militias. It's even hard to imagine UN or other international forces being able to establish the state's monopoly of violence in Yemen, yet democracy seems inconceivable without it.

National Unity

The Arab Winter provides strong support for arguments that posit the necessity of national unity, widespread commitment to a single political community, for analysis of democratization. Strong national unity helped Tunisians consolidate their democracy. It also helped prevent Egypt's descent into civil war after a military coup removed an elected Islamist government.

In contrast, Libya entered the Arab Spring as a weak nation-state with tribal and regional conflicts that had been repressed by Qaddafi. Unleashed after authoritarian breakdown, those conflicts turned into mini-civil wars across the country: pro-Qaddafi versus anti-Qaddafi tribes, Cyrenaicans fighting for independence, Amazigh (Berber) versus Arab, Black African Toubou against Arab and Berber.

National disunity, once suppressed by Saleh's regime in Yemen, flared up once he was removed. Instead of democratization,

Southerners are fighting to secede from the Republic of Yemen. The Houthis may be trying to reinstall their long-gone Imamate in North Yemen.

Historically bequeathed weaknesses in national unity in Iraq made the country an unlikely place for the United States to successfully impose democracy. Kurds do not want to be a part of Iraq regardless of how democratic it becomes. Distrust and a history of violent conflict challenge Sunni–Shia relations to the core. Policies during the United States' occupation made Iraqis view each other as ethnosectarian competitors instead of fellow Iraqis.

With the goal of democratic consolidation in mind, and based on Iraq's heterogeneous society, Post–Saddam Hussein Iraqi governments have been exceptionally unwise in their policies, political strategies, and institutional arrangements. Democratization in multinational states, like Iraq (and the United States) can be supported by federalism that provides some regional autonomy, but that does not threaten the sovereign state. The US-occupation's government-implemented policies and political strategies did the opposite, as did the Iraqi governments that followed it. Their policies reified regions and communal groups, beginning with Kurds and Kurdistan. Instead of encouraging cross-communal and cross-regional coalitions, the electoral rules, the political strategies, and the country's new constitution favored the ethnosectarian division of the country and deepened democratic consolidation challenges.

Democratic Consolidation: Military Pacts

Egypt's Arab Spring suggests additions to the democratic transitions literature's focus on the importance of a military pact – extricating the military from politics. Two are particularly important. First, Egypt's military authoritarian regime was characterized by a military that dominated the economy as much as it did the political system. The economic stakes made extricating the military from politics all the more difficult.

Second, there is a need to have sustained popular mobilization in efforts to extricate the military from politics. Egypt's cross-ideological broad revolution forced the Egyptian military to contemplate accepting democracy and an end to economic privileges, though they were loath to do so. At the height of the Arab Spring uprising in Egypt, it would have taken massive repression and bloodshed to deny steps toward the democracy and socioeconomic justice that Egyptians were clamoring for. The military was not willing to go down that bloody path.

However, in order to really uproot the Egyptian military from political and economic processes – and prevent their cagey return to power – civilian elected officials needed to have crafted institutions that permanently shifted power away from the military to bureaucracies they controlled. A number of strategies were available in this regard including creating institutions to watch over the military, presidential decrees, legislative action and legislative committees devoted to civilian–military relations, civilian ministers of defense, articles in new constitutions, constitutional court decisions, and establishing civilian control over the military budget. However, implementing any of those tactics requires sustained popular mobilization. Without it, why would the military cede dearly held prerogatives?

Elected President Morsi promised to bring the military budget under civilian control. He issued presidential decrees to protect his government from military and judicial interference. He changed the military's leadership. However, during the Egyptian transition it became clear that Morsi needed the support of sustained popular mobilization to permanently sideline the military from politics and the economy. For example, he could not follow through on bringing the military budget under civilian control without masses of people, of all stripes, in the streets clamoring for it. Instead, once they realized the scope of Islamist electoral power, the secular opposition began to side with the military and Mubarak's courts. Without a cross-ideological mass-coalition mobilized to sustain pressure to end military authoritarian rule for good, the military was able to reinstall and deepen its grip on the Egyptian political economy.

Democratic Consolidation: Political Pacts

By accommodating vital interests, political pacts during democratic transitions enable warring elite factions to deliberately reorganize their relations through negotiated compromises over their most basic disagreements. During the Arab Spring, leaders of political parties sought compromises over class, region, tribe, ethnicity, sect, and other conflicts that threatened to derail democratic outcomes. However,

Islamist–secularist polarization posed the most frequent challenge to emerging democratic bargains.

In Tunisia, the most successful case of democratic consolidation during the Arab Spring, an Islamist–secularist alliance called the Troika asserted that it should serve as a model during transitions across the region because their coalition helped to overcome the secular–Islamist divide that threatened democratic progress everywhere in the Arab world.

The Troika's reasoning was sound. Comparatively positive Islamist–secularist relations in Tunisia helped the country reach a compromise on the role of *Sharia* in politics and the constitution (There is none, despite the dreams of most Islamists that won founding elections). Islam is mentioned as the religion of the Tunisian nation.

The Islamist–secularist coalition represented by the Troika also helped build trust among secularists in general that they do not need to fear mainstream Islamists' commitment to democracy, despite their electoral strength. Trust helped prevent secularists from turning to the streets, violence, and a call to the military for a coup when Islamists won competitive elections in Tunisia. Islamists rewarded the trust, when they peacefully turned over power after losing subsequent elections to secularists. In essence, the vast majority of Tunisian Islamists and secularists learned to tolerate each other in a new democracy.

Mainstream Tunisian Islamists, when they had the electoral advantage, also made the powerful case for shared rule during transitional elections because they recognized that elections that determine matters such as the nature of the constitution and the country's new political system were different from elections in mature democracies that can be dominated by temporary majorities.

Of course, radical Islamists are the most potent contributors to secular–Islamist polarization, which prevents or interrupts democratic consolidation. Mainstream Tunisian Islamists argue that open and inclusive debate and negotiations can help in this regard because moderate Islamists can take on the role of persuading Salafis – Quietist, Jihadi, and Takfiri – to accept moderation and democracy. In contrast, absolute repression closes the door on evolution in Salafi thought toward the legitimacy of democracy. However, all Salafis could not be convinced to eschew violence in Tunisia, leading the Troika and Ennahdha to take on a much more robust security policy toward their country's radical Islamists.

Egyptian Islamists and secularists struggled much more than Tunisians at developing the twin tolerations in an emerging democracy. The Muslim Brotherhood in Egypt, much more of an electoral juggernaut than Ennahdha, proved to be insensitive to seeking broad consensus in transitional governments, the Constituent Assembly, and constitution-writing. Egyptian secularists, for their part, never developed trust in the intentions of the Muslim Brotherhood in Egypt and turned to the streets, violence, and the military to overturn democratic electoral outcomes. Failing to forge the twin tolerations in Egypt provided the Egyptian military with the opportunity to reinstall a military authoritarian regime.

Despite achieving greater success than in Egypt, the Tunisian case also demonstrates that Islamist–secularist coalitions designed to sustain democratic progress – over-time – can become counterproductive. Secularists in the coalition Nidaa Tounes defeated Islamists in Tunisia's second round of parliamentary elections. They, then, formed a government and brought in Ennhada as junior partners. The Nidaa Tounes–Ennahdha grand coalition was justified by claiming it would prevent instability and deliver desperately needed socioeconomic results by working together.

It did neither. For many Tunisians, both parties have little to offer but strong-arm security and the promises of the same liberal economic reforms that operated as corrupt crony capitalism under Ben Ali, and they seem to have offered little more than painful austerity since his departure from the scene. Tunisians are now clamoring for a more developed political party system with political parties that offer competing political and economic agendas that can provide hope for a different future. The very instability that Tunisian politicians Caid Essebsi and Rachid Ghannouchi had hoped to avoid through consensus is instead manifesting in an even less controllable form through the regular protests of angry, frustrated youth.

The Arab Winter also exposes the vast number of political parties with armed militias during the Middle East and North Africa's democratic transitions. Political parties in Libya, Yemen, and Iraq *all* have armed wings and need to be disarmed to facilitate democratic consolidation. Political pact-making is difficult when political parties are so well equipped to use violence to alter unfavorable electoral results. This is especially true because the tumult of Arab Spring democratic transitions also provided opportunities for aggrandizement by armed radical Islamists who reject both democracy and the world's nation-state system.

Democratic Consolidation: Socioeconomic Pacts

The Arab Winter provides evidence that, in addition to extricating the military from politics and getting political parties to compete according to the rules of political democracy, new socioeconomic pacts are needed to consolidate emerging democratic regimes.

Economic transitions can support democratic transitions. To do so, in the Arab world, most transitional elites and the International Financial Institutions (IFIs) have gravitated toward a modified market reform strategy that takes advantage of the opportunities for economic growth provided by global markets and a vigorous private sector, while avoiding the simpleminded application of market liberalization, privatization, and a minimal state that resulted in deeply corrupt, crony-capitalist forms of authoritarian rule prior to the Arab Spring.

In that light, the diagnosis of what is needed in terms of an economic transition begins with eliminating elite capture – the shaping of rules of the game and institutions of the state for the benefit of a few. This includes getting private sector actors to set aside rent-seeking activities and direct all their energy to production and innovation. The International Financial Institutions, the International Monetary Fund (IMF) and the World Bank (WB), can contribute to this process by explaining why they validated and supported the old, pre–Arab Spring autocratic regimes, even in the face of rampant corruption and deteriorating governance. In addition, the IFIs can undertake their own analyses of corruption, cronyism, and the potential capture of the state by special interest groups, and work more closely with civil society and emerging democratic parliaments in the region.

One of the most disturbing conclusions of the Arab Spring's political and economic transitions is that instead of using the opportunity provided by authoritarian breakdown and a democratic transition to improve, corrupt, stagnant economies and promote inclusive economic growth based on their own self-proclaimed modified market reform model, elites in the region are returning to the crony capitalism of the past.

Despite Tunisia's considerable success at democratic consolidation, 10 years in, the Tunisian economy, for most Tunisians, has not changed from the Ben Ali era. A small number of rent-seeking families and corrupt political elites are shaping the rules of the economic game for the benefit of the few. The IMF and WB in Tunisia undertook their own analyses of corruption and cronyism in Tunisia, and concluded that both have gotten worse since the Ben Ali era.

The resurgence of Ben Ali era political and economic elites has contributed – a lot – to forging a "political democracy" in Tunisia while reestablishing crony capitalism. Doing so has been nothing but volatile. Hundreds of strikes and demonstrations occur monthly. Instead of directing all their energy into production and innovation, Tunisian capitalists are taking the more lucrative rent-seeking route that their affiliated political elite – former President Caid Essebsi among them – is reestablishing for them.

Tunisia's democracy is in trouble. It's in trouble because its economy has not changed at all. It's the same Ben Ali economy that infuriated a nation. Tunisians today face the same corrupt, rent-seeking, crony-capitalist economy that had stagnated, benefited the few, provided little hope for the future for the young and educated, and fueled the Arab Spring revolution.

Egypt's transition took a similar path before the military coup. Initially, crony capitalists and the old political and military elite were on the defensive. Millions of people were in the streets clamoring for socioeconomic justice and an end to corruption. Momentum toward a more effective market reform strategy that could provide inclusive economic growth, or any other economic development model, ended when the old political, judicial, military, and economic elite, including President El-Sisi, regained the upper hand and retook power. El-Sisi has used the political opening to entrench an even more military-dominated crony-capitalist economy than the one under Mubarak. These socioeconomic conditions in Egypt make the country ripe for another revolution.

Democratic Consolidation: Transitional Justice, National Reconciliation, Human Rights, and Rule of Law Pacts

The Arab Spring began with a simple demand for dignity (*karamah*). Tunisian street vendor, Mohamed Bouazizi, could no longer stand the contempt displayed by a local official, Faida Hamdi, who allegedly humiliated Bouazizi by spitting at him, confiscating his wares, and slapping him in the face when he could not afford to pay a bribe. When other government officials treated him similarly, he had had enough and set himself on fire, despite being his family's sole breadwinner. Bouazizi's declaration that he had had enough of a cruel regime that treated citizens as subjects without rights inspired mass uprisings across the region by millions of people who felt the same way and were willing to risk their lives to reinvent the region into one defined by respect for human rights, the rule of law, and justice.

Reinvention, in this regard, requires judicial and security sector reforms that have largely not taken place. In the Arab autocracies, instead of being the cornerstone of the rule of law, the judiciary has been one of the institutions that autocrats have used to establish and maintain power. To establish the rule of law, protect human rights, and support democratic consolidation, the judiciary may have to be dismantled and reconstructed. Old regime figures resistant to change have to be removed.

Security sector reforms are critical as well. The mission of the security sector has to be redefined from a brutal instrument of internal repression designed to protect authoritarian rule and narrow patronage networks to a neutral public authority that protects citizens' rights and safety. Members of the security sector have to be subject to the rule of law. Citizens have to trust the police, not fear them.

One of the great disappointments of the Arab Spring is the lost opportunity to improve human rights and establish the rule of law. Even in Tunisia, judicial and security sector reforms have been slow to materialize. There have been multiple delays in establishing a Constitutional Court. In Egypt, respect for human rights has deteriorated under El-Sisi as have efforts to establish the rule of law. Libya and Yemen are in the midst of civil wars.

In sum, the violations and abuses of the *Mukhabarat* (spy) state, which defined the region and inspired the Arab Spring, continue. The long history of human rights violations and abuses also made transitional justice and national reconciliation key to democratic consolidation in the region.

Arab Spring transitions largely failed to strike the right balance between transitional justice and national reconciliation. Iraq never recovered from the decision to alienate and punish all Sunni Muslims by dismantling the Baathist military and bureaucracy. A civil war and an insurgency ensued. Libya never recovered from its draconian political isolation law that was implemented more or less at gunpoint to change electoral results. A civil war ensued. Even in Tunisia, former regime political and economic elite have regained enough power to hinder transitional justice, especially for economic crimes.

Looking Ahead

Mass uprisings for democracy, respect for human rights, and socio-economic justice are currently taking place in Sudan and Algeria years after the end of the popular mobilizations of the Arab Spring. The lives of tens of millions of people would be vastly improved if the Algerian and Sudanese opposition succeed.

Unfortunately, what also immediately comes to mind are the steep – though not impossible for any national pact – challenges of extricating the Algerian and Sudanese militaries from their dominant positions in politics and the economy. Sudan has major nation and state issues. Both countries have violent histories of secular–Islamist polarization. Socioeconomic justice will be particularly difficult in a country as poor and corrupt as Sudan. Both Algeria and Sudan would have to undergo major transformations to establish transitional justice, respect for human rights, and the rule of law.

Index

The team was a damn good team, a very diverse team of whites, blacks, Asians, coloreds, rich, poor, community workers, trade unionists, a really interesting mix. We would work together and play together ... You go for a long walk after the day's work with Tito Mboweni on a mountain path and you just talk. Tito was the last sort of person I would have talked to a year before that. Very articulate, very bright; we did not meet blacks like that normally. I don't know where they were all buried but they were there. The only other blacks of that caliber that I had met were the trade unionists sitting opposite me in adversarial roles. This was new for me, especially how open-minded they were. These were not people who simply said: "Look, this is how it is going to be when we take over one day." They were prepared to say: "Hey, how *would* it be? Let's discuss it." But their pictures of the future and ours were not the same, and here was an opportunity, spread over a fairly lengthy period of time, for actually learning how other people think.

During one of the Mont Fleur workshops, Liebenberg was recording on a flipchart while Mosebyane Malatsi of the radical black Pan Africanist Congress—unofficial slogan: "One Settler [White Person], One Bullet"—was speaking. Liebenberg was calmly summarizing what Malatsi was saying: "Let me see if I've got this right. 'The illegitimate, racist regime in Pretoria . . .'" Liebenberg was able to hear and actually to articulate the inflammatory perspective of his opponent.

Liebenberg became friends with Gabriels, who had been his adversary throughout acrimonious and violent mining industry negotiations and strikes. Gabriels described how each man came to see the situation from the other's perspectives:

In 1987 we took 340,000 workers out on strike. Fifteen workers were killed and more than 300 workers got terribly injured, and when I say injured, I do not only mean little